THE LEGENDS AND MYTHS OF HAWAII

OF HAWAII

The Fables and Folk-Lore of a Strange People

Kalakaua

THE LEGENDS AND MYTHS OF HAWAII

The Fables and Folk-Lore
of a Strange People

by

HIS HAWAIIAN MAJESTY
KING DAVID KALAKAUA

edited and with an introduction by
HON. R. M. DAGGETT

and with an introduction to the new edition by
TERENCE BARROW, Ph.D.

CHARLES E. TUTTLE COMPANY
Rutland, Vermont & Tokyo, Japan

Representatives
Continental Europe: BOXERBOOKS, INC., *Zurich*
British Isles: PRENTICE-HALL INTERNATIONAL, INC., *London*
Australasia: PAUL FLESCH & CO., PTY. LTD., *Melbourne*
Canada: M. G. HURTIG LTD., *Edmonton*

Published by the Charles E. Tuttle Company, Inc.
of Rutland, Vermont & Tokyo, Japan
with editorial offices at
Suido 1-chome, 2-6, Bunkyo-ku, Tokyo, Japan

Copyright in Japan, 1972, by Charles E. Tuttle Co., Inc.

Library of Congress Catalog Card No. 72-77519

International Standard Book No. 0-8048-1032-X

First edition, 1888 by
Charles L. Webster and Co., New York
First Tuttle edition, 1972
Third printing, 1973

0293-000301-4615
PRINTED IN JAPAN

TABLE OF CONTENTS

TABLE OF CONTENTS

LIST OF ILLUSTRATIONS

LIST OF ILLUSTRATIONS

INTRODUCTION TO THE
NEW EDITION

The Legends and Myths of Hawaii, by His Hawaiian Majesty King David Kalakaua, is here reprinted for the first time since the original 1888 edition was published in New York by Charles L. Webster and Company. The work has become a classic of its kind but has been virtually unavailable to students in recent decades. The 1888 volume has become a rare book indeed, much sought after by collectors.

The author, King David Kalakaua, spearheaded a renaissance of traditional Hawaiian culture, partly as a means of offsetting the many disintegrating influences under which the Hawaiians had fallen. In the eyes of many of his contemporaries, especially the European business fraternity and the missionaries in Honolulu, he was advocating a return to paganism. But they were wrong, and Kalakaua was right. We now know that the dignity of a people rests largely in respect for their culture and the activities in which that culture is expressed.

In the extensive introduction by the Hon. R. M. Daggett there is a gloomy reference to the condition of the Hawaiians: "slowly sinking year by year...their footprints grow more dim." Indeed, to the Hawaiians of the nineteenth century it appeared that the gods of old were taking revenge on them and that they were doomed to extinction. The king was an optimist, however, and *The Legends and Myths of Hawaii* is one of many practical steps taken in the direction of reviving and preserving Hawaiian culture.

The traditional Hawaiian culture to which King Kalakaua was so devoted had suffered three major traumatic shocks that had crippled its original vitality: namely, the realization that there existed another culture of technical superiority (first evident on the arrival of Captain Cook's ships in 1778), the renunciation in 1819 (by the Hawaiians themselves) of ancient traditional religion and revered social laws based on taboos, and the inflow of aliens to Hawaii from the mid-nineteenth century onward. A fourth blow to Hawaiian confidence came in 1893, when financially ambitious Americans overthrew the Hawaiian monarchy. Already the inroads of imported diseases and the dispirited condition of the Hawaiians had reduced their numbers to a fraction by the time of King Kalakaua's reign.

Fortunately, in the twentieth century, the number of native Hawaiians has increased, and there is a growing awareness of the value of their past. Today Hawaii is the fiftieth State of the U.S.A., a conglomeration of ethnic groups and racial admixtures. The Hawaiian is, however, still under the burden of an unequal battle with circumstances over the past two hundred years. The cry for identity that King Kalakaua put up has more meaning today than ever before, and it seems clear that right use of traditional Hawaiian culture will contribute tremendously to the life of modern Hawaii. The basic means of the study of Hawaiian culture today is literature, and no doubt King Kalakaua's book has a distinctive role to play.

Anthropology was an infant subject in Kalakaua's day, while Polynesian archaeology as a science was half a century in the misty future. The Polynesians are not, as he believed, Aryan wanderers out of "Asia Minor or Arabia" who reached Polynesia via India. In fact they are a racially mixed group whose ancestors ventured out from the eastern limits of the Southeast Asian islands and coasts in voyages of ever increasing length. Some eight hundred years after Christ it appears they had found and populated every habitable island from New Zealand in the south to Hawaii in the north and from Fiji to Easter Island. The entry of the Polynesian ancestors into Polynesia began some centuries before Christ. Hawaii itself was settled by migrations which seem to have originated first in the Marquesas Islands about 750 and then about 1250 in the Society Islands.

Modern scholars will also be critical of Kalakaua's belief that the first Western discoverers of Hawaii were Spanish. It seems clear that Captain James Cook was the first rediscoverer of

Hawaii following its initial discovery by the first Hawaiians. Captain Cook was unquestionably the greatest Western explorer of the Pacific, humane and much loved by the Polynesians. One may say that Hawaiian history is dominated by two great symbolic figures. They are King Kamehameha I and Captain James Cook. The story in this book entitled "Kaiana, the Last of the Hawaiian Knights" concerns them both, but Kalakaua's description of Cook's character as "exacting, dictatorial, and greedy" is uninformed. One feels that Kalakaua was reflecting a fashion of the time to downgrade the contribution of Captain Cook and to justify Hawaiian treatment of him.

King David Kalakaua was born in 1836, when memories of old Hawaiian ways and beliefs were still fresh. He was a man of both past and present, singularly colorful in character. Robert Louis Stevenson, who became his friend, found in him a cultured intellectual of unusual mental powers. His warmth of feeling and his unsurpassed ability to absorb alcohol were evident to all in the kingdom.

Kalakaua sought a revival of traditional Hawaiian life along with a political and cultural revival elsewhere in Polynesia. In fact, he attempted to unify Polynesia into one state: an idea as impractical then as it would be today.

But the Hawaiian monarchy was soon to end. In 1893, two years after King Kalakaua died, Queen Liliuokalani, the sister who had succeeded him, was deprived of her throne. The sad story has been retold in varying lights, but the truth is that the end of the ruling high chiefs was as inevitable as the earlier rejection of the Hawaiian pantheon of gods, demigods, guardians, and ancestral spirits. The world of old Hawaii was then ended forever.

Finally it should be noted that *The Legends and Myths of Hawaii* is not all mythology. It is rich in historical narrative. King Kalakaua relates the stories of certain great events with such verve that one can readily imagine he was an eyewitness. No doubt he had heard the same tales from the sons and daughters of those who had been present on occasions such as the death of Captain Cook. Since the momentous Hawaiian rejection of the ancient gods took place only two decades before his birth, many of the people about him as he grew to manhood had lived under the old system. His sources of knowledge were direct indeed.

TERENCE BARROW, PH.D.

PREFACE

FOR material in the compilation of many of the legends embraced in this volume obligation is acknowledged to H. R. H. Liliuokalani ; General John Owen Dominis ; His Excellency Walter M. Gibson ; Professor W. D. Alexander ; Mrs. E. Beckley, Government Librarian ; Mr. W. James Smith, Secretary of the National Board of Education ; and especially to Hon. Abram Fornander, the learned author of " An Account of the Polynesian Race, its Origin and Migrations."

The legends, in the order of their publication, beginning with the first and ending with " The Destruction of the Temples," may be regarded, so far as they refer to the prominent political events with which they are associated, as in a measure historic. Those following have been selected as the most striking and characteristic of what remains of the fabulous folklore of the Hawaiian group.

HAWAIIAN LEGENDS: INTRODUCTION.

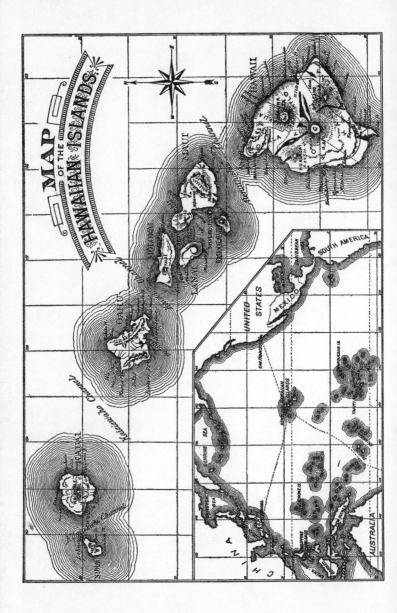

The Legends and Myths of Hawaii.

HAWAIIAN LEGENDS : INTRODUCTION.

Physical Characteristics of the Hawaiian Islands—Historic Outlines—The
Tabu—Ancient Religion—Ancient Government—Ancient Arts, Habits and Customs—The Hawaii of To-day.

GENERAL RETROSPECT.

THE legends following are of a group of sunny islands lying
almost midway between Asia and America—a cluster of
volcanic craters and coral-reefs, where the mountains are man-
tled in perpetual green and look down upon valleys of eternal
spring ; where for two-thirds of the year the trade-winds, sweeping down from the northwest coast of America and softened in
their passage southward, dally with the stately cocoas and spreading palms, and mingle their cooling breath with the ever-living
fragrance of fruit and blossom. Deeply embosomed in the silent
wastes of the broad Pacific, with no habitable land nearer than
two thousand miles, these islands greet the eye of the approaching mariner like a shadowy paradise, suddenly lifted from the
blue depths by the malicious spirits of the world of waters,
either to lure him to his destruction or disappear as he drops
his anchor by the enchanted shore.

The legends are of a little archipelago which was unknown
to the civilized world until the closing years of the last century,
and of a people who for many centuries exchanged no word or
product with the rest of mankind ; who had lost all knowledge,
save the little retained by the dreamiest of legends, of the great
world beyond their island home ; whose origin may be traced to
the ancient Cushites of Arabia, and whose legends repeat the
story of the Jewish genesis ; who developed and passed through

an age of chivalry somewhat more barbarous, perhaps, but scarcely less affluent in deeds of enterprise and valor than that which characterized the contemporaneous races of the continental world ; whose chiefs and priests claimed kinship with the gods, and step by step told back their lineage not only to him who rode the floods, but to the sinning pair whose re-entrance to the forfeited joys of Paradise was prevented by the large, white bird of *Kane ;* who fought without shields and went to their death without fear ; whose implements of war and industry were of wood, stone and bone, yet who erected great temples to their gods, and

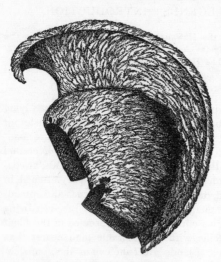

constructed barges and canoes which they navigated by the stars ; who peopled the elements with spirits, reverenced the priesthood, bowed to the revelations of their prophets, and submitted without complaint to the oppressions of the *tabu ;* who observed the rite of circumcision, built places of refuge after the manner of the ancient Israelites, and held sacred the religious legends of the priests and chronological *meles* of the chiefs.

MAHIOLE, OR FEATHERED WAR-HELMET.

As the mind reverts to the past of the Hawaiian group, and dwells for a moment upon the shadowy history of its people, mighty forms rise and disappear—men of the stature of eight or nine feet, crowned with helmets of feathers and bearing spears thirty feet in length. Such men were Kiha, and Liloa, and Umi, and Lono, all kings of Hawaii during the fifteenth and sixteenth centuries ; and little less in bulk and none the less in valor was the great Kamehameha, who conquered and consolidated the several islands under one government, and died as late as 1819. And beside Umi, whose life was a romance, stands his humble

WAR-CLUB.

PAHOA, OR WOODEN DAGGER.

SHARK'S-TEETH KNIFE.

FLINT-EDGED KNIFE.

STONE BATTLE-AXE.

STONE BATTLE-AXE.

IHE, OR JAVELIN, 6 TO 8 FEET LONG.

SPEAR, 16 TO 20 FEET LONG.

GROUP OF ANCIENT WEAPONS.

friend Maukaleoleo, who, with his feet upon the ground, could
reach the cocoanuts of standing trees ; and back of him in the
past is seen Kana, the son of Hina, whose height was measured
by paces.

And, glancing still farther backward through the centuries,
we behold adventurous chiefs, in barges and double canoes a
hundred feet in length, making the journey between the Hawaiian and more southern groups, guided only by the sun and
stars. Later we see battles, with dusky thousands in line.
The warriors are naked to the loins, and are armed with spears,
slings, clubs, battle-axes, javelins and knives of wood or ivory.
They have neither bows nor shields. They either catch with
their hands or ward with their own the weapons that are
thrown. Their chiefs, towering above them in stature, have
thrown off their gaudy feather cloaks and helmets, and, with
spear and stone halberd, are at the front of battle. The opposing forces are so disposed as to present a right and left
wing and centre, the king or principal chief commanding the
latter in person. In the rear of each hostile line are a large
number of women with calabashes of food and water with which
to refresh their battling fathers, husbands and brothers. While
the battle rages their wails, cries and prayers are incessant, and
when defeat menaces their friends they here and there take part
in the combat. The augurs have been consulted, sacrifices and
promises to the gods have been made, and, as the warring lines
approach, the war-gods of the opposing chiefs, newly decorated
and attended by long-haired priests, are borne to the front.
War-cries and shouts of defiance follow. The priests retire, and
the slingers open the battle. Spears are thrown, and soon the
struggle is hand-to-hand all over the field. They fight in groups
and squads around their chiefs and leaders, who range the field
in search of enemies worthy of their weapons. No quarter is
given or expected. The first prisoners taken are reserved as
offerings to the gods, and are regarded as the most precious of
sacrifices. Finally the leading chief of one of the opposing
armies falls. A desperate struggle over his body ensues, and his
dispirited followers begin to give ground and are soon in retreat.
Some escape to a stronghold in the neighboring mountains, and
a few, perhaps, to a temple of refuge ; but the most of them are
overtaken and slain. The prisoners who are spared become the

slaves of their captors, and the victory is celebrated with feasting and bountiful sacrifices to the gods.

This is a representative battle of the past, either for the supremacy of rival chiefs or in repelling invasion from a neighboring island. But here and there we catch glimpses of actual conflicts indicative of the warlike spirit and chivalry of the early Hawaiians. Far back in the past we see the beautiful Hina abducted from her Hawaiian husband by a prince of Molokai, and kept a prisoner in the fortress of Haupu until her sons grow to manhood, when she is rescued at the end of an assault which leaves the last of her defenders dead. Later we see the eight hundred helmeted chiefs of the king of Hawaii, all of noble blood, hurling themselves to destruction against the spears of the armies of Maui on the plains of Wailuku. And then, less than a generation after, Kamehameha is seen in the last battle of the conquest, when, at the head of sixteen thousand warriors, he sweeps the Oahuan army over the precipice of Nuuanu and becomes the master of the archipelago. Finally we behold Kekua-okalani, the last defender in arms of the Hawaiian gods and temples, trampling upon the edict of the king against the worship of his fathers, and dying, with his faithful wife Manono, on the field of Kuamoo.

In the midst of these scenes of blood the eye rests with relief upon numerous episodes of love, friendship and self-sacrifice touching with a softening color the ruddy canvas of the past. We see Kanipahu, the exiled king of Hawaii, delving like a common laborer on a neighboring island, and refusing to accept anew the sceptre in his old age because his back had become crooked with toil and he could no longer look over the heads of his subjects as became a Hawaiian king. We see Umi, a rustic youth of royal mien and mighty proportions, boldly leap the palace-walls of the great Liloa, push aside the spears of the guards, enter the royal mansion, seat himself in the lap of the king, and through the exhibition of a forgotten token of love receive instant recognition as his son. And now Lono, the royal great-grandson of Umi, rises before us, and we see him lured from self-exile by the voice of his queen, reaching him in secret from without the walls of the sovereign court of Oahu, to return to Hawaii and triumph over his enemies. These and many other romantic incidents present themselves in connection with the

early Hawaiian kings and princes, and are offered in the succeeding pages with every detail of interest afforded by available
tradition.

PHYSICAL CHARACTERISTICS.

A few general remarks concerning the physical characteristics of the Hawaiian Islands would seem to be appropriate in
presenting a collection of legends dealing alike with the history
and folk-lore of their people. The islands occupy a place in a
great waste of the Pacific between the nineteenth and twenty-
third degrees of north latitude, and the one hundred and fifty-
fourth and one hundred and sixty-first degrees of longitude west
from Greenwich. They are two thousand one hundred miles
southwest from San Francisco, and about the same distance
from Tahiti.

The group consists of ten islands, including two that are little
more than barren rocks. The farthest are about three hundred
miles from each other, measuring from their extreme boundaries,
and their aggregate area is a little more than six thousand one
hundred square miles. Of the eight principal islands all are
habitable, although the small islands of Niihau and Kahoolawe
are used almost exclusively as cattle-ranges.

The most of the shores of the several islands are fringed
with coral, but their origin seems to be indisputably shown in
the numerous craters of extinct volcanoes scattered throughout
the group, and in the mighty fires still blazing from the moun-
tain-heights of Hawaii.

By far the larger part of the area of the islands is mountainous; but from the interior elevations, some of them reaching
altitudes of from ten to fourteen thousand feet, flow many small
streams of sweet water, widening into fertile valleys as they reach
the coast, while here and there between them alluvial plateaus
have been left by the upland wash.

With rare exceptions the mountain-sides are covered with
vegetation, some of sturdy growth, capable of being wrought into
building materials and canoes, while lower down the *ohia*, the
palm, the banana, and the bread-fruit stand clothed in perpetual
green, with groves of stately cocoas between them and the sea.

Once the fragrant sandal-wood was abundant in the mountains, but it became an article of commerce with the natives in

their early intercourse with the white races, and is now rarely seen. Once the valleys and plateaus were covered with growing *taro* and potatoes ; now the cane and rice of the foreigner have usurped the places of both, and in the few shaded spots that have been left him the forgiving and revengeless Hawaiian sadly chants his wild songs of the past.

Neither within the memory of men nor the reach of their legends, which extend back more than a thousand years, has there been an active volcano in the group beyond the large island of Hawaii, which embraces two-thirds of the solid area of the archipelago. The mighty crater of Haleakala, more than thirty miles in circumference, on the island of Maui, has slept in peace among the clouds for ages, and hundreds of lesser and lower craters, many of them covered with vegetation, are found scattered among the mountains and foot-hills of the group ; but their fires have long been extinct, and the scoria and ashes buried at their bases tell the story of their activity far back in the past.

It must have been a sight too grand for human eyes to witness when all these dead volcanic peaks, aglow with sulphurous flames, lit up the moonless midnights of the eight Hawaiian seas with their combined bombardment of the heavens !

On the island of Hawaii alone have the fires of nature remained unextinguished. At intervals during the past thousand years or more have Mauna Kea, Mauna Hualalai and Mauna Loa sent their devastating streams of lava to the sea, and to-day the awful, restless and ever-burning caldron of Kilauea, nearly a mile in circumference, is the grandest conflagration that lights up the earth. Within its lurid depths, in fiery grottoes and chambers of burning crystal, dwell *Pele* and her companions, and offerings are still thrown to them by superstitious natives. Do they yet believe in these deities after more than sixty years of Christian teaching ? after their temples have been leveled and their gods have been destroyed ? after their *tabus* have been broken and their priesthood has been dethroned and dishonored ? The only answer is, " The offerings are still made."

Although the channel and ocean coasts of the islands are generally bold, rocky and precipitous, there are numerous bays and indentations partially sheltered by reefs and headlands, and many stretches of smooth and yellow beach, where the waves, touched by the *kona*, or the trade-wind's breath, chase each other high up among the cocoa's roots and branches of the humble *hau*-tree clinging to the sands. The harbor of Honolulu, on the island of Oahu, is the only one, however, where passengers and freights of ocean crafts may be received or landed without the aid of lighters.

The most of the useful and ornamental growths of the trop-ics now flourish on the islands. The indigenous plants, how-ever, are confined to the banana, plantain, cocoanut, breadfruit, *ohia*, sugar-cane, arrow-root, yam, sweet potato, *taro*, strawberry, raspberry and *ohelo*. The lime, orange, mango, tamarind, pa-paia, guava, and every other edible product, aside from those named as indigenous, are importations of the past century.

The only domestic animals of the ancient Hawaiians were dogs, swine and fowls, and the most formidable four-legged creatures found in their fields and forests were mice and liz-ards. Wild geese, including a species peculiar to the islands, ducks, snipe and plover were abundant in their seasons, but seem to have been sparely eaten; and owls, bats, and a few varieties of birds of simple song and not over-brilliant plumage made up about the sum total of animal life on the islands a hundred years ago. But the native could well afford to be content with this limited provision, since it did not include snakes, mosquitoes, centipedes, tarantulas, or scorpions.

To what processes of creation or isolation do the Hawaiian Islands owe their existence? Were they raised from the depths of the ocean by volcanic action, as plainly suggested by their formation? or are they a part of a great sunken continent which speculation, sustained by misty tradition, claims once occupied the Polynesian seas? Hawaiian *meles* mention islands no longer to be found, and the facility with which communication was maintained between the Hawaiian and more southern groups previous to the twelfth century renders plausible the assump-tion that this intercourse was abruptly terminated six or seven centuries ago by the disappearance of a number of intervening atolls or islands which had served as guides to early Polynesian navigators. The gigantic ruins of temples and other structures found on Easter and one or two other islands of the equatorial Pacific are almost unanswerable arguments in favor of the theory of a sunken Polynesian continent; but the question will proba-bly never be removed beyond the field of surmise.

HISTORIC OUTLINES.

The source and early history of the Hawaiian people, and, in fact, of the Polynesian race, of which they are a part, are involved in doubt. They have generally been regarded as an offshoot of the great Malayan family; but more recent as well as more thorough investigation, particularly by Judge Fornander, the learned and conscientious historian, with reasonable conclusiveness shows the Polynesian and Malayan races to be of distinct and widely different origin.

Accepting this conclusion, we trace the strictly Polynesian tribes to an Aryan beginning, somewhere in Asia Minor or Arabia. There, in the remote past, it is assumed, they were brought in close contact with early Cushite and Chaldeo-Arabian civilizations. Subsequently drifting into India, they to some extent amalgamated with the Dravidian races, and, following the channels of the great Chaldean commerce of that period, at length found a home in the Asiatic archipelago from Sumatra to Luzon and Timor.

The exact time of their settlement on the large coast islands of southern Asia cannot be definitely determined, but their legends and genealogies leave little room to doubt that it was contemporaneous with the Malay and Hindoo invasions of Sumatra, Java, and other islands of the archipelago, during the first and second centuries of the Christian era, that the Polynesians were pushed out—not at once in a body, but by families and communities covering a period of years—to the smaller and more remote islands of the Pacific.

Their first general rendezvous was in the Fiji group, where they left their impress upon the native Papuans. Expelled from, or voluntarily leaving, the Fijis, after a sojourn there of several generations, the Polynesians scattered over the Pacific, occupying by stages the several groups of islands where they are now found. Moving by the way of the Samoan and Society Islands, the migratory wave did not reach the Hawaiian group until about the middle of the sixth century.

Nanaula, a distinguished chief, was the first to arrive from the southern islands. It is not known whether he discovered the group by being blown northward by adverse winds, or in deliberately adventuring far out upon the ocean in search of new lands. In either event, he brought with him his gods, priests, prophets and astrologers, and a considerable body of followers and retainers. He was also provided with dogs, swine and fowls, and the seeds and germs of useful plants for propagation. It is probable that he found the group without human inhabitants.

During that period—probably during the life of Nanaula—other chiefs of less importance arrived with their families and followers either from Tahiti or Samoa. They came in barges and large double canoes capable of accommodating from fifty to one hundred persons each. They brought with them not only their priests and gods, but the earliest of Polynesian traditions. It is thought that none of the pioneers of the time of Nanaula ever returned to the southern islands, nor did others immediately follow the first migratory wave that peopled the Hawaiian group.

For thirteen or fourteen generations the first occupants of the Hawaiian Islands lived sequestered from the rest of the world, multiplying and spreading throughout the group. They erected temples to their gods, maintained their ancient religion, and yielded obedience to their chiefs. The traditions of the period are so meagre as to leave the impression that it was one of uninterrupted peace, little having been preserved beyond the genealogies of the governing chiefs.

But late in the tenth or early in the beginning of the eleventh century the Hawaiians were aroused from their dream of more than four centuries by the arrival of a party of adventurers from the southern islands, probably from the Society group. It was under the leadership of Nanamaoa. He was a warlike chief, and succeeded in establishing his family in power on Hawaii, Maui and Oahu. But stronger leaders were soon to follow from the south. Among the first was the high-priest Paao, from Samoa. He arrived during the reign of Kapawa, the grandson of Nanamaoa, or immediately after his death. The people were in an unsettled condition politically, and Paao, grasping the situation, either sent or returned in person to Samoa for Pili, a distinguished chief of that island. Arriving with a large following, Pili assumed the sovereignty of the island of Hawaii and founded a new dynasty. Paao became his high-priest, and somewhat disturbed the religious practices of the people by the introduction of new rites and two or three new gods. However, his religion did not seem to differ greatly from that of the native priests, and from him the last of the priesthood, seven hundred years after, claimed lineage and right of place.

The intercourse thus established between the Hawaiian and southern groups by Nanamaoa, Paao and Pili continued for about one hundred and fifty years, or until the middle or close of the twelfth century. During that period several other warlike families from the south established themselves in the partial or complete sovereignty of Oahu, Maui and Kauai, and expeditions were frequent between the group and other distant islands of Polynesia. It was a season of unusual activity, and the legends of the time are filled with stories of love, conquest and perilous voyages to and from the southern islands.

In that age, when distant voyages were frequent, the Polynesians were bold and intelligent navigators. In addition to large double canoes capable of withstanding the severest weather, they possessed capacious barges, with planks corded and calked upon strong frames. They were decked over and carried ample sail. Their navigators had some knowledge of the stars ; knew the prominent planets and gave them names ; were acquainted with the limits of the ecliptic and situation of the equator. With these helps, and keenly watchful of the winds and currents, of ocean drifts and flights of birds, they seldom failed to reach their destination, however distant.

Near the close of the twelfth century all communication between the Hawaiian and southern groups suddenly ceased. Tradition offers no explanation of the cause, and conjecture can find no better reason for it than the possible disappearance at that time of a number of island landmarks which had theretofore served as guides to the mariner. The beginning of this period of isolation found the entire group, with the exception, perhaps, of Molokai and a portion of Oahu, in the possession of the southern chiefs or their descendants.

It has been observed that the first discovery and occupation of the islands by Polynesians from the Society and Samoan groups occurred in the sixth century, and that more than four hundred years later a second migratory tide from the same and possibly other southern islands reached the coasts of Hawaii, continuing for more than a century and a half, and completely changing the political, and to some extent the social, condition of the people. Although nearly five centuries elapsed between the first and second migratory influxes from the south, during which the inhabitants of the group held no communication with the rest of the world, it is a curious fact that the Pili, Paumakua, and other chiefly families of the second influx traced back their lineage to the ancestors of the chiefs of the first migration, and made good their claim to the relationship by the recital of legends and genealogies common to both.

At the close of the second migratory period, which concluded their intercourse with the world beyond them for more than six hundred years, or from A.D. 1175 to 1778, the people of the group had very generally transferred their allegiance to the newly-arrived chiefs. The notable exceptions were the Maweke and Kamauaua families of Oahu and Molokai, both of the ancient Nanaula line. Although they were gradually crowded from their possessions by their more energetic invaders, the high descent of the prominent native chiefs was recognized, and by intermarriage their blood was allowed to mingle with the royal currents which have flowed down the centuries since they ceased to rule.

A mere outline of the political history of the islands from the twelfth century to the nineteenth is all that will be given here. The legends following will supply much that will be omitted to avoid repetition.

Until the final conquest of the group by Kamehameha I. at the close of the last century, the five principal islands of the archipelago—Hawaii, Maui, Oahu, Kauai and Molokai—were each governed, as a rule, by one or more independent chiefs. The smaller islands of Lanai and Kahoolawe were usually subject to Maui, while Niihau always shared the political fate of Kauai.

On each island, however, were descendants of distinguished ancient chiefs and heroes, who were recognized as of superior or royal blood, and with them originated the supreme chiefs, kings, or *mois* of the several islands, whose lines continued in authority, with interruptions of insurrection and royal feuds, until the consolidation of the group by Kamehameha. No one was recognized as a *tabu* chief unless his genealogical record showed him to be of noble blood, and intermarriage between the ruling fami-

Princess Liliuokalani.

lies, as well as between the lesser chiefs of the several islands, in time united the entire aristocracy of the group by ties of blood, and gave to all of royal strain a common and distinguished ancestry. The nobility and hereditary priesthood claimed to be of a stock different from that of the common people, and their superior stature and intelligence seemed to favor the assumption. To keep pure the blood of the chiefly classes, far back in the past a college of heraldry was established, before which all chiefs were required to recite their genealogies and make good their claims to noble descent.

The legends of the group abound in stories of romantic and sanguinary internal conflicts, and political and predatory wars between the islands ; but down to the time of Kamehameha but a single attempt had been made to subjugate the entire archipelago. This bold scheme was entertained by a king of the island of Hawaii who reigned during the latter part of the thirteenth century. He succeeded in overrunning Maui, Oahu and Molokai, but was defeated and taken prisoner on Kauai.

Without further reference to the intervening years from the twelfth century to the eighteenth—a long period of wars, festivals, tournaments, and royal and priestly pageantry—we will now glance at the condition of the islands at the time of their discovery by Captain Cook, a little more than a century ago. It was estimated that the islands then contained a population of four hundred thousand souls. This estimate has been considered large. But when it is noted that fifteen years later there were between thirty and forty thousand warriors under arms in the group at the same time, with large reserves ready for service, the conclusion is irresistible that the population could scarcely have been less. Kamehameha invaded Oahu with sixteen thousand warriors, principally drawn from the island of Hawaii. He was opposed by eight or ten thousand spears, while as many more awaited his arrival on Kauai. According to the figures of the Rev. Mr. Ellis, who travelled around the island of Hawaii in 1821 and numbered the dwellings and congregations addressed by him in the several coast districts through which he passed, the number of people on that island alone could not have been less than one hundred and fifteen thousand.

At the time of the arrival of Captain Cook, Kalaniopuu, of the ancient line of Pili, was king of the large island of Hawaii, and also maintained possession of a portion of the island of Maui. Kahekili, "the thunderer," as his name implied, was *moi* of Maui, and the principal wife of Kalaniopuu was his sister. Kahahana, who was also related to Kahekili, was the king of Oahu and claimed possession of Molokai and Lanai. Kamakahelei was the nominal queen of Kauai and Niihau, and her husband was a younger brother to Kahekili, while she was related to the royal family of Hawaii. Thus, it will be seen, the reigning families of the several islands of the group were all related to each other, as well by marriage as by blood. So had it been for many generations. But their wars with each other were none the less vindictive because of their kinship, or attended with less of barbarity in their hours of triumph.

At that time Kahekili was plotting for the downfall of Kahahana and the seizure of Oahu and Molokai, and the queen of Kauai was disposed to assist him in these enterprises. The occupation of the Hana district of Maui by the kings of Hawaii had been the cause of many stubborn conflicts between the chivalry of the two islands, and when Captain Cook first landed on Hawaii he found the king of that island absent on another warlike expedition to Maui, intent upon avenging his defeat of two years before, when his famous brigade of eight hundred nobles was hewn in pieces.

Connected with the court of Kalaniopuu at that time was a silent and taciturn chief, who had thus far attracted but little attention as a military leader. He was a man of gigantic mould, and his courage and prowess in arms were undoubted ; yet he seldom smiled or engaged in the manly sports so attractive to others, and his friends were the few who discerned in him a slumbering greatness which subsequently gave him a name and fame second to no other in Hawaiian history. He was the reputed and accepted son of Keoua, the half-brother of Kalaniopuu, although it was believed by many that his real father was Kahekili, *moi* of Maui. But, however this may have been, he was of royal blood, and was destined to become not only the king of Hawaii, but the conqueror and sovereign of the group. This chief was Kamehameha.

Such, in brief, was the political condition of the islands when Captain Cook arrived. He was an officer in the English navy, and, with the war-ships *Resolution* and *Discovery*, was on a voyage in search of a northwest passage eastward from Behring's Straits. Leaving the Society group in December, 1777, on the 18th of the following month he sighted Oahu and Kauai. Landing on the latter island and Niihau, he was received as a god by the natives, and his ships were provided with everything they required. Without then visiting the other islands of the group, he left for the northwest coast of America on the 2d of February, 1778, and in November of that year returned to the islands, first sighting the shores of Molokai and Maui. Communicating with the wondering natives of the latter island, he sailed around the coasts of Hawaii, and on the 17th of January dropped his anchors in Kealakeakua Bay. He was hailed as a reincarnation of their god *Lono* by the people, and the priests conducted him to their temples and accorded him divine honors. Returning from his campaign in Maui, the king visited and treated him as a god, and his ships were bountifully supplied with pigs, fowls, vegetables and fruits. The ships left the bay on the 4th of February, but, meeting with a storm, returned on the 8th for repairs. Petty bickerings soon after occurred between the natives and white sailors, and on the 13th one of the ships' boats was stolen by a chief and broken up for its nails and other iron fastenings. Cook demanded its restoration, and, while endeavoring to take the king on board the *Resolution* as a prisoner, was set upon by the natives and slain. Fire was opened by the ships, and many natives, including four or five chiefs, were killed. The body of Cook was borne off by the natives, but the most of the bones were subsequently returned at the request of Captain King, and the vessels soon after left the island.

If Captain Cook was not the first of European navigators to discover the Hawaiian Islands, he was at least the first to chart and make their existence known to the world. It has been pretty satisfactorily established that Juan Gaetano, the captain of a Spanish galleon sailing from the Mexican coast to the Spice Islands, discovered the group as early as 1555. But he did not make his discovery known at the time, and the existence of an old manuscript chart in the archives of the Spanish government is all that remains to attest his claim to it.

Native traditions mention the landing of small parties of white men on two or three occasions during the latter part of the sixteenth century ; but if the faces and ships of other races were seen by the Hawaiians in the time of Gaetano, their descendants had certainly lost all knowledge of both two hundred or more years later, for Cook was welcomed as a supernatural being by the awe-stricken islanders, and his ships were described by them as floating islands. A simple iron nail was to them a priceless jewel, and every act and word betrayed an utter ignorance of everything pertaining to the white races.

Kalaniopuu, the king of Hawaii, died in 1782, and Kamehameha, through the assistance of three or four prominent chiefs, succeeded, after a struggle of more than ten years, in securing to himself the supreme authority over that island. This done, encouraged by the prophets, assisted by his chiefs, and sustained by an unwavering faith in his destiny, he conquered Maui, Oahu, Kauai and their dependencies, and in 1795 was recognized as the sole master of the group.

Although of royal stock, the strain of Kamehameha from the old line of kings was less direct than that of his cousin, Kiwalao, from whom he wrested the Hawaiian sceptre ; but his military genius rallied around him the warlike chiefs who were dissatisfied with the division of lands by the son and successor of Kalaniopuu, and in the end his triumph was complete. To farther ennoble his succession he married the daughter of his royal cousin, and thus gave to his children an undoubted lineage of supreme dignity.

The existence of the Hawaiian Islands became generally known to the world soon after the final departure of the *Resolution* and *Discovery*, but it was not until 1786 that vessels began to visit the group. The first to arrive after the death of Captain Cook were the English ships *King George* and *Queen Charlotte*, and the same year a French exploring squadron touched at Maui. In 1787 several trading vessels visited the group, and the natives began to barter provisions and sandal-wood for firearms and other weapons of metal.

In 1792, and again in 1793, Captain Vancouver, of an English exploring squadron, touched and remained for some time at the islands. He landed sheep, goats and horned cattle, and distributed a quantity of fruit and garden seeds. His memory is gratefully cherished by the natives, for his mission was one of peace and broad benevolence. Thenceforward trading-vessels in considerable numbers visited the group, and during the concluding wars of Kamehameha the rival chiefs had secured the assistance of small parties of white men, and to some extent had learned the use of muskets and small cannon, readily purchased and paid for in sandal-wood, which was then quite abundant on most of the timbered mountains of the islands. The harbor of Honolulu was first discovered and entered by two American vessels in 1794, and it soon became a favorite resort for the war, trading and whaling vessels of all nations.

In the midst of these new and trying conditions Kamehameha managed the affairs of his kingdom with distinguished prudence and sagacity. He admonished his people to endure with patience the aggressions of the whites, and to retain, as far as possible, their simple habits. With his little empire united and peaceful, Kamehameha died on the 8th of May, 1819, at the age of about eighty; and his bones were so secretly disposed of that they have not yet been found.

Liholiho, the elder of his sons by Keopuolani, the daughter of his cousin Kiwalao, succeeded his warlike father with the title of Kamehameha II. Some knowledge of the Christian religion had reached the natives through their white visitors, but the old chief died in the faith of his fathers.

The death of Kamehameha was immediately followed by an event for which history affords no parallel. In October, 1819—six months before the first Christian missionaries arrived on the islands—Liholiho, under the inspiration of Kaahumanu, one of the widows of his father, suddenly, and in the presence of a large concourse of horrified natives, broke the most sacred of the *tabus* of his religion by partaking of food from vessels from which women were feasting, and the same day decreed the destruction of every temple and idol in the kingdom. He was sustained by the high-priest Hewahewa, who was the first to apply the torch; and within a few weeks idols, temples, altars, and a priesthood which had held prince and subject in awe for centuries were swept away, leaving the people absolutely without a religion.

But all did not peacefully submit to this royal edict against their gods. In the twilight of that misty period looms up a grand defender of the faith of Keawe and Umi and the altars of the Hawaiian gods. This champion was Kekuaokalani, a nephew, perhaps a son, of the first Kamehameha, and a cousin, perhaps a half-brother, of Liholiho. In his veins coursed the royal blood of Hawaii, and his bearing was that of a king. He

was above six and one-half feet in height, with limbs well proportioned and features strikingly handsome and commanding.
He was of the priesthood, and, through the bestowal of some
tabu or prerogative, claimed to be second in authority to Hewahewa, who traced his lineage back to Paao, the high-priest of
Pili. His wife, Manono, was scarcely less distinguished for her
courage, beauty and chiefly strain.

The apostasy of Hewahewa left Kekuaokalani at the head
of the priesthood—at least so he seems to have assumed—and
the royal order to demolish the temples was answered by him
with an appeal to the people to arm and join him in defence of
their gods. He raised the standard of revolt on the island of
Hawaii, and was soon at the head of a considerable army. A
large force was sent against him, and every effort was made to
induce him to lay down his arms. But he scorned all terms,
refused all concessions.

A battle was fought at Kuamoo, at first favorable to the
defenders of the gods ; but the fire-arms of the whites in the
service of the king turned the tide of war against them, and
they were defeated and scattered. Kekuaokalani was killed
on the field, and Manono, his brave and faithful wife, fighting
by his side, fell dead upon the body of her husband with a
musket-ball through her temples. A rude monument of stones
still marks the spot where they fell ; and it is told in whispers
that the *kona*, passing through the shrouding vines, attunes them
to saddest tones of lamentation over the last defenders in arms
of the Hawaiian gods.

Four or five months before the death of Kekuaokalani,
Kalaimoku, the prime minister of Liholiho, and his brother
Boki, were baptized under the formula of the Roman Catholic
Church by the chaplain of a French corvette on a passing visit
to the islands. They scarcely knew the meaning of the ceremony, and it is safe to say that, at the time of the destruction of
their temples and the repudiation of their gods, the Hawaiian
people knew little or nothing of any other religion. The abolition of the *tabu*, which had made them slaves to their chiefs
and priests, and held their fathers in bondage for centuries, was
hailed with so great a joy by the native masses that they did not
hesitate when called upon to consign the priesthood and their
gods to the grave of the *tabu*.

On the 30th of March, 1820—some months after this strange religious revolut on—the first party of Christian missionaries arrived at the islands from Massachusetts. They were well received. They found a people without a religion, and their work was easy. Other missionary parties followed from time to time, and found the field alike profitable to the cause in which they labored and to themselves individually. They acquired substantial possessions in their new home, controlled the government for the fifty or more years following, and their children are to-day among the most prosperous residents of the group. This is not said with a view to undervalue the services of the early missionaries to Hawaii, but to show that all missionary fields have not been financially unfruitful to zealous and provident workers.

And now let it be remarked with emphasis that the value of missionary labors in the Hawaiian group should not be measured by the small number of natives who to-day may be called Christians, but rather by the counsel and assistance of these thrifty religious teachers in securing and maintaining the independence of the islands, and by degrees establishing a mild and beneficent constitutional government, under which taxation is as light and life and property are as secure as in any other part of the civilized world. They were politicians as well as religious instructors, and practical examples of the value of Christian discipline when prudently applied to the acquisition of the needful and inviting things of life, and the establishment of a civil system capable of protecting the possessor in his acquired rights.

In 1824 Liholiho and his queen died while on a visit to England, and their remains were sent back to the islands in an English man-of war. Kauikeaouli, a youth of ten years, and brother of the deceased king, was accepted as the rightful heir to the throne under the title of Kamehameha III., and Kaahumanu, one of the wives of Kamehameha I., acted as regent and prime minister.

In 1827, and ten years later, Roman Catholic missionaries arrived, and were sent away by order of the government; but in 1839 the priests of that denomination were finally landed under the guns of a French frigate and allowed to remain. Meantime churches, schools and printing-presses had been established, the Hawaiian had become a written language, and the laws and decrees of the government were promulgated in printed form.

In 1840 the first written constitution was given to the people, guaranteeing to them a representative government. In February, 1843, Lord Paulet, of the English navy, took formal possession of the islands, but in the July following their sovereignty was restored through the action of Admiral Thomas. In November of the same year France and England mutually agreed to refrain from seizure or occupation of the islands, or any portion of them, and the United States, while declining to become a party to the agreement, promptly acknowledged the independence of the group.

Kamehameha III. died in 1854 and was succeeded by Kamehameha IV. The latter reigned until 1863, when he died and was succeeded by Prince Lot, with the title of Kamehameha V. In 1864 Lot abrogated the constitution of 1840 and granted a new one. He reigned until 1872, and died without naming a successor, and the Legislative Assembly elected Lunalilo to the throne. He was of the Kamehameha family, and with his death, in 1873, the Kamehameha dynasty came to an end. He, too, failed to designate a successor, and as but two of the accepted descendants of the first Kamehameha remained—one a sister of Kamehameha V. and the other a female cousin of that sovereign —David Kalakaua was elected to the throne by the Legislative Assembly in 1874, receiving all but five votes of that body, which were cast for the queen-dowager Emma, widow of Kamehameha IV.

Provision having been made for the event by a previous Legislative Assembly, King Kalakaua, with his queen, Kapiolani, was formally crowned on the 12th of February, 1883, in the presence of the representatives of many of the nations of the Old World and the New. Since the coronation the last of the Kamehamehas has passed away, including the queen-dowager Emma, and King Kalakaua remains the most direct representative in the kingdom of the ancient sovereigns of Hawaii. He draws his strain from Liloa through the great I family of Hawaii, who joined their fortunes with the first Kamehameha in the conquest of the group. His queen, Kapiolani, is a granddaughter of the last independent sovereign of Kauai, and is thus allied in blood with the early rulers of the group. She is childless, and the Princess Liliuokalani, the elder of the two sisters of the king, has been named as his successor. She is the wife of His Excel-

Princess Kauilani.

lency John O. Dominis, an American by birth and present governor of the islands of Oahu and Maui. The only direct heir
in the families of the king and his two sisters is the Princess
Kaiulani, daughter of the Princess Likelike,* wife of Mr. Cleg-
horn, a merchant of Honolulu.

Following is a list of the sovereigns of Hawaii, with the dates
and durations of their several governments, from the eleventh to
the nineteenth century. It embraces only the rulers of the
island of Hawaii, who eventually became the masters of the
group. Until the reign of Kalaniopuu, which began in 1754,
the dates are merely approximate :

Pilikaeae,	from A.D.	1095 to 1120
Kukohau,	"	1120 to 1145
Kaniuhi,	"	1145 to 1170
Kanipahu,	"	1170 to 1195
Kalapana (including the usurpation of Kamaiole),	"	1195 to 1220
Kahaimoelea,	"	1220 to 1260
Kalaunuiohua,	"	1260 to 1300
Kuaiwa,	"	1300 to 1340
Kahoukapu,	"	1340 to 1380
Kauholanuimahu,	"	1380 to 1415
Kiha,	"	1415 to 1455
Liloa,	"	1455 to 1485
Hakau,	"	1485 to 1490
Umi,	"	1490 to 1525
Kealiiokaloa,	"	1525 to 1535
Keawenui,	"	1535 to 1565
Kaikilani and Lonoikamakahiki,	"	1565 to 1595
Keakealanikane,	"	1595 to 1625
Keakamahana,	"	1625 to 1655
Keakealaniwahine,	"	1655 to 1685
Keawe and sister,	"	1685 to 1720
Alapanui,	"	1720 to 1754
Kalaniopuu,		1754 to 1782
Kamehameha I.,	"	1782 to 1819
Kamehameha II.—Liholiho,	"	1819 to 1824
Kaahumanu regency,	"	1824 to 1833
Kamehameha III.—Kauikeaouli,	"	1833 to 1854
Kamehameha IV.,	"	1854 to 1863
Kamehameha V.—Lot,	"	1863 to 1872
Lunalilo,	"	1872 to 1873
Kalakaua,	"	1874 to ——

* The Princess Likelike died February 2, 1887.

Having thus briefly sketched the outlines of the prominent political events of the islands, the ancient religion of the Hawaiians will next be referred to ; and as the *tabu* was no less a religious than a secular prerogative, it may properly be considered in connection with the priesthood. A knowledge of the power, scope and sanctity of the *tabu* is essential to a proper understanding of the relations existing in the past between the people and their political and religious rulers, and this great governing force will now claim our attention.

THE TABU.

Strictly speaking, the ancient *tabu*, or *kapu*, was a prerogative adhering exclusively to political and ecclesiastical rank. It was a command either to do or not to do, and the meaning of it was, " Obey or die." It was common to the Polynesian tribes, and was a protection to the lives, property and dignity of the priesthood and nobility.

The religious *tabus* were well understood by the people, as were also the personal or perpetual *tabus* of the ruling families ; but the incidental *tabus* were oppressive, irksome and dangerous to the masses, as they were liable to be thoughtlessly violated, and death was the usual penalty.

Everything pertaining to the priesthood and temples was

sacred, or *tabu*, and pigs designed for sacrifice, and running at large with the temple mark upon them, could not be molested. It was a violation of perpetual *tabu* to cross the shadow of the king, to stand in his presence without permission, or to approach him except

THE PULOULOU, OR TABU MARK.

upon the knees. This did not apply to the higher grades of chiefs, who themselves possessed *tabu* rights.

Favorite paths, springs, streams and bathing-places were at intervals *tabued* to the exclusive use of the kings and temples, and squid, turtle, and two or three species of birds could be eaten only by the priests and *tabu* nobility.

Yellow was the *tabu* color of royalty, and red of the priesthood, and mantles of the feathers of the *oo* and *mamo* could be worn only by kings and princes. Feather capes of mingled red and yellow distinguished the lesser nobility.

Women were *tabued* from eating plantains, bananas, and cocoanuts ; also the flesh of swine and certain fish, among them the *kumu, moano, ulua, honu, ea, hahalua* and *naia ;* and men and women were allowed under no circumstances to partake of food together. Hence, when Liholiho, in 1819, openly violated this fundamental *tabu* by eating with his queen, he defied the gods of his fathers and struck at the very foundation of the religious faith of his people.

The general *tabus* declared by the supreme chief or king were proclaimed by heralds, while the *puloulou*—a staff surmounted by a crown of white or black *kapa*—placed at the entrance of temples, royal residences and the mansions of *tabu* chiefs, or beside springs, groves, paths, or bathing-places, was a standing notification against trespass. General *tabus* were declared either to propitiate the gods or in celebration of important events. They were either common or strict, and frequently embraced an entire district and continued from one to ten days.

During the continuance of a common *tabu* the masses were merely required to abstain from their usual occupations and attend the services at the *heiaus*, or temples.; but during a strict *tabu* every fire and every light was extinguished, no canoe was shoved from the shore, no bathing was permitted, the pigs and fowls were muzzled or placed under calabashes that they might utter no noise, the people conversed in whispers, and the priests and their assistants were alone allowed to be seen without their places of abode. It was a season of deathly silence, and was thought to be especially grateful to the gods.

Some of the royal *tabus*, centuries back in the past, were frivolous and despotic, such as regulating the wearing of beards and compelling all sails to be lowered on passing certain coast points ; but, however capricious or oppressive, the *tabu* was seldom violated, and its maintenance was deemed a necessary protection to the governing classes.

ANCIENT HAWAIIAN RELIGION.

The ancient religion of the Hawaiians, of which the *tabu* formed an essential feature, was a theocracy of curious structure. It was a system of idolatrous forms and sacrifices engrafted without consistency upon the Jewish story of the creation, the fall of man, the revolt of Lucifer, the Deluge, and the repopulation of the earth.

The legends of the Hawaiians were preserved with marvellous integrity. Their historians were the priests, who at intervals met in council and recited and compared their genealogical *meles*, in order that nothing might be either changed or lost. How did the Hawaiian priesthood become possessed of the story of the Hebrew genesis? It was old to them when the *Resolution*

ANCIENT GODS.

and *Discovery* dropped their anchors in Kealakeakua Bay; old to them when one or more chance parties of Spanish sailors in the sixteenth century may have looked in upon them for a moment while on their way to the Spice Islands; and it was probably old to them when the Hawaiians found their present home in the sixth century, and when the Polynesians left the coast of Asia four hundred years earlier.

One theory is that the story was acquired through Israelitish contact with the ancestors of the Polynesians while the latter were drifting eastward from the land of their nativity. But the more reasonable assumption seems to be that the Hawaiian theogony, so strangely perpetuated, is an independent and perhaps original version of a series of creation legends common in the remote past to the Cushite, Semite and Aryan tribes, and was handed down quite as accurately as the Jewish version before it became fixed in written characters. In fact, in some respects the Hawaiian seems to be more complete than the Jewish version.

From the beginning, according to Hawaiian story, a trinity of gods existed, who were the sole and all-pervading intelligences of chaos, or night—a condition represented by the Hawaiian word *Po*. These gods were :

Kane, the originator ;

Ku, the architect and builder ; and

Lono, the executor and director of the elements.

By the united will of *Hikapoloa*, or the trinity, light was brought into chaos. They next created the heavens, three in number, as their dwelling-places, and then the earth, sun, moon and stars. From their spittle they next created a host of angels to minister to their wants.

Finally, man was created. His body was formed of red earth mingled with the spittle of *Kane*, and his head of whitish clay brought by *Lono* from the four quarters of the earth. The meaning of Adam is red, and it will be remarked that the Hawaiian Adam was made of earth of that color. He was made in the image of *Kane*, who breathed into his nostrils, and he became alive. Afterwards, from one of his ribs, taken from his side while he slept, a woman was created. The man was called *Kumu-honua*, and the woman *Ke-ola-ku-honua*.

The newly-created pair were placed in a beautiful paradise called *Paliuli*. Three rivers of "the waters of life" ran through it, on the banks of which grew every inviting fruit, including the "*tabued* bread-fruit tree" and "sacred apple-tree," with which are connected the fall and expulsion of the man and woman from their earthly paradise. The three rivers had their source in a beautiful lake, fed by "the living waters of *Kane*." The waters were filled with fish which fire could not destroy, and on being sprinkled with them the dead were restored to life. Legends relate instances in which these waters were procured, through the favor of the gods, for the restoration to life of distinguished mortals.

As a specimen of the chants perpetuating these traditions and embellishing the plainer prose recitals, the following extract relating to the creation is given :

> " Kane of the great Night,
>   Ku and Lono of the great Night,
>   Hika-po-loa the king.
>   The tabued Night that is set apart,
>   The poisonous Night,
>   The barren, desolate Night,
>   The continual darkness of midnight,
>   The Night, the reviler.
>   O Kane, O Ku-ka-pao,
>   And great Lono dwelling in the water,
>   Brought forth are Heaven and Earth,
>   Quickened, increased, moving,
>   Raised up into Continents.
>   Kane, Lord of Night, Lord the Father,
>   Ku-ka-pao, in the hot heavens,
>   Great Lono with the flashing eyes,
>   Lightning-like has the Lord
>   Established in truth, O Kane, master-worker ;
>   The Lord creator of mankind :
>   Start, work, bring forth the chief Kumu-honua,
>   And Ola-ku-honua, the woman ;
>   Dwelling together are they two,
>   Dwelling in marriage (is she) with the husband, the brother."

Among the angels created was *Kanaloa*, the Hawaiian Lucifer, who incited a rebellion in heaven, with the results, strangely enough, related in immortal song by Milton. When man was created, *Kanaloa* demanded his adoration. This was refused by *Kane*, as angels and man were alike the creations of Deity, whereupon *Kanaloa* ambitiously resolved to create a man of his own who would worship him. *Kane* allowed him to proceed with his seditious work. He made a man in the exact image of *Kumu-honua*, but could not give it life. He breathed into its nostrils, but it would not rise ; he called to it, but it would not speak. This exasperated him, and he determined to destroy the man made by the gods. He therefore crept into *Paliuli* in the form of a *moo*, or lizard, and, through some deception not definitely stated by tradition, *Kumu-honua* and his mate committed some offence for which they were driven from paradise by the "large, white bird of *Kane*."

Kumu-honua had three sons, the second of whom was slain by the first. The name of the Hawaiian Cain is *Laka*. *Ka Pili* was the youngest son, and thirteen generations are named between him and the Deluge, whereas the Hebrew version records but ten on the corresponding line of Seth.

The Hawaiian Noah is called *Nuu*. At the command of the gods he constructed an ark, and entered it with his wife and three sons, and a male and female of every breathing thing. The waters came and covered the earth. When they subsided the gods entered the ark, which was resting on a mountain overlooking a beautiful valley, and commanded *Nuu* to go forth with all of life that the ark contained. In gratitude for his deliverance *Nuu* offered a sacrifice to the moon, mistaking it for *Kane*. Descending on a rainbow, that deity reproved his thoughtlessness, but left the bow as a perpetual token of his forgiveness.

Continuing the genealogical record, ten generations are given between *Nuu* and *Ku Pule*, who "removed to a southern country," taking with him as a wife his slave-woman *Ahu*. So was it with Abraham. *Ku Pule* established the practice of circumcision, and was the grandfather of *Kini-lau-a-mano*, whose twelve children became the founders of twelve tribes, from one of which —the *Menehune*—the Hawaiians are made to descend.

A story similar to that of Joseph is also given, and mention is made of the subsequent return of the *Menehune* people to the land set apart for their occupation by *Kane*. Two brothers led them over deserts and through waters, and after many tribulations they reached their destination.

This would seem to imply that the *Menehune* people were one of the tribes of Israel; yet it is more probable that they had their origin in some one of the other twelveships into which the early Asiatic tribes were in many instances divided, and that the stories of Joseph and the Exodus became a part of their folk-lore through contact with other races.

The genealogical line from the Hawaiian Adam to the grandson of *Ku Pule*—that is, until the time of Jacob—has been brought down through three distinct traditional channels. The agreement of the several versions is remarkable, but the one brought to the islands by the high-priest Paao in the eleventh

century, and retained by his ecclesiastical successors, is regarded
as the most authentic.   It was an heirloom of the priesthood, and
was never communicated beyond the walls of the temples.

With the settlement of the *Menehune* people in the land set
apart for them by *Kane*, the Hawaiian legends cease to remind
us of the later history of the Hebrews.   There the similarity of
historic incident abruptly ends, and, with an uncertain stride of
twelve or thirteen generations, the chiefly line is brought down to
Wakea and his wife *Papa*, mythical rulers of superhuman attributes, who must have existed before the Polynesians left the
Asiatic coast, although in some legends they are connected not
only with the first settlement of the Hawaiian archipelago, but
with the creation of its islands.

A few of the many legends relating to the creation and first
settlement of the islands will be noted.   One of them in substance is that *Hawaii-loa*, a distinguished chief, and fourth in
generation from *Kini-lau-a-mano*, sailed westward, and, guided by
the Pleiades, discovered the Hawaiian group.   He gave to the
largest island his own name, and to the others the names of his
children.

Another tradition refers to *Papa*, the wife of *Wakea*, as a
tabued descendant of *Hawaii-loa*, and superior in caste to her
husband.   Mutual jealousies embittered their lives and led to
strange events.   *Wakea* found favor with the beautiful *Hina*,
and the island of Molokai was born of their embrace.   In retaliation *Papa* smiled upon the warrior *Lua*, and the fruit of their
meeting was the fair island of Oahu.   Hence the old names of
Molokai-Hina and *Oahu-a-Lua*.

Quite as fanciful a legend relates that an immense bird laid
an egg on the waters of the ocean.   It was hatched by the warm
winds of the tropics, and the Hawaiian group came into being.
Shortly after a man and woman, with a pair each of dogs, hogs
and fowls, came in a canoe from Kahiki, landed on the eastern
coast of Hawaii, and became the progenitors of the Hawaiian
people.

Fifty-six generations are mentioned from *Wakea* to the present ruling family.   The legends of the twenty-nine generations
covering the period between *Wakea* and Maweke—which brings
the record down to the eleventh century, when the second migratory influx from the southern islands occurred—abound in

wars, rebellions and popular movements, in which giants, demi-gods, and even the gods themselves took part ; and it was doubt-less during that period that the idolatrous forms and practices of the Hawaiian religion, as it existed a century ago, were en-grafted upon an older and simpler creed confined to the worship of the godhead.

When the high-priest Paao arrived with Pili he introduced some new gods while recognizing the old, strengthened and en-larged the scope of the *tabu*, and established an hereditary priest-hood independent of, and second only in authority to, the supreme political head. Different grades of priests also came into exist-ence, such as seers, prophets, astrologers and *kahunas* of various function, including the power of healing and destroying. In fact, the priesthood embraced ten distinct grades or colleges, each possessing and exercising powers peculiar to it, and the mastery of all of them was one of the qualifications of the high-priesthood. The tutelar deity of the entire body was *Uli*.

The form of the *heiau*, or temple, was changed by Paao and his successors, and the masses mingled less freely in the cere-monies of sacrifice and other forms of worship. The high-priest-hood became more mysterious and exclusive, and assumed pre-rogatives above the reach of royalty. The old Hawaiian trinity —*Kane, Ku* and *Lono*—remained the supreme gods of the pan-theon, but *Kanaloa*, the spirit of evil, was accorded beneficent attributes and exalted among them.

The regions of *Po*, or death, were presided over by *Milu*, a wicked king who once ruled on earth, while the spirits of favorite chiefs were conveyed by the divine messenger *Kuahairo* to the presence of *Kaono-hio-kala*, whose beatific abode was somewhere in the heavens. Another belief was that the ruler of *Po* was *Manua*, and that *Milu* did not follow *Akea*, the first king of Ha-waii, to that place, but dwelt in a region far westward and be-neath the sea. Although significant of darkness, *Po* was not without light. Like Tartarus, it could be visited by favored mortals, and the dead were sometimes brought back from it to earth.

Pele, the dreadful goddess of the volcanoes, with her malig-nant relatives, was added to the Hawaiian deities during the sec-ond influx from the south, and temples were erected to her wor-ship all over the volcanic districts of Hawaii. At that period were also introduced *Laamaomao*, the god of the winds, the poison goddesses *Kalaipahoa* and *Kapo*, and many other deities.

But the worship of the Hawaiians was not confined to *Kane, Ku, Lono* and *Pele. Heiaus* were erected to the war-gods of

the kings, and great sacrifices were frequently made to them, generally of human beings, preceding, during, and following campaigns and battles.   Humbler temples were also maintained to fish, shark, lizard and other gods, where sacrifices of fish and fruits were offered.

To the superstitious masses the land abounded in gnomes and fairies, and the waters in nymphs and monsters, whose caprices are themes of a bountiful store of folk-lore. With almost every stream, gorge and headland is connected some supernatural story, and the bards and musicians of old earned an easy support by keeping alive these legends of the people.   To some supernatural powers were given, and malignant and beneficent spirits assumed human forms and flitted among the palms in the guise of birds.

The people made their own household gods, and destroyed them when they failed to contribute to their success.   For example, at Ninole, on the southeast coast of Hawaii, is a small beach called Kaloa, the stones of which, it was thought, propagated by contact with each other. From the large stones the people made gods to preside over their games.   When a stone

Ku - Kaili - Moku,
the War-God of
Kamehameha I.

was selected for a god it was taken to the *heiau*, where certain ceremonies were performed over it.   It was then dressed and taken to witness some game or pastime. If the owner was successful it was accepted as a god ; if unsuccessful more than once or twice, it was thrown away or wrought into an axe or adze. Sometimes a stone of each sex was selected, wrapped in *kapa*, and laid away.   In time a small pebble was found with them. It increased in size, and was finally taken to the *heiau* and formally made into a god.   Such is the story that is still told.

The people believed that the spirits of the departed continued to hover around their earthly homes, and the shades of their ancestors were appealed to in prayer. The owl and a bird called the *alae* were regarded as gods, and scores of other deities, controlling the elements or presiding over the several industries and amusements of the masses, were recognized and placated with sacrifices when in unfavorable moods. They had a god of the winds, of the husbandman, the warrior, the canoe-maker, the *hula* dancer, the distiller, the orator, the doctor and the sorcerer, and many gods of the sailor and the fisherman.

The services of the high-priest did not extend to these popular deities on any of the islands of the group. The *heiaus* over which he presided were dedicated either to the higher gods of the pantheon or to the war-god of the king or supreme chief. He was next to the king in authority, and always of distinguished blood. Surrounded by seers, prophets and assistants, and claiming to hold direct intercourse with the gods, he was consulted on all matters of state consequence, and the auguries of the temple were always accepted with respect and confidence. The high-priest sometimes had charge of the war-god of the king, and in such cases went with it to the field of battle.

Hua, one of the ancient kings of Maui, defied the priesthood and slew his high-priest. As a warning to ruling chiefs, the story of the consequences of Hua's madness has come down with great conciseness through the chroniclers of the priesthood. Hua's kingdom became a desolation. Wherever he traveled all vegetation perished, and he finally died of famine on Hawaii, and his bones were left to whiten in the sun.

There were several classes of priests, or *kahunas*, beside those who were connected with the temples. They were seers, doctors and dealers in enchantment, and subsisted by preying upon the people through their superstitions. All physical illness was attributed either to the anger of the gods, witchcraft, or the prayers of a malignant *kahuna*. The afflicted person usually sent for a *kahuna*, whose first business was to discover the cause of the malady through incantation. This ascertained, an effort was made to counteract the spells or prayers which were wearing away the life of the patient, and sometimes with so great success that the affliction was transferred to the party whose malice had invoked it.

The belief that one person might be prayed to death by another was universal with the ancient Hawaiians, and not a few of the race would turn pale to-day if told that one of priestly strain was earnestly praying for his death. In praying a person to death it was essential that the *kahuna* should possess something closely connected with the person of the victim—a lock of his hair, a tooth, a nail-paring, or a small quantity of his spittle, for example ; hence the office of spittoon-bearer to the ancient kings was entrusted only to chiefs of some rank, who might be expected to guard with care the royal expectoration.

The belief was general that the spirits of the dead might be seen and conversed with by the *kilos*, or sorcerers, and the spirits of the living, it was claimed, were sometimes invoked from their slumbering tabernacles by priests of exceptional sanctity. The spirit of the dead was called *unihipili*, while the disembodied and visible spirit of a living person was known as *kahoaka*.

Of all the deities *Pele* was held in greatest dread on the island of Hawaii, where volcanic irruptions were frequent. With her five brothers and eight sisters—all representing different elemental forces—she dwelt in state in the fiery abysses of the volcanoes, moving from one to another at her pleasure, and visiting with inundations of lava such districts as neglected to cast into the craters proper offerings of meats and fruits, or angered her in other respects. One of her forms was that of a beautiful woman, in which she sometimes sought human society, and numerous legends of her affairs of love have been preserved. She was regarded as the special friend of Kamehameha I., and the suffocation of a portion of the army of Keoua, near the crater of Kilauea, in 1791, was credited directly to her.

The last public recognition of the powers of *Pele* occurred as late as 1882 on the island of Hawaii. The village of Hilo was threatened. A broad stream of lava from Mauna Loa, after a devastating journey of twenty-five miles or more, reached a point in its downward course within a mile or two of the bay of Hilo. Its movement was slow, like that of all lava-streams some distance from their source, but its steadily approaching line of fire rendered it almost certain that the village, and perhaps the harbor, of Hilo would be destroyed within a very few days. Trenches were digged, walls were raised, and prayers were offered, but all to no purpose. Downward moved the awful avalanche of fire.

Ruth, a surviving sister of the fourth and fifth Kamehamehas, was then living in Honolulu. She was a proud, stern old chiefess, who thought too little of the whites to attempt to acquire their language. The danger threatening Hilo was reported to her. " I will save the fish-ponds of Hilo," said the old chiefess. "*Pele* will not refuse to listen to the prayer of a Kamehameha." She chartered a steamer, left Honolulu for Hilo with a large number of attendants, and the next day stood facing the still moving flow of lava. Ascending an elevation immediately back of the village, she caused to be erected there a rude altar, before which she made her supplications to *Pele*, with offerings fed to the front of the advancing lava. This done, she descended the hill with confidence and returned to Honolulu.

The stream of fire ceased to move, and to-day its glistening front stands like a wall around Hilo. " A remarkable coincidence," explained the whites. " The work of *Pele*," whispered the natives, although the last of the temples of that goddess had been destroyed sixty years before. Without discussing the cause —a natural one beyond a doubt—it may be remarked that the result has been something of a renewal with the natives of faith in the discarded gods of their fathers.

All of the minor gods of the Hawaiians seem to have been independent and self-controlling. It is not claimed that they derived their powers from, were directed by, or were responsible to the supreme godhead. Hence the mythology of the Polynesians, strong though it be in individual powers and personations of the forces and achievements of nature, presents itself to us in a fragmentary form, like an incongruous patchwork of two or more half-developed or half-forgotten religious systems.

KALAIPAHOA, POISON WAR-
GODDESS OF MOLOKAI.

One of the most noted of the independent deities of the group was *Kalaipahoa*, the poison-goddess of Molokai. Some centuries back she came to the islands, with two or three of her sisters, from an unknown land, and left her mark in many localities. She entered a grove of trees on the island of Molokai, and left in them a poison so intense that birds fell dead in flying over their branches. The king of the island

was advised by his high-priest to have a god hewn from one of
the poisoned trees. Hundreds of his subjects perished in the
undertaking, but the image was finally finished and presented to
the king, wrapped in many folds of *kapa*. It came down the
generations an object of fear, and was finally seized by the
first Kamehameha, and at his death divided among his principal
chiefs.

Kuula was the principal god of the fishermen on all the islands of the group. Rude temples were erected to him on the
shores of favorite fishing-grounds, and the first fish of every
catch was his due. His wife was *Hina*, and she was appealed
to when her husband withheld his favors. *Laeapua* and *Kaneapua* were gods worshipped by the fishermen of Lanai, and other
fish-gods were elsewhere recognized.

There were a number of shark and lizard gods. They
were powerful and malignant, and greatly feared by the classes
who frequented the sea. *Heiaus* were erected to them on promontories overlooking the ocean, and the offerings to them of
fish and fruits were always liberal. They assumed the forms
of gigantic sharks and lizards, and not unfrequently lashed the
waters into fury and destroyed canoes. *Moaalii* was the great
shark-god of Molokai and Oahu. *Apukohai* and *Uhumakaikai*
were the evil gods infesting the waters of Kauai. *Lonoakihi*
was the eel-god of all the islands, and *Ukanipo* was the shark-god
of Hawaii.

Among the celebrated war-gods of the kings of the group
was that of Kamehameha I. It was called *Kaili*, or *Ku-kaili-
moku*, and accompanied the great chief in all of his important
battles. It had been the war-god of the Hawaiian kings for
many generations, and was given in charge of Kamehameha
by his royal uncle, Kalauiopuu. It was a small wooden
image, roughly carved, and adorned with a head-dress of yellow feathers. It is said that at times, in the heat of battle, it
uttered cries which were heard above the clash of arms. It is
not known what became of the image after the death of Kamehameha.

The public *heiaus*, or temples, of the Hawaiians were usually
walled enclosures of from one to five acres, and generally irregular in form. The walls were frequently ten feet in thickness
and twenty feet in height, and the material used was unhewn

stone, without mortar or cement. They narrowed slightly from the base upward, and were sometimes capped with hewn slabs of coral or other rock not too firm in texture to be worked with tools of stone.

Within this enclosure was an inner stone or wooden temple of small dimensions, called the *luakina*, or house of sacrifice, and in front of the entrance to it stood the *lele*, or altar, consisting of a raised platform of stone. The inner temple was sacred to the priests. Within it stood the *anu*, a small wicker enclosure, from which issued the oracles of the *kaulas*, or prophets, and around the walls were ranged charms and gods of especial sanctity. Beside the entrance to this sacred apartment were images of the principal gods, and the outer and inner walls were surmounted by lines of stone and wooden idols.

The enclosure contained other buildings for the accommodation of the high-priest and his assistants ; also a house for the governing chief or king, some distance removed from the domiciles of the priest. It was used temporarily by him when on a visit of consultation to the temple, or as a place of refuge in a time of danger. On each side of the entrance to the outer enclosure was a *tabu* staff, or elevated cross, and near it was a small walled structure in which were slain the victims for the altar.

When an augury was required by the king he frequently visited the *heiau* in person and propounded his questions to the *kaulas*. If the answers from the *anu* were vague and unsatisfactory, other methods of divination were resorted to, such as the opening of pigs and fowls, the shapes of the clouds, the flights of birds, etc. After prayers by the priest the animals were killed, and auguries were gathered from the manner in which they expired, the appearance of the intestines—which were supposed to be the seat of thought—and other signs. Sometimes the spleens of swine were removed, if auguries of war were required, and held above the heads of the priests while prayers were offered.

Before engaging in war or any other important enterprise attended by doubt or danger, human and other sacrifices were made, of which there were fifteen different kinds, and the first prisoners taken in battle were reserved for the altar. The priests named the number of men required for sacrifice, and the king provided them, sometimes from prisoners and malefactors, and sometimes from promiscuous drafts along the highways. The victims were slain with clubs without the temple walls, and their bodies, with other offerings, were laid upon the altar to decay. When the king or other high chief made a special offering of an enemy, the left eye of the victim, after the body had been brought to the altar, was removed and handed to him by the officiating priest. After making a semblance of eating it the chief tossed it upon the altar.

During the construction of *heiaus* human sacrifices were usually offered as the work progressed, and when completed they were dedicated with great pomp and solemnity, and the altars were sometimes heaped with human bodies. In dedicating ordinary temples the *kaiopokeo* prayer was employed; but in consecrating *heiaus* of the first class the *kuawili* invocation was recited, a prayer continuing from sunrise to sunset. Oil and holy water were sprinkled upon the altars and sacred vessels, and the services were under the direction of the high-priest, and generally in the presence of the governing chief.

The ordinary services in the temples consisted of offerings of fruits and meats, and of chants, prayers and responses, in which the people sometimes joined. Women did not participate in the ceremonies of the temples, but the exclusion found ample compensation in their exemption from sacrifice when human bodies were required.

Temples of refuge, called *puhonuas*, were maintained on Hawaii, and possibly on Lanai and Oahu in the remote past; but concerning the latter there is some doubt. One of the *puhonuas* on Hawaii was at Honaunau, near the sacred burial-place of *Hale-o-Keawe*, and the other at Waipio, connected with the great *heiau* of *Paa-kalani*. Their gates were always open, and priests guarded their entrances. Any one who entered their enclosures for protection, whether chief or slave, whether escaping criminal or warrior in retreat, was safe from molestation, even though the king pursued. These places of refuge, with the right of circumcision, which existed until after the death of the first Kamehameha, suggest a Polynesian contact with the descendants of Abraham far back in the past, if not a kinship with one of the scattered tribes of Israel.

In further evidence of the wanderings of the early Polynesians in western and southern Asia, and of their intercourse with the continental races, it may be mentioned that a disposition toward phallic worship, attested by tradition and existing symbols, followed them far out into the Pacific ; and that connected with their story of the creation, so closely resembling the Hebrew version, is the Buddhist claim of previous creations which either ran their course or were destroyed by an offended godhead. Nor is Hawaiian tradition content with the mere advancement of the theory of successive creations. It makes specific reference to a creation next preceding that of their *Ku-mu-honua,* or Adam, and gives the names of the man and woman created and destroyed. They were *Wela-ahi-lani* and *Owe.*

It has been mentioned that the birds *pueo* and *alae* were sacred and sometimes worshipped. Among the sacred fish were the *aku* and *opelu.* How they became so is told in a legend relating to the high-priest Paao, who migrated to the islands in the eleventh century and induced Pili to follow him. Before visiting Hawaii, Paao lived near his brother, probably on the island of Samoa. Both were priests and well skilled in sorcery and divination. The name of the brother was Lonopele. Both were affluent and greatly respected. Lonopele's lands were near the sea and produced the choicest varieties of fruits. One season, when the fruits were ripening, Lonopele discovered that some one was surreptitiously gathering them in the night-time, and accused one of the sons of Paao of stealing them. Indignant at the charge, and discerning no better way of disproving it, Paao killed and opened his son, and showed his brother that there was no fruit in the stomach of the boy.

Grieved at the death of his son, and holding his brother accountable for· it, Paao concluded to emigrate to some other land, and built strong canoes for that purpose. About the time they were completed a son of Lonopele chanced to be in the neighborhood, and Paao, remembering the death of his own son, ordered the boy to be killed. He was missed, and search was made for him, and his body was finally found near Paao's canoes. Lonopele charged his brother with the murder. Paao did not deny it, and Lonopele ordered him to leave the island. To avoid further trouble Paao set sail at once with a party consisting of thirty-eight persons. One tradition says Pili was of the party ; but he must have left Samoa some years later, as Paao sent or went for him after reaching Hawaii.

As the canoes were moving from the shore several prophets, standing on the cliffs above, expressed a desire to join the party. "Very well," was the answer of Paao ; "if you are prophets, as you say, leap from the cliffs and I will take you aboard." Several leaped into the sea and were dashed against the rocks and drowned. Finally Makuakaumana, a prophet of genuine inspiration, who was to have accompanied the expedition, reached the shore and discovered the canoes of Paao far out on the ocean. Raising his voice, he hailed Paao and asked that a canoe might be sent back for him. "Not so," returned the priest in a loud voice, which the favoring winds bore to the belated prophet. "To return would be an omen of evil. There is room for you, but if you would go with us you must fly to our canoes." And, flying, the prophet reached the canoes in safety.

Observing the canoes of Paao as they were disappearing in the distance, Lonopele sent a violent storm to destroy them ; but the strong fish *Aku* assisted in propelling the canoes against the storm, and the mighty fish *Opelu* swam around them and broke the waves with his body. The malignant brother then sent the great bird *Kihahakaiwainapali* to vomit over the canoes and sink them ; but they were hastily covered with mats, and thus escaped destruction. After a long voyage Paao landed in Puna, on the coast of Hawaii. Thenceforth the *aku* and *opelu* were held sacred by Paao and his descendants.

Following is a list of the supreme and principal elemental, industrial and tutelar deities of the Hawaiian group :

The Godhead.

Kane, the organizer.
Ku, the architect and builder.
Lono, the executor.

Kanaloa, the Lucifer, or fallen angel.

Rulers in the realms of Po, or death.

Akea, the first Hawaiian king, who, after life, founded the island-kingdom of *Kapapahaunaumoku*, in the realms of *Po*, or death.

Milu, the successor of *Akea*, or who, according to another belief, accompanied *Akea* to *Po*, and became the perpetual ruler of a kingdom on its western confines.

Manua, referred to in some legends as the supreme sovereign of *Po*. With him abide the spirits of distinguished chiefs and priests, who wander among beautiful streams and groves of *kou* trees, and subsist upon lizards and butterflies.

General Dominis, Consort of the Heir-Apparent.

Minor Celestial Deities.

Kaonohiokala (the eyeball of the sun), a celestial god, with an abode somewhere in the heavens, and to whose presence the departed spirits of chiefs were conducted.

Kuahairo, the messenger who conducted the souls of distinguished chiefs to *Kaonohiokala.*

Olopue, a god of Maui, who bore the spirits of noted chiefs to the celestial paradise. Kamehameha sought to secure possession of a very sacred image of this god, inherited by Kahekili, *moi* of Maui.

The Volcanic Deities.

Pele, the ruling goddess of the volcanoes, with her sisters,

Hiiaka-wawahi-lani, the heaven-rending cloud-holder ;

Makoie-nawahi-waa, the fire-eyed canoe-breaker ;

Hiiaka-noho-lani, the heaven-dwelling cloud-holder ;

Hiiaka-kaalawa-maka, the quick-glancing cloud-holder ;

Hiiaka-hoi-ke-poli-a-pele, the cloud-holder kissing the bosom of Pele ;

Hiiaka-ka-pu-enaena, the red-hot mountain lifting clouds ;

Hiiaka-kaleiia, the wreath encircled cloud-holder ;

Hiiaka-opio, the young cloud-holder ; and their brothers,

Kamo-hoalii, or King Moho, the king of vapor or steam ;

Kapohoikahiola, god of explosions ;

Keuakepo, god of the night-rain, or rain of fire ;

Kane-kahili, the husband of thunder, or thundering god;

Keoahi-kamakaua, the fire-thrusting child of war.

[The last two were hunchbacks.]

Akuapaao, the war-god of Paao, taken from the temple of Manini by Umi.

Ku-kaili-moku, the war-god of Kamehameha I., bequeathed to him by Kalaniopuu.

Deities of the Elements.

Laamaomao, god of the winds, the Hawaiian Æolus, whose home was on Molokai.

Hinakuluiau, a goddess of the rain.

Hinakealii and

Hookuipaele, sisters of *Hinakuluiau.*

Mooaleo, a powerful gnome of Lanai, conquered by Kaululaau, a prince of Maui.

Kuula, a god of the fishermen.

Hina, wife of *Kuula.*

Laeapua and

Kaneapua, gods of the fishermen of Lanai.

Hinahele and her daughter

Aiaiakuula, goddesses of the fishermen of Hawaii.

Ukanipo, the great shark-god of Hawaii.

Moaalii, the principal shark-god of Molokai and Oahu.

Lonoakiki, the great eel-god of all the group.

Apukohai and

Uhumakaikai, evil shark or fish-gods of Kauai.

Gods of the Arts and Industries.

Akua-ula, the god of inspiration.

Haulili, a god of speech, special to Kauai.

Koleamoku, the deified chief who first learned the use of herbs and the art of healing from the gods. He was a patron of the *kahunas*.

Olonopuha and

Makanuiailono, deified disciples of *Koleamoku*.

Kaanahua, the second son of the high-priest Luahoomoe, and

Kukaoo, gods of the husbandman.

Lakakane, god of the *hula* and similar sports.

Mokualii, god of the canoe-makers.

Hai, god of *kapa* making.

Ulaulakeahi, god of distillation.

Kalaipahoa, a goddess who entered and poisoned trees.

Kapo and

Pua, sisters of *Kalaipahoa*, with like functions.

Kama, a powerful tutelar god of all the islands.

Laauli, the god who made inviolable laws.

Kuahana, the god who killed men wantonly.

Leleioio, the god who inflicted bodily pain.

Lelehookaahaa, wife of *Leleioio*.

Lie, a goddess of the mountains, who braided *leis*.

Maikahulipu, the god who assisted in righting upset canoes.

Pohakaa, a god living in precipitous places, and who rolled down stones, to the fright and injury of passers.

Keoloewa, a god worshipped in the *heiaus* of Maui.

Kiha, a goddess of Maui, held in great reverence.

Uli, the god of the sorcerers.

Pekuku, a powerful god of Hawaii.

Lonoikeaualii, a god worshipped in the *heiaus* of Oahu.

Kauakahi, a god of Maui and Molokai.

Hiaka, a mountain god of Kauai.

Kapo and

Kapua, and several others, messengers of the gods.

Ouli, the god appealed to by the *kahunas* in praying people to death.

Maliu, any deified deceased chief.

Akua noho, gods possessing the spirits of departed mortals, of which there were many.

Kiha-wahine and

Kalo, noted deities of the class of *akua-noho*.

Mahulu, a name common to three gods in the temples of *Lono*.

Manu, the names of two gods at the outer gates of *heiaus* dedicated to *Lono*.

Puea, the god worshipped in the darkness.

Kaluanuunohonionio, one of the principal gods of the *luakina*, or sacrificial house of the temple.

Kanenuiakea, a general name for a class of thirteen gods connected with the larger *heiaus*.

ANCIENT HAWAIIAN GOVERNMENT.

Previous to the eleventh century the several habitable islands of the Hawaiian group were governed by one or more independent chiefs, as already stated. After the migratory influx of that period, however, and the settlement on the islands of a number of warlike southern chiefs and their followers, the independent chiefs began to unite for mutual protection. This involved the necessity of a supreme head, which was usually found in the chief conceded to be the most powerful ; and thus *alii-nuis, mois* and kings sprang into existence. So far as tradition extends, however, certain lines, such as the Maweke, Pili and Paumakua families, were always considered to be of supreme blood. They came to the islands as chiefs of distinguished lineage, and so remained.

Gradually the powers of the *mois* and ruling chiefs were enlarged, until at length they claimed almost everything. Then the chiefs held their possessions in fief to the *moi,* and forfeited them by rebellion. In time the king became absolute master of the most of the soil over which he ruled, and assumed *tabu* rights which rendered his person sacred and his prerogatives more secure. All he acquired by conquest was his, and by partitioning the lands among his titled friends he secured the support necessary to his maintenance in power. Certain lands were inalienable both in chiefly families and the priesthood ; they were made so by early sovereign decrees, which continued to be respected ; but with each succeeding king important land changes usually occurred.

Although the king maintained fish-ponds and cultivated lands of his own, he was largely supported by his subject chiefs. They were expected to contribute to him whatever was demanded either of food, raiment, houses, canoes, weapons or labor, and in turn they took such portions of the products of their tenants as their necessities required. The *ili* was the smallest political division ; next above it was the *ahapuaa,* which paid a nominal or special tax of one hog monthly to the king ; next the *okana,* embracing several *ahapuaas ;* and finally the *moku,* or district, or island.

The laboring classes possessed no realty of their own, nor could they anywhere escape the claim or jurisdiction of a chief or landlord. They owed military and other personal service to their respective chiefs, and the chiefs owed theirs to the king. If required, all were expected to respond to a call to the field, fully armed and prepared for battle.

Caste rules of dress, ornamentation and social forms were rigidly enforced. The entire people were divided into four general classes : first, the *alii*, or chiefly families, of various grades and prerogatives ; second, the *kahunas*, embracing priests, prophets, doctors, diviners and astrologers ; third, the *kanaka-wale*, or free private citizens ; and, fourth, the *kauwa-maoli*, or slaves, either captured in war or born of slave parents.

The laws were few and simple, and the most of them referred to the rights and prerogatives of the king, priesthood and nobility. Property disputes of the masses were settled by their chiefs, and other grievances were in most instances left to private redress, which frequently and very naturally resulted in prolonged and fatal family feuds, in the end requiring chiefly and sometimes royal intervention.

This, in brief and very general terms, was the prevailing character of the government and land tenure throughout the several islands of the group until after the death of Kamehameha I. in 1819, and the relinquishment by the crown of its ancient and sovereign rights in the soil.

The leading chiefs and high-priesthood claimed a lineage distinct from that of the masses, and traced their ancestry back to *Kumuhonua*, the Polynesian Adam. The *iku-pau*, a sacred class of the supreme priesthood, assumed to be the direct descendants from the godhead, while the *iku-nuu* were a collateral branch of the sacred and royal strain, and possessed only temporal powers. It was thus that one of the families of the Hawaiian priesthood, in charge of the verbal genealogical records, exalted itself in sanctity above the political rulers.

Proud of their lineage, to guard against imposture and keep their blood uncorrupted, the chiefs allowed their claims to family distinction to be passed upon by a college of heraldry, established by an early *moi* of Maui. Reciting their genealogies before the college, composed of *aliis* of accepted rank, and receiving the recognition of the council, chiefs were then regarded as members of the grade of *aha-alii*, or chiefs of admitted and irrevocable rank.

Meeting Place of an Ancient Secret Society.

(FROM A PAINTING IN THE ROYAL PALACE.)

The chiefs inherited their titles and *tabu* privileges quite as frequently through the rank of one parent as of the other. As Hawaiian women of distinction usually had more than one husband, and the chiefs were seldom content with a single wife, the difficulty of determining the rights and ranks of their children was by no means easy ; but the averment of the mother was generally accepted as conclusive and sufficient evidence in that regard.

For political purposes marriage alliances were common between the royal and chiefly families of the several islands, and thus in time the superior nobility of the entire group became connected by ties of blood. The political or principal wife of a king or distinguished chief was usually of a rank equal to that of her husband, and their marriage was proclaimed by heralds and celebrated with befitting ceremonies. Other wives were taken by simple agreement, and without ceremony or public announcement. Very much in the same manner the masses entered into their marriage unions. With the latter, however, polygamy was not common. When husband and wife separated, as they frequently did, each was at liberty to select another partner. The political wife of a chief was called *wahine-hoao ;* the others, *haia-wahine*, or concubine.

In the royal families, to subserve purposes of state, father and daughter, brother and sister, and uncle and niece frequently united as man and wife. The children of such unions were esteemed of the highest rank, and, strange to say, no mental or physical deterioration seemed to result from these incestuous relations, for all through the past the *mois* and nobles of the group were noted for their gigantic proportions.

There were five or more grades of chiefs connected with the royal lines. First in order, and the most sacred, was the *alii-niaupio* (the offspring of a prince with his own sister) ; next, the *alii-pio* (the offspring of a prince with his own niece) ; next, the *alii-naha* (the offspring of a prince or king with his own daughter) ; next, the *alii-wohi* (the offspring of either of the foregoing with another chiefly branch) ; and next, the *lo-alii* (chiefs of royal blood). Any of these might be either male or female.

To these grades of chiefs distinct personal *tabus* or prerogatives were attached, such as the *tabu-moe, tabu-wela, tabu-hoano* and *tabu-wohi*. These *tabus* could be given or bequeathed to others.

by their possessors, but could not be multiplied by transmission. The *meles*, or ancestral chants of a family, passed in succession to the legal representatives, and became exclusively theirs ; but the government, *tabus* and household gods of the king were subject to his disposal as he willed, either at his death or before it. The child of a *tabu* chief, born of a mother of lower rank, could not, according to custom, assume the *tabu* privileges of his father, although in some instances in the past they were made to inure to such offspring, notably in the case of Umi, King of Hawaii.

Before an *alii-niaupio*, clothed with the supreme function of the *tabu-moe*, all, with the exception of *tabu* chiefs, were compelled to prostrate themselves. When he appeared or was approached his rank was announced by an attendant, and all not exempt from the homage were required to drop with their faces to the earth. The exemptions were the *alii-pio*, the *alii-naha*, the *alii-wohi* and the *lo-alii*. They, and they alone, were permitted to stand in the presence of a *niaupio* chief. An *alii-pio* was also a sacred chief, so much so that he conversed with others only in the night-time, and on chiefesses of that rank the sun was not allowed to shine.

The kings lived in affluence in large mansions of wood or stone, in the midst of walled grounds adorned with fruit and shade trees and other attractive forms of vegetation. The grounds also contained many other smaller buildings for the accommodation of guests, retainers, attendants, servants and guards. They were attended by their high-priests, civil and military advisers, and a retinue of favorite chiefs, and spent their time, when not employed in war or affairs of state, in indolent and dignified repose.

The personal attendants of an ancient Hawaiian king were all of noble blood, and each had his specified duty. They were known as *kahu-alii*, or guardians of the person of the king. They consisted of the *iwikuamoo*, or rubber of the person ; the *ipukuha*, or spittoon-bearer ; the *paakahili*, or *kahili*-bearer ; the *kiaipoo*, or sleep-watcher ; and the *aipuupuu*, or steward. Other inferior chiefs, called *puuku*, with messengers, spies, executioners, prophets, astrologers, poets, historians, musicians and dancers, were among his retainers. Connected with the palace was an apartment used as a *heiau*, or chapel, which was sometimes in charge of the high-priest.

During festival seasons brilliant feasts, tournaments and *hula* and musical entertainments were given in the royal grounds, and the court was splendid in displays of flowers, feathers and other gaudy trappings. The king not unfrequently took part in the manly games and exercises of the chiefs, and sometimes complimented the *hula* dancers and musicians by joining in their performances.

To render the kings and higher nobility still more exclusive, they had a court language which was understood only by themselves, and which was changed in part from time to time as its expressions found interpretation beyond the royal circle. Some portions of this court language have been preserved.

ARTS, HABITS AND CUSTOMS.

All implements of war or industry known to the early Hawaiians were made either of wood, stone, or bone, as the islands are destitute of metals ; but with these rude helps they laid up hewn-stone walls, felled trees, made canoes and barges, manufactured cloths and cordage, fashioned weapons, constructed dwellings and temples, roads and fish-ponds, and tilled the soil. They had axes, adzes and hammers of stone, spades of wood, knives of flint and ivory, needles of thorn and bone, and spears and daggers of hardened wood. They wove mats for sails and other purposes, and from the inner bark of the paper mulberry-tree beat out a fine, thin cloth called *kapa*, which they ornamented with colors and figures.

Their food was the flesh of swine, dogs and fowls ; fish, and almost everything living in the sea ; *taro*, sweet potatoes and yams, and fruits, berries and edible sea-weed of various kinds. *Poi*, the favorite food of all classes, was a slightly fermented paste made of cooked and pounded *taro*, a large bulbous root, in taste resembling an Indian turnip. They made a stupefying beverage by chewing the *awa* root, and from the sweet root of the *ti* plant fermented an intoxicating drink. The soft parts of the sugar-cane were eaten, but, with the exception of the manufacture of a beer called *uiuia*, no other use seems to have been made of it. Their food, wrapped in *ti* leaves, was usually cooked in heated and covered pits in the earth. Their household vessels were shells, gourd calabashes of various shapes and sizes, and platters and other containers made of wood.

The dress of the ancient Hawaiian was scant, simple and cool. The principal, and generally the only, garment of the male was the *maro*, a narrow cloth fastened around the loins. To this was sometimes added, among the masses, a *kihei*, or cloth thrown loosely over the shoulders. The females wore a *pau*, or skirt of invariably five thicknesses of *kapa*, fastened around the waist and extending to the knees. When the weather was cool a short mantle was sometimes added. Ordinarily the heads of both sexes were without coverings, and in rare instances they wore *kamaas*, or sandals of *ti* or pandanus leaves.

With the *maro*, which was common to the males of all ranks, the king on state occasions wore the royal *mamo*, a mantle reaching to the ankles, and made of the yellow feathers of a little sea-bird called the *mamo*. When it is mentioned that but a single yellow feather is found under each wing of the *mamo*, and that tens of thousands, perhaps, entered into the fabrication of a single mantle, some idea of the value of such a garment may be gathered. A few of these royal cloaks are still in existence, one of which was worn by King Kalakaua during the ceremonies of his late coronation. Pure yellow was the royal color. The shorter capes or mantles of the chiefs were of yellow feathers mixed with red. The color of the priests and gods was red.

PALAOA, A TALISMAN WORN AROUND THE NECK.

The ornaments of the nobility consisted of head-dresses of feathers, *palaoas*, or charms of bone suspended from the neck, and necklaces and bracelets of shells, teeth and other materials. Many of them were tattooed on the face, thighs and breast, but the practice was not universal. Flowers were in general use as ornaments, and at feasts, festivals and other gatherings garlands of fragrant leaves and blossoms crowned the heads and encircled the necks of all. This is among the beautiful customs still retained by the Hawaiians.

The dwellings of the masses were constructed of upright posts planted in the ground, with cross-beams and rafters, and roofs and sides of woven twigs and branches thatched with leaves. The houses of the nobility were larger, stronger and more pretentious, and were frequently surrounded by broad verandas. It was a custom to locate dwellings so that the main entrance would face the east, the home of *Kane*. The opposite entrance looked toward Kahiki, the land from which Wakea came.

The homes of well-conditioned Hawaiians consisted of no less than six separate dwellings or apartments : 1st, the *heiau*, or idol-house ; 2d, the *mua*, or eating-house of the males, which females were not allowed to enter ; 3d, the *hale-noa*, or house of the women, which men could not enter ; 4th, the *hale-aina*, or eating-house of the wife ; 5th, the *kua*, or wife's working-house ; and 6th, the *hale-pea*, or retiring-house or nursery of the wife. The poorer classes followed these regulations so far as their means would admit, but screens usually took the place of separate dwellings or definite apartments.

When war was declared or invasion threatened, messengers, called *lunapais*, were despatched by the king to his subject chiefs, who promptly responded in warriors, canoes, or whatever else was demanded. A regular line-of-battle consisted of a centre and right and left wings, and marked military genius was sometimes displayed in the handling of armies. Sea-battles, where hundreds, sometimes thousands, of war-canoes met in hostile shock, were common, and usually resulted in great loss of life. Truces and terms of peace were ordinarily respected, but few prisoners were spared except for sacrifice.

The weapons of the islanders were spears about twenty feet in length, javelins, war-clubs, stone axes, rude halberds, knives, daggers and slings. The slings were made either of cocoa fibre or human hair. The stones thrown were sometimes a pound or more in weight, and were delivered with great force and accuracy. The spears were sometimes thrown, while the javelins were reserved for closer encounter. Shields were unknown. Hostile missiles were either dodged, caught in the hands, or dexterously warded. The chiefs frequently wore feather helmets in battle, but the person was without protection.

The athletic sports and games of the people were numerous.

The muscular pastimes consisted in part of contests in running, jumping, boxing, wrestling, swimming, diving, canoe-racing and surf-riding. Roll-

SURF BOARD.

ing round stone disks and throwing darts along a prepared channel was a favorite sport; but the most exciting was the *holua* contest, in which two or more might engage. On long, light and narrow sledges the contestants, lying prone, dashed down long and steep declivities, the victory being with the one who first reached the bottom. The goddess *Pele* enjoyed the game, and frequently engaged in it. But she was a dangerous contestant. On being beaten by Kahavari, a chief of Puna, she drove him from the district with a stream of lava. Sham battles and spear and stone throwing were also popular exercises.

Among the in-door games were *konane*, *kilu*, *puhenehene*, *punipiki*, and *hiua*. *Konane* resembled the English game of draughts. *Puhenehene* consisted of the adroit hiding by one of the players of a small object under one of several mats in the midst of the party of contestants, and the designation of its place of concealment by the others. *Kilu* was a game somewhat similar, accompanied by singing. *Punipiki* was something like the game of "fox and geese," and *hiua* was played on a board with four squares. These were the most ancient of Hawaiian household games.

The musical instruments of the island-ers were few and simple. They consisted of *pahus*, or drums, of various sizes; the *ohe*, a bamboo flute; the *hokio*, a rude clarionet; a nasal flageolet, and a reed in-strument played by the aid of the voîce. To these were added, on special occasions, castanets and dry gourds containing peb-bles, which were used to mark the time of chants and other music. They had many varieties of dances, or *hulas*, all of which

PAHU, OR DRUM.

were more or less graceful, and a few of which were coarse and licentious. Bands of *hula* dancers, male and female, were among the retainers of the *mois* and prominent chiefs, and their services were required on every festive occasion.

The mourning customs of the people were peculiar. For days they wailed and feasted together over a dead relative or friend, frequently knocking out one or more teeth, shaving portions of their heads and beards, and tearing their flesh and clothes. But their wildest displays of grief were on the death of their kings and governing chiefs. During a royal mourning season, which sometimes continued for weeks, the people indulged in an unrestrained saturnalia of recklessness and license. Every law was openly violated, every conceivable crime committed. The excuse was—and the authorities were compelled to accept it—that grief had temporarily unseated the popular reason, and they were not responsible for their misdemeanors.

The masses buried their dead or deposited the bodies in caves, but the bones of the kings were otherwise disposed of. There were royal burial-places—one at Honaunau, on the island of Hawaii, and another, called Iao, on Maui—and the tombs of many of the ancient *mois* and ruling chiefs were in one or the other of those sacred spots ; but they probably contained but few royal bones. In the fear that the bones of the *mois* and distinguished chiefs might fall into the hands of their enemies and be used for fish-hooks, arrow-points for shooting mice, and other debasing purposes, they were usually destroyed or hidden. Some were weighted and thrown into the sea, and others, after the flesh had been removed from them and burned, were secreted in mountain caves. The hearts of the kings of the island of Hawaii were frequently thrown into the crater of Kilauea as an offering to *Pele.* The bones of the first Kamehameha were so well secreted in some cave in Kona that they have not yet been found, and the bones of Kualii, a celebrated Oahuan king of the seventeenth century, were reduced to powder, mingled with *poi,* and at the funeral feast fed to a hundred unsuspecting chiefs.

The ancient Hawaiians divided the year into twelve months of thirty days each. The days of the month were named, not numbered. As this gave but three hundred and sixty days to their year, they added and gave to their god *Lono* in feasting and festivity the number of days required to complete the sidereal year, which was regulated by the rising of the Pleiades. The new

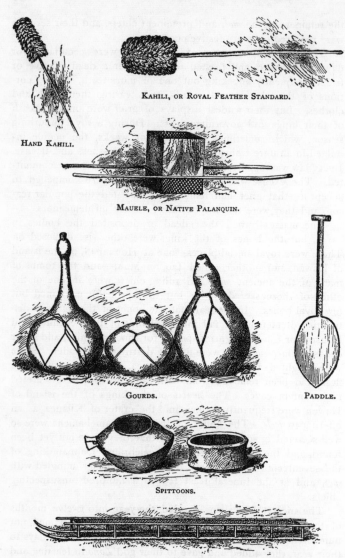

KAHILI, OR ROYAL FEATHER STANDARD.

HAND KAHILI.

MAUELE, OR NATIVE PALANQUIN.

GOURDS.

PADDLE.

SPITTOONS.

KEPIE, OR SLEDGE USED IN THE GAME OF HOLUA.

GROUP OF NATIVE IMPLEMENTS.

year began with the winter solstice. They also reckoned by lunar months in the regulation of their monthly feasts. The year was divided into two seasons—the rainy and the dry—and the day into three general parts, morning, noon and night. The first, middle and after parts of the night were also designated.

As elsewhere mentioned, they had names for the five principal planets, which they called "the wandering stars," and for a number of heavenly groups and constellations. It was this knowledge of the heavens that enabled them to navigate the ocean in their frail canoes.

In counting, the Hawaiians reckoned by fours and their multiples. Their highest expressed number was four hundred thousand. More than that was indefinite.

After what has been written it would seem scarcely necessary to mention that the Hawaiians were not cannibals. Their legends refer to two or three instances of cannibalism on the islands, but the man-eaters were natives of some other group and did not long survive.

THE HAWAII OF TO-DAY.

With this somewhat extended reference to the past of the Hawaiian Islands and their people, it is deemed that a brief allusion to their present political, social, industrial and commercial condition will not be out of place. The legends presented leave the simple but warlike islanders standing naked but not ashamed in the light of civilization suddenly flashed upon them from across the seas. In the darkness behind them are legends and spears ; in the light before them are history and law. Let us see what the years since have done for them.

The Hawaiian government of to-day is a mild constitutional monarchy, the ruling family claiming descent from the most ancient and respected of the chiefly blood of Hawaii. The departments of the government are legislative, executive and judicial.

The Legislative Assembly, which meets every two years, consists of representatives chosen by the people, nobles named by the sovereign, and crown ministers. They act in a single body, choosing their presiding officer by ballot, and their proceedings are held jointly in the English and Hawaiian languages, and in both are their laws and proceedings published. As the elective franchise is confined to native and naturalized citizens, the most of the representatives chosen by the people are natives, all of whom are more or less educated, and many of whom are graceful and eloquent debaters. White representatives of accepted sympathy with the natives are occasionally elected, and a majority of the nobles and ministers are white men. The English common law is the basis of their statutes, and their civil and criminal codes are not unlike our own. The Legislature fixes tax, excise and customs charges, and provides by appropriation for all public expenditure. The representatives are paid small salaries, and the Legislature is formally convened and prorogued by the king in person.

Although the present sovereign was elected by the Legislature, for the reason heretofore mentioned, the naming of a successor is left to the occupant of the throne. The king is provided at public expense with a palace and royal guard, and appropriations of money amounting to perhaps forty thousand dollars yearly. He has also some additional income from what are known as crown lands. The two sisters of the king and the daughter of one of them receive from the treasury an aggregate of fifteen thousand five hundred dollars yearly. The king entertains liberally, is generous with his friends and attendants, and probably finds his income no more than sufficient to meet his wants from year to year. His advisers are four Ministers of State and a Privy Council. The Ministry is composed of a Minister of Foreign Affairs, who ranks as premier, Minister of Finance, Minister of Interior, and Attorney-General. The Privy Council is composed of thirty or forty leading citizens appointed by the Crown. In certain matters they have original and exclusive powers. They are convened in council from time to time, but receive no compensation. The most of the Privy Councillors are white men, and embrace almost every nationality. The majority of the ministers of state are usually white men of ability, and their salaries are six thousand dollars per annum each.

The judiciary is composed of a Supreme Court of three members, one of whom is chief-justice and chancellor, Circuit Courts holden in different districts, and minor magistrates' courts in localities where they are required. The Supreme and Circuit judges are all white men, and but few magistrates are natives. The salaries of the superior judges are respectable, and the most of them are men of ability. The laws, as a rule, are intelligently administered and promptly executed, and life and property are amply protected.

Public schools are numerous throughout the islands, and are largely attended by native children. A considerable proportion of the adult natives are able to read and write their own language, and a number of native newspapers and periodicals are sustained. The English press of Honolulu—the only point of publication—is respectable in ability and enterprise.

Leprosy was brought to the islands by the Chinese about forty years ago, and has become a dangerous and loathsome scourge. Lepers are seldom encountered, however, as they are removed, whenever discovered, to the island of Molokai, where they are humanely cared for by the government. It is a cureless but painless affliction, and is doubtless contagious under certain conditions. Nine-tenths or more of the lepers are either natives or Chinese, and the whole number amounts to perhaps twelve hundred. It is not thought that the malady is increasing, and it is hoped that a careful segregation of the afflicted will in time eradicate the disease from the group.

The commerce of the islands is largely in the hands of foreigners, and the sugar plantations are almost exclusively under their control. There are but few native merchants, the large dealers being Americans, Germans, English and French, while the smaller traders are generally Portuguese and Chinese. There are native lawyers, clerks, mechanics, magistrates and policemen ; but the most of the race who are compelled to labor for their support find employment as farm and plantation laborers, stevedores, sailors, coachmen, boatmen, fishermen, gardeners, fruit-pedlars, waiters, soldiers and house-servants, in all of which capacities they are generally industrious, cheerful and honest.

The products of the islands for export are sugar, molasses, rice, bananas, fungus, hides and wool, of an aggregate approximate value of eight million dollars annually. The principal product, however, is sugar, amounting to perhaps one hundred thousand tons yearly. Nine-tenths of the exports of the group find a market in the United States, and four-fifths or more of the imports in value are from the great Republic. The receipts and expenditures of the government are a little less than one million five hundred thousand dollars annually, derived principally from customs duties and direct taxation.

The population of the islands is a little more than eighty thousand, of which about forty-five thousand are natives. The Americans, English, Germans, Norwegians and French number perhaps ten thousand, and Chinese, Japanese and Portuguese from the Azores constitute the most of the remainder.

The postal facilities of the islands are ample and reliable. Inter-island steamers, of which there are many, convey the mails throughout the group at regular intervals, and the San Franciscan and Australian steamers afford a punctual and trustworthy service with the rest of the world. The islands have a postal money-order system reaching within and beyond their boundaries, and are connected with the Universal Postal Union.

Over twenty thousand of the inhabitants of the group are centred in Honolulu, the capital of the kingdom, and its beautiful and dreamy suburb of Waikiki. The business portions of the city, with their macadamized and lighted streets, and blocks of brick and stone buildings, have a thrifty and permanent appearance, while the eastern suburbs, approaching the hills with a gentle ascent, abound in charming residences embowered in palms. Small mountain streams run through the city and afford an abundant supply of sweet water, which is further augmented by a number of flowing artesian wells. With a temperature ranging from seventy to ninety degrees, Honolulu, with its substantial churches and public buildings, its air of affluence and dreamy quiet, is a delightful place of residence to those who enjoy the heat and languor of the tropics.

In the midst of these evidences of prosperity and advancement it is but too apparent that the natives are steadily decreasing in numbers and gradually losing their hold upon the fair land of their fathers. Within a century they have dwindled from four hundred thousand healthy and happy children of nature, without care and without want, to a little more than a tenth of that number of landless, hopeless victims to the greed and vices of civilization. They are slowly sinking under the restraints and burdens of their surroundings, and will in time succumb to social and political conditions foreign to their natures and poisonous to their blood. Year by year their footprints will grow more dim along the sands of their reef-sheltered shores, and fainter and fainter will come their simple songs from the shadows of the palms, until finally their voices will be heard no more for ever.

And then, if not before—and no human effort can shape it otherwise—the Hawaiian Islands, with the echoes of their songs and the sweets of their green fields, will pass into the political, as they are now firmly within the commercial, system of the great American Republic.

February, 1887.

HINA, THE HELEN OF HAWAII.

CHARACTERS.

HAKALANILEO, a chief of Hawaii.
HINA, wife of Hakalanileo.
ULI, a sorceress, mother of Hina.
NIHEU and ⎫
KANA, ⎭ sons of Hina.
KAMAUAUA, King of Molokai.
KEOLOEWA and ⎫
KAUPEEPEE, ⎭ sons of Kamauaua.
NUAKEA, wife of Keoloewa.
MOI, brother of Nuakea.

HINA, THE HELEN OF HAWAII.

I.

THE story of the *Iliad* is a dramatic record of the love and hate, wrong and revenge, courage and custom, passion and superstition, of mythical Greece, and embraces in a single brilliant recital events which the historic bards of other lands, lacking the genius of Homer, have sent down the centuries in fragments. Human nature has been substantially the same in all ages, differing only in the ardor of its passions and appetites, as affected by the zone of its habitat and its peculiar physical surroundings. Hence almost every nation, barbarous and civilized, has had its Helen and its Troy, its Paris and its Agamemnon, its Hector and its demi-gods ; and Hawaii is not an exception. The wrath of no dusky Achilles is made the thesis of the story of the Hawaiian abduction, but in other respects the Greek and Polynesian legends closely resemble each other in their general outlines.

The story of Hina, the Hawaiian Helen, and Kaupeepee, the Paris of the legend, takes us back to the twelfth century, near the close of the second and final era of migration from Tahiti, Samoa, and perhaps other islands of Polynesia—a period which added very considerably to the population of the group, and gave to it many new chiefs, a number of new customs, and a few new gods. That the tale may be better understood by the reader who may not be conversant with the legendary history of the Hawaiian Islands, it will be necessary to refer briefly to the political and social condition of the group at that time.

Notwithstanding the many sharply drawn and wonderfully-preserved historic legends of the Hawaiians, the early settlement of the little archipelago is shrouded in mystery. The best testimony, however, warrants the assumption that the islands were first discovered and occupied by a people who had drifted from southern Asia to the islands of the Pacific in the first or second

century of the Christian era, and, by migratory stages from the
Figis to Samoa and thence to Tahiti, had reached the Hawaiian
group in about A.D. 550. The first discovery was doubtless the
result of accident ; but those who made it were able to find their
way back to the place from which they started—either Tahiti or
Samoa—and in due time return with augmented numbers, bearing
with them to their new home pigs, fowls, dogs, and the seeds
of such fruits and vegetables as they had found to be wanting
there.

The little colony grew and prospered, and for nearly five hundred years had no communication with, or knowledge of, the
world beyond. At the end of that time their geographical traditions had grown so faint that they spoke only of Kahiki, a place
very far away, from which their ancestors came. First landing
on the large island of Hawaii, they had spread over the eight
habitable divisions of the group. The people were ruled by district chiefs, in fief to a supreme head on some of the islands, and
on others independent, and the lines dividing the masses from
the nobility were less strictly drawn than during the centuries
succeeding. Wars were frequent between neighboring chiefs, and
popular increase was slow ; but the *tabus* of the chiefs and priests
were not oppressive, and the people claimed and exercised a de-
gree of personal independence unknown to them after the eleventh century.

In about A.D. 1025, or perhaps a little earlier, the people of
the group were suddenly aroused from their long dream of six
centuries by the arrival of a large party of adventurers from Tahiti. Their chief was Nanamaoa. Their language resembled
that of the Hawaiians, and their customs and religions were not
greatly at variance. They were therefore received with kindness,
and in a few years their influence began to be felt throughout the
group. They landed at Kohala, Hawaii, and Nanamaoa soon
succeeded in establishing himself there as an influential chief.
His sons secured possessions on Maui and Oahu, and on the
latter island one of them—Nanakaoko—instituted the sacred
place called Kukaniloko, in the district of Ewa, where it was the
desire of future chiefs that their sons should be born. Even
Kamehameha I., as late as 1797, sought to remove his queen
thither before the birth of Liholiho, but the illness of the royal
mother prevented. This became the sacred birth-place of princes,

as Iao, in Wailuku valley, on the island of Maui, became their *tabu* spot of interment.

It was at Kukaniloko that Kapawa, the son of Nanakaoko, was born. His principal seat of power was probably on Hawaii, although he retained possessions on Maui and Oahu. It was during his life that the celebrated chief and priest Paao made his appearance in the group. He came from one of the southern islands with a small party, bringing with him new gods and new modes of worship, and to him the subsequent high-priests of Hawaii traced their sacerdotal line, even down to Hevaheva, who in 1819 was the first to apply the torch to the temples in which his ancestors had so long worshipped. Paao was a statesman and warrior as well as a priest, but he preferred spiritual to temporal authority ; and when Kapawa died and was buried at Iao, leaving his possessions without a competent ruler and his subjects in a state bordering upon anarchy, Paao did not assume the chieftaincy, as he manifestly might have done, but despatched messengers—if, indeed, he did not go himself—to the land of his birth, to invite to Hawaii a chief capable of re-storing order.

Such a leader was found in Pilikaekae, of Samoa, who mi-grated to Hawaii with a goodly number of retainers, and was promptly established in the vacant sovereignty, while Paao con-tinued in the position of high-priest. Pili extended his authority over the six districts of Hawaii ; but beyond Kohala and the northern part of the island the recognition of his sovereignty was merely nominal, and internal wars and revolts were frequent.

The next arrivals of note from the southern islands were the two Paumakua families, one of which settled in Oahu and Kauai and the other in Hawaii and Maui. Whether, as averred by con-flicting traditions, they arrived contemporaneously or two or three generations apart, is a question in nowise pertinent to our story. The legend is connected with the Hawaii branch alone, and the order of their coming need not, therefore, be here dis-cussed.

The Paumakua family, which became so influential in Hawaii and Maui, arrived during the early part of the reign of Pili, in about A.D. 1090. A large party accompanied the family, and they brought with them their gods, priests, astrologers and prophets. They first landed and secured possessions in Maui ;

but the sons and other relatives of Paumakua were brave and ambitious, and soon by conquest and marriage secured an almost sovereign footing both in Maui and Hawaii.

One of the nephews of Paumakua, Hakalanileo, who was the son of Kuheailani, as an entering wedge to further acquisitions became in some manner possessed of a strip of land along the coast in the district of Hilo, Hawaii. It was a large estate, and the owner availed himself of every opportunity to extend its boundaries and increase the number of his dependents. His wife was the beautiful Hina of Hawaiian song and daughter of the seeress Uli, who had migrated from Tahiti with some one of the several expeditions of that period—possibly with the Paumakua family, although tradition does not so state.

At that time Kamauaua, a powerful chief of the ancient native line of Nanaula, held sway over the island of Molokai. He proudly traced back his ancestry to the first migration in the sixth century, and regarded with aversion and well-founded alarm the new migratory tide which for years past had been casting upon the shores of the islands a flood of alien adventurers, whose warlike and aggressive chiefs were steadily possessing themselves of the fairest portions of the group. He had sought to form a league of native chiefs against these dangerous encroachments ; but the wily invaders, with new gods to awe the masses and new customs and new traditions to charm the native nobility, had, through intermarriage and strategy rather than force, become the virtual rulers of Hawaii, Maui, Oahu, and Kauai, and he had abandoned all hope of seeing them supplanted. Molokai alone rem ined exclusively under native control, and its resolute old chief had from their infancy instilled into his sons a hatred of the southern spoilers and a resolution to resist their aggressions to the bitter end.

The eldest of the sons of Kamauaua was Kaupeepee. He was a warlike youth, well skilled in arms and mighty in strength and courage, and so profound was his detestation of the alien chiefs that he resolved to devote his life to such warfare as he might be able to make upon them and their subjects. With this view he relinquished his right of succession to his first brother, Keoloewa, and, gathering around him a band of warriors partaking of his desperation and courage, established a stronghold on the promontory of Haupu, on the north side of the island, be-

Type of Ancient King in State.

tween Pelekunu and Waikolo. At that point, and for some miles on each side of it, the mountains hug the ocean so closely as to leave nothing between them and the surf-beaten shores but a succession of steep, narrow and rugged promontories jutting out into the sea, and separated from each other by gorge-like and gloomy little valleys gashing the hills and, like dragons, for ever swallowing and ejecting the waves that venture too near their rocky jaws.

One of the most rugged of these promontories was Haupu. It was a natural fortress, precipitously fronting the sea with a height of five hundred feet or more, and flanked on the right and left by almost perpendicular declivities rising from narrow gulches choked with vegetation and sweetening the sea with rivulets of fresh water dashing down from the mountains seamed by their sources. It was connected with the range of mountains back of it by a narrow and rising ridge, which at a point something less than a mile inland, where opposite branches of the two flanking gulches approached each other closely, was contracted to a neck of not more than fifty paces in width. The summit of the point abutting the ocean was a comparatively level plateau, or rather series of three connecting terraces, embracing in all an area of nearly a hundred acres. Surrounded on three sides by almost perpendicular walls, and accessible on the fourth only by a narrow and easily-defended ridge extending to the mountains, little engineering skill was required to render the place well-nigh impregnable.

Setting himself earnestly to the task, Kaupeepee soon transformed the promontory of Haupu into one of the strongest fortresses in all the group. He surrounded the plateau with massive stone walls overlooking the declivities, and across the narrow neck leading to the mountains raised a rocky barrier ten feet in thickness and twenty feet in height, around which aggression from without was rendered impracticable by the excavation of precipices leading to, and in vertical line with, the ends of the wall. Instead of a gate, a subterranean passage-way led under the wall, the inside entrance being covered in times of danger with a huge flat stone resting on rollers.

Although the passage was rough and in unfavorable weather attended with danger, canoes could enter the mouths of both gulches and be hauled up beyond the reach of the waves, and be-

yond the reach of enemies as well ; for above the entrances, and
completely commanding them, frowned the broad battlements of
Haupu, from which might be hurled hundreds of tons of rocks
and other destructive missiles.   With ingenuity and great labor
narrow foot-paths were cut leading from the middle terrace to
both gulches, some distance above their openings, and affording
a means of entering and leaving the fortress by water.   These
paths connected with the terrace through narrow passage-ways
under the walls, and a single arm could defend them against a
host.

Within the walls buildings were erected capable of accommodating in an emergency two or three thousand warriors, and on
the lower terrace, occupied by Kaupeepee and his household, including his confidential friends and captains, a small *heiau* overlooked the sea, with a priest and two or three assistants in
charge.   Mountain-paths led from the fortress to Kalaupapa and
other productive parts of the island ; and as fish could be taken
in abundance, and Kaupeepee and many of his followers controlled *taro* and other lands in the valleys beyond, it was seldom
that the stronghold was short of food, even when foraging expeditions to the neighboring islands failed.

The services of the courageous alone were accepted by Kaupeepee, and it was a wild and daring warfare that the little band
waged for years against the alien chiefs and their subjects.   They
could put afloat a hundred war-canoes, and their operations, although usually confined to Oahu, Maui, and Hawaii, sometimes
in a spirit of bravado extended to Kauai.   Leaving their retreat,
they hovered near the coast selected for pillage until after dark,
and then landed and mercilessly used the torch and spear.   This
part of their work was quickly done, when they filled their canoes
with the choicest plunder they could find or of which they were
most in need, and before daylight made sail for Haupu.   Women
were sometimes the booty coveted by the buccaneers, and during
their raids many a screaming beauty was seized and borne to
their stronghold on Molokai, where in most instances she was so
kindly treated that she soon lost all desire to be liberated.   Occasionally they were followed, if the winds were unfavorable to
their retreat, by hastily-equipped fleets of canoes.   If they allowed themselves to be overtaken it was for the amusement of
driving back their pursuers ; but as a rule they escaped without

pursuit or punishment, leaving their victims in ignorance alike of the source and motive of the assault.

A prominent chief of Oahu, whose territory had been ravaged by Kaupeepee, traced the retiring fleet of the plunderers to the coast of Molokai, when it suddenly disappeared. He landed and paid his respects to the venerable Kamauaua, then at Kalaupapa, and craved his assistance in discovering and punishing the spoilers, who must have found shelter somewhere on the island. The old chief smiled grimly as he replied : " It is not necessary to search for your enemies. You will find them at Haupu, near the ocean. They are probably waiting for you. They do not disturb me or my people. If they have wronged you, land and punish them. You have my permission."

The Oahu chief offered his thanks and departed. He made a partial reconnoissance of Haupu, ascertained that it was defended by but a few hundred warriors, and shortly after returned with a large fleet of canoes to capture and retain possession of the place. Arriving off the entrance to the gulches, and discovering a number of war-canoes drawn up on their steep banks, he opened the campaign by ordering their seizure. Sixty canoes filled with warriors rode the surf into the gulches, where they were met by avalanches of rocks from the walls of the fortress, which dashed the most of them in pieces. The chief was startled and horrified, and, believing the gods were raining rocks down upon his fleet, he rescued such of his warriors as were able to reach him from the wrecked canoes, and hastily departed for Oahu, not again to return.

It is said that Kamauaua watched this assault upon Haupu from the hills back of the fortress, and, in token of his pleasure at the result, sent to Kaupeepee a feather cloak, and gave him the privilege of taking fish for his warriors from one of the largest of the royal ponds on the island. He also quietly presented him with a barge, than which there were few larger in the group. It would accommodate more than a hundred warriors and their equipments, and was intended for long and rough voyages.

These barges were constructed of planks strongly corded together over a frame, and calked and pitched. They were sometimes ten or more feet in width, and were partially or wholly decked over, with a depth of hold of six or eight feet. It was in vessels of this class, and in large double canoes of equal or

greater burden, that distant voyages were made to and from the
Hawaiian Islands during the migratory periods of the past, while
the single and double canoes of smaller dimensions, hollowed
from the trunks of single trees, were used in warfare, fishing, and
in general inter-island communication. After the final suspension of intercourse, in the twelfth century, between the Hawaiian and Society Islands—the possible result of the disappearance
of a guiding line of small islands and atolls dotting the ocean at
intervals between the two groups—the barges referred to gradually went out of use with the abandonment of voyages to distant
lands, and were almost unknown to the Hawaiians as early as
one or two centuries ago. Their spread of sail was very considerable, but oars were also used, and the mariner shaped his
course by the sun and stars, and was guided to land by the
flights of birds, drifting wood, and currents of which he knew
the direction.

Some of the double canoes with which the barges were supplanted were scarcely less capacious and seaworthy than the
barges themselves. They were hollowed from the trunks of
gigantic pines that had drifted to the islands from the northern
coast of America, and when one was found years sometimes
elapsed before wind and current provided a proper mate. One
of the single-trunk double canoes of Kamehameha I. was one
hundred and eight feet in length, and both single and double
canoes of from fifty to eighty feet in length were quite common
during his reign, when the native forests abounded in growths
much larger than can now be found. But the native trees never
furnished bodies for the larger sizes of canoes. They were the
gifts of the waves, and were not unfrequently credited to the
favor of the gods.

Kaupeepee was delighted with the present of the barge. It
gave him one of the largest vessels in all the eight Hawaiian seas,
and rendered him especially formidable in sea-encounters. He
painted the sails red and the hull to the water-line, and from the
masthead flung a saucy pennon to the breeze, surmounted by a
kahili, which might have been mistaken for Von Tromp's broom
had it been seen a few centuries later in northern seas. He provided a large crew of oarsmen, and made a more secure landing
for it in one of the openings near the fortress.

With this substantial addition to his fleet Kaupeepee enlarged the scope of his depredations, and his red sails were known and feared on the neighboring coasts of Oahu and Maui. Haupu was filled with the spoil of his expeditions, and the return of a successful raiding party was usually celebrated with a season of feasting, singing, dancing, and other boisterous merriment. Nor were the gods forgotten. Frequent festivals were given to *Kane*, *Ku*, and *Lono;* and *Moaalii*, the shark-god of Molokai—the god of the fisherman and mariner—was always the earliest to be remembered. A huge image of this deity overlooked the ocean from the north wall of the *heiau* of Haupu, and *leis* of fresh flowers adorned its shoulders whenever a dangerous expedition departed or returned. On one occasion this god had guided Kaupeepee to Haupu during a dark and rainy night, and on another had capsized a number of Oahuan war-canoes that had adroitly separated him from his fleet ·in Pailolo channel.

At that period the islands were generally ruled by virtually independent district chiefs. They recognized a supreme head, or *alii-nui*, but were absolute lords of their several territories, and wars between them were frequent ; but they were wars of plunder rather than of conquest, and sometimes continued in a desultory way until both parties were impoverished, when their chiefs and priests met and arranged terms of peace. But Kaupeepee was inspired by a motive higher than that of mere plunder. He hated the southern chiefs and their successors, and his assaults were confined exclusively to the territories over which they ruled. His sole aim was to inflict injury upon them, and the spoils of his expeditions were distributed among his followers. Brave, generous and sagacious, he was almost worshipped by his people, and treason, with them, was a thing unthought of.

It was indeed a wild and reckless life that Kaupeepee and his daring associates led ; but it lacked neither excitement abroad nor amusement at home. On the upper terrace a *kahua* channel had been cut, along which they rolled the *maika* and threw the blunted dart. They played *konane, puhenehene*, and *punipeki*, and at surf-riding possessed experts of both sexes who might have travelled far without finding their equals. The people of the island were friendly with the dashing buccaneers, and the fairest damsels became their wives, some of them living with their husbands at Haupu, and others with their relatives in the valleys.

II.

We will now return to Hina—or Hooho, as she was some-times called—the beautiful wife of Hakalanileo, nephew of Pau-makua, of Hawaii. Hakalanileo had acquired his possessions in Hilo partly through the influence of his own family, and partly through his marriage with the sister of a consequential district chief. Later in life he had seen and become enamored of Hina, the daughter of Uli, and prevailed upon her to become his wife The marriage was not acceptable to Uli. The position and family connections of Hakalanileo were sufficiently inviting, but Uli, who dealt in sorcery and magic, saw disaster in the proposed union and advised her daughter against it. After much persuasion, however, her consent was obtained ; but she gave it with this injunction :

"Since you will have it so, take her, Hakalanileo ; but guard her well, for I can see that some day the winds will snatch her from you, and you will behold her not again for many years."

"Be it even as you say," replied Hakalanileo, " I will take the hazard. We do not well to reject a treasure because, per-chance, it may be stolen. Hina shall be my wife."

And thus it was that Hina became the wife of the nephew of Paumakua—Hina, the most beautiful maiden in all Hawaii ; Hina, whose eyes were like stars, and whose hair fell in waves below the fringes of her *pau ;* Hina, whose name has come down to us through the centuries garlanded with song. And for years she lived happily with Hakalanileo, who loved her above all others—lived with him until she became the mother of two sons, Kana and Niheu ; and then the winds snatched her away from her husband, just as Uli had predicted six years before. But the winds that bore her hence filled the sails of the great barge of Kaupeepee.

The chief of Haupu had heard of her great beauty, and re-solved to see with his own eyes what the bards had exalted in song. Travelling overland from Puna in disguise, he reached her home in Hilo, and saw that the poets had done her no more than justice. She was beautiful indeed, and the wife of one to whose blood he had vowed undying enmity. Returning to Puna, where his barge lay in waiting for him, he hovered around the coast of Hilo for some days, watching for an opportunity to seize the woman whose charms had enraptured him.

At last it came. After sunset, when the moon was shining, Hina repaired to the beach with her women to bathe. A signal was given—it is thought by the first wife of Hakalanileo—and not long after a light but heavily-manned canoe dashed through the surf and shot in among the bathers. The women screamed and started for the shore. Suddenly a man leaped from the canoe into the water. There was a brief struggle, a stifled scream, a sharp word of command, and a moment later Kau-peepee was again in the canoe with the nude and frantic Hina in his arms.

The boatmen knew their business—knew the necessity of quick work—and without a word the canoe was turned and driven through the surf like an arrow. The barge, with a man at every oar and the sails ready to hoist, was lying a short distance out at sea. A speck of light guided the boatmen, and the barge was soon reached. All were hastily transferred to it. The sails were spread, the men bent to their oars, the canoe was taken in tow ; and, while the alarm-drum was sounding and fires were appearing on shore, Hina, wrapped in folds of soft *kapa*, sat sobbing in one of the apartments of the barge, and was being swiftly borne by wind and oar toward the fortress of Haupu.

The return to Haupu occupied a little more than two days. During that time Hina had mourned continually and partaken of no food. Kaupeepee had treated her with respect and kindness ; but she was bewildered with the shock of her abduction, and begged to be either killed or returned to her children.

The party landed a little before daylight. The sea was rough, but the moon shone brightly, and the passage into the mouth of one of the gulches was made without accident. In the arms of Kaupeepee Hina was borne up the rock-hewn path to the fortress, and placed in apartments on the lower terrace provided with every comfort and luxury known to the nobility of the islands at that period. They had been especially prepared for her reception, and women were in attendance to wait upon her and see that she wanted for nothing, except her liberty. The large private room of the three communicating apartments— the one designed for her personal occupation—was a model of barbaric taste and comfort, and to its adornment many of the exposed districts of Oahu and Maui had unwillingly contributed. Its walls were tapestried with finely-woven and brilliantly-colored mattings, dropping from festoons of shells and underlapping a carpet of hardier material covering the level ground-floor. The beams of the ceiling were also studded with shells and gaudily stained. On one side of the room was a slightly-raised platform, thickly strewn with dry sea-grass and covered with many folds of *kapa*. This was the *kapa-moe*, or sleeping-couch. Opposite was a *kapa*-covered lounge extending along the entire side of the room. In the middle of the apartment were spread several thicknesses of mats, which served alike for eating and lounging purposes. Light was admitted through two small openings immediately under the eaves, and from the door when its heavy curtains were looped aside. On a row of shelves in a corner of the room were carved calabashes and other curious drinking-vessels, as well as numerous ornaments of shells, ivory and feathers; and in huge calabashes under them were stores of female attire of every description then in use. In fact, nothing seemed to be wanting, and, in spite of her grief, Hina could scarcely repress a feeling of delight as she was shown into the apartment and the *kukui* torches displayed its luxurious appointments.

Declining food, Hina dismissed her attendants, and, throwing herself on the *kapa-moe*, was soon folded in the soft mantle of sleep and carried back in dreams to the home from which she had been ravished. The room was dark, and she slept for many hours. Awaking, she could not for a moment recollect where she was; but gradually the events of the preceding three days came to her, and she appreciated that she was a prisoner in the hands of Kaupeepee, of whose name and exploits she was not ignorant, and that repining would secure her neither liberation nor kind treatment. Therefore, with a sagacity to be expected of the daughter of Uli, and not without a certain feeling of pride as she reflected that her beauty had inspired Kaupeepee to abduct her, she admitted her attendants, attired herself becomingly, partook heartily of a breakfast of fish, *poi*, potatoes and fruits, and then sent word to Kaupeepee that she would be pleased to see him.

Kaupeepee expected a storm of tears and reproaches as he entered the room, but was agreeably disappointed. Hina rose, bowed, and waited for him to speak.

"What can I do for you?" inquired Kaupeepee in a kindly

tone, while a just perceptible smile of triumph swept across his handsome face.

"Liberate me," replied Hina promptly.

"You are free to go anywhere within the walls of Haupu," returned Kaupeepee, moving his arms around as if they embraced the whole world.

"Return me to my children," said Hina; and at thought of them her eyes flashed with earnestness.

"Impossible!" was the firm reply.

"Then kill me!" exclaimed Hina.

"Did you ever see me before I had the pleasure of embracing you in the water on the coast of Hilo?" inquired the chief, evasively.

"No," replied Hina, curtly.

"Well, I saw you before that time," continued Kaupeepee—"saw you in your house; saw you among the palms; saw you by the waters. I made a journey overland from Puna to see you—to see the wife of my enemy, the most beautiful woman in Hawaii."

Hina was but a woman, and of a race and time when the promptings of the heart were not fettered by rigid rules of propriety. Kaupeepee was the handsome and distinguished son of a king, and his words of praise were not unpleasant to her. She therefore bent her eyes to the floor and remained silent while he added:

"Hina would think little of the man who would risk his life to possess himself of such a woman, and then kill or cast her off as not worth the keeping. You are like no other woman; I am like no other man. Such companionship has the approval of the gods, and you will leave Haupu only when its walls shall have been battered down and Kaupeepee lies dead among the ruins!"

To this terrible declaration Hina could offer no reply. The fierceness of this prince of the old line of Nanaula, this enemy of her people, this scourge of the southern chiefs, alike charmed and frightened her, and with her hands to her face she sank upon the lounge of *kapa* beside which she had been standing.

The chief regarded her for a moment, perhaps with a feeling of pity; then, placing his hand upon her shoulder, he softly said:

" You will not be unhappy in Haupu."

" Will the bird sing that is covered with a calabash ? " replied Hina, raising her eyes.   " I am your prisoner."

" Not more my prisoner than I am yours," rejoined the chief, gallantly.   " Therefore, as fellow-prisoners, let us make the best of walls that shut out no sunshine, and of gates that are a bar only against intrusion."

" How brave, and yet how gentle ! " mused Hina, as Kaupee-pee, feeling that he had said enough, turned and left the room. " How strangely pleasant are his words and voice !   No one ever spoke so to me before.   I could have listened longer."

After that Hina harkened for the footsteps of Kaupeepee, and lived to forget that she was a prisoner in the fortress of Haupu. His love gently wooed her thoughts from the past and made sweet the bondage which he shared with her.

III.

The sudden disappearance of Hina created a profound excitement among the people of that part of the coast of Hilo from which she had been abducted. The women who had been permitted to escape ran screaming to the house of Hakalanileo with their tale of woe, and soon for miles around the country was in arms. When questioned, all they could tell was that a canoe filled with armed men suddenly dashed through the surf, and their mistress was seized and borne out to sea. This was all they knew.

Canoes were suddenly equipped and sent in pursuit, but they returned before morning with the report that nothing had been seen of the abductors. Messengers were despatched to the coast settlements of Hamakua, Hilo and Puna, but they brought no intelligence of the missing woman. Uli was consulted, but her divinations failed, for the reason, as she informed the unhappy husband, that the powers that had warned her against the marriage of her daughter and foreshadowed the result could not be prevailed upon to impart any information that would interfere with the fulfilment of the prophecy. Uli, therefore, sat down in gloom to await the developments of time, and Hakalanileo started on a systematic search through the group for his lost wife.

After visiting every district and almost every village on Hawaii, he proceeded with a small party of attendants to Maui, and thence to Molokai, Oahu, Kauai and Niihau, and back to Lanai and Kahoolawe; but no trace of Hina could be discovered. He was well received by the various chiefs, and assistance was freely offered and sometimes accepted; but all search was in vain, and he returned disheartened to Hawaii after an absence of more than two years.

But his first search was not his last. During the fifteen years that followed he made frequent voyages to the different islands on the same errand, and always with the same result. He offered sacrifices in the temples, made pledges to the gods, and consulted every *kaula* of note of whom he had knowledge; but his offerings and promises failed to secure the assistance of the unseen powers, and the *kilos* and astrologers could gather nothing of importance to him from their observations.

Meantime Kana and Niheu, the sons of Hina, grew to manhood and prepared to continue the search for their mother, which Hakalanileo had at last abandoned as hopeless. Again and again had their grandmother told them the story of the abduction of Hina, and as often had they vowed to devote their lives to a solution of the mystery of her fate. It was vouchsafed to Uli to see that her daughter lived, but beyond that her charms and incantations were fruitless. But when the beards of her grandsons began to grow she felt that the time was approaching when Hina's hiding-place would be discovered, and she inspired them to become proficient in the use of arms and the arts of war. And to their assistance she brought the instruction of supernatural powers.

Niheu became endowed not only with great personal strength and courage, but with unerring instincts of strategy and all the accomplishments of a successful military leader. To Kana were given powers of a different nature. He could contract his body to the compass of an insect, and expand or extend it almost indefinitely; but he was permitted to do neither except in cases of imminent personal peril, as the faculty was rarely imparted to mortals, and in this instance was accorded by *Kanaloa* without the knowledge of the powers to which that deity was subject.

Finally, after a season of long and patient inquiry, it was developed to Uli that her daughter was secreted in the fortress of

Haupu and could be recovered only by force, as she had long been the wife of Kaupeepee and would not be surrendered peacefully. Hakalanileo regarded the development with distrust; for while at Kalaupapa, on the island of Molokai, less than three years before, word was brought to him from Kaupeepee, offering to open the fortress of Haupu to his inspection. Hence, when his sons set about raising a large force to attack that stronghold, he gave them every assistance in his power, but declined to accompany the expedition.

Before noting with greater detail the warlike preparations of Hina's sons, let us refer briefly to the changes which the years leading them to manhood had brought to others connected with the events of this legend. Hina had been a not unhappy captive at Haupu for nearly seventeen years, during which Kaupeepee had continued his desultory assaults upon the usurping chiefs of the neighboring islands. His name had become known throughout the entire group, and several combined attacks upon Haupu had been repulsed—the last by land, led by a distinguished Maui chief, with a slaughter so great that the adjoining gulches were choked with the slain. The venerable Kamauaua had passed away, leaving the government of Molokai to his son, Keoloewa, who had married Nuakea, daughter of the powerful chief, Keaunui, of Oahu, and sister of Lakona, of the strain of Maweke. Moi, another of Nuakea's brothers, had joined Kaupeepee at Haupu, and became not only his steadfast friend and adviser, but his *kaula*, or prophet, as well.

Paumakua had died at a very old age, and was buried at Iao, leaving his titles, *meles* and possessions to his son, Haho; but the change did not seem to affect the holdings of Hakalanileo in Hilo, although it brought to his sons some support in their subsequent war with Kaupeepee. Haho was a haughty but warlike chief, and refused to recognize the titles of many of the native nobles ; and, to permanently degrade them, he founded the *Aha-alii*, or college of chiefs, which embraced the blue-blooded of the entire group, and remained in vogue as late as the beginning of the present century. To be recognized by this college of heraldry, it was necessary for every chief to name his descent from an ancestor of unquestioned nobility ; and when his rank was thus formally established, no circumstance of war or peace could deprive him of it. There were gradations of rank and *tabu* within the *Aha-alii*, and all received the respect to which their rank entitled them, without regard to their worldly condition. No chief could claim a higher grade than the source from which he sprang; nor could he achieve it, although through marriage with a chiefess of higher rank he might advance his children to the grade of the mother. The *Aha-alii* had a language which was not understood by the common people, and which was changed whenever it became known to the *makaainana,* and it w.,s their right on all occasions to wear the insignia of their rank, the feather wreath (*lei-hulu*), the feather cape (*aha ula*), and the ivory clasp (*palaoa*); and their canoes might be painted red and bear a pennon. The royal color was yellow.

Although Kaupeepee was of the undoubted blood of Nanaula, and would not have been denied admission to the *Aha-alii,* he treated with contempt the institution of nobility founded by Haho, declaring that the blood of the founder himself was ennobled only through the thefts of his low-born grandfather. This was doubtless correct; but Kaupeepee's hatred of the southern invaders would not allow him to be just, even to their ancestors.

Such was the condition of affairs when the sons of Hina began to prepare for their expedition against Haupu. They sent emissaries to Oahu and Maui, and were promised substantial co-operation by the leading chiefs of those islands, the most of whom had suffered from the raids of the scourge of Molokai. They collected a mighty fleet of canoes and a force of six thousand warriors. As many more were promised from Oahu and Maui, which, were Keoloewa's permission obtained, would be landed at Molokai to operate in conjunction with the army from Hawaii.

As an attack on Haupu from the sea side was not considered practicable, even with the overwhelming force that was being organized against it, messengers were despatched to Molokai to prevail upon Keoloewa to permit a portion of the united armies to land on the south side of the island and assault the fortress from the mountain. His sympathies were with his brother, and he hesitated; but when he learned of the formidable force organizing for the reduction of Haupu, he appreciated that he was unable to successfully oppose the movement, and, with the assurance that his subjects would be neither disturbed nor despoiled of their property during the conflict, and that the invading armies would be withdrawn from the island at the end of the campaign against Haupu, he consented to the landing. Had he known the real motive of the assault he would have advised his brother to surrender his fair prisoner and save both from possible ruin ; but, conceiving that Kaupeepee's depredations had become unendurable, and that the chiefs of the great islands had at length united to crush him, for his own safety he felt compelled to leave him to his fate.

This resolution accorded with the advice of Kaupeepee. Many days before his faithful *kaula* had told him of the approaching invasion, of the combination of chiefs against him, and the doubtful result of the struggle ; and before the messengers reached his brother he had gone to and advised him to offer no opposition to the landing of his enemies on the island. "Opposition would be useless," argued Kaupeepee, "for my enemies are coming in great force. I have slain them and blasted their lands, and single-handed will meet the consequences. Do not embroil yourself with me, but save to our blood the possessions of our fathers."

"Perhaps you are right," said Keoloewa ; "but why not abandon Haupu and save yourself, if you are not able to hold it?"

"Never!" exclaimed Kaupeepee. "For more than twenty years its walls have stood between me and my enemies, and I will not desert them now. I have a thousand brave men who will triumph or die with me. Should Haupu be taken, go and count the corpses around its walls, and you will not blush to see how a son of Kamauaua died!"

"So let the will of the gods be done!" replied the brother. "But we may not meet again."

"True," returned Kaupeepee, with a strange smile—"true, my good brother, for my sepulchre at Haupu needs ornamenting before the mourners come."

"In my name take anything required for your defence," said Keoloewa, still holding the hand of his brother, as if reluctant to part with him ; "my heart, if not my arm, will be with you!"

"We shall be well prepared," were the words of Kaupeepee at parting ; and before he reached the top of the *pali* on his return to Haupu, the messengers from Hawaii landed at Kalaupapa.

With this concession from Kèoloewa the arrangements for the campaign were speedily made. The main body of the united forces was to concentrate at Kaunakakai, on the north side of the island, and move under the supreme leadership of Niheu, while a large detachment, embracing the best seamen of the several quotas, was to blockade the sea-entrances to Haupu, destroy the canoes of the fortress to prevent escape or succor, and co-operate generally with the land forces. This dangerous service was entrusted to the command of Kana.

At the appointed time the Hawaiian army set sail for Molokai in a fleet of over twelve hundred canoes, many of them double, and carrying a large supply of provisions. The assistance of the gods had been invoked with many sacrifices, and the omens had been favorable. In one of the large double canoes was Uli. Her form was bent with age, and her hair, white as foam, covered her shoulders like a mantle. In youth she was noted for her stateliness and beauty ; but age and care had destroyed all traces of her early comeliness, and her wrinkled face, and black eyes glistening through the rifts of her long, white hair, gave her the appearance of one who dealt with things to be feared. She was surrounded with charms and images, and before her, on a stone-bordered hearth of earth, burned a continual fire, into which she at intervals threw gums and oily mixtures, emitting clouds of incense. Her canoe followed that of the sons of Hina, with their priest and war-god, and red pennon at the masthead ; and as the fleet swept out into the ocean, with thousands of oars in the waves and thousands of spears in the air, Uli rose to her feet and began a wild war-chant, which was taken up by the following hosts and borne far over the waters.

The day following a number of expeditions left various openings on the coasts of Oahu and Maui—none of them approaching the Hawaiian army in strength, but together adding an aggregate of nine hundred canoes of all sizes and about four thousand warriors to the invading force. All of them reached the landing at Kaunakakai on the day appointed for their arrival, and Niheu found himself in command of ten thousand warriors and over two thousand canoes. No such number of spears was ever before seen massed on Molokai ; but the people had been assured that they would not be injured either in person or property so long as they remained peaceful, and the terms of the agreement with Keoloewa were faithfully observed. Among the invaders the people found many friends and relatives, for intercourse between the islands at that time was free and frequent ; and although their sympathies were with Kaupeepee, they soon came to regard the projected capture of Haupu as a great game of *konane*, played by agreement between two champions, during which the spectators were to remain silent and make no suggestions.

The tents of the chiefs, around which were encamped their respective followers, extended along the shore for more than two miles, while the beach for a greater distance was fringed with canoes, many of the larger painted red and bearing gaudy pennons of stout *kapa*. As plundering had been forbidden, provisions of dried fish, potatoes, cocoanuts, *taro*, and live pigs and fowls had been brought in considerable quantities in extra canoes ; but as the duration of the campaign could only be surmised, rolls of *kapa* and matting, shell wreaths, ivory, feather capes, calabashes, mechanical tools, ornaments, and extra arms were also brought, to be fairly exchanged from time to time for such supplies as might be wanted.

IV.

Everything being in readiness for an advance upon the stronghold of Kaupeepee, a war-council of the assembled chiefs was called. Among them were several who were well informed concerning the approaches to Haupu, and the main features of the campaign were arranged without discussion. Signals and other means of communication between the two divisions having been agreed upon, the next morning a detachment of two thousand men, occupying five hundred canoes, under the command of Kana, moved around the island to blockade the entrances to Haupu, and immediately after the main army, leaving a strong reserve to guard the canoes and look after supplies, broke camp and took up its line of march across the island to the mountains back of the fortress. The trails were rough, but at sunrise the next morning the land division, stretched along the summit of the hills two miles back of Haupu, looked down and saw the fleet of Kana drawn like a broad, black line around the ocean entrances to the doomed stronghold.

Meantime Kaupeepee had not been idle. Every movement of the enemy had been watched ; and when word came to him that the shores of Kaunakakai were so crowded with warriors that the number could not be told, he grimly answered : " Then will our spears be less likely to miss ! "

The walls of the fortress had been strengthened and replenished with missiles ; large quantities of provisions had been secured, and sheds of ample space were finally erected for the collection of rain-water, should communication be interrupted with the streams in the gulches below. Before the enemy had reached positions completely cutting off retreat from the fortress, Kaupeepee had called his warriors together and thus addressed them :

" Warriors and friends !—for all, indeed, are warriors and friends in Haupu !—for years you have shared in the dangers of Kaupeepee and have never disobeyed him. Listen now to his words, and heed them well. A mighty army is about to surround Haupu by land and sea. It already blackens the shores of Kaunakakai, and will soon be thundering at our gates. The fight will be long and desperate, and may end in defeat and death to the most or all of us. I cannot order, cannot even ask you to face such peril for my sake. The gates are open. Let all leave with my good-will whose lives are precious to them. Let your acts answer at once, for the enemy is approaching and no time can be lost ! "

For a moment not a warrior of the thousand present moved. All stood staring at their chief and wondering that he should doubt. Then a confused hum of voices, rising louder and louder, swelled into a united shout of " Close the gates ! " and Kaupeepee was answered. And a braver answer was never given than that which came from the stout hearts and unblanched lips of the thousand fearless defenders of Haupu. The gates were closed, with not a single warrior missing, and the fortress was soon environed with its enemies.

Halting his army on the summit of the mountains overlooking Haupu, Niheu despatched a messenger to the fortress with a signal of peace, to ascertain with certainty whether Hina was a prisoner there, and, if so, to demand the surrender of the captive. The messenger returned in safety, bearing this message from Kaupeepee : " Hina is within the walls of Haupu. Come with arms in your hands and take her ! "

Communication was established with the fleet in front of Haupu, and Kana was advised to enter the gulches in force the next morning, destroy the canoes of the fortress, and maintain a footing there, if possible, while a strong division of the land forces would move down and draw attention to the rear defences by taking a position within attacking distance.

In pursuance of this plan, early next morning Niheu despatched a formidable force down the mountain in the rear of Haupu, with orders to menace but not to assault the defences. Arriving near the walls, a little skirmishing ensued, when the detachment took a position beyond the reach of the slingers, and began the construction of a stone wall across the ridge.

Meantime Kana's fleet of canoes, which had been hovering nearer and nearer the walls of Haupu since daylight, with a wild battle-cry from the warriors crowding them suddenly dashed through the surf, and partially succeeded in effecting a landing in one of the gulches flanking the fortress. So rapid had been the movement, and so thoroughly had the attention of the besieged been engrossed with the diversion from the mountains, that a division of the assaulting party managed to reach the canoes of the fortress, and another to secure a lodgment among the rocks on the opposite side of the gulch, before meeting with serious opposition. The score or two of warriors left to guard the canoes of the fortress were quickly overpowered and slaughtered, and then the work of destruction began. With loose rocks and heavy stone hammers the canoes were being hastily broken in pieces, including the great war-barge of Kaupeepee, when from the walls above the destroyers was precipitated a bewildering and murderous avalanche of rocks of all sizes and heavy sections of tree-trunks. As the missiles rolled and bounded down the steep declivity, sweeping it at almost the same moment for two hundred yards or more in length, the ground trembled as with an earthquake, and the gorge was filled with a dense cloud of dust.

The thunder of the avalanche ceased, and in the awful silence that succeeded Kaupeepee, at the head of two hundred warriors, dashed down the narrow path leading from the middle terrace to finish the dreadful work with spear, knife and battle-axe. The sight was appalling, even to the chief of Haupu. The gulch was choked with the bodies of the dying and the dead. Panic-stricken, those posted on the opposite hillside had abandoned their only place of safety, and perished in large numbers in attempting to reach their canoes. The few left alive and able to retreat were wildly struggling to escape seaward from the gulch in such canoes of their wrecked fleet as would still float, or by plunging desperately into the surf.

With exultant shouts Kaupeepee and his warriors sprang over their dead and dying enemies and swept down upon the unarmed and escaping remnant of the invaders. Although a considerable reserve of canoes came to their rescue from without, protected from assault from above by the presence of Kaupeepee and his party, the most of the fugitives would have been cut off but for the extraordinary efforts of Kana, who led the attacking party, but miraculously escaped unhurt. In the surf, in the deep entrance to the gulch, everywhere he moved around with his head and shoulders above the water. He assisted the canoes through the breakers, rescued exhausted and drowning swimmers, and from the bottom of the ocean reached down and gathered huge rocks, which he hurled at intervals at Kaupeepee's warriors to keep them in check. These wonderful exploits awed the attacking party, and greater still was their astonishment when they saw the strange being finally walk through the deep waters, erect and with his head and breast exposed, and step into a canoe quite half a mile from the shore. Turning to his warriors, with these words Kaupeepee answered their looks of inquiry : " He is Kana. I have heard of him. I am glad he escaped."

Kana returned with his shattered fleet and still worsely shattered army to Kaunakakai. As the most of his canoes had been destroyed, Kaupeepee was unable to follow the retreating enemy to sea, but, hearing the shouts of conflict above, at once mounted with his warriors to the fortress, to assist in repelling an attack on the rear wall which had been hastily begun to save, if possible, the sea party from destruction. With Kaupeepee at the front the assault was quickly repulsed, the enemy retiring in confusion behind the lines of defence from which the advance had been made.

The wounded in the gulch were despatched, six of the least injured being reserved for sacrifice, and the night following the fortress of Haupu was ablaze with savage joy. As the first-fruits of the victories of the day, the six wounded prisoners were slain with clubs and laid upon the altar of the *heiau* as offerings to the gods, and chants of defiance were sent through the night air to the discomfited enemy beyond the walls.

These disasters did not dishearten Niheu. The canoes of the fortress had been destroyed, and that was something of a compensation for the loss of nearly two thousand of his best warriors and a considerable part of his fleet. Plans for further assaults from the sea were abandoned, and a regular siege, with a final entrance by the rear wall, was suggested and in the end agreed to by the chiefs in council.

Lines of pickets were accordingly stationed along the summits of the mountains flanking the fortress, in order to prevent the entrance into it of reinforcements or supplies, and the main body of the attacking force was moved down and placed in positions within slinging distance of the rear wall. This was not done without loss, for the wall was manned with expert slingers; but in less than a week the besiegers had advanced their main line of wooden defences within a hundred paces of the rear bulwark of the fortress and were daily gaining ground.

This movable line of assault and defence was a device as ingenious as it was effective. Timbers twenty feet in length, or corresponding with the height of the wall, were firmly corded together side by side until they stretched across the narrow summit leading to the fortress. To the top of each fourth or fifth timber was lashed a movable brace thirty feet in length, and then the wooden wall was raised into the air nearly erect, and securely held in that position by its line of supporting braces. It was a formidable-looking structure. Against it the missiles of the besieged fell harmless, and behind it the besiegers worked in safety.

Section by section and foot by foot this moving line of timber was advanced, until the warriors on the wall could almost touch it with their spears. Several desperate sorties, to destroy or prostrate it, had been made, but nothing beyond the cutting of a few of the lower fastenings had been achieved; and the defenders of Haupu, with tightened grasp of their weapons, grimly awaited the final assault, which they felt would not long be delayed. Day after day, night after night, they watched; but the wooden wall did not move, and they could only guess at what was going on behind it.

Finally a night of inky darkness came—a night "as dark as the farthest confines of *Po*"—bringing with it a storm of wind and rain. In the midst of the storm the wooden wall began to move, but so noiselessly that the advance was not perceived by the fortress sentinels. Midnight came and went ; the storm continued, and nearer and nearer to the wall of stone was crowded the wall of timber. Just as coming day began to streak the east the bases of the two walls came together, the backward inclination of both leaving them a few feet apart at their tops. Hundreds of men then laid hold of the braces, and in a moment the wooden wall was shoved over and stayed against the other.

The alarm was given within, and warriors from all parts of the enclosure sprang toward the menaced wall. But the movement of their enemies was not less prompt. Up the braces they swarmed in such numbers that the few who had succeeded in reaching the top of the wall from within were hurled from it, and after them poured a cataract of spears against which the opposing force was powerless. The huge stone was rolled back, the gate was opened, and soon the upper terrace was cleared and five thousand warriors, led by Niheu in person, were sweeping down to complete their work of slaughter.

But their victory was not to be cheaply purchased. They had slain two or three hundred on the wall and around the gate, but thrice as many more, under the desperate leadership of Kaupeepee, were stretched like a wall across the middle terrace, with a resolution to contest every pace of the ground with their lives. They might have escaped, perhaps, down the paths leading from that terrace to the gulches ; but they preferred to die, as they had for years lived, in defence of Haupu.

Down the terrace swept the victorious horde in the gray dawn of the morning. Niheu vainly tried to hold his warriors in check, for he knew the main body of the fortress force was still before him, and would have advanced with prudence ; but the voices of the leaders were drowned in the battle-shouts of the surging throng, which in a few minutes struck Kaupeepee's wall of spears and battle-axes, and rolled back like a storm-wave broken against the front of Haupu. But the check was only momentary, for immediately behind the shattered column was a forest of advancing spears, and with a wild tumult of shouts and clashing weapons the entire force was precipitated upon Kaupee-pee's thin but resolute lines of defence.

The slaughter was frightful ; but the unequal conflict could have but one result. Kaupeepee and the fifty or less of his followers left standing were crowded, fighting step by step, into the lower terrace, and thence to the *heiau*, and finally to the temple as a last place of defence. There the struggle was brief. The roof of the temple was fired, and as Kaupeepee and the last of his devoted band sprang from the blazing building to die at the throats of their enemies they were struck down with their javelins in the air. A spear penetrated the breast of Kaupeepee. As a last act he poised his *ihe* to hurl at a helmeted chief who had just struggled to the front. The chief was Niheu. By his dress or face, which bore a resemblance to the features of Hina, Kaupeepee must have recognized him. He looked, but his arm did not move. " Not for your sake, but for hers ! " exclaimed the dying warrior, dropping his weapon to the earth and falling lifeless beside it.

Not one of the defenders of Haupu escaped, but more than one-half of Niheu's army perished in the various assaults upon the fortress. Hina was found uninjured, and, while there was great joy to her in the embrace of her sons and aged mother, she wept over the death of Kaupeepee, who with his love had made light her long imprisonment.

The body of Kaupeepee was given to Keoloewa for interment, as were also the remains of Moi, who was among the last to fall. The walls of Haupu were levelled, never to be raised again, and Hina returned to her husband in Hilo, after a separation of nearly eighteen years, thus bringing to a close one of the most romantic legends of early Hawaiian chivalry.

THE ROYAL HUNCHBACK.

CHARACTERS.

KANIPAHU, king of Hawaii.
KALAPANA, son of Kanipahu.
KAMAIOLE, a usurper of the throne, chief of Kau.
IOLA, sister of Kamaiole.
MAKEA, daughter of Iola.
WAIKUKU, a military chief, abductor of Iola.
NANOA, a chief in the royal household.

THE ROYAL HUNCHBACK.

I.

ABOUT the period of A. D. 1160 Kanipahù was the nominal sovereign of the island of Hawaii. He was the grandson of Pili, who near the close of the previous century came from Samoa, at the solicitation of the high-priest Paao, to assume the *moiship* left vacant by the death of Kapawa, whose grandfather was probably the first of the southern chiefs who came to the Hawaiian group during the important migratory movements of the eleventh and twelfth centuries.

Although the sovereignty of the entire island was claimed by the Pili family, disturbances were frequent in the time of Kanipahu, and a few of the native chiefs of the old stock of Nanaula, which held sway in the group for nearly six centuries, refused to yield allegiance to the new dynasty. To strengthen his power and placate the native chiefs and people, Kanipahu took to wife Hualani, the fifth in descent from Maweke, of the Nanaula line, and subsequently Alaikaua, who was probably of the same native strain.

The *makaainana*, or common people, however, seem to have been better satisfied with their new rulers than were their former chiefs who had been supplanted in authority, and it was therefore with difficulty that they could be aroused to a resistance to political conditions which imposed upon them no hardships which they had not borne under their old rulers, and no responsibilities with which they were not already familiar. And, besides, the new-comers from the south had introduced new laws, new customs and new products of the soil, as well as new gods and new forms of worship. They had brought with them the *kaeke*, or sacred drum, and *puloulou*, or inviolable *tabu* staff, crowned with balls of white or black *kapa*. They had also instituted the title of *moi*, or supreme sovereign, whereas the several islands before had been ruled by scores of independent chiefs, each claiming and holding as large a district as he was able to defend. They had established the *Aha-alii*, or college of chiefs, through which the rank of every noble might find recognition, and be perpetuated in his family. They had constructed grander *heiaus*, or temples, and shut the populace from the observance of many of their religious ceremonies. The *tabus* of the chiefs and priests had been enlarged and rendered more strict, and the priesthood had become more powerful and independent. The persons of the *mois* and high chiefs had become more sacred, and they exercised their functions with increased display and ostentation.

These additional exactions on the part of the new rulers, however, were partially if not wholly compensated for to the laboring masses by the protection brought to them through the political change against the oppressions of their petty chiefs and land-owners ; and it is therefore probable that, on the whole, their social and industrial condition was quite as tolerable under the new as under the old or native *régime*.

Kanipahu resided principally in Kohala, where his grand-father had taken up his abode, and constructed mansions consistent with his sovereign state. And it was there that the high-priest Paao, who brought Pili to the group, established himself and family, after first landing in Puna and erecting to his god the temple of Wahaula, the ruins of which are still seen near the village of Kahawalea. After the arrival of Pili it is probable that Paao removed with him to the more populous district of Kohala, and there remained as his high-priest and adviser. At Puuepa he erected the large *heiau* of Mookini, the stones for which were passed from hand-to-hand from Niulii, a distance of nine miles—a circumstance indicating the presence of a large population on Hawaii at that time. As it was one of the largest temples in the group—its walls, enclosing an irregular parallelogram, having an aggregate length of 817 feet, with a height of 20 feet, and a breadth of 8 feet at the top—a vast amount of labor must have been required to transport the material over so long and rough a road, with no appliance more effective than human muscle. But the walls are so well built that they are standing to-day, and from a secret crypt in the wall of the south side of the *heiau* were taken but a few years ago, and are still preserved, two finely-polished stone disks of a diameter of eight or ten inches, which it is not improbable were the two strange idols which tradition says Paao brought with him over the great waters from Upolu, and which were hidden by some faithful *kahu* or servant of the *heiau* when the ancient worship of the people was abolished by the second Kamehameha in 1819.

Kanipahu was a just and considerate sovereign, and sought by every peaceful means to harmonize the conflicting interests of the chiefs and strengthen and consolidate his power. To this end, as already stated, he allied himself by marriage to the Na-naula line of chiefs, and attached to his person and household a number of prominent nobles of native lineage. The result was that for some years he ruled in peace, and race jealousies were gradually wearing away, when a circumstance occurred which suddenly terminated the reign of Kanipahu and drove him into exile.

It was a sultry afternoon, near the time of the annual feast of *Lono*, perhaps in 1172, that Kanipahu, after having despatched the business of the day, was reclining on a couch of mats in the cool shade of a palm-grove within the walled enclosure of the palace grounds—if, indeed, two large wooden and thatched build-ings, each a hundred or more feet in length by forty in breadth, with eight or ten smaller houses among the banana growths in the rear, may be called a palace. The grounds were thickly studded with shade and fruit trees, embracing almost every variety of value found on the island. Here and there were shaded walks and vine-wreathed nooks in which rude seats had been constructed ; and as the sentinels lounged lazily at the entrance, and the *kahus* of the king languidly administered to his wants, the scene was a picture of royal power and barbaric comfort peculiar to the Polynesian islands, but scarcely less imposing than the forms and architectural environments of the jarls and princes of northern and central Europe at that period. Each of the personal attendants of the king was of the lesser nobility, and his office was one of honor. Over the head of the drowsing sovereign the *paakahili*, or *kahili*-bearer, at brief inter-vals waved his tuft of painted plumes, while at a respectful dis-tance stood the spittoon-bearer (*ipakuha*) and head steward (*aipuupuu*).

The king was suddenly aroused by a tumult at the outer

gate. There was a sound of angry voices mingled with a clashing of spears, and immediately after a tall chief, clad in *maro*, feather cape and helmet, and bearing a stout *ihe*, or javelin, strode toward the royal mansion, followed by a number of excited chiefs and their retainers. Reaching the palace, the chief turned and faced his clamoring pursuers with a look of defiance. To shed blood there was an offence which no one was bold or reckless enough to commit, and, after one of the number had first been despatched to the king to ascertain his pleasure, the entire party of chiefs repaired to the royal presence, leaving their weapons behind in the hands of the guards who had hurried toward the scene of disturbance.

Bowing low before the king, who had risen to a sitting posture on his couch, the chiefs waited for him to break the silence. Slowly scanning his auditors, all but one of whom he knew and trusted, Kanipahu finally fixed his eyes upon the face of the stranger and quietly said :

"Your face is strange to me. Who are you, and what brings you here?"

"Great chief, I am Kamaiole, a chief of Kau," was the reply, "and I came to Kohala in search of my sister, Iola, who was stolen and brought here about the close of the last season of rain."

"Have you found her?" inquired the king.

"I have found her," replied Kamaiole, bowing his head.

"Who took your sister away from Kau?" resumed the king.

"That man," said Kamaiole, pointing to one of the chiefs present; "at least, so I presume, since he was seen in Kau about the time of her disappearance, and I found her in his possession here."

The chief designated was a large and well-favored young man, with a palm-tree tattooed upon each of his muscular thighs, and wearing a number of gaudy ornaments around his neck. He was an *alii koa*, or military chief, without possessions and in the service of the king, to whom he was distantly related. Turning toward him, Kanipahu said :

"Speak, Waikuku, and answer the words of the chief of Kau."

Glancing savagely at Kamaiole, Waikuku bowed to the king and replied :

"It is true that Iola came with me from Kau, where I went

Type of Scenery—on the Road to Kilauea, Hawaii.

to visit the brother of my mother; but she came willingly, although I admit without the consent of Kamaiole."

"Waikuku is of the blood of noble chiefs," said the king in a tone of conciliation; "why not permit your sister, since it is her will, to remain with him in peace?"

"She may remain," was Kamaiole's grim reply.

"And well may she remain!" exclaimed Waikuku bitterly. "Iola is dead! To-day, even a few breaths past, her brutal brother found and with his own hand killed her!"

"Killed her?" repeated the king.

"Yes, killed her," continued Waikuku; "and but that her cowardly murderer sought the protection of the royal enclosure, my spear would have tasted his blood!"

"Speak, and give good reason for this murder of the wife of Waikuku," said the king, sternly addressing Kamaiole, "or, by great *Lono!* I will downward command your face!"

When a prisoner of war or malefactor was brought before an ancient Hawaiian king, if his order was "Downward the face!" the prisoner was taken away and slain at once by one of the royal executioners; but if it was "Upward the face!" his life was spared, either for complete pardon, slavery or sacrifice to the gods.

Giving little regard to the threat of the king, but burning with wrath at the insulting language of Waikuku, Kamaiole proudly answered:

"I am of the *aha-alii* of Hawaii. My war-canoes are red, and pennons float at their mast-tips. The blood of Nanaula is in my veins, and my ancestors were of the *alii-nui*—were kings here generations before Pili landed at Kohala or the Paumakuas blasted the shores of Hilo. With a rank befitting it was my purpose to mate my sister. But she secretly became the wife of a marauding *puuku*—possibly by force, probably by the charm of lies and the glitter of shells—and I followed and slew her, that her blood and mine might not be degraded by being mingled with that of Waikuku!"

"*Puuku!*" hissed Waikuku, enraged at the low rank contemptuously given him by Kamaiole, and making a hostile menace toward the speaker.

Kamaiole regarded Waikuku for a moment with a look of disdain, and then continued:

"The occupation of this Waikuku—this woman-stealer—is

that of war, I have been informed. He boasted that his spear
would have tasted the blood of Kamaiole had he not sought the
protection of the royal grounds. I came here through no fear
of his arm or the spears of his friends, but to explain to the king
why I had shed blood within sight of the royal *hale*. But since
he talks so bravely of blood and spears, I challenge him to make
good his words with me beyond the palace walls. The matter
is solely between us. I am prepared to answer to him in words
of combat for what I have done to-day. Or if, as I suspect, he
lacks the courage to give his warlike training a test so public, I
will ward a spear with such of his friends, one by one, as may
feel disposed to make his grievance theirs."

The chiefs looked at each other in amazement at the broad
challenge of Kamaiole, and the king seemed to be scarcely less
astounded. But the proposal could not be deemed either unfair
or unusual, since, according to the usage of the time, Kamaiole
was answerable to Waikuku for the death of Iola.

The stinging remarks of the dauntless Kau chief left to Waikuku no pretext or excuse for declining the challenge, and the
king somewhat reluctantly consented to a settlement of the matter by the arbitrament of single combat, with such weapons as
might be mutually agreed upon.

Among the members of the royal household who witnessed
this remarkable interview with the king was a chief of the old
native line called Nanoa. Admiring the cool courage of Kamaiole, and feeling for him something of a sympathy of lineage,
he proffered to stand his friend and adviser in the forthcoming
encounter ; and the arrangements finally made were that the
hostile parties were to meet just at sunset in a grove immediately
back of the palace enclosure. They were to be armed each with
two spears and a javelin. The spears were first to be used when
the combatants approached within twenty paces of each other.
These being thrown without ending the battle, the parties were
to advance to close encounter with their javelins, with the discretion of either throwing or retaining them in hand. No other
weapons were to be used, and the conditions of the meeting were
such that the king, who proposed to be present, did not deem it
probable that there would be loss of life, especially as he had
resolved to put an end to the combat with the first wound received by either.

Promptly at the time appointed the principals were on the ground. The attendants of Kamaiole were nowhere to be seen. By his orders they had quietly left the village two hours before, and the only friend at his side was Nanoa. He had thrown aside his cloak and helmet, and stood stern and motionless at the place assigned him, with a spear in his right hand, and another, with a javelin, at his feet. With limbs and shoulders bare, and beard and hair black as midnight veiling his neck, Kamaiole leaned upon his spear a picture of barbaric strength and courage.

Thirty paces in front of Kamaiole stood Waikuku, similarly armed and clad, but less calm than his adversary. Around him were a score or more of high chiefs, some rallying and others advising him ; but he remained gloomily silent, nervously awaiting the arrival of the king and the word for action.

In a few minutes Kanipahu, accompanied by a number of armed attendants, arrived and took a seat prepared for him at a point about equally distant from the two combatants. It being announced that everything was in readiness, the king signaled the word to be given, and the hostile chiefs, advancing five paces each, were in a moment balancing their long spears for flight. The spear of Waikuku first shot through the air in a line direct for his adversary's breast ; but the latter adroitly turned it from its course with a touch from his own weapon, which he in turn launched at Waikuku without effect. The second spears were thrown to the injury of neither, when they grasped their javelins and slowly and warily began to advance. It was an exciting moment. As each had gripped his weapon with both hands, it was apparent that neither *ihe* would be thrown, and a hand-to-hand struggle was inevitable.

The king drew nearer to obtain a better view of the closing conflict, and the spectators eagerly watched every movement of the advancing chiefs. Approaching within striking distance— the javelins being about six feet in length—a few feints were made, and Waikuku ventured a desperate thrust at the breast of his opponent. The movement was evidently expected, perhaps invited, for like a flash the point of the *ihe* was thrown into the air, and the next moment Waikuku received a thrust through the side. He fell, javelin in hand, and Kamaiole was lifting his weapon to strike his prostrate enemy to the heart when " Stop ! " came the command of the king.

Heedless of the royal order, or too greatly excited to be able to restrain his hand, Kamaiole savagely drove his javelin into the breast of Waikuku, inflicting a death-wound.

"Downward the face!" thundered the king, exasperated at Kamaiole's apparent defiance of his order.

The chiefs began to move forward to seize or slay the offender. Knowing that his death had been decreed, Kamaiole recklessly poised his *ihe*, red with the life-blood of Waikuku, and with a wild cry of "Yes, downward the face!" hurled it at the heart of Kanipahu.

With exclamations of rage and horror the spectators sprang toward Kamaiole, the most of them dropping their unwieldy spears and grasping their *pahoas*, or daggers of ivory or hardened wood, as they advanced.

For an instant Kamaiole hesitated whether to defend himself to the death with the javelin of the dying chief, or take the almost equally desperate chances of escape by breaking through the lines of his encircling enemies. He chose the latter, and, grasping the javelin, started toward the king, with the view of drawing his assailants in that direction. This object being accomplished, he suddenly turned to the right, and charged and made an opening through the throng at a point that seemed to be the weakest. As he flew past the yielding line he miraculously escaped the spear and knife thrusts aimed at him, and succeeded in putting himself beyond the reach of spear and sling before real pursuit was made.

The javelin hurled at the king was received in the shoulder of a faithful attendant who had opportunely thrown himself in front of his royal master; and so rapid and confusing were the movements following that Kanipahu had scarcely recovered from his consternation at the bold assault upon his life before he learned that Kamaiole had escaped. Giving orders for a vigorous pursuit of the fugitive, the king walked to the body of Waikuku, and, discovering that life was extinct, directed its respectful removal, and then proceeded sadly to the royal mansion.

Kamaiole was not overtaken. He was strong and fleet of foot, and, as darkness soon intervened in his favor, he was able to elude his pursuers. He reached the coast in safety, and, boarding a canoe awaiting him in charge of his attendants, set sail for Kau. This provision for a hasty flight from Kohala renders it certain that Kamaiole meditated desperate work on landing there, and the relation of his subsequent exploits has shown how successfully he performed it.

II.

Kamaiole supposed he had killed his sister, and Waikuku, who had seen her just before his unfortunate encounter, thought she had but a few minutes to live ; but the wounds inflicted did not prove fatal, and Iola finally recovered and became the mother of a daughter to her dead husband. Tradition attributes her recovery to the especial prayers of the high-priest, but careful nursing and a good constitution were probably the saving means, assisted by the fortunate escape of the vital organs from serious injury.

Returning to Kau, Kamaiole began to prepare for war at once, not doubting that Kanipahu, defied and assaulted at the very gates of the royal mansion, would feel it his duty to bring him to submission. Sending emissaries through the several districts, he appealed to the native chiefs and people to join him in a revolt against Kanipahu, for the purpose of transferring the sovereignty of the island to a ruler of the old Nanaula line, and restoring to them the simple worship of their fathers and the possessions of which they had been despoiled by the southern invaders.

The appeal was not without effect. Substantial aid was promised in Kona, Kau, Puna and Hilo, and in less than three months Kamaiole found himself at the head of an army large enough not only to protect him at Kau, which was doubtless the original purpose of the movement, but to carry the war into Kohala and effect a general revolution.

Whatever may have been the plans of Kanipahu concerning the rebellious Kau chief, he certainly seemed to be in no haste to put them in execution, for when Kamaiole arrived in Kohala at the head of his forces he was but feebly opposed. Tradition fails to account for the apathy of Kanipahu in the face of the supreme danger confronting him. All we are told is that, finding it impossible to raise an army strong enough to suppress the formidable revolt, he left his sons with a trusted friend in the valley of Waimanu, in the district of Hamakua, and sought refuge for

himself on the island of Molokai. Iola, fearing to meet her brother, or that he might learn that she still lived, also found an
asylum with the young sons of Kanipahu in the secluded valley
of Waimanu.

Thus Kamaiole assumed the sovereignty of Hawaii almost
without opposition, and Kanipahu lived quietly and unknown at
Kalae, on the small island of Molokai. He dressed and comported himself as a simple commoner, performing his own work,
bearing his own burdens, and accepting all the hardships to
which the poor and untitled were subject. He won the love of
his neighbors for his kindness, and on two occasions took up
arms to assist them in repelling plundering raids from Maui; and
so well did he use his weapons that his humble friends were
astonished, and thought he must have been trained in the arts
of war, even if he was not of chiefly blood. It is well known
that the chiefs, as a class, were physically larger than the masses,
so much so that they claimed, and still claim, a descent distinct
from that of the common people. Kanipahu was nearer seven
than six feet in height, and his size was suggestive of rank; but
he habitually stooped his head and shoulders, that his height
might be subject to less remark, and labored more industriously
than any of his neighbors in order to convince them that he was
reared to toil. And in the end, as the years came and went, toil
became a comfort to him, for it occupied his thoughts and gave
him dreamless and refreshing slumber.

Let us now pass over a period of eighteen years from the accession of Kamaiole to the sovereignty of Hawaii. Kanipahu
was still a laborer on the island of Molokai, and his sons had
grown to manhood in the secluded valley of Waimanu, their rank
and family ties known only to a few who could be trusted. One
of these sons was Kalapana, and he had married Makea, the
daughter of Iola. Her father was the dead Waikuku, and her
uncle was Kamaiole, the *moi* of Hawaii.

Kamaiole's reign had been eighteen years of almost continual
domestic turmoil and popular dissatisfaction. He was cruel, selfish and arrogant; but he was also a cool and sagacious soldier,
and his craft and courage had thus far enabled him to thwart the
organization of discontent and enforce obedience to his authority. He had even succeeded in securing the allegiance of every
prominent chief in the six districts of Hawaii—a political condi-

tion such as had never before been achieved by any of his pre-
decessors.

Wide-spread changes in feudatory tenures were the principal
causes of internal trouble. Under the Pili dynasty the land
boundaries of the native chiefs had been greatly shifted and
narrowed to make room for the chiefs of the new *régime*. In
attempting to restore the old feudal boundaries as far as possible, and adjust the new, Kamaiole had not only stirred up bitter strifes among the nobles, but had unwittingly disturbed the
vassalage of the masses and thereby rendered all classes restless
and distrustful.

Finally the discontent became so general among the *makaainana* that they appealed to the head of the Paao family, the
high-priest of the kingdom, for advice and assistance. They declared that they would no longer submit to the tyranny of Kamaiole and the exactions of his favored chiefs, and demanded a
new ruler. Tradition ascribes this movement almost wholly to
the laboring people, but it is more than probable that the priesthood took an early if not the initiatory part in it, since the high-
priest seems to have known that Kanipahu was still living, and at
once despatched a messenger to Molokai, informing the exiled
king that the people were ripe for rebellion, and advising him to
repair to Hawaii at once and place himself at the head of the
discontented thousands who would rejoice at his coming. Fearful of treachery, Kanipahu declined to make any promises to the
messenger, and, in disguise, the high-priest himself proceeded to
Kalae and urged the old chief to return and reassert his authority on Hawaii.

Kanipahu was profoundly moved at the words of the high-
priest, and no longer doubted the sincerity and good faith of the
tempting offer ; but he declined to accept it, and, when urged
for the reasons, rose sadly to his feet and said :

" Look at these hands, hardened and crooked with toil ; look
at this face, begrimed and wrinkled with exposure to the sun and
rain ; behold my bent head, and the unsightly hump that old age
and stooping labor have placed upon my shoulders ! Is this the
figure of a king? No ! The *oo* better becomes the hand of
Kanipahu now than the staff of sovereignty. Here have I contentedly dwelt for many years, and here it is my will to peacefully die."

" Then are we without hope," replied the priest, in a tone of unfeigned sadness.

" No, not without hope," returned Kanipahu. " My sons are in the valley of Waimanu. I have heard from them many times. They are worthy of their blood. Seek out Kalapana. He is brave, manly, sagacious. Tell him that upon his shoulders Kanipahu, his father, places the burden of the war against Kamaiole, and in advance bequeaths to him all his valor may win, even the sovereignty of Hawaii."

" You are right, great chief ! " said the priest. " We are not without hope. Kalapana shall answer for his father, and from every *heiau* in Hawaii shall prayers be spoken for his success."

The priest received the directions necessary to enable him to communicate with the sons of Kanipahu, and secretly returned to Hawaii to fan the smouldering fires of rebellion and prepare for the coming struggle.

Although the high-priesthood had become too firmly established in the Paao family to be changed by Kamaiole, he could not disguise his dislike for the innovations made by the southern line upon the simpler worship of his fathers, and neither confidence nor cordiality existed between the political and religious authorities. The rebellion against Kamaiole was therefore secretly but earnestly assisted by the entire priesthood, and when Kalapana raised the standard of revolt the people flocked to his support by thousands.

The rebellion was organized with extraordinary rapidity, and when Kalapana suddenly made his appearance in Kohala at the head of a large army, Kamaiole was in no condition to meet him. He hurriedly despatched his *lunapais*, or war-messengers, to the chiefs of Kohala, Kona, Hamakua and Hilo, commanding their prompt assistance, and summoned the priests and diviners of the *heiau* of Mookini to make unusual sacrifices to the gods and to bring him at once the auguries of the uprising. But the chiefs responded with no alacrity to his call, and the diviners informed him that triumph to his arms was possible only in Kona. Kamaiole therefore abandoned Kohala, and, with such force as he was able to assemble, fell back into North Kona, where the quotas of warriors from the neighboring districts were ordered to join him.

Amidst great popular enthusiasm Kalapana marched into

Northern Kohala without opposition, and took possession of the royal mansion from which his father had been driven into exile eighteen years before. Kanipahu had not overestimated the capacity of his son. By instinct he was a soldier, and from the moment that he appeared at the head of his army the chiefs who had been rallied to his support by the priesthood saw that the quiet and dreamy recluse of Waimanu was made to command; and their enthusiasm in his cause, which was soon shared by the people, made easy his way to victory.

Learning that Kamaiole had fallen back into Kona, Kalapana resolved to follow him without delay, and, if possible, bring him to battle before reinforcements could reach him from the south. The auguries were more than favorable. They were not even ambiguous. They expressly declared that Kamaiole would be killed in Kona. It was, therefore, with confidence and enthusiasm that Kalapana and his steadily increasing army started on their march for the adjoining district of Kona.

Meantime Kamaiole was not inactive. He had succeeded in gathering a force of eight thousand men, and, learning that Kalapana was advancing from Kohala, resolved to give him battle at a place called Anaehoomalu, not far from the northern line of Kona. The point was selected for its strategical advantages, and there Kamaiole, doubtful of the result—for he could see that the tide had set in against him—determined to end the struggle.

There was but a two days' march between the hostile camps, and Kalapana pushed forward with cautious haste. The priests and *kaulas* had promised him success, and the most influential chiefs of Hamakua and Kohala were at his side. He had brought with him from Waimanu, where it had been secreted for eighteen years, the war-god of Pili, which had been redecorated, and was borne in front of him in charge of the high-priest. And with him, to share his fate, went his young wife, Makea, to care for him if wounded, to fight by his side, perhaps, should the tide of battle turn against him; for at that time, and later, the more courageous of the wives and daughters of the chiefs not unfrequently, in emergencies, took an active part in the field.

On the morning of the third day after Kalapana's departure from Kohala the two armies confronted each other, and Kalapana immediately organized his forces for battle. Kamaiole saw that he was outnumbered, and resolved to await the attack behind his defences. In the face of the great odds against him in numbers he was by no means hopeful; and, besides, the auguries were unsatisfactory, and three times the night before he had heard the scream of the *alae*, the bird of evil omen. But no feeling of fear affected him. Filled with gloomy courage, he cheered his warriors with promises of victory, and, armed with a javelin and heavy *laau-palau*, or rude halberd, placed himself at the most exposed point of his defences and awaited the attack.

The battle opened, and with a wild rush a heavy division of Kalapana's forces, armed with spears, clubs, and stone axes, was hurled against the rough stone wall, four or five feet in height, behind which the enemy found partial protection. The wall was leveled in places, and desperate hand-to-hand conflicts followed, but the assault was finally repulsed. Rallied and reinforced, a second charge was made, but with no better success. The loss of life was great, and the result began to look doubtful.

But Kalapana was not discouraged by these costly failures. Withdrawing and strengthening the attacking division, and announcing that he would lead the next assault in person, he ordered an attack in the rear of the enemy by his entire reserve. This involved a rapid march of two or three miles, and the passage of a deep ravine which Kamaiole relied upon as a complete defence of his right flank. While this movement was being executed Kalapana kept the enemy employed with heavy lines of skirmishers and frequent menaces of more decided assault.

For more than an hour this desultory fighting continued, Kalapana impatiently watching for the appearance of his flanking column on the hill above the enemy. At length he discovered the first of its advancing spears, and a few minutes later the entire body came into view and began to pour down the slope. The final assault in front was then ordered, Kalapana taking command in person.

The sudden attack in the rear carried consternation to Kamaiole's warriors; but their undaunted leader coolly and resolutely prepared for the worst. Hastily taking from the front defences such spears as could be spared, he summoned the entire reserve, and with the united force sprang like a lion to meet the attack from the hill. It came like an avalanche and could not be stayed. The struggle was desperate. As his warriors fell on every side of him, Kamaiole moved like a tower of destruction through the conflict. He seemed to bear a charmed life, and men fell like grass before the sweep of his *laau-palau.*

Suddenly an old man of large mould, with head bent and long, white hair and beard sweeping his breast and stooping shoulders, stepped in front of Kamaiole, and with a heavy spear-pointed club calmly but dexterously warded a blow of the terrible *laau-palau* aimed at his head, and, answering quick as thought, felled the royal warrior to the earth like a forest tree. Around and over the body of the fallen chief a desperate struggle ensued. But it was of short duration. Under the command of Kalapana the front defences had been carried, and such of the royal army as had escaped slaughter were soon wildly leaping over the walls and retreating in confusion in all directions.

Pressing toward the rear at the head of his victorious warriors, Kalapana was attracted to the fierce hand-to-hand conflict taking place over the body of Kamaiole. Without stopping to inquire the cause, he promptly plunged into the thickest of the combat, backed by a few resolute followers, and speedily relieved the old white-haired warrior from a struggle which was taxing his strength to the utmost. This was the last stand made by the enemy in a body ; what remained of the battle was a merciless massacre of the wounded, and the capture and retention alive of a few prisoners for sacrifice.

Resting for a moment and taking a survey of the field, Kalapana's eyes fell upon the old warrior. With one foot upon the breast of Kamaiole, he was leaning upon his war-club and scanning the face of Kalapana. His ponderous weapon still dripped with gore, and his wrinkled face was splashed with the blood of his enemies.

" Where is Kamaiole ? " suddenly inquired Kalapana, grasping his weapon, as if his work of death had not yet been finished. " Where is Kamaiole ? " he repeated to those around him. " Who has seen him ? "

" Here is Kamaiole," replied the old warrior, pointing with bloody finger to the face of the dying king.

Kalapana abruptly turned, and for a moment gazed in silence upon the face of his fallen enemy. Although wounded to the death, Kamaiole was still living, and his eyes showed that he was conscious of what was transpiring around him.

" By whose hand did he fall ? " inquired Kalapana.

"By mine," briefly answered the old man.

"And who are you?" continued Kalapana, with something of a feeling of awe, "who have thus come unsummoned, in the guise of a god from our sacred temples, to strike for the son of Kanipahu?"

The old man slowly raised his head, and, brushing back the white hairs from his face, was about to speak, when the high-priest, with *kahus* bearing the war-god of Kalapana, approached to greet his victorious chief. Recognizing the venerable warrior, the astounded high-priest dropped on his knees before him, exclaiming, "Kanipahu! Kanipahu!"

Almost in a dream, Kalapana, making himself known, embraced his father, whom he had not seen for eighteen years, and then respectfully chided him for coming secretly from Molokai and joining the army as a common warrior, when his rank and abilities entitled him to supreme command.

The old chief smiled sadly as he replied:

"The purpose of my coming has been accomplished. With my own hand I have answered in blood to the treachery of Kamaiole, and paid him for the hump he has placed upon my shoulders. I shall return to Molokai, and there the old hunchback will spend his few remaining days in peace."

These words were heard and doubtless understood by Kamaiole, for he closed his eyes, and a smile of defiance played for a moment about his lips.

Just then Makea joined her husband, and was overjoyed to find him victorious and unhurt. With the first lull of battle she had started in search of him with a calabash of water, and to reach him had been compelled to pick her way through ghastly heaps of dead. At the sound of her voice, sweetly replacing the din of battle, Kamaiole opened his eyes and fixed his gaze upon her face. Finally his lips moved as if he would speak. Instinctively she approached the dying chief, and, kneeling, poured into his open mouth a few swallows of water.

Kalapana turned and smiled at Makea's humanity, unusual on barbarous battle-fields. A grateful look came into the eyes of Kamaiole, and with a questioning glance he faintly syllabled "Iola!" the name of his sister, and the mother of Makea, whom she closely resembled. Kalapana caught the word, and, understanding its meaning, in a tone not far from kind replied:

"No, not Iola, your sister, whom you failed to kill, but Makea, her daughter, who is Kalapana's wife."

Kamaiole convulsively raised his head and arms—whether in a spirit of rage or conciliation will never be known—and then dropped back dead.

The remainder of the story may be briefly told. In disregard of all persuasion, Kanipahu returned at once to Molokai, where he lived and died in obscurity, earning his own living and assuming no rank.

Kalapana was anointed king of Hawaii on his return to Kohala, and a hundred prisoners were sacrificed to the gods at Mookini. His reign was conciliatory and peaceful, and with Makea, whose full name was Makeamalamaihanae, he became the ancestor of Kamehameha the Great.

THE TRIPLE MARRIAGE OF LAA-MAI-KAHIKI.

CHARACTERS.

MULIELEALII, chief of western Oahu.

KUMUHONUA,
OLOPANA, and } sons of Mulielealii.
MOIKEHA,

LAA-MAI-KAHIKI, adopted son of Moikeha.

LUUKIA, wife of Olopana.

LAAMAOMAO, god of the winds.

MOOKINI, a high-priest.

KAMAHUALELE, an astrologer and poet.

PUNA, the principal chief of Kauai.

HOOIPO, daughter of Puna.

KILA, son of Moikeha and Hooipo.

HOAKANUI,
WAOLENA, } the three brides of Laa.
MANO,

AHUKINI-A-LAA,
KUKONA-A-LAA, and } the three children of Laa.
LAULI-A-LAA,

THE TRIPLE MARRIAGE OF LAA-MAI-KAHIKI.

THE LEGENDS OF MOIKEHA AND THE ARGONAUTS OF THE
ELEVENTH AND TWELFTH CENTURIES.

I.

TRADITION abounds in bold outlines, here and there interspersed with curious details, of the many prominent expeditions to the Hawaiian Islands, from the beginning of the eleventh to the latter part of the twelfth centuries, of adventurous Tahitian, Samoan and Georgian chiefs. Learning of the existence and approximate location of the group, and perhaps guided to an extent by intervening islands and atolls that have since disappeared, they came with large fleets of barges and double canoes, bearing their families and attendants, their priests, astrologers and musicians, and by degrees possessed themselves or their immediate descendants with the fairest portions of the little archipelago. For a century or more bitter feuds and frequent wars followed ; but in the end the invaders and the invaded, both of the same Polynesian race, became assimilated through concession, intermarriage and fundamental identity of religious cult, and thenceforth in a united and homogeneous stream flowed down the years. The genealogies of the prominent chiefs and priests were alone preserved ; and while, in after-generations, some of them traced their lines of rank to the native stock of Nanaula, and others to the chiefs of the second migratory influx from the south, the ruling families of the entire group had become so united in blood by intermarriage that it was difficult to find a chief of distinction who could not trace his lineage back to both.

But during the migratory period referred to, especially marked by the coming of Nanamaoa, Pili, Paao and the Oahu and Maui Paumakuas, the Hawaiian group was not the only scene of foreign adventure among the central islands of the Pacific. The native chiefs of Hawaii, whose ancestors had reached the group more than five hundred years before, were quite as adventurous and skilled in navigation as their southern invaders ; and thus while the latter, continually augmented in numbers by fresh arrivals, were steadily possessing themselves of the lands and governing forces of the Hawaiian Islands, a few resolute chiefs of the old line, either in a spirit of retaliation or because the way had been pointed out, boldly spread their sails for the abandoned homes of their aggressors, and by conquest or other means acquired lands and influence in the distant islands of the south.

The *mooolelo* about to be related embraces the romantic story of one of these expeditions of native Hawaiian chiefs to the southern islands, and presents an interesting picture of the manners, customs and aspirations of the mid-Pacific Argonauts of that period.

Somewhere about the year A.D. 1040 Maweke, a native chief of the line of Nanaula—the first of the family that is brought prominently to view in the chronology of the second influx—was the *alii-nui*, or nominal sovereign, of the island of Oahu. He had three sons—Mulielealii, Keaunui and Kalehenui. On the death of Maweke, the eldest son, Mulielealii, acceded to the title of *alii-nui*, occupying the western side of the island. Kalehenui was given possessions at Koolau, and Keaunui was established in the district of Ewa. The latter became the ancestor of a line of powerful chiefs in that district, and is credited with having cut or opened the navigable channel near the Puuloa salt-works, by which the estuary now known as Pearl River, not far from Honolulu, was rendered accessible to navigation. No further reference need here be made to this branch of the family beyond the remark that Keaunui became the father of Lakona, and also of Nuakea, the wife of Keoloewa, King of Molokai, and of the prophet Moi, who fell with Kaupeepee in defence of the fortress of Haupu, as related in the legend of "*Hina, the Helen of Hawaii.*"

Mulielealii had three sons—Kumuhonua, Olopana and Moikeha—and one daughter, named Hainakolo. As the eldest son and successor of his father, Kumuhonua in time acceded to the patrimonial estates and titles ; but the younger brothers, not content, as they grew to manhood, with the small allotments which must necessarily have been accorded them, concluded to seek for ampler and more inviting possessions elsewhere.

The Pali, near Honolulu.

The Paumakua family occupied a large part of the eastern side of the island, and, although they were of the stock of the second influx, their relations with the native chiefs and people seem to have been peaceful and satisfactory. Paumakua, who first appeared in native annals two generations before the time of Olopana and his brothers, either as an immigrant from one of the southern islands or the son or grandson of a chief of recent arrival, was one of the most restless and dashing of the prominent leaders of that period. The legends of the time glow with stories of his marvellous exploits and adventures in foreign lands, and the friendly feeling entertained for his immediate successors was doubtless due in a great measure to the respect established for them through his rank and prowess.

It is claimed by tradition that Paumakua visited all the foreign lands then known to the Hawaiians, and brought back with him many things that were strange. From one of his voyages he returned with two white priests, Keakea and Maliu, from whom several ecclesiastical families subsequently claimed descent and authority. At another time he brought back Malela, a noted prophet and sorcerer, and three other persons of a strange race, one of whom was a woman. Tradition somewhat minutely describes them as "foreigners of large stature, bright, staring, roguish eyes, and reddish faces."

As the voyages of this adventurous chief were sometimes of many months' duration, and he is said to have prosecuted his researches in almost every direction, it is not impossible that the foreigners with "roguish eyes and reddish faces" were aborigines of North America. But, leaving this to conjecture, tradition permits no doubt that Paumakua was a skilful and fearless explorer, and through his enterprise acquired renown for himself and respect for his descendants, one of whom is about to be presented to the reader.

As already stated, the younger sons of Mulielealii, Olopana and Moikeha, not content with their prospects in Oahu, resolved to seek fame and fortune elsewhere. Both were unmarried, but, through some circumstance or for some purpose not mentioned by tradition, Moikeha had adopted a young son of Ahukai, the great-grandson and successor of Paumakua. The name of the boy was Laa, or Laa-mai-kahiki, to which it was subsequently extended. The child-chief could not have been without political prospects, for he is referred to in the chants as "Chief of Kapaahu and Lord of Nualaka." Although the custom was common then, as now, among Hawaiians of every rank and condition, of exchanging and adopting children, the adoption of so promising a scion of the Paumakua line by a grandson of Maweke must have been the result of some extraordinary compact, all reference to which has disappeared from tradition.

Taking leave of their relatives on Oahu, Olopana and Moikeha, with a considerable number of attendants, embarked for the island of Hawaii, and established themselves at once in the beautiful valley of Waipio, in the district of Hamakua. What chief, if any, they found in possession there is not stated; but it was not long before the valley was ruled by Olopana, with Moikeha as his principal captain and adviser. The young chief Laa accompanied his foster-father to Waipio, and there Moikeha began to instruct him in the manly accomplishments for which in after-years he became distinguished.

To strengthen his rule and protect himself against the encroachments of neighboring chiefs, Olopana married Luukia, granddaughter of Hikapaloa, chief of Kohala, and a descendant of the ancient line of Nanaula, to which Olopana himself belonged by lineage still more direct. He urged his brother to follow his example and connect himself by marriage with some one of the ruling families of Hamakua. Such an alliance could have been readily made by Moikeha, for his strain was undoubted, and in manly beauty and courtly graces he had scarcely a peer in all the group ; but he declared that he had a wife in his spear and an heir in Laa, and would not create a jealousy in the family by adding to either.

But the brothers did not remain long in Waipio. A terrible hurricane, followed by storms and floods, completely devastated the valley, compelling the inhabitants to abandon their homes and seek refuge elsewhere. Moikeha had never been satisfied with Waipio, and in the midst of the ruin around them found little difficulty in persuading his brother to make a bold push for the misty and far-off land of Kahiki. Preparations for the journey were immediately made, and in five large double canoes the brothers, with Laa and a considerable body of attendants, set sail for the islands of the south. They knew the general direction, and the sun and stars guided them in their course.

A prosperous wind wafted them to the Society group, and they finally landed on the island of Raiatea, and forcibly took, or in some other manner secured, possession of the district of Moaula. Olopana was accepted as sovereign of the district, and soon became a ruler of opulence and distinction. Moikeha, still his chief adviser, built a sumptuous residence and *heiau* for himself, called *Lanikeha*, or " the heavenly resting-place," and became noted for his hospitality.

For some time—perhaps for four or five years—the brothers dwelt together in harmony, and then misunderstanding and trouble came between them—it need scarcely be said, through a woman—which drove Moikeha again to the sea and separated them for ever. A meddlesome native chief named Mua, who was jealous of the popularity of Moikeha and desirous of supplanting him in the favor of Olopana, called the attention of Luukia on several occasions to Moikeha's affluent style of living, and intimated that his purpose was to thereby secure the friendship of influential chiefs, and in the end wrest the sovereignty of the district from his brother. Alarmed at last, she bore the tale to her husband, and at length succeeded in arousing his suspicions. A coldness toward Moikeha very naturally followed. Olopana could not help but note his brother's increasing popularity, and one day took occasion to rebuke him for his extravagance and love of display, suggesting, at the same time, that a more modest style of living would comport better with his position. Moikeha, who had never harbored a thought that was not loyal to his brother, was profoundly grieved at these words of suspicion, and resolved to leave Raiatea at once and return to the Hawaiian Islands. Feeling that he had gone too far in thus indirectly accusing his brother of meditated treachery, Olopana endeavored to persuade him to remain ; but Moikeha's resolution could not be shaken, and he set about preparing at once for his return to the Hawaiian group.

The number of canoes manned and provisioned for the voyage is not stated ; but tradition avers that the fleet was equipped under the superintendence of Moikeha's famous prophet and astrologer, Kamahualele ; and, with the priest Mookini, Laamaomao, the director of the winds, and a large party of chiefs and retainers, the expedition set sail for Hawaii, the young chief Laa being left behind with Olopana.

It was one of the most imposing fleets that had ever sailed out of the harbor of Opoa. The large double canoe bearing Moikeha and his priests, gods, astrologer, principal navigator, wind director and personal attendants, was the same in which he had sailed for Kahiki. The *kaulua* was nearly a hundred feet in length, and afforded ample accommodations for the forty or more persons assigned to it. It was painted red, and at the masthead floated the pennon of a Polynesian *alii*.

Moikeha embarked with a number of distinguished companions, but the most noted was Laamaomao—a name signifying, perhaps, the sacred bluish green or wind clouds. He was the director of the winds, which were stored in his *ipu*, or calabash, and went forth at his bidding. He bore a close resemblance to the Æolus of the Greeks. After accompanying Moikeha to the Hawaiian Islands he took up his abode near a place called Hale-a-Lono, a well-known eminence of Kaluakoi, on the island of Molokai, and was subsequently deified and worshipped as an *aumakua*, or god of the winds.

With musicians and drummers to enliven the spirits of the voyagers, and favoring winds from the *ipu* of Laamaomao, the journey seems to have been prosperous, and no incident of note occurred until the island of Hawaii was sighted. As the green hills of Kau came to view songs and shouts of joy went up from the canoes. A voyage of over twenty-five hundred miles in open boats had tested the patience of the party, and land at last was a joyous sight to them all. Many leaped into the water and swam beside the canoes. Mookini, the high-priest, burned incense before the gods, at the same time addressing them a prayer of thanksgiving, and Kamahualele, the astrologer and poet, recited an inspiring chant in further celebration of the occasion. The chant has been preserved by tradition.

Some of the early poetic accounts of the first appearance of the islands of Hawaii above the surface of the ocean mention Hawaii, the largest of the group, as suddenly rising from the great deep and becoming a part of a row or cluster of islands "stretching to the farthest ends of Kahiki," from which it is conjectured that, centuries back in the past, islands now no longer existing marked the way at intervals between the Society and Hawaiian groups. The other islands of the Hawaiian cluster are referred to as natural births, their parents being demi-gods or distinguished chiefs. Thus, in the language of an old chant :

> " Rising up is Hawaii-nui-akea !
> Rising up out of the night (*Po*) !
> Appeared has the island, the land,
> The string of islands of Nuuamea,
> The cluster of islands stretching to the farthest ends of Kahiki.
> To Kuluwaiea of Haumea, the husband,
> To Hina-nui-a-lana, the wife,
> Was born Molokai, a god, a priest,
> The first morning light from Nuuamea.
> Up stands Akuhinialaa,
> The chief from the foreign land ;
> From the gills of the fish
> From the overwhelming billows of Halehale-kalani,
> Born is Oahu, the *wohi*,
> The *wohi* of Akuhinialaa,
> And of Laamealaakona the wife."

Kamahualele began by repeating an ancient story of the origin of the several islands of the group, and concluded his chant with these hopeful words :

> " O Haumea Manukahikele,
> O Moikeha, the chief who is to reside,
> My chief will reside on Hawaii—a !
> Life, life, O buoyant life !
> Live shall the chief and priest,
> Live shall the seer and the slave,
> Dwell on Hawaii and be at rest,
> And attain old age on Kauai.
> O Kauai is the island—a !
> O Moikeha is the chief !"

Thus sang the poet, with his face toward the verdant slopes of Kau, while the canoes of the fleet gathered around him, that all might hear the words of one who read the fate of mortals in the stars.

II.

The prediction of Kamahualele, inspired by a sudden view of the coast of Hawaii, was verified. A landing was made in the district of Kau, the most southerly point of the island. There securing supplies of provisions and water, the next landing was effected at Cape Kumukahi, in the district of Puna ; but a recent eruption from the crater of Kilauea, or a subterranean channel connected with it, had devastated a wide strip of country near the coast, and after a brief stay sail was made for Kohala. Landing in that district, Moikeha and his party were well received by Kaniuhi, the *alii-nui* and grandson of Pili, and permission to offer sacrifices in behalf of the expedition in the great *heiau* of Mookini was accorded the high-priest of Moikeha, whose name, by singular coincidence, was identical with that of the temple, erected by the high-priest Paao more than two generations before.

Leaving Kohala, Moikeha next touched at Hanuaula, on the island of Maui ; but, without stopping to exchange courtesies with Haho, the noted *moi* of that division of the island, he sailed immediately for Oahu. His purpose was to visit his royal father, Mulielealii, whose residence was at Ewa ; but his priest and seer so strongly protested against the visit, declaring it to be contrary to the will of the gods, that he directed his course around the northern side of the island, touching at Makapuu and Makaaoa, and then sailing directly for the island of Kauai.

On the evening of the second day after leaving Oahu, Moikeha anchored his canoes in a roadstead not far from Kapaa, Kauai, where Puna, the governing *alii* of the island, held his court, surrounded by the chiefs of his family and a large number of retainers. Puna was one of the most popular rulers in the group, and, strict as he may have been in the exercise of his prerogatives, was always merciful in dealing with offences thoughtlessly or ignorantly committed. He would pardon the humble laborer who might inadvertently cross his shadow or violate a *tabu*, but never the chief who deliberately trespassed upon his privileges or withheld a courtesy due to his rank. His disposition was naturally warlike, but as the condition of the island was peaceful, and military force was seldom required except in repelling occasional plundering raids from the other islands, he kept alive the martial spirit of his chiefs and subjects by frequent sham fights, marine drills, and the encouragement of athletic games and friendly contests at arms, in which he himself sometimes took part. Feasting and dancing usually followed these

warlike pastimes, and the result was that the court of Puna became somewhat noted for the chivalry of its chiefs and the
splendor of its entertainments.

Puna had but one child, a daughter named Hooipo. Tradition describes her as having been, like the most of royal daughters painted by the poets, a very comely maiden. She was therefore the pride and glory of the court, and as she grew to a marriageable age her favor was sought by a number of aspiring chiefs
whose rank entitled them to consideration ; but, flattered by the
contest for her smiles, and naturally vain of a face which the un-
ruffled waters told her was attractive, she evinced no haste in
making choice of a husband.

This tardiness or indecision was but very gently rebuked by
Puna. Although one tradition gives him two daughters, Hooipo
was doubtless his only child, and he was therefore indisposed to
hasten an event which would probably lead to their separation.
But, as time passed, the suitors of the young chiefess became so
persistent, and the rivalry for her assumed so bitter and warlike
an aspect, that Puna deemed it prudent for her to restore harmony among the rivals by making a choice at once. But for no
one of them did she seem to entertain a decided preference, and
therefore suggested that, since a choice must be made, she was
willing to leave it to the arbitrament of such manly contest between the rivals as might comport with their dignity and the
character of the prize at stake. Puna eagerly accepted the suggestion, as it opened the way to a selection without incurring the
enmity of all but the one chosen.

But what should be the nature of the contest ? Each of the
rival chiefs was probably noted for his skill in some especial accomplishment, and the difficulty was in naming a trial that would
seem to be just to all. Unable to decide the matter himself,
Puna appealed to the high-priest, and the next day announced
that his *palaoa*—a talisman consisting of a whale's tooth, carved
and sanctified—would be sent by a trusty messenger to the little
island of Kaula ; that four days thereafter the rival chiefs should,
each in his own canoe, start at the same time and place from
Kauai, and the one who returned with the *palaoa*, which the messenger would be instructed to give to the first of the contesting
chiefs to land and claim it on the rocks of Kaula, should be the
husband of Hooipo, and the others must remain his friends.

The size of the canoes was left to the discretion of the several contestants, but as no more than four assistants would be allowed to each, very large canoes, of course, would not be used. Any means of speed might be employed, including oars, paddles and sails.

The contest was admitted to be as fair as any that could be devised, and the rival chiefs declared themselves satisfied with it, and began to prepare for the race by securing suitable canoes and skilful and stalwart assistants. It promised to be an exciting contest, and the whole of Kapaa was on tiptoe to witness the start.

After a few days of preparation the messenger of Puna was despatched with the *palaoa* to Kaula, with instructions to place it in the hands of the first of the contesting chiefs to claim it on that island. The messenger had been gone two days, and had probably reached his destination, as the distance to be travelled was but little more than a hundred miles, and the rival chiefs had everything in readiness to bend their sails for Kaula, when Moikeha, as already stated, anchored his fleet in the evening off Kapaa.

Early next morning, with his double canoe flying the standard of his rank and otherwise becomingly dressed, Moikeha went ashore, where he was cordially received by the chiefs of the district, and in due time escorted to the sovereign mansion and presented to Puna. Without referring to his family connections, he simply announced that he was a chief from the distant land of Kahiki, and was traveling through the Hawaiian group on a tour of observation and pleasure. He wore a *maro* fringed with shells, a *kihei* or mantle of finely-woven and decorated cloth, and on his head a *lei-alii* of brilliant feathers, while from his neck was suspended by a cord of plaited hair a curious ornament of mother-of-pearl set in ivory. He was a handsome representative of savage manhood, and his bearing was dignified, correct and courtly.

During his audience with Puna, Moikeha met Hooipo—most likely by accident, but he was so charmed by her bright eyes that he did not leave the mansion until he found occasion to exchange a few pleasant words with her. They seemed to be mutually pleased with each other, and Moikeha accepted the invitation of the chief to consider himself his guest until the next day, at the same time allowing him to send fresh provisions to his people, whose canoes had been drawn up on the beach.

A brilliant entertainment of feasting, music and dancing in honor of the distinguished stranger followed in the evening, during which Moikeha was favored with the companionship of Hooipo, and learned of the contest about to take place between the rival chiefs of Kauai to determine to whom she should be given in marriage.

Hilarity and feasting were the order of the next day and evening, for on the morning following the contesting chiefs were to start for Kaula under the eye of Puna. Their well-equipped canoes were on the beach, and their crews, drilled to work sail and oar together, were in readiness.

Morning came, and with it a large concourse of people to witness the departure of the chiefs. The canoes and their attending crews were examined, and many wagers laid on the result of the race. Finally the contesting chiefs made their appearance, followed shortly after by Puna and the most of his household, including Hooipo, who was conveyed to the beach in a *manele* borne on the shoulders of four stout attendants. She was attired in an embroidered *pau*—a short skirt of five thicknesses of thin *kapa* cloth reaching to the knees—and a cape or short mantle trimmed with feathers. Her hair was braided in a single strand at the back ; her head and neck were adorned with *leis* of flowers and feathers, and her limbs were ornamented with circlets of shells and tinted seeds.

Everything being in readiness, the contending chiefs, eight in number, appeared before the *alii-nui*, and, bowing low, proceeded in turn to recite their *kuauhaus*, or genealogies, as they had been called upon to do, to show in a formal manner that all their strains were noble. As each concluded he again bowed, giving Hooipo a smile and look of confidence, and stepped back to await the signal of departure.

The last of them had given his pedigree, the terms of the contest had again been announced in form by a herald, and Puna was about to order the simultaneous launching of the canoes, when Moikeha, whose presence had not before been observed by the chiefs, suddenly presented himself before the *alii-nui*, and, bowing first to him and then courteously to the chiefs, said :

"Great chief, as this trial seems to be free to all of noble blood, I accept the terms, and ask permission to present myself as a contestant for the prize."

The chiefs exchanged glances of surprise, and a pleased expression lighted up the face of Hooipo, who until that moment had manifested but little interest in what was transpiring around her.

Puna hesitated a moment, and then graciously replied :

"Noble stranger, if your rank is level with the conditions, and the chiefs now ready for departure urge no objection, my consent will not be withheld."

A hurried consultation among the chiefs showed that some of them objected ; but as the stranger, with no knowledge of the coast and apparently no canoe or crew in readiness, did not seem to be a competitor to be feared, it was finally agreed that, should he be able to establish his rank, which a few of them doubted, he might be admitted to the contest.

This resolution having been communicated, Moikeha gracefully bowed his thanks, and then began to recite his genealogy. Curious to learn the strain of the courtly stranger, the chiefs pressed around him, eagerly listening to every word. He began with Wakea, away back in the past, when his ancestors were residents of other lands referred to in Hawaiian story. Giving the record of thirteen generations, he brought the connection down to Nanamaoa, the pioneer of the first migratory influx to the Hawaiian group seven hundred years before. Thence, generation by generation, naming father, mother and heir, he traced down a line of sixteen successors to Maweke. Pausing a moment, while a look of surprise and wonder was exchanged by the listening chiefs, Moikeha continued :

"Maweke the husband,
"Naiolaukea the wife ;
"Mulielealii the husband,
"Wehelani the wife ;
"Moikeha the husband,
"Hooipo the wife."

Applause followed this announcement by the stranger that he was the son of Mulielealii, the *alii-nui* of Oahu, and the jesting and good-natured manner in which he concluded the *kuauhau* by predicting his success in the coming contest, and marriage with Hooipo, made him no enemies among the competing chiefs. Hooipo was now sure that she could make a choice without the trouble and excitement of a race to Kaula ; but the canoes were ready, and all she could do was to hope and pray that Moikeha would bring back the *palaoa*.

But what were Moikeha's preparations for the race ? When asked by Puna, he pointed to a small canoe with an outrigger drawn up on the beach, and a single long-haired man of strange aspect standing motionless beside it with a paddle in his hand. Puna shook his head doubtingly, and Hooipo looked disappointed. Others who noted the stranger's slim preparations for the race imagined that he was treating the contest as a jest ; but he announced himself in readiness, and the signal for departure was given.

The chiefs sprang toward the beach, and in a few minutes had launched their canoes and passed through the heavy surf, when with strong and steady pulling the race began in earnest for the open sea. Moikeha alone seemed to be in no haste. He took formal leave of Puna, and, noting Hooipo's look of impatience, smilingly said to her as he turned toward the beach : " I will bring back the *palaoa !* " The assurance contented her. The other canoes were beyond the surf, but she believed him and was happy.

Satisfying himself that the sail was ready for use and everything required for the voyage aboard, Moikeha and his assistant shoved their canoe into the water, and with a few vigorous strokes of their paddles dashed through the surf. The passage was so adroitly made as to attract the attention of the many who witnessed it from the shore. For a few minutes the canoe remained almost motionless, except as it was tossed from wave to wave. Then the sail was spread. This movement was unaccountable to those on shore, for the little wind stirring was directly from the west, to which point the canoe was bearing for an offing to round the southern capes of the island. But if the witnesses were surprised at the spreading of a sail under such circumstances, they were little less than astounded when they saw the sail fill with wind and the canoe suddenly speed out to sea as if driven by a hurricane.

Moikeha's long-haired companion was Laamaomao, god of the winds, who had accompanied him from Raiatea. Behind the

sail sat the friendly deity, from whose exhaustless *ipu* of imprisoned winds a gale was sent forth which carried the canoe to
Kaula before daylight the next morning. Effecting a landing
soon after sunrise, Puna's messenger was found, and at once delivered to Moikeha the *palaoa*, which he had been instructed to
surrender to the chief first demanding it. Content in the possession of the talisman, Moikeha and his companion remained on
the island for refreshment until past midday, and then started on
their return to Kauai, favored by the same winds that had borne
them to Kaula, but proceeding with less haste. Toward night
the eight other chiefs landed within a few hours of each other,
and great was their astonishment on learning that the *palaoa*
had been delivered to a chief claiming it early that morning.

" He must have had wings," said one of them.

"He was surely helped by the gods," suggested another, who
had been the first to land after Moikeha. "But for that the
palaoa would have been mine, as you all know. But who can
struggle with the gods ? Let us not incur their anger by complaint."

As it was easy for the others to reconcile themselves to Moikeha's success, good-humor was soon restored, and the next
morning, in company with the messenger, they all re-embarked
for Kauai. On the evening of the same day Moikeha landed at
Kapaa, and hastened to place in the hands of Puna the talisman
which made him the husband of Hooipo. Now assured of the
rank of the victor, Puna was gratified at his success, and Hooipo
made no disguise of her joy. Tradition says she fell in love
with the handsome stranger on first beholding him ; but be that
as it may, when he returned from Kaula with the *palaoa* she was
frank enough to confess that his success had made her happy.

In the course of a few days all of the defeated chiefs returned
to Kapaa, and Moikeha invited them to a feast, over which they
forgot their rivalry and renewed the pledges of friendship embraced in the terms and made a condition of the contest. They
sought by many ingenious ways to draw from Moikeha the secret of his success ; but he failed to enlighten them, and they
were compelled to content themselves with the belief that he had
been assisted by some supernatural power, possibly by *Apukohai*,
the great fish-god of Kauai, who sometimes seized canoes and
bore them onward with almost incredible velocity.

In due time Hooipo became the wife of Moikeha, who, on the death of Puna, succeeded him as the *alii-nui* of Kauai, where he remained to the end of his life. He was blessed with a number of sons, through one of whom, it may be mentioned, the sovereignty of the island was continued in the family after Moikeha was laid under the black *kapa*.

III.

Tradition next refers to Moikeha about twenty-five years after his marriage with Hooipo. The death of Puna had left him the sovereignty of Kauai, and his principal residence was at Waialua. He had seven sons, and his court, like that of his predecessor, was noted for the distinguished chiefs, priests, prophets and poets connected with it.

As the life of Moikeha was drawing to a close a strong desire possessed him to see once more his foster-son Laa, whom, on his departure from Raiatea, he had left with his brother Olopana, whose presumptive heir and successor the young chief had become. In preparation for a journey thither he ordered a number of large double canoes to be repaired and put in order for the open sea, and had some time before despatched a large party of hunters to the cliffs along the coast for the feathers of the *mamo*, from which to fabricate a royal mantle for the ward of his youth.

As but a single small yellow feather of the kind used in a royal mantle is found under each wing of the *mamo*, the task of securing the many thousands required was by no means a brief or easy service ; but in time the feathers were gathered and the cloak was completed. As the choicest feathers alone were used, the garment was one of the most brilliant and elaborate ever made on Kauai, and represented the labor of a hundred persons for a year.

But when everything was in readiness for his departure for the south, Moikeha concluded that he was too old and feeble to undertake the voyage. In this conclusion he was sustained by the auguries of the prophets and the persuasion of his sons.

His third son was Kila. He was distinguished for his capacity and courage, and especially for his skill as a navigator, and it was finally decided that he should make the journey to Raiatea as the messenger of Moikeha, and invite Laa to revisit the Hawaiian group, assuring him of the feeble health of his foster-father and of his anxiety to embrace him before death separated them for ever.

Kila was delighted with the mission. For several years intercourse between the Hawaiian and southern groups had been almost completely suspended, but from boyhood his dreams had been of visits to the far-off and misty shores of Kahiki, of which he had heard Moikeha speak ; and now that an opportunity was presented for gratifying his appetite for adventure in unknown seas, his joy was boundless, and so vigorously did he push the work of preparation that in a few days the canoes were equipped and provisioned for the voyage. The provisions consisted, in long voyages of that period, of dried fish, dried bananas and plantains, cocoanuts, yams and potatoes, with *poi* and *paiai*, fresh fruits and cooked fowls and pigs, for early consumption. Large calabashes of fresh water were also provided, but frequent baths largely diminished the craving for that necessity.

Sacrifices were offered, the auguries were pronounced favorable, and the fleet of double canoes set sail for the south. Kila was accompanied by three of his brothers, and, more important still, by the venerable Kamahualele, the friend and astrologer of Moikeha, who had borne him company from Raiatea more than a quarter of a century before, and chanted his inspired visions of the future off the coast of Kau. He went as Kila's chief navigator and especial counsellor.

The fleet passed through the group and took its final departure from the most southern point of the island of Hawaii. Wind and weather were both favorable, and without a mishap of consequence the expedition arrived in due time at Raiatea, first touching for guidance at some of the other islands of the southern group.

Kila landed at Opoa through the sacred entrance of Avamoa. His flag and state were recognized by Olopana, who was still living, and the sons of Moikeha and their personal attendants were ceremoniously conducted to the royal mansion, where Kila made known the purpose of his visit. Olopana was greatly interested in the story of Moikeha's successful establishment on

Kauai, but refrained from referring to the circumstances which led to their separation many years before. He was also informed of the death of his father, Mulielealii, and the succession of his brother Kumuhonua to the rank and authority of *alii-nui* of Oahu.

With the affectionate greetings of Moikeha, Kila presented to Laa the brilliant *mamo*, or royal mantle, of which he was made the bearer, and expressed the hope that he would comfort the few remaining days of his foster-father by returning with him on a visit to Kauai. Olopana strongly objected to the proposed journey, urging his advanced years and the probability of his early death ; but when assured by Laa of his speedy return he reluctantly consented, and after a round of hospitable feasts and entertainments, in his own double canoes, and attended by his priest, astrologer, master of ceremonies, musicians, and a number of knightly and noble friends, Laa accompanied Kila and his party back to Hawaii.

The voyage was made in good time, and as the combined fleet, with canoes of royal yellow and pennons flying, coursed through the group to Kauai, stopping at several points to exchange courtesies with the ruling chiefs, it attracted unusual attention ; and when Laa landed at Waialua, on the island of Oahu, to greet his relatives, and the people learned that the son of Ahukai had returned from the distant land of Kahiki rich in honors and possessions, they strewed his path with flowers and welcomed him as if he were a god.

Proceeding to Kauai, after a brief stay at Waialua, Laa was affectionately received by Moikeha, his foster-father, who had left him a child in Kahiki, and for a month or more the Kauaian court blazed nightly with feasts and festivals given in his honor.

Returning to Oahu, Laa took up his residence for a time at Kualoa. A large mansion was constructed for him, with ample accommodations for his friends and retainers, and the chiefs of the island esteemed it an honor to share his friendship and accept his hospitality.

There was no jealousy of Laa, for it was known that he would soon return to Raiatea, there to permanently remain as the heir and successor of Olopana. In his veins ran the noblest blood of Oahu. He was the son of the great-grandson of the great Paumakua in direct and unchallenged descent, and the adopted heir of the grandson of Maweke, the proud descendant of the Nanaula dynasty of kings.

It was not deemed well that the line of Paumakua, through so distinguished a representative as Laa, should be perpetuated solely on a foreign soil. From a suggestion the matter came to be seriously discussed by the leading chiefs, and finally Laa was approached on the subject. Being a young man, the patriotic proposal of the chiefs very naturally accorded with his tastes, and, without great persuasion, he expressed a willingness to comply with what seemed to be a general request.

But the approval of Laa did not quite settle the delicate question, as the chiefs at once observed on casting around for a suitable wife for so desirable a husband. The most of them had daughters or sisters of eligible rank and age. But which one of them should they select? Whose family should be so honored? They were willing to leave the choice to Laa, but, sagaciously anticipating the result, he declined to make the selection.

As usual in momentous cases of doubt, the high-priest was consulted, and the matter was settled in a manner quite satisfactory to Laa. It was agreed that he should marry three wives, all on the same day, and the maidens selected were Hoakanui, daughter of Lonokaehu, of Kualoa; Waolena, daughter of a chief of Kaalaea; and Mano, daughter of a chief of Kaneohe. All were noted for their beauty and distinguished blood.

The three brides were brought to the mansion of Laa, at Kualoa, on the day fixed for the triple marriage, and the event was celebrated with splendor and enthusiasm. The *hoao*, or marriage agreement, was made public by a herald, as was then the custom among the nobility; the brides, attired becomingly and decked with garlands, were delivered in form to the bridegroom, and in the evening a feast was served on the grounds to more than a thousand guests, with *hula, mele,* and other festive accompaniments, including *mele-inoas,* or songs of personal application to the new wives and their husband.

This triple marriage is one of the most thoroughly-established incidents of remote Hawaiian tradition. After his marriage Laa remained a year at Kualoa, and then began to prepare for his return to Raiatea. He looked forward to his departure with mingled feelings of regret and satisfaction, for his brief married life had been singularly as well as most bountifully blessed. On

the same day he had been presented with a son by each of his
three wives, and an ancient chant thus refers to the event:

> " O Ahukai, O Laa-a, O Laa,
> O Laa from Kahiki, the chief;
> O Ahukini-a-Laa,
> O Kukona-a-Laa,
> O Lauli-a-Laa, the father
> The triple canoe of Laa-mai-kahiki,
> The sacred first-born children of Laa,
> Who were born on the same one day."

Moikeha died soon after, and Laa bade farewell to the Hawaiian Islands and returned to Raiatea just in time to receive
the dying blessing of Olopana. As he had promised, he left his
three wives and their sons in Oahu, where they were well cared
for. The names of the children, as mentioned in the chant quot-
ed, were Ahukini-a-Laa, Kukona-a-Laa, and Lauli-a-Laa, from
whom it was in after-generations the pride and glory of the governing families of Oahu and Kauai to trace their lineage. From
Ahukini-a-Laa Queen Kapiolani, wife of Kalakaua, the present
sovereign of the islands, is recorded in descent through a line of
Kauaian chiefs and kings.

Kila, after his return from Raiatea, established himself in the
valley of Waipio, on the island of Hawaii, and became prosperous in the possessions abandoned by his uncle Olopana a generation before. He was the ancestor of several prominent Hawaiian families, who traced their descent to him as late as during
the reign of Kamehameha I.

With the return of Laa to Raiatea all communication between
the Hawaiian and southern groups seems to have abruptly terminated, and for a period of about six hundred years, or until
the arrival of Captain Cook in 1778, the Hawaiians learned nothing of the great world beyond their little archipelago, and knew
that lands existed elsewhere only through the mysterious *mooolelos* of their priests, and a folk-lore consisting of broken chains of
fables and tales of the past in which the supernatural had finally
become the dominant feature.

THE APOTHEOSIS OF PELE.

CHARACTERS.

PELE, goddess of the volcanoes.

MOHO,
KAMAKAUA and } brothers of Pele.
KANEHEKILI,

KALANA, a chief from the southern islands.

KAMAUNUI, wife of Kalana.

HINA, daughter of Kalana and Kamaunui.

OLOPANA, chief of Oahu and husband of Hina.

KAHIKIULA, brother of Olopana.

KAMAPUAA, the monster son of Hina.

THE APOTHEOSIS OF PELE.

THE ADVENTURES OF THE GODDESS WITH KAMAPUAA.

I.

IN the pantheon of ancient Hawaiian worship—or, rather, of the worship of the group from the twelfth century to the nineteenth—the deity most feared and respected, especially on the island of Hawaii, was the goddess Pele. She was the queen of fire and goddess of volcanoes, and her favorite residence was the vast and ever-seething crater of Kilauea, beneath whose molten flood, in halls of burning adamant and grottoes of fire, she consumed the offerings of her worshippers and devised destruction to those who long neglected her or failed to respect her prerogatives.

Her assistants and companions, as related by tradition, were her five brothers and eight sisters, all of them clothed with especial functions, and all but little less merciless and exacting than Pele herself. The first in authority under Pele was *Moho*, king of steam. The others were charged, respectively, with the duties of creating explosions, thunders and rains of fire, moving and keeping the clouds in place, breaking canoes, fighting with spears of flame, hurling red-hot masses of lava, and doing whatever else the goddess commanded.

As the family claimed tribute of the entire island of Hawaii, to receive it they frequently visited the active and extinct craters of other districts, and earthquakes heralded their departure from Kilauea. The temples of Pele were numerous, particularly in the neighborhood of old lava-flows, and their priests were always well sustained. The crater of Kilauea was especially sacred to the goddess, and the earth around it could not be safely disturbed. An offering was first made of a part of everything eaten there, and fruits, pigs, fowls, fish, and sometimes human beings, were thrown into the crater to appease the wrath of the goddess and avert a threatened overflow.

The Pele family was neither connected with, nor controlled

by, the supreme gods of Hawaiian worship, nor was it a part either of the ancient or later theocracy of the group, as brought down by the priesthood of *Hika-paloa*, the godhead and trinity of original creation. It was an indigenous and independent development of the twelfth century, until which period the family was unknown on Hawaii; and the strong hold it secured and for centuries maintained in the native heart was due partly to a popular faith in, and worship of, the spirits of departed chiefs and ancestors, and partly to the continued and ever-visible evidences of the power and malignity of the volcanic deities. And so, indeed, was it with the many other deities of Hawaiian adoration. While *Kane* was deemed the creator and undoubted superior of them all, they were seldom restrained in the exercise of their several functions, and individual appeals to them through their priests were necessary to secure their favor or placate their wrath.

With this brief reference to the worship and attributes of the terrible goddess and her family, the story of their mortal lives will now be told, and a plain relation given of the strange events which led to their apotheosis. Every tradition refers to them as deities at the time of their arrival at Hawaii and occupation of Kilauea, and all abound in marvellous tales of their exploits, the most wonderful being connected with the Oahuan warrior Kamapuaa, one of the lovers of Pele, who was transformed by the bards into a supernatural monster—a being half-man and half-hog—with powers almost equal to those of Pele herself. A careful analysis, however, of the various *mooolelos* of Pele and her family renders it plain that they came to the group as simple human beings, and as human beings lived and died, as did also Kamapuaa, and that superstition subsequently elevated their mortal deeds to the realms of supernatural achievement.

The Pele family came to Hawaii during the reign of Kamiole, the usurper, from one of the southern islands—probably Samoa—in about the year A.D. 1175. It was of chiefly blood, and also of priestly lineage, and, to escape the penalties of defeat, had, at the close of a long and disastrous war, fled northward and found a home on Hawaii. The head of the family had fallen in battle, and Moho, the eldest of the sons, assumed the direction of what remained of the once powerful household.

The fugitives first landed at Honuapo, in the district of Kau,

Type of Scenery—on the Island of Kauai.

but, finding no lands there available, coasted along to the southern shores of Puna, and finally located in the valleys back of Keauhou, among the foothills of Mauna Loa, including the crater of Kilauea. A few miles to the westward an overflow had reached the sea the year before, and as the volcano was still active, and earthquakes were of frequent occurrence in the neighborhood, the valleys had been deserted, and the new-comers who boldly settled there were soon spoken of as being under the especial protection of the gods, since they seemed to fear neither earthquakes nor threatened inundations of fire. Under the circumstances almost everything they did was credited to supernatural agencies, and it was not long before Pele, Moho and Kamakaaa—the three most influential members of the little community—were regarded as *kahunas* of unusual sanctity and power.

The Pele family proper consisted, at that time, of Pele, her two brothers, Moho and Kamakaua, and a younger sister named Ulolu, who was after her apotheosis known as *Hiiaka-ika-pali-o-pele*. With them, however, were a number of relatives—principally females, whose protectors had perished in the struggle preceding their departure from Samoa—and about thirty attendants. The brothers were large, stalwart men, who had distinguished themselves in arms in their native land, and their attendants were warriors of tried courage and capacity. From these companions and assistants were created the three additional brothers and seven sisters of Pele mentioned in the *meles* of the bards. One of the former—*Kanehekili*—is said to have been a hunchback, as was also Kamakaua, but the fighting qualities of neither seem to have been impaired by the deformity.

Pele was as courageous as she was personally attractive. She had taken an active part in the wars of her father, and with her own hand had slain a chief who attempted to abduct her. Her brothers were devoted to her, and her bright eyes and queenly presence commanded the respect and homage of all who approached her.

And now, cultivating their lands in the valleys back of Keauhou, and living contentedly and without fear of molestation, we will leave the little colony for a time and refer to another important character in the story we are telling—Kamapuaa, the traditional monster of Oahu, whose deeds so aggrandize the folk-lore of that island. In some *meles* he is depicted as a hog with a human head, and in others as a being with a human form and head of a hog ; but in all he is described as a monster of prodigious bulk and malicious and predatory propensities.

II.

Glancing back a half-century or more before the landing of the Pele family in Puna, we note the arrival in the group of a number of independent parties of immigrants or adventurers from the southern islands. Among them were the chiefs Kalana and Huma. They came with considerable of a following, including the beautiful Kamaunui and a few of her relatives. The party landed on the island of Maui, and, after some wandering and change of locations, finally settled in Waihee, a spot noted for its beauty and natural advantages. Huma loved the fair Kamaunui. He had whispered soft words to her on their long journey from Kahiki, and fed her with the choicest food to be found among the stores of his great double canoe ; but she loved Kalana better, and, when she became his wife, Huma abruptly left Waihee, returning, it is supposed, to his native land.

The only child of this marriage was Hina, who on reaching womanhood became the wife of Olopana, a chief of the island of Oahu. Although of the same name, he was in nowise related to the Olopana who was the brother of Moikeha and grandson of Maweke. This chief had arrived from the south a few years before his marriage with Hina, and, with his younger brother, Kahikiula, settled in Koolau, or on the Koolau side of the island of Oahu, where he had acquired very considerable possessions. By what chance he met Hina, or through what influence he won her, tradition does not mention, but as his wife she went with him to Oahu, and there remained.

Hina was fair, and Kahikiula, unlike his brother, was young and handsome. They were happy in the society of each other, and were therefore much together. She went with him to the hills for wild fruits and berries, and he followed her to the seashore to gather shells and limpets. The jealousy of Olopana was at last aroused, and when Hina presented him with a son he charged Kahikiula with its paternity and refused to accept the child as his own. This estranged the brothers and made the lot of Hina miserable.

From its birth Olopana disliked the child, and in his resentment named it Kamapuaa, signifying a hog-child, or child of a hog. As the infant showed no marked physical characteristics of that animal, it is probable that Olopana fastened upon it the graceless appellation in a spirit of retaliation. But, whatever may have prompted its bestowal, the child certainly bore the name through life thus giving to the bards who chanted the story of his acts the cue and pretext for shaping him into the monster depicted by tradition.

Having no love for Kamapuaa, Olopana took little interest in his growth from year to year to the mighty manhood which he finally attained, and which excited the admiration of all others. The more Kamapuaa was praised the greater dislike did Olopana feel for him, and at length the presence of the young giant became so obnoxious to him that he ordered him, under penalty of death, to leave the district.

Failing to understand the cause of this unnatural hatred, the anger of Kamapuaa was at last aroused, and he strode away from the home of his youth with his heart filled with bitterness and vows of vengeance. As he left, Kahikiula presented him with a long and finely-finished spear tipped with bone, and his mother threw over his broad shoulders the feather cape of a chief, and hung around his neck a *palaoa*, or talisman carved from the tooth of some great animal of the sea.

Kamapuaa knew of a large cavern in the hills some miles distant from Koolau, the name by which will be designated the place of his birth, and thither he repaired and took up his residence. He led a wild, predatory life, and was soon joined by others as reckless as himself, until the party numbered fifty or sixty in all. Made bolder by this following, Kamapuaa began to harass the estates of Olopana. He stole his pigs, fowls and fruits, and whatever else his little band required, and delighted in breaking his nets, cutting adrift his canoes and robbing his fish-ponds. In a spirit of youthful bravado he had his body, from his loins upward, tattooed in black, shaved his head and beard to the resemblance of bristles, and hung from his shoulders a short mantle of tanned hog-skin, the hair being left to be worn on the outer side. In this guise his name did not seem to be altogether inappropriate, and he was pleased at the terror his appearance inspired.

Becoming still bolder, Kamapuaa resolved to inaugurate a more vigorous warfare upon Olopana, and began to cut down his cocoanut-trees and destroy his growing crops. This brought the matter to a crisis, as such acts were always regarded as a declaration of war. The depredations of Kamapuaa were invariably committed at night, and it was some time before the real aggressors were discovered. Koolau was filled with stories of the marauding exploits of a lawless band, led by a monster half-man and half-hog, and the *kahunas* were called upon to ascertain the character of the spoilers, and, if found to be supernatural, placate them with sacrifices.

While the *kilos* were plying their arts the mystery was suddenly solved in a more practical manner. Detected one night in destroying the walls of one of Olopana's fish-ponds, Kamapuaa and a number of his party were secretly followed to their hiding-place in the hills. This information was brought to Olopana, and he promptly equipped a small force of warriors to follow and capture or destroy the plundering band, which, he was enraged beyond all measure in learning, was under the leadership of his outcast son or nephew, Kamapuaa.

But the task of capturing or destroying Kamapuaa and his band was by no means an easy one. Of the party first sent to attack them in their mountain stronghold all were killed with the exception of a single warrior, and he was allowed to return to tell the tale of the slaughter and take to Olopana the defiance of Kamapuaa.

This satisfied the chief that Kamapuaa's purpose was rebellion as well as pillage, and a force of six hundred warriors was organized and sent against the outlaws. This forced Kamapuaa to change his tactics, and, leaving their retreat, in which they might have been surrounded and brought to submission by famine, the rebels retired farther back into the mountains, where they for months defied the whole force of Olopana. Frequent skirmishes occurred and many lives were lost, but every attempt to surround and capture the desperate band was frustrated by the dash and sagacity of their leader.

Once, when closely pursued and pressed against the verge of a narrow gorge, the rebels crossed the chasm and escaped to the other side by some means unknown to their pursuers, and the story was told and believed that Kamapuaa, taking the form of a gigantic hog, had spanned the gorge and given his followers speedy passage over his back to the other side, when he leaped across at a single bound and escaped with them. The spot marking this marvellous achievement is still pointed out at Hauula, and the tracks of the monster in the solid rock are shown.

It is difficult to say just how long this desultory fighting continued, but in the end the rebels were surrounded and nearly destroyed, and Kamapuaa was captured unhurt and delivered over to Olopana, to the great joy and relief of the people of Koolau. Olopana had erected a *heiau* at Kaneohe, where Lonoaohi officiated as high-priest, and thither he resolved to take his rebellious son or nephew, and offer him as a sacrifice to the gods. Hina pleaded for the life of Kamapuaa, but Olopana could not be moved. Satisfied that he would listen to no appeals for mercy, she determined to save her son, even at the sacrifice of her husband, and to that end secured the assistance of the high-priest, through whose treachery to Olopana the life of Kamapuaa was saved.

On the day fixed for the sacrifice Kamapuaa, carefully bound and strongly guarded, was taken to the *heiau*, followed by Olopana, who was anxious to witness the ghastly ceremonies, and with his own eyes see that his troublesome enemy was duly slain and his body laid upon the altar. In offering human sacrifices the victim was taken without the walls of the *heiau* and slain with clubs by the assistants of the high-priest. The body was then brought in and placed upon the altar in front of the entrance to the inner court, or sanctuary, when the left eye was removed by the officiating priest, and handed, if he was present, to the chief who had ordered the sacrifice. This being done, the offering was then ceremoniously made, and the body was left upon the altar for the elements to deal with.

Standing, with three or four attendants, at the door of his *tabued* retreat, within forty or fifty paces of the altar, Olopana saw his victim preliminarily led to the place of sacrifice, and a few minutes after motioned for the ceremonies to begin. Kamapuaa was taken without the walls of the temple to be slain. He was in charge of three assistant priests, one of them leading him by a stout cord around his neck, another keeping closely behind him, and the third walking silently at his side with the club of execution in his hand. Passing beyond the outer wall, the party entered a small walled enclosure adjoining, and the executioner raised his club and brought it down upon the head of his victim. Kamapuaa smiled, but did not move. Twice, thrice with mighty sweep the club descended upon the head of Kamapuaa, but scarcely bent the bristly hairs upon his crown.

With a semblance of wonder the executioner, whose tender blows would have scarcely maimed a mouse, dropped his club and said :

"Three times have I tried and failed to slay him! The gods refuse the sacrifice !"

"It is so, it is so, it is so !" chimed his companions. "The gods indeed refuse the sacrifice ! We have seen it !"

Therefore, instead of slaying Kamapuaa, the assistants, as they had been secretly instructed to do by the high-priest, removed the cords from his limbs, smeared his hair, face and body with the fresh blood of a fowl, and on their shoulders bore him back and placed him upon the altar as if dead.

The high-priest approached the apparently lifeless body, and bent for a moment over the face, as if to remove the left eye ; then placing on a wooden tray the eye of a large hog, which had been procured for that purpose, he sent an assistant with it to Olopana, at the same time retiring within the inner court, and leaving by the side of Kamapuaa, and near his right hand, as if by accident, the sharp ivory *pahoa*, or dagger, with which he had, to all appearance, been operating.

Giving but a single glance at the eye presented to him by the assistant of the high-priest, Olopana passed it to an attendant without the customary semblance of eating it, and approached the altar alone. Kamapuaa did not breathe. His face was streaked with blood, his eyelids were closed, and not a single muscle moved to indicate life.

Olopana looked at the hated face for a moment, and then turned to leave the *heiau*, not caring to witness the ceremonies of the formal offering. As he did so Kamapuaa clutched the dagger beside his hand, and, springing from the altar, drove the blade into the back of Olopana. Again and again he applied the weapon until the chief, with a groan of anguish, fell dead at the feet of his slayer.

Horrified at what they beheld, the attendants of Olopana

sprang toward their fallen chief. But their movements, whatever their import, did not disturb Kamapuaa. He had been
accustomed to meeting and accepting odds in battle, and when
he had secured possession of the *ihe* and huge axe of stone con-
veniently placed for his use behind the altar, he boldly approached and invited an encounter.

But the challenge was not accepted. The attendants of the
chief did not ordinarily lack courage, but they were unnerved
at the sight of a victim, slain, mutilated and laid upon the altar
by the priest, coming to life and springing to his feet full-armed
before his enemies.

Appearing upon the scene, the high-priest expressed great
surprise and horror at what had occurred, and his assistants
wildly clamored at the sacrilege ; but no hand was laid upon
Kamapuaa, and the friends of Olopana finally left the *heiau*, taking his body with them.

This tragedy in the *heiau* of Kawaewae created a profound
excitement in the district. Had Kamapuaa been at all popular
with the masses the death of Olopana at his hands would have
occasioned but little indignation ; but as many beside the dead
chief had suffered through his plundering visitations, and hundreds of lives had been sacrificed in his pursuit and final capture,
the people rose almost in a body to hunt him down and destroy him.

Hina attempted to save her son from the wrath of his
enemies, but her influence was insufficient to protect him, and
he again sought refuge in the mountains ; but his following was
small, and he finally crossed the island, and, with a party of
forty or fifty reckless and adventurous spirits, set sail for the
windward islands in a fleet of eight or ten canoes which he
in some manner obtained from the people of Ewa.

III.

More than one tradition avers that Kamapuaa traveled to
foreign lands after leaving Oahu, even to the lands where the
sky and sea were supposed to meet ; but he made no such
journey at that time. He spent some months in sight-seeing
among the islands southeast of Oahu, and pretty nearly cir-
cumnavigated them all. Sometimes, for the lack of better occu-

pation, he and his companions engaged in the petty wars of the districts visited by them ; but they generally led a roving, careless life, maintaining peaceful relations with all, and plundering only when every other means of securing supplies failed.

And thus they journeyed from island to island until they reached Hawaii. Kamiole, the usurper, had but just been defeated and slain by Kalapana, the son of Kanipahu, the hunchback, and Kohala, where Kamapuaa first landed, was still suffering from the effects of the war. He therefore proceeded southward along the coast, touching at several points in Kona ; then rounding the southern cape of the island, he sailed along the shores of Kau to Honuapo, where he landed and spent several weeks.

It was while he was there that Kamapuaa first learned of the Pele family in the adjoining district of Puna, and became acquainted with the many stories of enchantment and sorcery connected with the little colony. Pele was described to him as a woman of unusual personal beauty, and the lands occupied by the family and its retainers were said to be secure against lava inundations from Kilauea through the especial favor and protection of the gods.

These strange stories interested Kamapuaa, and he resolved to satisfy himself of their truth by visiting the mysterious colony. He accordingly set sail with his companions for Puna, and, landing at Keauhou, took up his abode near the sea-shore, not far from the lands occupied by Pele and her relatives.

As the colonists seemed to pay but little attention to the new-comers, at the expiration of three or four days Kamapuaa concluded to open a way to an acquaintance with them by visiting their settlement in person, and with a few of his companions appeared one morning before the comfortable *hale* of Pele and her family.

Moho received the strangers courteously, inquired the purpose of their visit to Keauhou and from what part of the country they came, and hospitably invited them to a breakfast of meat, potatoes, *poi* and fruits. The invitation was not declined, and during the repast Moho learned from Kamapuaa that he was the chief of the party, and that the visit of himself and companions to Puna had no especial object beyond that of observation and pleasure.

The tattooed body and bristly hair and beard of Kamapuaa imparted to his otherwise handsome person a strangely ferocious and forbidding appearance, and at the mention of his name and place of nativity Moho at once recognized in him, from report, the monster of Oahu, who had ravaged the estates of Olopana and finally assassinated that chief in the *heiau* of Kawaewae. His presence, therefore, in that part of Puna, was considerably less welcome than the words of Moho implied ; but no act of the latter indicated a suspicion that the ulterior purposes of his visitors were possibly otherwise than peaceful, and when they took their departure for the beach it was with mutual assurances of friendship.

But Kamapuaa did not take his leave that morning until he saw Pele. He found a pretext for prolonging his visit until she finally appeared, and when Moho made them known to each other Kamapuaa comported himself with a grace and gallantry never before observed in him by his companions. He admitted to himself that the reports of Pele's beauty had not been exaggerated, and wondered how it happened that she had remained for years unmarried.

The thought then came to Kamapuaa—perhaps not for the first time—that he would marry Pele himself and settle permanently in Puna. The idea of marriage had seldom occurred to him, but after he saw Pele he could think of little else. He greatly admired her appearance, and could see no reason why she should not be equally well pleased with his. No mirror, save the uncertain reflection of the waters, had ever shown him his hideously-tattooed face and bristly hair and beard, and the hog-skin still worn over his stained shoulders was regarded by him as a manly and warlike covering, well calculated to impress with favor a woman of Pele's courage and accomplishments.

But Kamapuaa did not urge his suit at once. He visited Moho almost every day for half a month or more, and endeavored to render himself agreeable to Pele by sending her baskets of choice wild fruits, fish from the sea which women were allowed to eat, and strings of beautiful and curious shells gathered from the shores and caverns of the coast. He saw her occasionally, and observed that she avoided him ; but he attributed her seeming repugnance to him to a coyishness common to her sex, and drew from it no augury unfavorable to his suit.

The companions of Kamapuaa soon discovered the attraction that was keeping him so long in the neighborhood of Keauhou, where food was becoming the reverse of abundant, and urged him to return to Honuapo ; but he silenced their clamors with promises of good lands and lives of ease in the valleys back of them, and they hopefully struggled on with their unsatisfactory fare.

Kamapuaa finally made a proposal of marriage to Pele ; but she refused to entertain it, and was promptly and heartily sustained by her brothers. But a simple refusal did not satisfy Kamapuaa. He urged that his blood was noble, and that the proposed union was in every way fitting and proper, and would prove mutually beneficial. Enraged at his presumption and persistency, Pele boldly expressed her contempt for him and aversion to his presence. In return Kamapuaa threatened to seize her by force and desolate the colony. Tradition asserts that she thereupon defied his power, and denounced him to his face as "a hog and the son of a hog."

But, whatever may have been the precise language used on the occasion by Pele, it was sufficiently definite and insulting not only to destroy the last hope of Kamapuaa, but to arouse in his heart the bitterest feelings of revenge, and he retired in wrath to the beach to plan and speedily execute a terrible scheme of retaliation.

Without referring to his final interview with Pele and her brothers, Kamapuaa informed his companions that he was at last ready to move—not to Honuapo, however, but to the cultivated valleys immediately back of them, occupied by a family of foreign interlopers and their adherents, who recognized the authority neither of Kalapana nor the governing chief of Puna, and might therefore be dispossessed without incurring the reproach or hostility of any power competent to punish. The project pleased them, but they doubted their ability to drive from their lands so large a number, the most of whom were doubtless skilled in the use of arms.

But Kamapuaa promised to make the way clear to an easy victory. He said he had carefully noted the number of the settlers, and observed the places where the most of them lodged. His plan was to suddenly fall upon them in the night and massacre all the male adherents of the family. This done, they would be masters of the situation, and able to treat on their own terms with the few who remained. It was proposed to include the governing family in the slaughter, but Kamapuaa opposed the suggestion, declaring that one of the brothers of Pele was a priest of great sanctity, whose death by violence would kindle the wrath of the gods ; and his counsel prevailed.

Several days elapsed without any movement being made. Kamapuaa was waiting, not only for a relaxation of the vigilance which his incautious threats may have inspired, but for the dark of the waning moon. Finally the blow was struck. Under the favoring cover of darkness Kamapuaa and his companions left the beach and secreted themselves near the scattered huts of the settlers, and at a signal, some time past midnight, rose and massacred every man within reach of their weapons. But few escaped. The screams of the women, who had been spared, rang through the valleys as they fled toward the mansion of Pele and her brothers for protection, and the band of murderers returned satisfied to the beach.

It was the purpose of Kamapuaa to surround the home of the surviving family the next day, and capture Pele by force, as he had threatened, or otherwise bring her and her haughty relatives to terms. But, after what had occurred, Moho readily understood the plans of the assassins, and early next morning abandoned the family cluster of houses, which could not be successfully defended, and sought refuge in a cavern in the hills, about three miles up the valley, accompanied by the entire family and the few others who had escaped the massacre of the night before. There was water in the cavern, and as the fugitives took with them a considerable quantity of provisions, and the opening to the retreat was small and easily defended, they hoped to be able, even if discovered and besieged, to protect themselves until the arrival of relief or the abandonment of the siege as hopeless by their enemies.

The cavern was of volcanic formation and had never been fully explored. It embraced a number of large connecting chambers, with ragged avenues leading back into and up the hill. The only light came through the front entrance, into which, from the inside, were hastily rolled heavy boulders of lava, found here and there detached, leaving openings through which spears and javelins could be thrust. A tiny rivulet of water trickled in somewhere from the darkness, and, after filling a shallow basin in the floor of one of the chambers, ran out through the opening. As air came in from the back of the cavern, it must have been connected with the surface through some one or more of the dark avenues referred to ; but not a glimmer of light, so far as the occupants had been able to penetrate the depths, indicated the possibility of an escape in that direction should the cavern be rendered untenable by assault. The party numbered, in all, seven men and eighteen women and children, and they had taken to their retreat a goodly supply of arms and provisions enough to sustain them for some weeks. Thus prepared they gloomily awaited their fate.

But they had fled to the hills not a moment too soon, for early in the day Kamapuaa and his companions appeared and surrounded the deserted habitations of the family. Discovering that his victims had escaped, Kamapuaa promptly divided his followers into small parties, and despatched them to the hills in search of the fugitives or of traces of their flight. He also joined in the search, but went unattended.

In the course of the day all returned to the deserted huts, where they had taken up their quarters, and reported that no traces of the missing colonists had been discovered, and the general opinion was that they had escaped across the mountains. Kamapuaa waited until all the rest had told the stories of their fruitless wanderings, when he announced that he had found what they had lacked the sagacity to discover. He informed them that the fugitives were secreted in a cavern some distance up one of the valleys, where they could be surrounded and captured without difficulty ; but he did not mention that he had made the discovery by shrewdly following a dog into the hills, and watching the animal until it stopped in front of the entrance to the cavern. He was willing that his companions should believe that his success was due to some inspiration or prescience of his own.

A guard was immediately detailed to watch the cavern and see that no one escaped, and the next day the place was surrounded and formally besieged. Following these preparations, visible to Moho and his handful of warriors, Kamapuaa approached the entrance sufficiently near to be heard within, and demanded the surrender of the party, promising that the lives of all would be spared.

The demand was refused with words of insult and defiance, and Kamapuaa ordered an assault upon the entrance. Several attempts were made to force the protecting rocks from the opening, but their interstices bristled with spear-points, and, after a number of the assailants had been wounded, that plan of attack was abandoned as impracticable.

A large quantity of dry wood, leaves and grass was then heaped in front of the entrance and fired, in the hope of suffocating the inmates with the heat and smoke of the conflagration ; but the draught of air through the cavern kept the smoke from entering, and, although the heat for a time became oppressive immediately around the opening, the connecting chambers were but slightly affected by it. The fire was allowed to die out, and Kamapuaa, on too closely approaching the entrance to note its effects, was made keenly aware of the failure of the project by receiving a sharp spear-thrust in the arm.

As fire and assault had proved unavailing, and a long siege did not accord with his purposes, Kamapuaa next endeavored to effect a breach through the top of the cavern in the rear of the entrance. As this necessitated the removal of an overlying mass of ten or fifteen feet of soil and rocks, the undertaking involved a very considerable amount of hard labor. But the plan met with general favor, and, with *oos* and other implements obtained from the valleys below, the besiegers entered upon the task of excavating through into the cavern.

For several days the work progressed almost uninterruptedly, and a large pit had been lowered to a depth of eight or ten feet, when the earth began to tremble violently, and a few minutes after the air was filled with sulphurous smoke and ashes. But this was not the most appalling sight beheld by Kamapuaa and his companions. Looking up the valley, which at that point was little more than a narrow gorge, they saw a flood of lava, full a hundred feet in width, bursting from the hillside and pouring down the ravine, its high-advancing crest aflame with burning timber, and sweeping before it a thundering avalanche of half-molten boulders.

With exclamations of dismay they started in full flight down the valley, closely followed by the devouring flood. On, on they sped, past the deserted huts of their victims, past the sandy foothills, past the cocoa-trees that fringed the beach. Turning at the water's edge, they beheld the awful stream spreading its mantle of death over the broadening valley, and speeding to the sea in broken volumes. Leaping into their canoes, they plunged through the surf and paddled out to sea. Setting sail for Honu-apo, Kamapuaa saw, as they left the coast, that the upper part of the valley from which they had fled was filled with lava, and knew that the cavern in which Pele and her companions had sought refuge from his wrath had been deeply buried by the flood.

When the news of the eruption reached Honuapo, the people, who had heard so many strange stories of Pele and her family, did not believe that they had perished. On the contrary, they declared that the eruption had been invoked by Pele to drive Kamapuaa from the district, and that if she had permitted her lands to be destroyed it was with the view of taking up her residence in the crater of Kilauea. This opinion soon crystalized into a belief which spread throughout the island of Hawaii, and another generation saw temples erected to Pele, the goddess of fire, and priests sanctified to her service. All but three of her brothers and sisters were the creations of her early priests, and their attributes gradually grew and took form as they floated down the stream of tradition.

Many adventures are related of Kamapuaa after his flight from Keauhou, but the most or all of them are the dreams of the poets of after-generations ; and further reference here to this most striking of the early heroes of the group may be properly concluded with the remark that, shortly after his experiences with the Pele family, he immigrated with a considerable following to one of the southern islands, where he married, distinguished himself in arms, and finally died without revisiting the Hawaiian archipelago.

Bird's-eye View of the Crater of Kilauea.

HUA, KING OF HANA.

CHARACTERS.

HUA, king of Hana, Maui.

LUUANA, a priest of the king's household.

LUAHOOMOE, the supreme high-priest.

KAAKAKAI and
KAANAHUA,   } sons of Luahoomoe.

OLUOLU, wife of Kaakakai.

KAAKOA, and
MAMULU, his wife, } friends of Oluolu.

NAULA-A-MAIHEA, a high-priest of Oahu.

HUA, KING OF HANA.

THE LEGEND OF THE GREAT FAMINE OF THE TWELFTH CENTURY.

I.

WITH the reign of Hua, an ancient king of Hana, or eastern Maui, is connected a legendary recital of one of the most terrible visitations of the wrath of the gods anywhere brought down by Hawaiian tradition. It is more than probable that the extent of the calamities following Hua's defiant and barbarous treatment of his high-priest and prophet was greatly colored and exaggerated in turn by the pious historians who received and passed the *moooelo* down the centuries; but the details of the story have been preserved with harrowing conciseness, and for more than six hundred years were recited as a solemn warning against wanton trespass upon the prerogatives of the priesthood or disregard of the power and sanctity of the gods.

In some of the genealogies Hua is represented as having been the great-grandfather of Paumakua, of Maui. This record, if accepted, would remove him altogether from the Hawaiian group, since Paumakua himself was undoubtedly an immigrant from Tahiti or some other of the southern islands. As he was contemporaneous with the distinguished priest and prophet Naula, who is said to have accompanied Laa-mai-kahiki from Raiatea, he must have appeared two or three generations later than Paumakua, and probably belonged to a collateral branch of the great Hua family from which Paumakua drew his strain.

It may therefore be assumed that as early as A.D. 1170 Hua was the *alii-nui*, or virtual sovereign, of eastern Maui. He is referred to as the king of Maui, but it is hardly probable that his sway extended over the western division of the island, as it was not until the reign of Piilani, nearly three centuries later, that the people of Maui became finally united under one government. Previous to that time, except at intervals of temporary conquest or occupation, eastern and western Maui were ruled by distinct and frequently hostile lines of kings. Hence the sovereignty of

Hua could scarcely have reached beyond the districts of Koolau, Hana, Kipahulu and Kaupo, while the remainder of the island must have recognized the authority either of Palena, the grandson of Paumakua, or of Hanalaa, the distinguished son and successor of Palena, since the later *mois* of Maui traced their genealogies uninterruptedly through this branch of the Paumakua family.

But, from whatever source Hua may have derived his rank and authority, he was a reckless, independent and warlike chief. Having access to the largest and finest timber in the group, his war-canoes were abundant and formidable, and when not engaged in harassing his neighboring frontiers he was employed in plundering expeditions to the coasts of Hawaii and Molokai. Tradition makes him the aggressor in the earliest remembered war between Maui and Hawaii. Although the name of the war (*Kanuioohio*) has been preserved, it probably did not reach beyond the limit of a powerful marauding excursion to the coast of Hilo, Hawaii, resulting in the defeat of the chiefs of that district by Hua, but in nothing more than a temporary seizure and occupation of their lands; for at that time Kanipahu was the *moi* of Hawaii, and would scarcely have permitted a permanent hostile lodgment in Hilo, whose chiefs acknowledged his suzerainty and were therefore entitled to his protection.

The high-priest of Hua was Luahoomoe. He claimed to be an *iku-pau*—that is, a direct descendant from *Kane*—and as such was strict in claiming respect for his person and sacred prerogatives. He did not approve of many of Hua's marauding acts, advising him instead to lead his people in happier and more peaceful pursuits, and not provoke either the retaliation of his enemies or the anger of the gods. This opposition to his aggressive methods exasperated Hua, and a feeling of suspicion and ill-will gradually grew up between him and the priesthood. He began to attribute his occasional failures in arms to deliberately-neglected prayers and sacrifices by Luahoomoe, and on one occasion, after having returned from an unsuccessful expedition to Molokai, he placed his *tabu* on a spring of water set apart for the use of the *heiau*, and on another wantonly speared a *puaa-hiwa*, or black *tabued* hog, sacred to sacrifice. When expostulated with for thus inviting the wrath of the gods, he threatened the high-priest with similar treatment.

Hua resided principally at Hana, where he constructed one of the largest royal mansions in the group, and all the leisure spared from his warlike pastimes was given to revelry. He had a hundred *hula* dancers, exclusive of musicians and drummers, and his monthly feasts were prolonged into days and nights of debauchery and unbridled license. Drunk with *awa*, an intoxicating drink made from a plant of that name, he kept the whole of Hana in an uproar during his frequent seasons of pleasure, and the attractive wives and daughters of his subjects were not unfrequently seized and given to his favorite companions.

The annual festival of *Lono* was approaching—an event marking the winter solstice, and which was always celebrated impressively on every island of the group. It was an occasion not only for manifesting respect for the nearest and most popular deity of the godhead, but for celebrating, as well, the ending of the old year and the beginning of the new. The ancient Hawaiians divided the year into twelve months of thirty days each. Each month and day of the month was named. They had two modes of measuring time—the lunar and sidereal. The lunar month began on the first day that the new moon appeared in the west, and regulated their monthly feasts and *tabu* days. Their sidereal month of thirty days marked one of the twelve divisions of the year; but as their two seasons of the year—the *Hooilo* (rainy) and *Kau* (dry)—were measured by the Pleiades, and their twelve months of thirty days each did not complete the sidereal year, they intercalated five days at the end of the year measured by months, in order to square that method of reckoning with the movements of the stars. This annual intercalation was made about the 20th of their month of *Welehu* (December), at the expiration of which the first day of the first month (*Makalii*) of the new year commenced. This was their *Makahiki*, or new-year day. The five intercalated days were a season of *tabu*, and dedicated to a grand yearly festival to *Lono*.

In preparation for this festival Hua had called for unusually large contributions from the people, and, in anticipation of another hostile expedition to Hawaii, had ordered quotas of warriors, canoes and provisions from his subject chiefs, to be reported at Hana immediately after the beginning of the new year. These exactions caused very general dissatisfaction, and the priesthood assisted in promoting rather than allaying the popu-

lar discontent.   All this was reported to Hua, and he resolved to
liberate himself at once and for the future from what he conceived to be an officious and unwarranted intermeddling of the
priesthood/with the affairs of state, by deposing or taking the life
of Luahoomoe.   In this desperate resolution he was sustained by
Luuana, a priest who had charge of the *heiau* or chapel of the royal
mansion, and who expected to succeed Luahoomoe as high-priest.

Hua sought in every way for a pretext for deposing or slaying Luahoomoe ; but the priest was old in years, exemplary in
his conduct, and moved among the people without reproach.
Finally, at the instigation of Luuana, who assumed that the advice was a divine inspiration, Hua created a bungling and absurd
pretence for an assault upon Luahoomoe.   The dishonesty of the
scheme was exposed, but it resulted, nevertheless, in the death of
the unoffending priest.

As tradition tells the story, Hua found occasion in a public
manner to order some *uwau*, or *uau*, to be brought to him from
the mountains.   The *uau* is a water bird, and seldom found in
the uplands.   As neither its flesh for eating nor its feathers for
decorating could have reasonably been required, the object of
despatching snarers in quest of it must have been a subject of
comment ; but kings then, as later, did not always deign to give
reasons for their acts, and preparations were at once made by the
household servants and retainers of the king to proceed upon the
hunt.

"Be careful that the birds come from the mountains," said
Hua, addressing the trusted *hoalii* in charge of the hunting
party—"only from the mountains," he repeated ; "I will have
none from the sea."

"But can they be found in the mountains?" ventured the
hoalii, looking inquiringly toward Luahoomoe, who was standing
near and watching a flight of birds which seemed to be strangely
confused and ominous of evil.

"Do you inquire of me?" said the priest, after a pause, and
finding that the king did not answer.

"I inquire of any one who thinks he knows," returned the
hoalii.

"Then the birds you seek will not be found in the mountains
at this season of the year," returned the priest, "and you must set
your snares by the sea-shore."

"Is it so that you would attempt to countermand my orders?" exclaimed Hua, in apparent anger. "I order my servants to go to the mountains for the *uau*, and you tell them to set their snares by the sea-shore!"

"I humbly ask the king to remember that I have given no orders," calmly replied the priest.

"But you have dared to interfere with mine!" retorted the king. "Now listen. My men shall go to the mountains in search of the birds I require. If they find them there I will have you slain as a false prophet and misleader of the people!"

With this savage threat the king walked away with his *hoalii*, while the priest stood in silence with his face bowed to the earth. He knew the import of Hua's words. They meant death to him and the destruction of his family. The bloody purpose of the king had been told to him at the sacrificial altar, had been seen by him in the clouds, had been whispered to him from the *anu* of the sanctuary.

"Since the gods so will it, I must submit to the sacrifice," was the pious resolution of the priest; "but woe to the hand that strikes, to the eyes that witness the blow, to the land that drinks the blood of the son of Laamakua!"

Luahoomoe had two sons, Kaakakai and Kaanahua. Both were connected with the priesthood, and Kaakakai had been instructed in all the mysteries of the order in anticipation of his succession, on the death of his father, to the position of high-priest. They were young men of intelligence, and their lives had been blameless. Knowing that they would not be spared, Luahoomoe advised them to leave Hana at once and secrete themselves in the mountains, and suggested Hanaula, an elevated spur of the mighty crater of Haleakala, as the place where they would be most likely to escape observation.

But a few weeks before Kaakakai had become the husband of the beautiful Oluolu, the daughter of a distinguished chief who had lost his life in Hua's first expedition against Hilo. Twice had she sought the *heiau* for protection against the emissaries of Hua, who had been ordered to seize and bring her to the royal mansion, and in both instances Luahoomoe had given her the shelter of the sacred enclosure. It was there that Kaakakai first met her, and, charmed no less by her beauty than her abhorrence of the lascivious intents of the king, he soon persuaded her to become his wife. But, even as his wife, Kaakakai did not deem her secure from the evil designs of the king, and had found an asylum for her in the humble home of a distant relative in a secluded valley four or five miles back of Hana, where he frequently visited her and cheered her with assurances of his love.

As the danger was imminent, Luahoomoe urged his sons to leave Hana without delay, promising Kaakakai that he would visit Oluolu the next day, and apprise her of her husband's flight and the place to which he had fled for concealment. But the old priest did not live to fulfil his promise, and Oluolu was left in ignorance of the fate of her husband.

Early next morning the bird-hunters returned, bringing with them a large number of birds, including the *uau* and *ulili*, all of which, they averred, had been caught in the mountains, when in reality they had been snared on the sea-shore.

Hua summoned the high-priest, and, pointing to the birds, said : " All these birds were snared in the mountains. You are therefore condemned to die as a false prophet who has been abandoned by his gods, and a deceiver of the people, who are entitled to the protection of their king."

Taking one of the birds in his hand, the priest calmly replied : " These birds did not come from the mountains; they are rank with the odor of the sea."

But the *hoalii* of the king steadfastly maintained that the birds had been snared in the mountains, and Hua declared the assurance of the hunters to be sufficient to outweigh the flimsy testimony of the priest.

Luahoomoe saw that he was doomed, and that the hunters had been schooled to sustain the lying assertion of the *hoalii ;* yet he resolved to disconcert them all and make good his position, no matter what might be the result. He therefore asked permission to open a few of the birds, and the king sullenly granted it.

"Select them yourself," said the priest to the *hoalii,* and the latter took from the heap and handed to him three birds. The priest opened them, and the crops of all were found to be filled with small fish and bits of sea-weed.

" Behold my witness ! " exclaimed the priest, pointing to the eviscerated birds, and turning toward the *hoalii* with a look of triumph.

Confounded and enraged at the development, Hua seized a javelin, and without a word savagely drove it into the breast of Luahoomoe, killing him on the spot. A shudder ran through the witnesses as the venerable victim fell to the earth, for violence to a high-priest was a crime almost beyond comprehension ; but the king coolly handed the bloody weapon to an attendant, and, with a remorseless glance at the dying priest, leisurely walked away.

Sending for Luuana, he immediately elevated him to the dignity of high-priest, and ordered the body of Luahoomoe to be laid upon the altar of the *heiau*. The house of the dead priest was then burned, in accordance with ancient custom, and the king's executioners were despatched with attendants in search of the sons of Luahoomoe.

Proud of his newly-acquired honors, Luuana made preparations for extensive sacrifices, and then proceeded to the *heiau* with the body of Luahoomoe. As he approached the gate of the outer enclosure, the tall *pea*, or wooden cross indicative of the sanctity of the place, fell to the ground, and on reaching the inner court the earth began to quake, groans issued from the carved images of the gods, and the altar sank into the earth, leaving an opening from which issued fire and smoke. The attendants dropped the body of the priest and fled from the *heiau* in dismay, followed by the no less frightened Luuana.

The priests of the temple, who knew nothing of the death of Luahoomoe until they beheld his body about to be offered in sacrifice, stood for a moment awe-stricken at what was transpiring around them. They had been taught that the *heiau* was the only place of safety for them in a time of danger, and after the flight of Luuana and his attendants they tenderly conveyed the body of the high-priest to a hut within the enclosure to prepare it for burial.

Luuana repaired in haste to the *halealii* to report to the king what had occurred at the *heiau*. But his story excited but little surprise in Hua, for events quite as overwhelming were occurring all around them. The earth was affected with a slight but continuous tremor ; a hot and almost suffocating wind had set in from the southward ; strange murmurs were heard in the air ; the skies were crimson, and drops of blood fell from the clouds ; and finally reports came from all parts of Hana that the streams, wells and springs were no longer yielding water, and a general flight of the people to the mountains had commenced.

Such chiefs as could be found were hastily called together in council. Hua was completely subdued, and admitted that he had angered the gods by killing Luahoomoe. But what was to be done? Perhaps the sons of the martyred priest might be appealed to. But where were they? No one knew. It was suggested that a hundred human sacrifices be offered, but Luuana declined to appear again at the *heiau*, and resigned his office of high-priest. Another was appointed, and the sacrifices were ceremoniously offered. The *mu* had no difficulty in obtaining victims, for the people were desperate and offered themselves by scores. But the drought continued, and the general suffering increased from day to day. All other signs of the displeasure of the gods had passed away.

Other sacrifices were offered in great profusion, and an *imuloa* was constructed, where human bodies were baked and in that form presented to the gods. But the springs and streams remained dry, and the clouds dropped no rain.

The gods were redecorated, and the erection of a new *heiau* was commenced, but the people remaining in the district were too few and too weak to complete it; and a strict *tabu* was declared for a season of ten days, but the people were too desperate to observe it, and no attempt was made to punish those who disregarded it. Many drowned themselves, insane from thirst, and such as could procure the poisonous mixture died from the effects of *koheoheo* administered by their own hands.

The drought extended to the mountains, and the people fled beyond; but wherever they went the streams became dry and the rains ceased. The pestilence became known in western Maui, and the famishing refugees were driven back in attempting to enter that district.

After vainly attempting to stay the dreadful scourge, and seeing his kingdom nearly depopulated, Hua secretly embarked with a few of his attendants for Hawaii. He landed in the district of Kona; but the drought followed him. Wherever he went the fresh waters sank into the earth and the clouds yielded no rain. And so he journeyed on from place to place, carrying famine and misery with him, until in the course of his wanderings, occupying more than three years, he rendered almost one-half of the island of Hawaii a desolation. Finally he died, as the gods had decreed, of thirst and starvation—one legend says in a temple of Kohala—and his bones were left to dry in the sun ; and the saying of "rattling are the bones of Hua in the sun," or "dry are the bones of Hua in the sun," has come down to the present as a significant reference to the fate of one high in power who defied the gods and persecuted the priesthood.

But rainless skies and drought did not mark alone the footsteps of Hua and his attendants. Wherever the despairing people of the district went the same affliction followed. Some of them sailed to Hawaii, others to Molokai and Oahu, and a few to Kauai ; but nowhere could they find relief. Everywhere the drought kept pace with them, and famine and suffering were the result throughout the entire group. The diviners had discovered the cause of the scourge, but neither prayers nor sacrifices could avert or ameliorate it. And so it continued for nearly three and a half years.

II.

During all the long years of famine and death what had befallen Oluolu, the young wife of Kaakakai, left in the secluded valley back of Hana ? She saw the blight that suddenly fell upon the land ; saw the springs and streams go dry around her humble home ; saw the leaves of the banana wither and the grass turn yellow in the valley ; saw famishing men, women and children madly searching for water, and tearing down cocoanuts for the little milk they afforded ; and then by degrees she learned of all that had transpired and was still transpiring in Hana, including the sad story of the death of Luahoomoe and the flight of Kaakakai. But whither had he fled ? No one could tell her ; but, wherever he might be, she knew that, if alive, he would some day return to her, and therefore struggled on as best she could to live.

Her home was with Kaakao, whose wife was Mamulu. They had been blessed with three sons, all of whom had perished in Hua's useless wars, and now in their old age they were occupying a little *kuleana*, so far up the narrow valley winding into the hills that no land for cultivation was found above them. They had small patches of *taro* and potatoes, a score or two of cocoanut-trees of old growth, and plantains and bananas enough for their use. In the hills back of them were *ohias* and other wild fruits, and, with pigs and fowls in abundance, there was never any lack of food in the house of Kaakao.

But when the drought came, accompanied by the scorching south wind, Kaakao shared the fate of his neighbors. His pigs and fowls scattered in search of water, and did not return. The ripening plantains and bananas, together with a few bulbs of *taro*, were hastily gathered, and the food supply stored in the house was adequate to the wants of the occupants for some weeks to come ; but fresh water was nowhere to be found, and the cocoanuts were stripped from the trees and laid away to meet, as far as possible, the terrible emergency.

Thus passed nearly half a month, during which time harrowing reports from the valleys below reached the *kuleana* through parties vainly searching everywhere among the hills for water. Then Kaakao saw that his supply of cocoanut-milk was nearly exhausted, and resolved to visit the sea-shore, where he knew of a spring in times past dripping from the rocks almost on a level with the waves. "Surely," he thought, "that spring cannot be dry, with all the water around it." And, swinging two water-calabashes over his shoulders, he started for the sea-shore. But he never returned. In passing to the coast he was seized, among others, and offered as a sacrifice in the *heiau*.

For two days his return was awaited at the *kuleana*. Then Mamulu solemnly said : "Kaakao is dead. We have no more water and but little food. Why suffer longer ? Let us drink *koheoheo* and die."

"Not to-day, my good friend Mamulu," replied Oluolu, soothingly. "We will talk of it to-morrow. Last night in my dreams a whisper told me not to despair. Let us wait."

The next morning Oluolu rose at daylight. The last of the cocoanut-milk was gone, and the mouths of both were dry and feverish. There was a strangely cheerful light in Oluolu's eyes as she bent over the suffering but patient Mamulu, and, holding up a calabash, said : "I shall soon return with this filled with water !—think of it, Mamulu !—filled with pure, fresh water ! "

"Poor child ! " replied Mamulu, not doubting that her mind was wandering. "But where will you go for it ? "

"Only a short walk—right up the valley ! " returned Oluolu. "You know the little cavern among the rocks. The mouth is almost closed, but I can find it. The water is in the back part of the *ana*. It is running water, but it disappears in the darkness. Perhaps it comes from *Po ;* but no matter—it is sweet and good. Luahoomoe came to me last night, with his long, white hair smeared with blood, and told me he had sent the water there. It is for us alone. If others know of it or taste it, it will disappear. So we must be careful, Mamulu, very careful."

Leaving the woman almost in a daze at the words thus spoken in rapid and excited sentences, Oluolu left the hut and started up the narrow valley. A walk of three or four minutes brought her to the entrance of an abrupt and chasm-like ravine gashing the hills on the right. To its almost precipitous sides clung overhanging masses of ragged volcanic rock, from the crevices of which a sturdy vegetation had taken root, and in time past gloomily shaded the narrow channel ; but the interlacing branches of the trees were almost leafless, and all around were seen the footprints of death and desolation. Not a breath of wind cooled the sultry air, and no sound of living creature broke the silence of the heated hills. The mouth of the ravine was partially choked with huge boulders washed down by the freshets of centuries, and the ground was strewn with dead leaves and broken branches.

Casting her eyes around in every direction, to be sure that she was not observed, Oluolu quickly found a way over the boulders and ascended the ravine. Proceeding upward thirty or forty yards, and climbing a rocky bench, over which in seasons of rain had poured a little cascade, she stopped in front of an overhanging mass of vitreous rock, and the next moment disappeared in a stooping posture through a low opening almost concealed by decrepitations from above. The opening led to a cavern forty or fifty feet in depth, with an irregular width almost as great. The floor descended from the entrance, and was smooth and apparently water-worn. Two or three steps forward enabled her to stand upright ; but all beyond was darkness, and for a moment she remained undecided which way to proceed. She heard a sound like that of a bare and cautious footstep on the smooth floor. She was startled, but suffering had made her desperate, and she listened again. The same sound continued, but it was mellowed into the soft murmur of waters somewhere back in the darkness, and with a swelling heart she groped her way toward the silvery voice, sweeter to her than the strains of the *ohe* or the songs of birds.

Closer and closer she approached, every step making more distinct the joyful music, until at last she felt the spatter of cool water upon her bare feet. Stretching out her hand, it came in contact with a little stream gushing from the back wall of the cavern, and instantly disappearing where it fell upon a layer of loose gravel washed down from the entrance. She hastily drank from her palm, and found that the water was cool and sweet. Then she held the mouth of the calabash under the stream, and, after wetting her head and drinking until prudence counseled her to stop, refilled the vessel, cautiously emerged from the opening, and hastened back to the hut.

Hesitating without the door, to satisfy herself that no one had arrived during her absence, Oluolu noiselessly entered, and, stealing to the *kapa-moe* upon which Mamulu was half-deliriously dreaming, poured a quantity of water upon her head, and, as she opened her eyes with a bewildered stare, dropped a swallow into her parched and open mouth.

Half-rising, Mamulu dreamily felt of her dripping hair, and then stared vacantly at Oluolu, who stood smilingly beside her with the calabash in her hand. In a moment she recalled all that had occurred before she dropped into the troubled sleep from which she had been so strangely aroused.

"Then it is not a dream!" she murmured, clasping her wasted hands upon her breast. "The gods have sent us water!" And she reached for the calabash.

"No," said Oluolu kindly, withdrawing the vessel. "We have plenty, but you are weak and would drink too much. Now lie down, with this roll of *kapa* under your head, and while I am giving you a swallow at a time I will tell you all about the water and how I found it."

And so, slowly feeding Mamulu with the precious fluid, and at the same time bathing her head and throat, Oluolu related to her everything that had occurred.

"But will the stream continue?" anxiously inquired Mamulu. "Would it not be well to fill all the calabashes in the house, and all we can procure, and so keep them, that we may not be left without water should the stream disappear?"

"I think it would not be well to anger the gods by doubting

them," replied Oluolu. "The water was sent, not to prolong
our sufferings, but to save our lives ; and I am sure it will continue so long as we guard the secret and allow no others to
use it."

Oluolu's faith was rewarded. Without any diminution in
volume the little stream continued to flow and sink in the darkness of the cavern until the wrath of the gods was appeased and
the rains finally came again. But Oluolu and her companion
could not subsist on water alone. The parched earth produced
no food ; but they did not despair. Every day they cautiously
watered a little patch of mountain *taro* in the ravine above the
cavern, and at intervals of four or five days went to the sea-shore
and returned with fish, crabs, limpets and edible sea-weed.

And so they managed to live without suffering, while the
valleys became almost depopulated, and all others in Hana were
stricken with famine. They seldom saw a human face in their
journeys to and from the sea, and never in the valley where they
lived, and the few they met avoided them, fearful, no doubt,
that the miserable means of subsistence to which they resorted
might become known to others.

III.

It was near the end of the terrible scourge that the district
of Ewa, on the island of Oahu, became its victim. It followed
the appearance there of a Hana chief and a few of his retainers,
who had been driven from Molokai. At that time there lived
at Waimalu, in the district of Ewa, the celebrated priest and
prophet Naula-a-Maihea. No one in the Hawaiian priesthood
of the past was ever more feared or respected. It was thought
by some that he had visited the shadowy realms of *Milu*, and
from *Paliuli* had brought back the waters of life. He must
have been well on in years, for, as already mentioned, he is credited with having been the priest of Laa-mai-kahiki on the romantic journey of that prince from the southern islands.

In evidence of the great sanctity of Naula, tradition relates
that his canoe was upset during a journey from Waianae, Oahu,
to Kauai. He was swallowed by a whale, in whose stomach he
remained without inconvenience until the monster crossed the
channel and vomited him up alive on the beach at Waialua,

Kauai, the precise place of his destination. At another time, when crossing to Hawaii, and beset with adverse winds, two huge black sharks, sent by *Mooalii*, the shark-god of Molokai, towed him to Kohala so swiftly that the sea-birds could scarcely keep him company.

He built a *heiau* at Waimalu, the foundations of which may still be traced, and in the inner temple of the enclosure it is asserted that *Lono* conversed with him freely; and at his bidding the spirits of the living (*kahaoka*) as well as the shades of the dead (*unihipili*) made their appearance; for it was believed by the ancient Hawaiians that the spirits or souls of the living sometimes separated themselves from the body during slumber or while in a condition of trance, and became visible in distant places to priests of especial sanctity.

Consulting with the gods, Naula discovered the cause of the drought, and, becoming alarmed at the threatened destruction of the entire population of the group, undertook to stay the ravages of the spreading scourge. With a vision enlarged and intensified by sacrifice and prayer, he ascended the highest peak of the Waianae Mountains. Far as the eye could reach the skies were cloudless. He first looked toward Kaala, but discerned no sign of rain around its wooded summits. He turned toward Kauai, but not a cloud could be seen above the mountains of that island. Cloudless, also, were the mountains of Molokai. Finally, casting his eyes in the direction of Maui, he saw a small, dark spot like a rain-cloud hanging above the peak of Hanaula. "It may disappear," he thought; "I will wait." Midday came. He looked again, and the spot was still there. The sun grew red in the west. Again he looked and found that the cloud had neither disappeared nor moved. "Surely the sons of Luahoomoe are there," he said to himself. "I will go to them; they will listen to me, and the waters will come again."

Naula descended from the mountain, and the same night embarked alone in a canoe for Maui. He spread no sail, used no paddle, but all night his *waa* skimmed the waves with the speed of the wind, and at sunrise the next morning he landed at Makena, above which, a few miles inland, towered the peak of Hanaula, with the dark spot still hanging over it.

There, indeed, were the sons of Luahoomoe. Nurtured by the rains that had fallen alone on the peak of Hanaula, there they had remained unseen for three and a half years, waiting for the wrath of the gods to be appeased and for a summons to descend. A strange light accompanied the canoe of Naula in the darkness. From their elevated retreat they noted it far out upon the ocean, and watched it growing brighter as it approached, until it went out on the beach at Makena. They knew it to be the signal of their deliverance, and hastened down the mountain to meet the messenger of the gods. One account says they met Naula at Kula ; but the meeting occurred not far from the Makena landing, where the priest, inspired with a knowledge of their coming, awaited their arrival. As they approached, the venerable *kahuna*, his white hair and beard falling to his waist and a *tabu* staff in his hand, advanced to meet them. They bowed respectfully, and, returning the salutation, Naula said :

"I know you to be the sons of Luahoomoe, whose death by the hands of Hua, King of Hana, has been avenged by the gods upon the people of all the islands of Hawaii. The earth is still parched, and thousands are seeking in vain for food and water. Hua is dead ; his bones lie unburied in the sun. Scattered or dead are the people of Hana ; their lands are yellow, and their springs and streams yield nothing but dust and ashes. Great was the crime of Hua, and great has been the punishment. I am Naula-a-Maihea, the high-priest of Oahu, and have come to ask, with you, that the gods may be merciful and no longer scourge the people."

At the mention of his name the sons of Luahoomoe bowed low before the aged prophet of whose sanctity report had years before apprised them, and then Kaakakai replied :

"Great priest, willingly will we add our voices to your supplication to the gods, whose vengeance has indeed been terrible. But since our retreat was revealed to you and nothing seems to be hidden from your understanding, let me ask if you know aught of the fate of Oluolu. She was my wife, and I left her in a little valley in the mountains back of Hana. I loved her greatly, and am grieved with the fear that she is dead."

Without replying the priest seated himself upon the ground, and, unbinding the *kihei* from his shoulders, threw it over his head, shutting the light from his face. While one hand pressed the mantle closely to his breast, the other held to his forehead what seemed to be a talisman of stone suspended by a short cord from his neck. He remained motionless in that position for some minutes ; then throwing off the *kihei* and rising to his feet, he turned to Kaakakai and said :

"I was not wrong in my thought. The presence here of the sons of Luahoomoe has sanctified the spot to communion with the spirits of the air. Oluolu, alone with a woman much her elder, still lives where you left her and hopefully awaits the coming of Kaakakai—for such I now know to be your name. The spirit of Luahoomoe has nourished and protected her."

"Great Naula, most favored of the gods !" exclaimed Kaakakai, grasping the hand of the priest. "You have made my heart glad ! Now ask of me what you will !"

On the very spot from which the priest had risen they proceeded to erect a rude altar of stones. When it was completed Naula brought from his canoe a combined image of the godhead —the *Oie* of the early priesthood—and a small enclosed calabash of holy water—*ka-wai-kapu-a-Kane.* Removing the *kapa* covering, the image was placed beside the altar, and while the priest recited the solemn *kaiokopeo,* or prayer of consecration, Kaakakai intoned the invocation and continued at intervals to sprinkle the altar with holy water.

The dedication ceremonies were at length concluded ; but what was there to offer as a sacrifice ? The hills were bare and parched. Far as the eye could reach the lands were deserted, and no living thing beside themselves was visible. Suddenly there appeared among the leafless shrubbery near them a large black hog sacred to sacrifice. The brothers exchanged looks of wonder, but the priest did not seem to be greatly surprised. The animal was immediately seized, killed and placed upon the altar, and sacrificial prayers were devoutly offered.

In the midst of these services a wind set in from the south. Black clouds began to gather, from which the answering voice of thunder came, and then a gentle rain began to fall upon the sere and hungry earth. Raising his face into the baptism, Naula with emotion exclaimed :

"The sacrifice is accepted ! The gods are merciful, and the people are saved !"

And the rains continued, not there alone but all over the islands, until the grass grew green again and the banana put forth its shoots. Everywhere the rejoicing was great. The people returned to their deserted lands, and the valleys of Hana, even, blossomed as before. But Hua and his family had perished from the earth, and a new dynasty came into being to claim the sovereignty of eastern Maui.

The sons of the martyred Luahoomoe returned at once to Hana, and in the arms of Kaakakai the brave and faithful Oluolu recited the story of her sufferings and deliverance. With largely-augmented possessions Kaakakai became the high-priest under the new *régime*, and for generations his descendants continued to be among the most influential of the families of eastern Maui. Kaanahua became the god of the husbandman.

The political events immediately following the death of Hua are but vaguely referred to by tradition, and the few particulars known doubtless owe their preservation to the care taken by the priesthood—to which class the historians of the past usually belonged—to bring down, with all its terrible details, the fate of Hua, as a warning to succeeding sovereigns who might be disposed to trespass upon the sacred domain of the spiritual rulers who, in a measure, divided the allegiance of their subjects.

THE IRON KNIFE.

CHARACTERS.

KALAUNUIOHUA, king of Hawaii.
KAMALUOHUA, king of Maui.
HUAPOULEILEI, *alii-nui* of Oahu.
KAHOKUOHUA, king of Molokai.
KUKONA, king of Kauai.
KAHEKA, queen of Hawaii.
KUAIWA, son of the king of Hawaii.
KAPAPA, daughter of the king of Hawaii.
WAAHIA, a renowned prophetess.
KUALU, adopted son of Waahia.
WAKALANA, an influential chief of Maui.

KALUIKI-A-MANU,
HAKOA and   } males,
HIKA,   } shipwrecked foreigners.
NELEIKE and
MALAEA,   } females,

MANOKALANIPO, son of the king of Kauai.

THE IRON KNIFE.

I.

TWO or three attempts to consolidate under one general government the several islands of the Hawaiian group were made by ambitious and war-like chiefs previous to the final accomplishment of the project, at the close of the last century, by Kamehameha I.; but all these early schemes of conquest and aggrandizement proved unsuccessful, and were especially unfortunate in affording excuses for retaliatory raids and invasions, sometimes extending, with more or less persistency and bitterness, to generations thereafter.

The most disastrous of these ambitious ventures was the first, and connected with it were a number of strange and dramatic incidents, giving to the story of the enterprise something more than a historic interest. It occurred in about A.D. 1260, and the bold warrior who attempted it was Kalaunuiohua, king of the island of Hawaii. He was the grandson of Kalapana, who reconquered the kingdom from Kamaiole, the usurper, as related in the story of "The Royal Hunchback."

At that time Kamaluohua, the seventh in descent from Paumakua, was the *moi* of Maui, or rather of the western and greater part of the island. Huapouleilei, the eighth in line from Maweke, was the *alii-nui* of Oahu, his possessions embracing the districts of Ewa, Waianae and Waialua, while the Koolau and Kona divisions were ruled, respectively, by Moku-a-Loe and Kahuoi. The *moi* of Molokai was Kahokuohua, the fourth in descent in the old Nanaula line from Keoloewa, the brother of Kaupeepee, the abductor of Hina and desperate defender of the fortress of Haupu, as told in the legend of "Hina, the Hawaiian Helen." Kukona was the sovereign of Kauai. He was the great-grandson of Ahukini-a-Laa, one of the three sons of the three wives of Laa-mai-kahiki, as mentioned in the story of "The Triple Marriage of Laa-mai-kahiki."

The contemporary rulers of the several islands are thus referred to for the reason that they all appear as prominent actors in the several legends from which have been gathered the historic features of the story about to be related, and also for the purpose of keeping partially in view the conspicuous and succeeding representatives of the sovereign families of the group.

Kalaunuiohua—or, as he will be called hereafter, Kalaunui—inherited something of the military spirit of his warlike grandfather, and is referred to by tradition as an ambitious and aggressive sovereign, courageous in enterprise, but lacking in judgment and discretion. This estimate of his character is abundantly sustained by the record of his acts.

Waipio had been made the focus of sovereign authority by Kahaimoelea, the royal father of Kalaunui, and continued to be the most attractive and consequential point in the kingdom. The royal grounds and edifices had been enlarged and improved from time to time, until barbaric taste and skill seemed to be able to add nothing more to their grandeur or beauty. Not far from the royal mansion was the great *heiau* of Pakaalani, partially built by Kalapana, and completed by his successor. Its *tabus* were the most sacred on Hawaii, and a descendant of Paao officiated there as high-priest. It was connected with the palace enclosure by a sacred stone pavement, which it was death for any but royal and privileged feet to touch, and on its walls were over a hundred gods.

Kalaunui was proud of his ancestry, which carried back his lineage both to Pili and Maweke, and united in his veins the foremost blood of the pioneers of the fifth and eleventh centuries. He had two children—a son named Kuaiwa, and a daughter, Kapapa, whose full name was Kapapalimulimu. At the time of which we are writing she was fifteen, and her brother was three or four years older. Both had been carefully reared. The son had been instructed in all the manly accomplishments of the time, and from her infancy the daughter had been guarded with the most jealous watchfulness. She had grown almost to womanhood without betrothal, for the reason that a husband suited to her rank and personally deserving of her beauty could with difficulty be found in the kingdom.

Among the number of the king's retainers of various grades of rank—beginning with the *wohi*, or chief counsellor of royal blood next to the throne, and ending with the *kahu-alii* and *puuku*, or personal and other attendants at the palace—was the young chief Kualu. He was large, muscular and handsome, with a bearing indicative of good blood, and through his courage and capacity at arms had been raised to the military position of *pukaua*, or captain, and placed in charge of the palace guard—an office which gave him, if he did not before possess it, the privilege of an *aialo*, or the right to eat food in the presence of the king.

Kualu was a chief without possessions. His grandfather, a chief of the old line of Nanaula, had been killed in the battle which restored Kalapana to the throne of his fathers, and on the sudden death of his father, twenty years before, he had been adopted by Waahia, a *kaula*, or prophetess, renowned in tradition for her foresight and influence. He was recognized by the *Aha-alii*, or college of chiefs of established lineage, as of noble blood, but belonged to that class of chiefs who, lacking the influence of family and estates, were compelled to rely upon their own efforts for advancement.

Although it is claimed that Waahia was of chiefly lineage, nothing is positively known, even of her parents. She first appeared in Waipio more than a generation before, and, through an almost undeviating verification of her prophecies, in time became noted and feared by the people, not only as a favored devotee of *Uli*, the god of the sorcerers, but as a medium through whom the *unipihili*, or spirits of the dead, communicated. She lived alone in a hut in a retired part of the valley of Waipio, and it is said that a large *pueo*, or owl, which, with the white *alae*, was sacred and sometimes worshipped, came nightly and perched upon the roof of her lonely habitation.

Of course a *kaula* of her sanctity wanted for nothing. The people were only too happy to leave at her door anything of which she might stand in need, and the best of everything in the valley came unbidden to her board. Of her abundance she gave to the needy, and, while she seldom spoke to any one, her looks and acts were kind to all. The priesthood recognized her power, and the king and chiefs consulted her in matters of moment when the *kilos* of the temple were in doubt.

She had reared Kualu with the greatest care, and saw him grow to a manhood of which she was proud. She loved him as if he had been her own child, and he repaid her affection by heeding her advice in all things, and by kindness comforting her declining years. She had schooled him in a lore which but few possessed, and the most skilful had instructed him in the martial and courtly accomplishments consistent with his chiefly rank. At the age of twenty he became attached to the household of the king, and in time was advanced, as already stated, to the high grade of captain of the palace guard. Although his abilities had commended him to advancement, his early favor with the king was doubtless due to some extent to the influence of his foster-mother.

Kualu's intimate connection with the royal household brought him into frequent companionship with Kuaiwa and his sister, and as the latter grew to womanhood a romantic attachment sprang up between her and the handsome captain of the guard. It was romantic only because it was to every appearance hopeless, for there was a wide gulf between Kualu and the daughter of the proudest *moi* in all the group, and for whom there seemed to be no fitting mate.

The home of Kualu was within the palace enclosure; yet he frequently visited Waahia in her lonely retreat, to cheer her with words of affection and see that she wanted for nothing. It was during one of these visits, not long before the beginning of the leading events of this legend, that the *kaula* abruptly said to him :

" Kualu, I can see that you are thinking much of Kapapa."

" We sometimes meet," replied Kualu, evasively.

"It is not well for you to try to gather berries from the clouds," returned the *kaula*, kindly. " A *niapio* of the highest rank alone can reach that fruit. "

" The flying spear brings down what the hand cannot reach," was Kualu's significant answer.

Waahia smiled at the dauntless spirit of her ward, and after a long pause, during which she sat thoughtfully, with her eyes fixed upon the ground, said :

" Your hopes are bold, but the gods are great. Come to me to-morrow."

The next day Kualu was made joyful by the words of Waahia. She told him that she had been given a view of something of his future, and that the auguries promised so much that she could not discourage even the most audacious of his aspirations ; but that coming events affecting his life were so mingled with wars, and strange faces of a race she had never seen except in dreams, that she could then advise no definite course of action.

With these vague words of encouragement Kualu returned to the palace, and authoritatively learned, what had for some time been rumored, that preparations were to be speedily made for an invasion of Maui, and possibly of the other islands of the group. Having brought all the districts of Hawaii under his control, Kalaunui entertained the ambitious design of uniting the several islands of the archipelago under one government. In this grand scheme of conquest and consolidation he was sustained by the leading chiefs of Hawaii, hungering for foreign possessions, and large quotas of canoes and warriors were promised.

A general plan of action having been adopted, a fleet of two thousand canoes of all sizes and an army of twelve thousand warriors were speedily collected. Sacrifices were made at the great temple of Pakaalani; the favor of the gods was invoked, and the auguries were satisfactory. The king was to lead the expedition in person, and the chivalry of the kingdom rallied to his support. His double canoe, nearly forty paces in length, was gorgeous in royal colors and trappings, and more than a hundred others bore at their mast-heads the ensigns of distinguished chiefs. No such warlike display had been seen by the generation witnessing it, and the confidence and enthusiasm of the king and his commanding officers were fully shared by the people.

Leaving the government in the hands of his young son Kuaiwa, with Kaheka, the queen-mother, as principal adviser, Kalaunui ordered the warriors to their canoes, and with his aids and personal attendants repaired to the beach to superintend the departure of the expedition in person. In charge of his high-priest, his newly-decorated war-god had been taken aboard, and the king was about to follow, when Waahia, whose foster-son was one of the leaders in the enterprise, approached the royal *kaulua*. She was clad in a *pau* and short mantle, and her long, white hair fell below her shoulders. Her form was bent, and she carried a staff for support.

At the sight of the venerable figure, familiar to every one in Waipio, the king turned and said:

"I am glad you are here. Encouragement comes from the temple. What says Waahia?"

"Good in the beginning! bad in the end!" was the blunt response of the prophetess.

"I am instructed by your cheering assurances," adroitly returned the king, observing that her words had been overheard. "The true meaning is that it would be bad to abruptly end a good beginning." Saying which, with something of a scowl he hastily stepped into his *kaulua* and gave the signal for departure.

Without replying, Waahia, fully believing that disaster would overtake the expedition in the end, and anxious to be near Kualu when it came, entered one of the many canoes set apart for the women and other camp-followers of the invading army, and with the fleet set sail for Maui.

II.

While the Hawaiian army, cheered by chants of battle and beating of war-drums, is buffeting the waves on its way to Maui, let us glance again at the *moi* of that island and the political condition of his possessions. While Kamaluohua was the nominal sovereign of the island, the extreme eastern portion of it continued to be governed by independent chiefs. The principal chief of the windward side was Wakalana, whose residence was at Wailuku. He was a cousin of the *moi*, and their relations were exceedingly friendly.

Two years before a remarkable event had occurred at Wailuku. It was the second appearance in the group of a vessel bearing people of a strange race, described by tradition as "white, with bright, shining eyes." Mention is made of other white people who were brought to the islands on one or more occasions by the argonauts of earlier generations, notably by Paumakua, of Oahu, who near the close of the eleventh century returned from one of his exploring voyages with three white persons of an unknown race; but this was the second time that a vessel of a people other than Polynesian had been seen in Hawaiian waters. The first made a landing near Makapu Point, on the island of Oahu, more than a hundred years before. Tradition has preserved the name of the vessel (*Ulupana*) and of the captain (*Mololano*) and his wife (*Malaea*); but as it is not mentioned that they remained in the country, it is probable that they soon re-embarked.

The second arrival is more distinctly marked by tradition. It was a Japanese vessel that had been dismantled by a typhoon, driven toward the North American coast until it encountered the northwest trade-winds, and then helplessly blown southward to the coast of Maui. It was late in the afternoon that word had been brought to Wakalana that a strange vessel was approaching the coast. As it was high out of water and drifting broadside before the wind, it appeared to be of great size, and little disposition was shown by the people to go out in their canoes to meet the mysterious monster. Wakalana hastened to the beach, and, after watching the vessel intently for some time, saw that it was drifting slowly toward the rocky coast to the westward. Seaman enough to know that certain destruction awaited it in that direction, Wakalana hastily manned a stout canoe and started out to sea in pursuit. The waters were rough and his progress was slow, but he succeeded in reaching the vessel a few minutes after it struck the cliffs and was dashed in pieces. Seizing whatever they could find to assist them in floating, those on board leaped into the sea. It was hazardous to approach the wreck too nearly, but Wakalana succeeded in rescuing from the waves and returning to Wailuku with five persons, but not before he saw the last fragment of the wreck disappear in the abyss of raging waters.

There is nothing in the names preserved, either of the vessel or its rescued passengers, to indicate their nationality. The name of the vessel is given as *Mamala*, which in the Hawaiian might mean a wreck or fragment. The name of the captain was Kaluiki-a-Manu ; the four others were called Neleike, Malaea, Haakoa and Hika—all names of Hawaiian construction. Two of them—Neleike and Malaea—were women, the former being the sister of the captain.

They landed almost without clothing, and the only novelties upon their persons were the rings and bracelets of the women, and a sword in the belt of the captain, with which he had thoughtlessly leaped into the sea from the sinking vessel. They were half-famished and weak, and by gestures expressed their gratitude to Wakalana for his gallantry in rescuing them, and asked for food and water. Both were provided in abundance, and two houses were set apart for their occupation. They attracted great attention, and people came from all parts of the island to see the white strangers. It was noted with astonishment by the natives that these men and, women ate from the same vessels, and that nothing was especially *tabu* to either sex ; but Wakalana explained that their gods doubtless permitted such freedom, and they should therefore not be rebuked for their apparent disregard of Hawaiian custom.

The comfort of the strangers was made the especial care of Wakalana, and they soon became not only reconciled but apparently content with their situation.   But the kindness of the chief, however commendable, was not altogether unselfish.   He was charmed with the bright eyes and fair face of Neleike, the sister of the captain.   He found a pleasure that was new to him in teaching her to speak his language, and almost the first use she made of *oia* was to say " yes " with it when he asked her to become his wife.   Her marriage was followed by that of Malaea to a native chief, and of her brother and his two male companions to native women of good family.   And here, as well as anywhere, it may be mentioned that, through her son Alooia, Neleike became the progenitor of a family which for generations showed the marks of her blood, and that the descendants of the others were plentiful thereafter, not only on Maui but in the neighborhood of Waimalo, on the island of Oahu.

The object of the rescued Japanese which attracted most attention was the sword accidentally preserved by the captain. No such terrible knife had ever before been seen or dreamed of by the natives.   They had *pahoas*, or daggers of wood or ivory, and knives of sharply broken flint and sharks' teeth ; they had stone adzes, axes, hatchets and hammers, with which they could fell trees, hollow canoes from tree-trunks, build houses, manufacture implements of war and industry, and hew stone of softer composition ; they had spears and javelins with points of seasoned wood hard enough to splinter a bone ; but iron and other metals had for ages been practically unknown to their race, and the long, sharp sword of the captain, harder than bone or seasoned wood, and from its polished surface throwing defiantly back the bright rays of the sun, engaged their ceaseless wonder and admiration.   As an ornament they regarded it with longing, and when they learned that it was a weapon of war they felt that the arm that wielded it in battle must be unconquerable.

The captain did not see fit to disabuse the minds of the superstitious natives in their disposition to attribute a power of almost unlimited slaughter to the simple weapon. On the contrary, he rarely exhibited it except to distinguished chiefs, and in a few months it began to be mentioned as a sacred gift of the gods and pledge of victory to him who possessed it. Nor was the knowledge of the existence of a talisman so wonderful long confined to the windward side of Maui. The fame of the terrible weapon spread from Hana to Kaanapali, and thence to the other islands of the group ; and if but few of the many who came to learn the truth of the report were favored with a view of the sword, all saw, at least, the strange people who were pointed out as the bearers of it from an unknown land, and the story of its powers was readily accepted. But he who possessed it did not come as a conqueror, and, as he showed no disposition to use it offensively, the weapon ceased to be regarded with alarm.

And now we will return to Kalaunui and his army of conquest, last seen on their way to Maui in a fleet of two thousand canoes. Sailing to the western division of the island, which was reached in two days, Kalaunui effected a landing of his army at Lahaina. Kamaluohua, the *moi* of the island, had learned of the projected invasion some days before, and made every preparation possible to meet and repel it. *Lunapais*, or war-messengers, had been despatched to the several district chiefs, and an army of seven or eight thousand warriors of all arms had been hastily collected. Wakalana had gone to the general defence with a force of eight hundred men, including Kaluiki, the Japanese captain, upon whose presence great reliance was placed by the warriors of Wailuku, if not by Wakalana himself.

Unable to land at Lahaina, which was in possession of the enemy, Kamaluohua marched his forces across the mountains, and a sanguinary battle was fought in the neighborhood of the village. But the Mauians, greatly outnumbered, were defeated and driven back to the hills, and their king was taken prisoner. Throughout the battle Kualu was especially conspicuous for his might and courage. Armed with a huge stone axe, everything human seemed to fall before him, and where he led the bravest alone followed, for he sought the very heart of danger.

The conflict was drawing to a close. The *moi*, gallantly fighting, had been taken prisoner, and his decimated battalions were steadily giving way, when Kualu encountered a body of two or three hundred men resolutely defending themselves behind a low stone wall. Several ineffectual attempts to dislodge them had been made, and they were sending forth shouts of victory and defiance. Something had inspired them with unusual courage and confidence. Did Kualu divine what it was? Perhaps he did, for, hastily rallying to his support a force of sturdy warriors, he fought his way over the wall, and a determined hand-to-hand struggle followed. Meantime a flanking party of spearsmen had made a circuit around the wall and were menacing its defenders in the rear. Observing the peril of the situation, and that an effort was being made to cut off their retreat to the hills, the Mauians began to fall back. As they did so Kualu was seen to dash forward and precipitate himself, almost unsupported, upon a score or two of warriors who had apparently rallied to the assistance of some chief in distress. Regardless of danger, he hewed his way through the battling throng until he stood face to face with Kaluiki, the white captain, in whose hand was the shining blade which had so nerved the arms of the warriors of Wailuku. With a blow of his battle-axe he struck the sword from the upraised hand of the strange warrior. As it fell to the earth he placed his foot upon it, and yielded no ground until the tide of battle swept around and past him, forcing to retreat the last to present a hostile front of the army of the captive king of Maui.

Left alone for a moment by the wild pursuit of the flying enemy, Kualu hurriedly stooped and thrust the sword into the earth, pressing it downward until the hilt was covered; then, placing a large rock upon the spot, he left the field, numbering, as he went, his paces to the wall behind which the Mauians had sought protection.

The victory was complete. The *moi* was a prisoner, and such of his army as had not escaped to the hills lay dead on the field. The country was given over to pillage, and at sunset twenty prisoners were slain and sacrificed in a *heiau* near the village. The sacrifices were made to his war-god, and Kalaunui witnessed the solemn ceremonies of the offering.

The night was spent in the wildest revelry by the victorious warriors, in the midst of which Kualu sought his foster-mother, who, with the women and non-combatants of the invading army, was encamped near the canoes on the beach. He hastily recited to her the events of the day, and concluded with the information that he had captured the long, bright knife of the strange chief of Wailuku, and, believing it to be of great value, had hidden it in the earth. At this intelligence the eyes of Waahia flashed with satisfaction.

"You have done well," said the *kaula*, rising to her feet. "I have seen that long knife in my dreams. It will have much to do with your future. But it will be unsafe in your possession. Give it to me. Give it to me at once," she repeated, "for should Kalaunui by any chance learn that it was taken in battle, he will claim it."

"But I am sure no one saw me hide it," replied Kualu.

"You talk like a boy," returned Waahia. "You must be sure of nothing of which there is a possibility of doubt. But no matter. It is not too dark to find the spot to-night. Let us go to it at once."

Excited by her words, Kualu now became no less anxious than the *kaula* that the sword should be placed in her keeping, and in an indirect way, to avoid observation, they repaired to the battle-field. Their only light was that of the stars, and after reaching the wall it was some time before Kualu was able to identify the exact place to which he had extended the line of his hasty measurement. The ground was strewn with the naked bodies of the slain, and occasional groans came from a few whose struggles with death were not quite over. But no emotion, either of dread or pity, disturbed the visitors.

Satisfied at length that he had found the desired place in the wall, Kualu took a careful bearing, and then stepped briskly toward the north, closely followed by Waahia. Measuring a hundred paces or more, he suddenly stopped, and with alarm discovered what seemed to be the form of a man crouching beside the rock marking the spot where the sword had been buried. Grasping his *pahoa*—the only weapon he had brought with him— Kualu sprang forward and placed his hand upon the object. It was cold and motionless; and the young warrior smiled as the thought came to him that some one of the many who had fallen under his axe that day had possibly crawled to the spot to guard his treasure in death. He lifted the body aside, removed the stone, and the next moment pulled from the earth and handed to Waahia the iron blade. She grasped it eagerly, and, with a hasty glance at its bright blade glistening in the starlight, wrapped it securely in a piece of *kapa* and placed it under her mantle.

Without attracting especial notice they returned to the beach. When importuned by Kualu to tell him something definite of his future, Waahia revealed to him much that would happen ; but all had not yet been given to her, and she admonished him to keep his lips closed and patiently await the development of the will of the gods. " I can see victories to come," said the *kaula,* " but in the end defeat and disaster."

" But if disaster is to come to us in the end," suggested Kualu, " why should it not mean defeat and death to me ? "

" I can give no reason why it should not ; but the gods seldom explain their acts to mortals, and I am content in seeing your star shining above the ruin of Kalaunui."

So spoke the *kaula,* and, cheered by her words, Kualu sought his tent of mats, and on a hard couch of *kapa* dreamed of a long, bright knife, and of battles in which he hewed down armies with it.

Taking his royal captive with him, the second day after the battle Kalaunui set sail with his army for the island of Molokai, of which Kahokuohua was the *alii-nui,* or governing chief. No force adequate to cope with the invading army could be rallied ; but the chivalrous descendant of the ancient kings of Hawaii was not a ruler to allow his subjects to be plundered without resist. ance, and, hastily gathering an army of four or five thousand warriors, he gave the invaders battle at Kalaupapa. But he was defeated and taken prisoner, and after ravaging the country for miles around, and destroying every captured canoe of which he could make no use, Kalaunui sailed for the conquest of Oahu with the two royal captives in his train.

Waahia still accompanied the expedition. But the iron knife was not with her. The king had from some source learned that its glitter had been seen on the battle-field at Lahaina, and she had hidden it in a cleft of the black rocks of the *pali* encircling Kalaupapa.

As already stated, Oahu was at that time governed by a number of practically independent chiefs. The most powerful of these, and possibly recognized *alii-nui* of the island, was Huapouleilei, chief of the Ewa and Waianae districts, to which division Kalaunui directed his fleet. Landing his forces at

Waianae, a sanguinary battle was fought near that place, resulting in the defeat of the Oahuans and the capture of Huapouleilei.

Elated with his successes, and deeming himself invincible,
Kalaunui next prepared for a descent upon Kauai and the conquest of the entire group. But his plans for so formidable an
undertaking were faulty. He took no steps to consolidate his
conquests or maintain possession of the lands subdued by his
arms. He left behind him no friend or stronghold on the conquered islands, blindly trusting, no doubt, that in the persons of
his royal prisoners he retained, for the time being, a sufficiently
firm hold upon their lands and subjects.

Before embarking for Kauai elaborate sacrifices were offered,
and every device known to the priesthood was exhausted to
secure a continuance of the favor of the gods. The *moi* of that
island was Kukona, the fourth in descent from the great Laa-
mai-kahiki. Kalaunui recognized that the defensive resources of
Kauai were not to be despised, but he as greatly underrated the
military abilities of Kukona as he overrated his own, and therefore did not doubt the result.

Waahia saw disaster approaching, but knew that Kalaunui
would not listen to her voice of warning, and therefore remained
silent when the *kilos*, anxious to please the king, shaped their
inauspicious auguries into promises of victory. Her greatest
solicitude was for Kualu. He had been entrusted with an important command, and could find no honorable pretext for
declining to accept the hazard of the final struggle on Kauai.
Waahia, therefore, did not advise him to remain, for she had seen
his star shining above the clouds of defeat. She had sought frequent and earnest counsel of the mysterious intelligences of the
earth and air. She had seen their answers in the smoke of burning incense, and within the circle of blood at midnight, when the
moon was dark, had heard their whispers. Hence it was with
confidence that she said to Kualu, on the evening before the departure of the fleet for Kauai:

"Yes, you must go. I can be of no service to you where the
air will be filled with spears and the canoes will be painted red
with blood. I will return to Hawaii. You will be defeated.
Kukona is a brave and skilful warrior, and the army of Kalaunui
will be rent in pieces and thrown into the sea. The slaughter

will be great, but circumstances will open a way and you will escape."

"And should I escape, where will I find you?" inquired Kualu.

"Among the owls in the old hut in Waipio," replied the *kaula.*

"And the long knife?"

"The long knife is where I alone can find it," answered Waahia. "Leave the secret to me; it will be of service to us yet."

Early next morning the army of Kalaunui set sail for Kauai, and with it, as prisoners, the *mois* of Maui and Molokai and the *alii-nui* of Oahu. At the same time Waahia embarked for Hawaii, taking with her the war-god of the king. Traditions differ concerning the circumstances under which the god was delivered to the prophetess. One asserts that she refused to hold her peace or leave the expedition without it; another that the king, annoyed by her ill-omened words and presence, purchased her departure with it; and a third that it was given to her in deference to her declaration that, if taken to Kauai, it would not return except at the head of a conquering army that would make a tributary kingdom of Hawaii. Certain it is, however, that Waahia returned to Hawaii from Oahu with the war-god of the king. It was the sacred *Akuapaao,* or war-god of Paao, and was held in great reverence by the priesthood. Borne over the waters by unseen forces, the canoe of Waahia was stranded on the beach at Koholalele, on the island of Hawaii. Not far off was the old *heiau* of Manini, and thither the god was conveyed, and placed in the custody of the high-priest of the temple, with the injunction that it was never to be removed from the inner court, or sanctuary, unless the kingdom was in peril. Six generations after it was taken from the *heiau* by the giant Maukaleoleo, and carried at the head of the victorious army of Umi, as mentioned in the legend of "Umi, the Peasant Prince of Hawaii."

Five hundred canoes had been added to the fleet of Kalaunui, and the imposing squadron seemed to stretch half across the wide channel separating the two islands. A landing was made at Koloa, and the entire army disembarked without opposition. The district seemed to be deserted, and not a hostile spear was visible. And so continued the peaceful aspect until daylight the next morning, when Kukona, supported by every prominent chief of

Kauai, suddenly precipitated upon the invaders from the surrounding hills an army of ten thousand warriors. Nor this alone. Along the westward coast was seen approaching a fleet of nearly a thousand war-canoes, with the manifest design of capturing or destroying the canoes of the Hawaiians and cutting off their retreat by sea. Hastily forming his lines to meet the avalanche from the hills, Kalaunui despatched Kualu to the beach with a force of three thousand warriors to protect the canoes.

The attacks by land and sea were almost simultaneous, and the battle was one of the most stubborn and sanguinary ever fought in the group. As predicted by Waahia, the air was filled with spears and the canoes were painted red with blood. Standing in the water to their hips, Kualu and his warriors met their enemies as they attempted to land, and a struggle of the wildest description followed. Canoes were upset ; men were hauled into them and killed, and out of them and drowned, and for a distance of three or four hundred yards in the surf along the beach raged a desperate conflict, dreadful even to savage eyes. In their fury they fought in, above and under the water, and hundreds fiercely grappled and without a wound sank to their deaths together. Neither would yield, and in the end resistance ceased, and Kualu saw the beach strewn with dead, a thousand tenantless canoes idly playing with the surf, and less than as many hundreds of warriors left as he had led thousands into the fight. He had saved the fleet, but the sacrifice of life had been terrible.

Despatching a messenger to the king, and speedily reorganizing the remnant of his force, Kualu was about to leave the beach for service where he might most be needed, when he discovered, with horror, that the Hawaiian army had been defeated, and in scattered fragments was seeking flight in all directions. Harassed by pursuit, a thousand or more were fighting and struggling to reach the beach. Satisfied that the battle was lost, to facilitate the escape of the fugitives Kualu ordered a large number of canoes to be hastily equipped and launched, and then started back to assist in covering the retreat. But his men refused to follow him. Knowing the danger of delay, all but a few of them leaped into canoes and paddled out to sea. As he could do nothing more, he selected a canoe suitable to the four persons who were to occupy it, and with his three remaining companions passed through the surf and headed for Oahu.

Kualu did not escape a moment too soon. He had scarcely stemmed the surf before the fugitives, abandoning all defence, made a precipitate dash for the canoes, closely followed by their pursuers. In their haste they shoved out in canoes some of which were overburdened and others but half-manned. A number of the former foundered in the surf, and such of the latter as succeeded in passing the breakers were overtaken by the canoes sent in pursuit. Nor did but few escape of the two or three hundred who preceded Kualu in his flight. Some of them embarked in double canoes which they were unable to manage, and others were either without sails or short of paddles. The result was that less than a hundred of the fugitives escaped capture, and of that number probably not more than twenty or thirty succeeded in reaching the other islands of the group, for the sea was rough and but few of them were skilled in navigation. Among these were Kualu and his companions.

Almost from the beginning the sudden attack of Kukona from the hills had been a slaughter. The withdrawal of three thousand spears for the protection of his canoes had weakened the lines of Kalaunui at an exposed point, and, breaking through them, the Kauaians so vigorously followed up the advantage that no effort could save the Hawaiians from defeat. They fought bravely and with desperation ; but the breaking of their lines had left them without arty definite plan of action, and defeat was inevitable. Kalaunui's courage was conspicuous, but after an hour's hopeless struggle he saw his brave battalions melting to the earth and giving way at all points. Recognizing that the battle was lost, and that what was left of his army would soon be in wild retreat, he attempted to cut his way through to the beach, but was intercepted and taken prisoner. Learning his rank, he was taken by his captors to Kukona, and a few minutes later the royal chiefs of Maui, Molokai and Oahu, with their arms corded behind their backs, appeared on the scene. Deserted by their guards, they had been found in a hut not far from the beach and brought to the victorious *moi*.

It was a historic group, that meeting on the battle-field of Koloa of the five principal sovereigns of the archipelago. Had Kukona been ambitious the means were at his command to become the supreme head of the island group ; but he thought only of the future peace of Kauai, and promptly dismissed from his mind all dreams of broader fields of empire, well knowing that, were he able to seize the mastery of the group, he could not hope to long maintain it.

Not a word of jeering or of triumph passed between Kalaunui and the captive chiefs as they stood before Kukona, for the *aha alii* of the period—the chiefs of accepted rank—commanded the respect, not only of the untitled, but of each other, even in bondage and in death. Kukona had met the *alii-nui* of Oahu in his own dominions some years before, and recognized him at once, but the kings of Maui and Molokai were strangers to him. Being informed of their rank and the circumstances of their captivity, he ordered them to be liberated at once, and with his own hands removed the cords from the arms of his royal friend from Oahu.

The rescued princes were at once returned with befitting escorts to their own possessions, but Kalaunui was retained as a prisoner of war. But few of the invading army escaped. The victory was celebrated with elaborate sacrifices and general rejoicing throughout the island. The captured arms and canoes were divided among the assisting chiefs, and peace reigned again on Kauai.

Kukona had secured the lasting friendship of the chiefs of Oahu, Maui and Molokai, and therefore did not fear the retaliation of Hawaii. But, as a guarantee of peace, he kept Kalaunui a prisoner, rightly surmising that, if the ruling powers of Hawaii really valued the life of the captive king, they would not imperil it by attempting his release by force, and if they did not greatly value it he would be left to his fate or the chances of peaceful negotiation.

III.

Escaping from Koloa, Kualu and his companions made sail for Hawaii, stopping for supplies at such intermediate points as they deemed safe on the coasts of Oahu, Molokai and Maui, and on the evening of the sixth day arrived at Waipio. They were the first to bring to Hawaii the news of the defeat of Kalaunui on Kauai, and when the people learned that the army had been destroyed the land was filled with wailing.

Appearing at once before Kaheka and her son, Kualu recited to them the story of the dreadful battle, but was unable to tell them definitely of the fate of Kalaunui.   The grief of the queen was great, and found strange and unreasonable expression in charging Kualu with cowardice and ordering him from the palace.   In vain he protested against the ungenerous treatment. She had never liked him, especially since discovering that he had secured something more than the good-will of Kapapa, and it seemed monstrous to her that he should have survived Kalaunui and the scores of gallant chiefs who fell with him.   She cruelly intimated that it was more than probable that, with the force sent to protect the fleet, he had embarked in the canoes without striking a blow, thus treacherously depriving the defeated army of its sole means of escape.

Had these monstrous charges been made by a man Kualu would have answered them with blows ; but, as they were the foolish and inconsiderate ravings of a woman, without venturing further reply he took his leave, and with a heart filled with stifled rage and anguish strode from the palace.

Proceeding up the valley, Kualu entered the hut of Waahia. He found the *kaula* alone, as usual.   She knew he was coming, but was none the less rejoiced to meet him.   With a word or two of greeting he sat down in silence.   The cruel words of Kaheka still stuck like thorns in his throat.   Waahia regarded him intently for a time, and then said :

"I know it all.   Kalaunui's army has been destroyed.   You escaped in a canoe with three others."

"And Kalaunui?" questioned Kualu, not a little amazed at the correctness of her information.

"Is a prisoner," replied the *kaula*.

"Thank the gods for that !" exclaimed the chief vehemently. "He must be liberated, for he can tell her that in escaping I acted neither with cowardice nor treachery ! "

"Tell whom ?" inquired the *kaula*.

"Kaheka," answered Kualu.   "She charges me with coward-ice and desertion."

"Then Kaheka accuses you of what I know to be false ! " said Waahia.

"Yes," returned the chief ; "but the witnesses to my fidelity are few and humble, and the words of the king can alone relieve me in the eyes of the *aha alii* of the disgrace with which the charges of Kaheka will cover me."

" True," replied the *kaula*, encouragingly ; " but the disgrace will not be lasting, for the king will return to do you justice."

" When will he return ? " eagerly inquired the chief.

" I cannot tell," answered Waahia ; " but I know that his rule is not yet at an end in Hawaii, and you must be patient."

And Kualu promised to be patient, and for a few days bore the neglect and frowns of his former friends, and the sneers and covert insults of his enemies. But when the heartless accusations of Kaheka, passing from tongue to tongue with the news of the dreadful slaughter, became generally known, and almost as generally believed, notwithstanding the statements of his three companions to the contrary, Kualu's indignation could no longer be restrained, and he challenged to combat and slew on the spot a chief who, in the presence of a party of friends, repeated the charges to his face. Great excitement followed, and in his desperation and wrath Kualu invited the friends of his fallen defamer, one and all, to test his courage then or thereafter.

As the life of Kualu was now in constant and undoubted peril, Waahia advised him to leave Hawaii for a time, and together they set sail for Molokai, and took up their residence at Kalaupapa. But before leaving Waipio the *kaula* called upon the high-priest, by whom she was held in great respect, and told him where she might be found on Molokai, should her services be required.

" And they will be required," said Waahia, significantly. " Kalaunui is not dead, and when you shall have failed in all your efforts to liberate him, tell Kaheka to think better of Kualu and send for me."

" How know you that Kalaunui still lives ? " inquired the priest.

"Should the high-priest of Pakaalani ask me that question ? " replied Waahia. " Where are his seers ? Where are the *kilos* of the temple, who in the heavens saw victory for Kalaunui where I beheld defeat ? Have they not been consulted ? "

" All do not see with the eyes of Waahia," returned the priest, evasively.

Flattered by this recognition of her superiority, the *kaula* said, as she turned to depart : " You will know more to-morrow ! " And an hour after, accompanied by Kualu, she left Waipio for Molokai.

The priest was not deceived by Waahia, for the day after

authentic intelligence was received from Maui to the effect that Kalaunui's campaign had been a failure in Kauai, and the king was a prisoner in the hands of Kukona. The leading chiefs were called together in council, and several projects for the liberation of the king were advanced and discussed. Kaheka was in favor of raising a powerful army at once, and bringing her royal husband back by force ; but when it was considered by cooler heads that Kukona was undoubtedly well prepared for war, and had secured the friendship, and in an emergency could command the support, of the chiefs of Maui, Oahu and Molokai, the suggestion was dismissed as dangerous and impracticable.

Under the circumstances it was finally resolved to attempt the liberation of Kalaunui through negotiation ; and to this end messengers were despatched to Kauai with offers of a large number of canoes, spears and other war materials in exchange for the royal prisoner. But the surrender of Kalaunui's fleet, and the capture of thousands of spears and other arms, had given Kukona a great abundance of both, and he declined the offer.

Failing in this, after a lapse of some months messengers were again sent to Kukona with a proffer of twenty full-sized *mamos,* or royal feather cloaks, a canoe-load of ivory and whalebone, and a thousand stone *lipis,* or axes, of a superior kind peculiar to Hawaii. The messengers were courteously received and listened to, but the offer was not accepted.

War was again urged by Kaheka, but the chiefs refused to embark in an undertaking so hazardous, and without their support she could do nothing. And so for more than two years Kalaunui remained in captivity, when a third attempt to ransom him was made. Kaheka despatched to Kauai two ambassadors of high rank, offering her daughter Kapapa in marriage either to Kukona or his son, Manokalanipo, and promising perpetual peace between the islands. This offer was also declined, and Kukona refused to name to the ambassadors the terms upon which he would treat for the liberation of their king.

It now became a question either of war or the abandonment of Kalaunui to his fate. In this dilemma the priests and *kaulas* were consulted, but their predictions were vague and their counsels unsatisfactory. Remembering the words of Waahia, the high-priest sought the presence of Kaheka, and advised her to send for the old prophetess, who was living with her foster-son at

Kalaupapa. This, after some persuasion, she consented to do, and, despatching a chief of high rank to Molokai, with the admission that she had accused Kualu unjustly, the *kaula* was induced to return with the messenger to Waipio. But Kualu did not accompany her. She was suspicious of Kaheka, and advised him to remain at Kalaupapa.

Arriving at Waipio, the *kaula*, feeling that the game was now in her own hands, informed the high-priest that she would communicate with the leading chiefs of the kingdom convened in council. The chiefs were accordingly assembled, and Waahia appeared before them. Kaheka was present, as the *kaula* desired.

With a staff in her hand, capped with the head of an owl, and her long, white hair falling to her waist, there was something weird and awe-inspiring in the appearance of the venerable prophetess as she entered the council-room and bowed low before Kaheka and the assembled chiefs. It was not her privilege to break the silence without permission, and when it had been formally accorded she raised her eyes, and, without especially addressing any one, said :

" Why have I been sent for ? "

No one could answer, not even Kaheka.

At length an old chief, after conferring with those around him, replied :

" You have been sent for on the word of the high-priest, and with the hope that you might be able to point out a way for the return of Kalaunui to Hawaii. Can you do so ? "

" I can speak of no way," answered the *kaula*.

" Then you can do nothing ? " returned the chief.

" My words were that I could speak of no way, nor can I," said the *kaula ;* " yet, keeping my own counsel, I might possibly be able to accomplish what you all desire."

" And will you undertake to do so ? " inquired Kaheka.

" Yes, on one condition," was the prompt reply.

" Well, what do you ask for attempting to save the life of your king ? " returned the queen, in a tone of rebuke.

Waahia did not like the spirit of the inquiry, and a scowl darkened her wrinkled face as she replied :

"I might ask that, if the gods willed that I should fail, Kaheka would not charge me with treachery ! "

This reference to the treatment of Kualu created a feeling of uneasiness among the chiefs ; but, without inviting remark or explanation, the *kaula* continued :

"What I require is a pledge from every chief here that, should I succeed in liberating Kalaunui, the terms of the release, whatever they may be, will be complied with."

The chiefs hesitated, as it was not impossible that the sovereignty of the island might be offered to Kukona by the prophetess, and they could not pledge themselves to a sacrifice involving their own ruin. Waahia relieved their apprehensions, however, by assuring them that the pledge would not be considered binding if the terms affected either the sovereignty of the island or the lives, possessions or prerogatives of its chiefs. With this assurance the members of the council, after briefly discussing the possibilities of the obligation, consented to accept it. Thereupon the pledge was carefully repeated thrice by the chiefs, and each in turn solemnly invoked upon himself, should he fail to keep and observe it in its fulness, the wrath of *Hikapoloa*, the divine trinity, and the swift and especial vengeance of *Kuahana*, the slayer of men.

"Are you satisfied now ?" inquired Kaheka.

"I am satisfied," replied the *kaula*.

"Do you require assistance ?" This inquiry came from more than one.

"Only of the gods !" was the impressive answer of Waahia, as she left the council and slowly wended her way up the valley.

All night long strange lights flashed at intervals through the weather-rent openings in the *kaula's* hut. Shadowy forms were seen to move noiselessly around it ; owls came and went as the lights vanished and reappeared ; and, just as the sun began to paint the east, Waahia proceeded to the beach, and with a single sturdy assistant of supernatural aspect embarked in a canoe which seemed to be equipped and provisioned for a long voyage. This was the ghostly narration of two or three of the nearest neighbors of the prophetess, and the truth of the story was not doubted, even when it reached the palace. Doubtless the plain facts were that Waahia spent the most of the night in preparing for the voyage, and set sail early in the morning with an assistant known to be trustworthy and familiar with the sea.

Waahia proceeded very leisurely to Kauai. The annual feast of *Lono* was approaching, and as she desired to arrive there during the festival, which would not be for some days, she spent the intervening time in visiting many sacred spots and noted temples on Maui, Oahu, Molokai and Lanai. Perhaps to commune with the honored dead, she made a pilgrimage to the sacred valley of Iao, on the island of Maui, where were buried many of the distinguished kings and chiefs of the group. She stopped at Kalaupapa, on Molokai, to confer with Kualu, and while there paid a visit to the home, near Kaluakoi, of *Laamaomao*, the wind-god, who came from the south with Moikeha more than a century before ; and in the same valley visited the dreaded spot where, in the reign of Kamauaua, the father of Kaupeepee, the abductor of Hina, near the close of the eleventh century, sprang up in a night the poisoned grove of *Kalaipahoa*, or, according to another tradition, where that goddess, belonging to a family of southern deities, visited the group with two of her sisters, and entered and poisoned a small grove of trees of natural growth.

From one of these poisonous trees the famous idol of *Kalaipahoa* was made. So poisonous was the wood that many died in cutting down the tree and carving the image, for all perished whose flesh was touched by the chips ; but the workmen finally covered their bodies with *kapa*, including masks for their faces and wraps for their hands, and thus succeeded in completing the dangerous task without farther loss of life. But a single image was made. It remained with the ruling family of Molokai until the subjugation of the group by Kamehameha I., when it came into his possession, and at his death, in 1819, was divided among a few of the principal chiefs. Two fragments of the image, it is said, are still preserved, but they are carefully guarded and never exhibited to eyes sceptical or profane. Long before Waahia visited the spot the last vestige of the grove had disappeared, but for many acres around where the terrible trees once stood the earth was black and bare. Within the dreaded area no living thing was seen, and birds fell dead in flying over it. But the *kaula* entered it and returned unharmed, to the amazement of more than one witness.

Waahia next visited the *heiau* of Kaumolu, which was then a *puhonua*, or place of refuge, and in another temple near the coast offered sacrifices to the shark-god *Mooalii*. By reputation she was generally known to the priesthood of the group, and was nowhere regarded as an intruder in places sacred to worship.

Stopping at Ewa, on the island of Oahu, she saw for the first time the hallowed enclosure of Kukaniloko, the creation of Nanakaoko, son of Nanamaoa, the earliest arrival from the south of the migratory stream of the eleventh century. Chiefs born there were endowed with especial prerogatives and distinctions, and the beating of a sacred drum called *hawea* gave notice without of the birth of a *tabu* chief.

IV.

The winter solstice, which marked the end of the Hawaiian year, was at hand, to be followed by the usual five days' feast of *Lono*, and Waahia so timed her voyage as to arrive on Kauai the day before the festival began. She quietly landed at Koloa, and as far as possible avoided observation by taking up her residence in a small hut secured by her companion well back in the neighboring hills.

These annual festivals of *Lono* were seasons of universal merriment and rejoicing. The god was crowned and ornamented with *leis* of flowers and feathers, and unstinted offerings of pigs, fowls and fruits were laid upon the altars of the temples consecrated to his worship. Chiefs and people alike gave themselves unreservedly over to feasting, dancing, singing and the indulgence of almost every appetite and caprice, and the Saturnalias of the old Romans gave to the masses scarcely more license than the festivals of *Lono*. Every instrument of music known to the people—and they possessed but four or five of the simplest kinds—was brought into requisition, and for five days there was almost an uninterrupted tumult of revelry. *Lakakane*, the *hula* god, was decorated and brought out, and every variety of the dance was given—some of them to the time of vocal recitations and others to the noisier accompaniment of pipes, drums and rattling calabashes. In the midst of these enjoyments long-bearded bards appeared before the king and distinguished chiefs, and while some of them recited wild historic tales of the past, others chanted the *mele-inoas* and sang of the personal exploits of their titled listeners. *Awa* and other intoxicating drinks were freely indulged in by those who craved them, and the festivals were usually followed by a week or more of general languor and worthlessness.

It was the third day of the festival at Koloa. The gates of the enclosure had been thrown open, and thousands of people thronged around the royal mansion in a grove near which large quantities of refreshments were spread on the ground in huge wooden trays and calabashes. The feast was free to all, and Kukona lounged on a pile of *kapa* in the deep shade of the trees in front of the palace, happy in witnessing the enjoyment of his subjects. Around him were standing a number of chiefs of high rank. A *kahili* of bright feathers was occasionally and unobtrusively waved above his head by the *paakahili*, and the *iwikuamoo, aipuu-puu* and other of his personal attendants, all of the lesser nobility, stood in readiness to respond to his slightest wishes. A guard of inferior chiefs kept the crowd from pressing too closely the distinguished group, but from time to time, as permission was granted, select bands of dancers and musicians and chanters of ability were allowed to approach and entertain the royal party with specimens of their skill and erudition.

A company of dancers had just retired, when Waahia, with a staff in her hand, and wearing a short mantle, indicating that she claimed privileges of dress which were not accorded to women generally, asked permission to be admitted to the presence of the king. Her strange appearance excited the curiosity of Kukona, and she was allowed to approach. Kneeling and touching her forehead to the ground, she rose and asked if it was the pleasure of the king to hear her. As these ceremonies, due to supreme authority, were usually waived on such occasions, it was surmised that the woman must be a stranger in Kauai. She was told to speak. A *moooelo*, or historic chant, was expected; but in a full, sharp voice she chanted these words :

> "O the long knife of the stranger,
> Of the stranger from other lands,
> Of the stranger with sparkling eyes,
> Of the stranger with a white face !
> O long knife of *Lono*, the gift of *Lono ;*
> It flashes like fire in the sun ;
> Its edge is sharper than stone,
> Sharper than the hard stone of Hualalai ;
> The spear touches it and breaks,
> The strong warrior sees it and dies !
> Where is the long knife of the stranger ?
> Where is the sacred gift of *Lono ?*

It came to Wailuku and is lost,
It was seen at Lahaina and cannot be found.
He is more than a chief who finds it,
He is a chief of chiefs who possesses it.
Maui cannot spoil his fields,
Hawaii cannot break his nets ;
His canoes are safe from Kauai ;
The chiefs of Oahu will not oppose him,
The chiefs of Molokai will bend at his feet.
O long knife of the stranger,
O bright knife of *Lono !*
Who has seen it ? Who has found it ?
Has it been hidden away in the earth ?
Has the great sea swallowed it ?
Does the *kilo* see it among the stars ?
Can the *kaula* find it in the bowels of the black hog ?
Will a voice from the *anu* answer ?
Will the priests of *Lono* speak ?
The *kilo* is silent, the *kaula* is dumb.
O long knife of the stranger,
O bright knife of *Lono,*
It is lost, it is lost, it is lost !"

At the conclusion of the chant, which was listened to with attention, the *kaula* bowed and disappeared in the crowd. Kukona had heard of the long knife, and Waahia's description of its powers interested him greatly. He despatched a messenger to the high-priest, ordering that the diviners at once be put to the task of discovering the hiding-place of the sacred weapon.

On the following afternoon Waahia appeared before the king and his chiefs, and with the same ceremonies repeated her chant of the day before. The high-priest was summoned, and informed the king that his diviners had as yet discovered no trace of the long knife.

The third day Waahia appeared and repeated her chant before the king, and silently withdrew, as before. Again the high-priest was summoned, but was able to offer no assurance that the long knife would be found by the *kahunas.* They had resorted to every means of inspiration and magic known to them, but could discover no clue to the mystery.

"Who is this woman who for three successive days has told us of the lost knife ? " inquired Kukona, addressing the chiefs surrounding him.

No one seemed to be able to answer. Finally the master of ceremonies stepped forward and replied :

"The woman, I think, is Waahia, the noted prophetess of Hawaii. I saw her fifteen years ago in Waipio, and am quite sure that I remember her face."

The name, if not the face, of the distinguished seeress was known to the king and many others present, and the high-priest, anxious to explain the failure of his magicians, bowed and said :

"The master of ceremonies has doubtless spoken truly. The woman must be Waahia. Her powers are great, and a secret in her keeping is beyond the reach of the *kaulas.*"

Accepting this explanation of the high-priest, Kukona order-ed the prophetess to be found and respectfully conducted to the royal mansion ; but after a fruitless search of two days it was reported that she had probably left the valley, and therefore could not be found.

Irritated at what seemed to be the inefficiency or neglect of his *kaulas* and chiefs, Kukona was about to attach a death-penalty to further failure when Waahia suddenly entered the royal enclosure and approached the palace. Her appearance was most welcome to the attending chiefs, and she was ushered at once into the presence of the king. So delighted was Kukona at the unexpected visit that he rose unconsciously to his feet and greeted the prophetess. This breach of courtly form amazed the attendants of the king, and suggested to them that the strange visitor must be of supreme rank ; but before any ex-planation could be gathered they were ordered to retire, even to the *paakahili*, and Kukona was left alone with the *kaula*.

The king motioned his visitor to a lounge of *kapa*, for she seemed to be old and feeble, and he had a favor to ask. Seating herself, as requested, the king approached, and, in a voice that could not well be overheard, said :

"Are you Waahia, the prophetess of Hawaii ? "

"I am Waahia," answered the *kaula*.

"You have chanted of the long knife of the stranger, of the bright knife of *Lono*, of the lost knife of Wailuku," resumed Ku-kona. "Our diviners can give me no information concerning it."

Waahia smiled significantly, but made no reply, and the king continued :

"They say you have *tabued* the secret, and others, therefore, cannot share it. Is it so?"

"Perhaps," was the brief reply.

"Then you can find the sacred knife?" eagerly suggested Kukona.

"I can find it," was the *kaula's* emphatic answer.

"Then find and bring it to Kukona, and for the service claim what you will," was the prompt proposal of the king.

With the way thus broadly opened, Waahia announced that the price of the knife must be the liberation of Kalaunui, and was astonished at the promptness with which the terms were accepted. It was manifest to Waahia that he either placed a very high value upon the talisman, or had kept his royal prisoner about as long as he cared to detain him or the peace of his kingdom required. In either event his unhesitating acceptance of the main consideration warranted Waahia in at once naming one or two other conditions, which were just as promptly agreed to by the king. One of these conditions was that Kalaunui should agree, as the only consideration for his release to be known to him, that his daughter Kapapa should be given in marriage to the chief Kualu, not only as a fitting union, but as a measure of atonement for the unjust and disgraceful charges made against that worthy young chief by Kaheka, and that Kukona and Kalaunui should mutually pledge themselves to the fulfilment of the compact. The other condition was that, on the delivery of the knife to Kukona, he was to release the captive king at once, and return him to Hawaii in company with three high chiefs of Kauai, who were to remain in Waipio until after the consummation of the marriage of Kapapa and Kualu.

Kalaunui was communicated with. For nearly three years he had been confined and closely but respectfully guarded within a square of high stone walls enclosing a single hut. Utterly unable to account for Kukona's interest in Kualu, he nevertheless accepted the terms submitted to him for his release, and Waahia started at once for Kalaupapa, promising to be back within six days. For the voyage she accepted a canoe larger and more commodious than her own, and the services of five additional rowers.

Arriving at Kalaupapa on the morning of the third day from Koloa, Waahia startled Kualu by informing him that Kalaunui was about to be released, and that in twelve days he must return without further notice to Waipio, where he would be relieved of all disgrace by the king, and become the husband of Kapapa. Coming from Waahia, he believed the words as if they had been flashed from the heavens, and asked for no confirmation as the *kaula* abruptly left him and proceeded alone toward the hills.

A few hours later Waahia re-embarked for Kauai, taking with her, securely wrapped in a number of *kapa* folds, the sword of Kaluiki. She reached Koloa within the time promised, and, proceeding to the palace, delivered to the king, in person and alone, the glittering blade which rumor had clothed with extraordinary sanctity and power.

Kalaunui renewed his pledge to Kukona, and the next morning embarked for Hawaii in a large double canoe, accompanied by three of the leading chiefs of Kauai and their attendants. Stepping into the *kaulua* as it was about to be shoved into the surf, Kalaunui caught sight of Waahia, for the first time for years, as she stood leaning upon her staff near the water. Kualu's part in the agreement with Kukona was explained at once by Waahia's presence in Koloa ; but what was Kualu to Kukona ? and, if nothing, what influences had the *kaula* been able to bring to effect his release upon such conditions? No matter. Kalaunui was too happy in his liberation to quarrel with the means through which it had been secured, and he turned with a look of gratitude toward the prophetess as the canoe shot out into the breakers.

The return of their captive king was joyously celebrated by the people of Hawaii, and a few days after Kapapa became the willing wife of Kualu. The union was distasteful to Kaheka, but she was powerless to prevent it. The agreement was faithfully fulfilled by Kalaunui, and he spent the remainder of his days in peace, leaving the kingdom to his only son, Kuaiwa, between whom and Kualu a lasting friendship was established.

Kualu, with Kapapa, became the head of an influential family, one of his direct descendants having been the wife of Makaoku, a son of Kiha and brother of Liloa, one of the most noted of the kings of Hawaii.

The sword of Kaluiki, the ransom of a king, remained for some generations with the descendants of Kukona ; but what became of it in the end tradition fails to tell.

THE SACRED SPEAR-POINT.

CHARACTERS.

KAKAE and
KAKAALANEO, } joint *mois* of Maui.

KAHEKILI, son of Kakae.

KAULULAAU, son of Kakaalaneo.

WAOLANI, a high-priest of Maui.

KALONA-IKI, king of Oahu.

LAIEA-A-EWA, sister of the queen of Oahu.

KAMAKAUA, a companion of Kaululaau.

KAUHOLANUI-MAHU, king of Hawaii.

NEULA, queen of Hawaii.

NOAKUA, a chief of Kohala, Hawaii.

PELE, goddess of Kilauea.

KEUAKEPO, brother of Pele.

MOOALEO, a gnome-god of Molokai.

PUEOALII, a winged demon of Oahu.

THE SACRED SPEAR-POINT.

THE ADVENTURES OF KAULULAAU, PRINCE OF MAUI.

I.

KAULULAAU was one of the sons of Kakaalaneo, brother of, and joint ruler with, Kakae in the government of Maui. The latter was the legitimate heir to the *moiship*, but, as he was weak-minded, Kakaalaneo ruled jointly with him and was the real sovereign of the little kingdom. The court of the brothers was at Lele (now Lahaina), and was one of the most distinguished in the group.

The mother of Kaululaau was Kanikaniaula, of the family of Kamauaua, king of Molokai, through his son Haili, who was the brother or half-brother of Keoloewa and Kaupeepee. The latter, it will be remembered, was the abductor of the celebrated Hina, of Hawaii, and the family was of the old strain of Maweke.

Kaululaau was probably born somewhere between the years 1390 and 1400. He had a half-sister, whose name was Wao, and a half-brother, Kaihiwalua, who was the father of Luaia, who became the husband of a daughter of Piliwale, *moi* of Oahu, and brother of Lo-Lale. He doubtless had other brothers and sisters, since his father was blessed with two or more wives, but the legends fail to refer to them.

Kahekili, son of Kakae, and who became his successor in the *moiship*, was of near the age of his cousin, Kaululaau, and the two princes grew to manhood together. They were instructed by the same teachers, schooled in the same arts and chiefly accomplishments, and chanted the same genealogical *meles*. Yet in disposition and personal appearance they were widely different.

From his youth Kahekili was staid, sober and thoughtful. Bred to the knowledge that he would succeed his father as *moi* of the island, he began early in life to prepare himself for the proper exercise of supreme authority, and at the age of twenty was noted for his intelligence, dignity and royal bearing. He had been told by a prophet that one of his name would be the last independent king of Maui, and the information rendered him solicitous for his future and drove many a smile from his lips. Yet, with all his austerity and circumspection, he was kind-hearted and affectionate, and his pastimes were such as comported with his dignity. In height he was somewhat below the chiefly medium, and his features were rugged and of a Papuan cast; but all knew that he was royal in heart and thought, and the respect due to him was not withheld.

Kaululaau was unlike his royal cousin in almost every respect. He was noted alike for his intelligence, his manly beauty and his rollicking spirit of mischief and merriment. He did not covet the sceptre. He thought more of a wild debauch, with music, dancing and a calabash of *awa*, than the right to command "downward" or "upward the face"; and since Kahekili was the designated successor of his father, he claimed the right, as a favored and *tabu* subject of the realm, to enjoy himself in such manner as best accorded with his tastes. As he could not make laws, he found a pleasure in breaking them. He was neither wantonly cruel nor malignant, but recklessly wild and mischievous, and neither the reproofs of his father nor the mild persuasions of his cousin were sufficient to restrain him. His bantering reply to the latter was: "When you become king I will act with more propriety. Two *mois* can afford one wild prince."

He had a congenial following of companions and retainers, who assisted him in his schemes of mischief. With feasting and *hula* dancing he would keep the village in an uproar for a dozen consecutive nights. He would send canoes adrift, open the gates of fish-ponds, remove the supports of houses, and paint swine black to deceive the sacrificial priests. He devised an instrument to imitate the death-warning notes of the *alae*, and frightened people by sounding it near their doors; and to others he caused information to be conveyed that they were being prayed to death.

Notwithstanding these misdemeanors, Kaululaau was popular with the people, since the chiefs or members of the royal household were usually the victims of his mischievous freaks. He was encouraged in his disposition to qualify himself for the priesthood, under the instruction of the eminent high-priest and prophet, Waolani, and had made substantial advances in the calling, when he was banished to the island of Lanai by his royal father for an offence which could neither be overlooked nor forgiven.

At that time Lanai was infested with a number of gnomes, monsters and evil spirits, among them the gigantic *moo*, Mooaleo. They ravaged fields, uprooted cocoanut-trees, destroyed the walls of fish-ponds, and otherwise frightened and discomfited the inhabitants of the island. That his residence there might be made endurable, Kaululaau was instructed by the *kaulas* and sorcerers of the court in many charms, spells, prayers and incantations with which to resist the powers of the supernatural monsters. When informed of these exorcising agencies by Kaululaau, his friend, the venerable high-priest, Waolani, told him that they would avail him nothing against the more powerful and malignant of the demons of Lanai.

Disheartened at the declaration, Kaululaau was about to leave the *heiau* to embark for Lanai, when Waolani, after some hesitation, stayed his departure, and, entering the inner temple, soon returned with a small roll of *kapa* in his hand. Slowly uncording and removing many folds of cloth, an ivory spear-point a span in length was finally brought to view. Holding it before the prince, he said :

"Take this. It will serve you in any way you may require. Its powers are greater than those of any god inhabiting the earth. It has been dipped in the waters of *Po*, and many generations ago was left by Lono upon one of his altars for the protection of a temple menaced by a mighty fish-god who found a retreat beneath it in a great cavern connected with the sea. Draw a line with it and nothing can pass the mark. Affix it to a spear and throw it, and it will reach the object, no matter how far distant. Much more will it do, but let what I have said suffice."

The prince eagerly reached to possess the treasure, but the priest withdrew it and continued :

"I give it to you on condition that it pass from you to no other hands than mine, and that if I am no longer living when you return to Maui—as you some day will—you will secretly deposit it with my bones. Swear to this in the name of Lono."

Kaululaau solemnly pronounced the required oath. The priest then handed him the talisman, wrapped in the *kapa* from which it had been taken, and he left the temple, and immediately embarked with a number of his attendants for Lanai.

Reaching Lanai, he established his household on the south side of the island. Learning his name and rank, the people treated him with great respect—for Lanai was then a dependency of Maui—assisted in the construction of the houses necessary for his accommodation, and provided him with fish, *poi*, fruits and potatoes in great abundance. In return for this devotion he set about ridding the island of the supernatural pests with which it had been for years afflicted.

In the legend of "Kelea, the Surf-rider of Maui," will be found some reference to the battles of Kaululaau with the evil spirits and monsters of Lanai. His most stubborn conflict was with the gnome god Mooaleo. He imprisoned the demon within the earth by drawing a line around him with the sacred spear-point, and subsequently released and drove him into the sea.

More than a year was spent by Kaululaau in quieting and expelling from the island the malicious monsters that troubled it, but he succeeded in the end in completely relieving the people from their vexatious visitations. This added immeasurably to his popularity, and the choicest of the products of land and sea were laid at his feet.

His triumph over the demons of Lanai was soon known on the other islands of the group, and when it reached the ears of Kakaalaneo he despatched a messenger to his son, offering his forgiveness and recalling him from exile. The service he had rendered was important, and his royal father was anxious to recognize it by restoring him to favor.

But Kaululaau showed no haste in availing himself of his father's magnanimity. Far from the restraints of the court, he had become attached to the independent life he had found in exile, and could think of no comforts or enjoyments unattainable on Lanai. The women there were as handsome as elsewhere, the bananas were as sweet, the cocoanuts were as large, the *awa* was as stimulating, and the fisheries were as varied and abundant in product. He had congenial companionship, and bands of musicians and dancers at his call. The best of the earth and the love of the people were his, and the *apapani* sang in the grove that shaded his door. What more could he ask, what more expect should he return to Maui? His exile had ceased to be a punishment, and his father's message of recall was scarcely deemed a favor.

However, Kaululaau returned a respectful answer by his father's messenger, thanking Kakaalaneo for his clemency, and announcing that he would return to Maui some time in the near future, after having visited some of the other islands of the group ; and three months later he began to prepare for a trip to Hawaii. He procured a large double canoe, which he painted a royal yellow, and had fabricated a number of cloaks and capes of the feathers of the *oo* and *mamo*. At the prow of his canoe he mounted a carved image of Lono, and at the top of one of the masts a place was reserved for the proud *tabu* standard of an *aha alii*. This done, with a proper retinue he set sail for Hawaii.

II.

On his visit to Hawaii, Kaululaau was accompanied by a number of companions of his own disposition and temperament. Among them was Kamakaua, a young Maui chief, who had followed him into exile and was thoroughly devoted to his interests. He was brave, courtly and intelligent, and in personal appearance somewhat resembled the prince. The crew and most of the attendants of the prince had been selected by Kamakaua, including the chief navigator and astrologer ; and however competent they may have been in their respective stations, it was discovered during the voyage that they were no less efficient as musicians and dancers. Hence there was no lack of amusement as the huge double canoe breasted the waves of Alenuihaha Channel, and on the morning of the third day stood off the village of Waipio, in the district of Hamakua, Hawaii.

At that time Kauholanui-mahu, father of the noted Kiha, was king of Hawaii. His wife was Neula, a chiefess of Maui, who had inherited very considerable possessions in the neighborhood of Honuaula, on that island. As the climate of the locality was salubrious, and the neighboring waters abounded abundantly in fish, the royal couple made frequent and sometimes lengthy visits thither. These visits were usually made without the knowledge of Kakaalaneo, and the unexplained attachment of the Hawaiian king to the comparatively small inheritance of his wife on a neighboring island began to be regarded with suspicion, and had become a theme for speculation and inquiry at the court of Lahaina.

At the time of the visit of Kaululaau to Waipio, Kauholanui

had been absent for some months on Maui, leaving Neula in charge of the government of Hawaii. Attributing the absence of the king to deliberate neglect, Neula had become greatly dissatisfied, and whispers of coming trouble were rife throughout the island. All this was doubtless known to Kaululaau, and, as the royal residence was at Waipio, it was upon the beach below it that he landed with his party and drew up his double canoe.

The presence and state of the strangers were soon heralded to the queen, and she promptly despatched messengers, courteously inviting the prince and his personal retainers to become her guests at the royal *hale*, at the same time giving orders for the accommodation of the humbler of his attendants and followers, as was the hospitable custom of the time.

Accepting the invitation, Kaululaau and four of his chiefly companions were provided with quarters within the palace enclosure, and their food was served from the royal table. In the afternoon Kaululaau was accorded an audience with the queen, during which he presented his friends, including Kamakaua.

The prince whiled away nearly a month at Waipio, and many formal entertainments were given in his honor. Neula was unusually agreeable, and was soon on terms of friendly intimacy both with the prince and Kamakaua. This was exactly what Kaululaau desired, since it enabled him to devise and assist in the execution of a scheme for bringing the king back from Maui and keeping him thereafter within his own kingdom.

Under the instructions of Kaululaau, Kamakaua assumed to be greatly smitten with the charms of the queen. As she was a comely woman, and somewhat vain of her personal appearance, the conquest of the handsome chief gratified her ; but his attentions developed the fact that he had a rival in Noakua, a chief of Kohala. This discovery simplified the plans of the prince, and relieved Kamakaua of a dangerous duty in the end. In pressing his suit he found a pretext for informing the queen that the continued absence of the king was due to the fact that he had taken another wife, with whom he was living at Honuaula, and that he had ceased to care either for his kingdom or his family.

While Kamakaua was pouring this poison into the ears of Neula, Kaululaau, who had made the acquaintance of Noakua, was planting in the mind of that chief the seeds of sedition. He flattered him with the opinion that he was made to rule, and by degrees developed to him a plan through which, with the favor of the queen, he could seize the government, unite the principal chiefs in his support, and prevent Kauholanui from returning to Hawaii.

The ambition of Noakua, and anger of the queen at the presumed neglect and infidelity of her husband, soon harmonized them in a plot against the absent king. Preparations for the revolt began to be observed, when Kaululaau, not wishing to be openly identified with the dangerous movement, quietly embarked with his party for Hilo, where he remained to watch the progress of the struggle which he had been instrumental in originating.

The prince had been in Hilo but a few days when a *lunapai* arrived from Waipio, summoning the chief of the district to repair thither with eight hundred warriors, and announcing the assumption of the sovereignty of the island by Neula. Similar notifications were sent to the chiefs of the other districts of the kingdom, and soon all was excitement from Kau to Kohala.

Hearing of the revolt, Kauholanui, who had been engaged in constructing a fish-pond at Keoneoio, in the neighborhood of Honuaula, left Maui at once with less than a hundred spears, and, landing in Kona, whose chief could be relied upon, he started overland for Waipio. The revolution was unpopular, and with great unanimity the chiefs and people rallied to the standard of the king. The struggle was brief. A battle was fought near Waimea, resulting in the defeat of the rebel army and the death of Noakua.

This ended the revolt. As a punishment to Neula the king took another wife. But the object of Kaululaau was accomplished, for Kauholanui never again visited Maui, although the queen spent much of her time thereafter at Honuaula, where her favorite guest and friend was Kamakaua.

Leaving Hilo, Kaululaau and his party leisurely drifted along the coasts of Puna until they reached the borders of Kau, when they landed at Keauhou to spend a few days in fishing and surf-riding.

Weary of the sport, Kaululaau left the bathers in the surf, one afternoon, and threw himself under the shade of a *hala* tree near the shore. Watching the clouds and the sea-birds circling in the heavens above him, he fell asleep, and when he awoke his eyes fell upon a beautiful woman sitting upon a rock not more than a hundred paces distant, and silently watching the swimmers as they came riding in on the crests of the rollers. Her skirts were a *pau* spangled with crystals, and over her shoulders hung a short mantle of the colors of a rainbow. Her long hair was held back by a *lei* of flowers, and her wrists and ankles were adorned with circlets of tiny shells of pink and white.

The appearance of the woman dazzled him, and after gazing for some time, and rubbing his eyes to be sure that he was not dreaming, he rose to his feet and approached the radiant being. Advancing within four or five paces of the woman, apparently unobserved, he stopped, and with a cough attracted her attention. Turning her face toward him, he greeted her courteously, and requested permission to approach nearer and converse with her. Her appearance indicated that she was a person of rank, and he did not feel like trespassing uninvited upon her privacy. She did not deign to make any reply to his request, but, after scanning him from head to foot, turned her face toward the sea again with a contemptuous toss of the head.

He hesitated for a moment, and then turned and strode rapidly down to the beach, where his double canoe had been safely drawn up on the sands. " In the guise of a bather," thought the prince, " she evidently mistakes me for a servant. I will approach her in the garb to which my rank entitles me, and see what effect that will have."

Entering the canoe, he girded his loins with a gaudy *maro*, hung round his neck a *palaoa*, and threw over his shoulders a royal mantle of yellow feathers. Then, crowning his head with a brilliant feather helmet, he selected a spear of the length of six paces and stepped from the canoe. As he did so he stumbled. " This means that I have forgotten or omitted something of importance," said the prince to himself, stopping and in detail scanning his equipments. At that moment a lizard ran across his path and entered a hole in the earth. This brought to mind his battle with the gigantic gnome on Lanai, and with a smile he re-entered the canoe. Taking from a calabash, where it had been for months secreted, the charmed spear-point of Lono, he affixed it firmly to the point of a javelin, and, thus equipped, again sought the presence of the fascinating being by whom he had been repulsed.

Advancing as before, he once more craved permission to

approach near enough to drink in the beauty of her eyes. But she seemed to be in no mood to consent. Scanning him in his changed apparel, with an air of indifference she said :

"You need not have taken the trouble to bedeck yourself with royal feathers. I knew you before, as I know you now, to be Kaululaau, son of Kakaalaneo, *moi* of Maui. I do not desire your company."

"Since you know who I am, I must claim the right to insist upon my request, unless you can show, indeed, that you are of equal or better rank." Saying this, the prince took a step forward.

"Then come," replied the woman, "since you are rude enough to attempt it. Sit at my feet and tell me of your love, and I will search the caves for squid and beat the *kapa* for you."

The prince advanced joyfully, and was about to seat himself at the feet of the lovely being, when with a cry of pain he sprang back. The rock he had touched was as hot as if it had just been thrown from the crater of a volcano.

"Come," said the woman tauntingly ; "do you not see that I am waiting for you ? "

Again the prince advanced, but the earth for two or three paces around her was glimmering with heat, and he hastily withdrew to where the ground and rocks were cool. He was now satisfied that he was dealing with some one wielding supernatural powers, and resolved to test the efficacy of the charmed point of his javelin.

"Why do you not come ? " continued the woman in a tone of mingled defiance and reproach.

"Because the earth where you are sitting is too warm for my feet," replied the prince, innocently. "Come where I am standing, and I will sit beside you." And with the point of his javelin he marked upon the ground the boundaries of a space around him.

"Retire some paces, and I will do so," replied the woman, confidently. The prince withdrew, as requested, and she quietly removed to the spot where he had been standing.

"Now come," said the woman, reseating herself ; "perhaps you will find it cooler here."

"I hope so," returned the prince, as he began cautiously to advance. He crossed the line marked by the point of his javelin, and felt no heat.   He took three more steps forward, and the earth was still cool.   Another step, which brought him within two paces of the enchantress, convinced him that her powers were impotent within the boundaries of the line he had drawn, and with a sudden leap forward he caught her in his arms.

Astounded at the failure of her powers, and humiliated at her defeat, the woman struggled to free herself from the embrace of the prince ; but within the charmed circle she possessed but the strength of a simple woman, and was compelled to yield to the supreme indignities of superior force.

Exasperated beyond measure, she at length succeeded in eluding his grasp and springing beyond the fatal line.   The prince followed, but she was now herself, and he could neither overtake nor restrain her.   Retreating some distance up the hill, she suddenly stopped and awaited his approach.   She permitted him to advance within forty or fifty paces of her, when in the space of a breath she abandoned her captivating disguise and stood forth in the form of Pele, the dreadful goddess of Kilauea. Her eyes were bright as the midday sun, and her hair was like a flame of fire.

The prince stopped in dismay.   The goddess raised her hand, and at her feet burst forth a stream of molten lava, rolling fiercely down upon the prince, as if to engulf him.   He started to escape by flight, but the stream widened and increased in speed as it followed.   Fearful that it would overtake him before he could reach the sea, he thought of his javelin, and with the point hastily drew a line in front of the advancing flood.   Continuing his flight and looking back, he discovered, to his great relief, that the stream had stopped abruptly at the line he had drawn, and could not pass it.   Passing into a ravine, the angry flow sought to reach the sea through its channel, and thus cut off the retreat of the prince ; but he crossed the depression, marking a line as he went, and the fiery avalanche was stayed at the limit.

Observing that she was thwarted by some power whose element seemed to be of the earth, Pele summoned her brother Keuakepo from Kilauea, and a shower of fire and ashes descended upon Kaululaau and his companions.   Leaping into the sea to avoid the fire, they dragged the double canoe from its moorings, and, swimming and pushing it through the breakers, escaped from the coast with but little injury.

III.

Having embroiled himself with the divine and political powers of Hawaii, Kaululaau rounded the southern point of La Lae and set sail for Molokai. He spent a month on that island with the royal relatives of his mother, by whom he was appropriately received and entertained. He visited the home of Laamaomao, the wind-god, the poisoned grove of Kalaipahoa, and the demolished fortress on the promontory of Haupu, where the gallant Kaupeepee, of whose blood he was, met his dramatic death. He then set sail for Oahu.

The island of Oahu was at that period one of the most prosperous in the group. It was under the government of Kalona-iki, one of the two sons of Mailikukahi, who during his reign had instituted a code of laws giving better protection to the poor, making theft punishable with death, and claiming as the wards of the government the first-born male children of all families, without regard to rank or condition.

Kalona continued the peaceful and intelligent policy of his father, and his court was noted alike for the brilliancy of its chiefs and the beauty of its women. His principal place of residence was Waikiki, although he had sumptuous temporary resorts at Ewa and Waialua.

Kaululaau first touched at Waialua, but, learning that the king was at Waikiki, he ordered his canoe to proceed around to the south side of the island in charge of his chief navigator, while he and Kamakaua concluded to make the journey overland. Dispensing with all insignia of rank, and habited like simple commoners, the prince and his companion started unattended for Waikiki. Both were armed with javelins, but the one borne by Kaululaau was tipped with the charmed point of Lono.

Proceeding along the foot of the Kaala range of mountains, in the afternoon they sat down to rest in the shade of a *hala* tree. In a ravine below them five or six men were working, and scattered along its banks were a number of huts. Soon a tumult of screams reached them, and men, women and children were seen running hither and thither in a state of great excitement.

The travelers sprang to their feet, and as they did so a gigantic bird swept immediately over their heads and winged its way

toward the hills.   It passed so closely that the branches of the
hala tree were swayed by the motion of its mighty pinions, and
its outspread wings seemed to measure scarcely less than twenty
long steps from tip to tip.

While watching the monster with amazement, a woman approached, and to the questions of the prince replied, between wails
of anguish, that the great bird—the *Pueoalii*, as she called it—had
just killed her only child in front of her hut, with a stab to the
heart resembling the cut of a knife.   She hurriedly gave the additional information that for many years past the same bird had at
intervals visited different districts of the island, killing children,
pigs and fowls, and that the priests had declared it to be a *pueo*,
or owl, sacred to the gods, and which could not, therefore, be
molested with safety, even if harm to it were possible from
human hands.

Better learned in the inspiration and purposes of such visitations—since he had been instructed by the eminent high-priest
Waolani—and having had many conflicts with malignant spirits,
he doubted that the monster he had just seen was of the sacred
pueo family, and requested that he be shown the dead child.   Proceeding to the hut and inspecting the wound, he observed that
the fatal cut was upward, and not downward, as it would have
been had it been made by the beak of an owl.   This confirmed
him in the correctness of his first impression, and, requesting
Kamakaua to follow him, he started toward the hills in the direction taken by the bird.

They could still see it in the distance, like a dark cloud against
the mountain.   After following it for some time the bird swooped
down to commit some fresh depredation, and then rose and
alighted upon a rocky ridge with precipitous face sweeping down
from the main summit of Kaala.

"Why go farther?" said Kamakaua.   "We cannot reach the
bird, and, if we could, our spears would be like straws to such a
monster."

As if by a strong hand, the javelin in the grasp of the prince
forcibly turned and pointed toward the bird.   Smiling at the
augury, Kaululaau replied :

"Look you carefully back and see if we are followed."

Kamakaua turned his face in compliance, and as he did so the
prince poised his javelin and hurled it in the direction of the bird.

In twenty paces the point did not droop ; in forty it did not fall to the ground ; in a hundred a new energy seized it, and like a flash of light it sped out of sight. A moment later the prince saw the bird sink and disappear.

"I can see no one," said Kamakaua, after carefully scanning the ground over which they had passed. "Nor can I now see the bird," he continued, looking toward the ridge. "Where can it be ?"

"At the foot of the cliff," replied the prince, "with the point of my javelin in his heart."

Having been with the prince on Molokai, Kamakaua received the strange information without question or great wonder, and, hastening to the base of the precipice, they found the monster dead, with the javelin buried in its breast. Removing the weapon, they cut off the head and one of the feet of the bird, pulled from its wings four of the longest feathers, and with them returned to the *hala* tree under which they had found shelter from the sun. The burden taxed their strength to the utmost. The weight of the head, which was borne by the prince, was scarcely less than that of his own body, while the feathers were seven paces in length, and the claws two paces between their extreme points.

Great excitement followed the spreading of the news that *Pueoalii* had been killed by strangers. The sufferers through its visitations were disposed to commend the act, and others condemned it as an insult to the gods, which would probably bring broadcast calamity upon the whole island. To placate the anger of the gods it was proposed to sacrifice the strangers at the nearest *heiau*, and, respectfully wrapping the head of the bird in *kapa*, Kaululaau and his companion were conducted with their trophies to the sacred temple of Kukaniloko, which was not far distant. They were accompanied by a crowd which constantly swelled in numbers as they proceeded, and on arriving at the *heiau* they were surrounded by four or five hundred men and women, many of them armed and clamoring for their blood.

Kaululaau was in nowise alarmed, but rather enjoyed the situation. The high-priest of the temple appeared and the matter was laid before him. Looking at the foot and mighty feathers of the bird, he turned to the strangers and said :

"You have slain a creature sacred to the gods, and my thought is that you should be sacrificed to avert their wrath."

"Be careful in your judgment, priest," replied the prince. "How know you that the bird was sacred?"

"For years it has been so regarded," returned the priest. "How know you that it was not?"

"Does it become the high-priest of Kukaniloko to ask such a question?" said the prince. "But I will reply to it when you answer this: With the javelin now in my hand I killed the bird at a distance farther than from where we stand to yonder hills. Could it have been done by human hand without the especial favor of the gods. If not, then how have the gods been angered?"

The priest was confounded, and when the prince proposed to submit the question of his guilt to the king, the suggestion was accepted. It now being near nightfall, Kaululaau and his companion were removed within the enclosure of the temple for safe-keeping, and, knowing that they would be deprived of their weapons, the prince removed the charmed point from his javelin and secreted it in the folds of his *maro*.

Early next morning the high-priest and his two prisoners, who were kept under no marked restraint, accompanied by a large concourse of people carrying the head, foot and feathers of *Pueo-alii*, started for Waikiki. Every one seemed to know that the great bird had been killed, and many stood by the wayside to see the feathers that had been torn from its wings, and catch a glimpse of its destroyer.

Near the middle of the day the great gathering arrived at Waikiki. As many carried spears, it resembled an army in its march, and messengers were despatched by the king to ascertain its meaning. Halting near the shores of the harbor, and not far from the royal mansion, to report the arrival of the prisoners and learn the pleasure of the king, the prince observed his double canoe drawn up on the beach, and requested permission to approach it, that he might secure the counsel of his master, Kaululaau, son of the *moi* of Maui.

The favor could not well be denied, and, under guard of two inferior priests of Kukaniloko, the prince was conducted to the canoe. As but three or four of the crew were present, and their attention was wholly absorbed in the gathering around the royal *hale*, the prince stepped, unobserved by them, into the canoe, and passed quickly into his private quarters—a close wicker-work apartment eight or ten feet in length by the breadth of both canoes, and with a height of six feet or more from their bottoms to the top screen.

Hurriedly investing himself with his regalia of rank, including helmet, feather mantle and spear, he stepped into view and sounded a blast upon a shell. Soon a number of his attendants made their appearance, and, with such following as befitted a prince, he started for the royal mansion. The guards who escorted him to the canoe did not recognize him as he left it, and after passing the crowd surrounding the palace his name and rank were announced to the king. He was promptly met and courteously welcomed at the door by Kalona, and informed that messengers of greeting and invitation would have been despatched to him had his presence at Waikiki been known.

Kaululaau then apprised the king that he had but just arrived overland from Waialua, while his double canoe had been sent around to meet him at Waikiki, and that it was his purpose to spend some days on Oahu. The hospitalities of the royal *hale* were then tendered and accepted, after which the king explained to his distinguished guest the cause of the large gathering around the palace, and invited him to an inspection of the head, feathers and claws of the mighty *Pueoalii*, and to listen to the story of the slayer of the sacred bird, should he deem it of sufficient interest.

Kaululaau accompanied the king to a large dancing pavilion within the royal enclosure, to which had been conveyed the severed parts of the gigantic bird. After the claws and feathers had been examined with awe and amazement, the king ordered the slayer of the bird to be brought before him. The high-priest of Kukaniloko bowed and turned to execute the order, when the guards placed over the prince came from the beach with the information that their prisoner had escaped.

The priest was savage in his disappointment. "Either find him or take his place upon the altar!" he hissed to the unfortunate guards, and then led Kamakaua before the king, with the explanation that the other prisoner had managed to elude the vigilance of his guards, but would doubtless soon be found.

Kamakaua discovered the prince at the side of the king, and could hardly restrain a smile. When questioned he denied that he killed the great bird, but admitted that he assisted in removing the head, feathers and one of the feet.

"This is trifling," said the king, turning to the priest with a scowl. "Where is the other prisoner?"

"He is here, great king!" exclaimed Kaululaau, bowing before Kalona, to the astonishment but great relief of the priest. "Favored by the gods, I slew the malignant monster your priests call by the sacred name of *Pueoalii*. Their skill should have instructed them differently. Will the king favor me by ordering the *kapa* covering to be removed from the head?"

The order was given, and the uncovered head was raised beak upward before the king.

In a moment it was observed that the head was not of a *pueo*, or owl; nor did it bear resemblance in form to that of any bird known. It was narrow between the eyes, which in color were those of a shark, and its long and pointed beak, both of the upper and under jaws, turned sharply upward.

"It is not a *pueo!*" was the general exclamation.

"Are you satisfied, priest?" inquired the prince.

"I think it is not a *pueo*," responded the priest, reluctantly.

"You *think* it is not a *pueo!*" exclaimed the king, indignantly. "Do you not *know* it? What *pueo* ever had such eyes and such a beak?"

The priest hung his head in confusion, and the prince, having completely discomfited him, now came kindly to his relief by remarking:

"The mistake might well have been made, for on the wing and at a distance the bird much resembled a *pueo*."

"You are kind to say so, prince," said the king; "but the priests and *kaulas* have been greatly at fault. For years the bird has preyed upon the people, and no one has dared to molest it. Since you killed it, knowing that it was not sacred, perhaps you may be able to tell me something of its unnatural birth and appetites."

Thus appealed to, Kaululaau modestly replied:

"If I may rely upon what seemed to be a dream last night, the bird was possessed by the spirit of Hilo-a-Lakapu, one of the chiefs of Hawaii who invaded Oahu during the reign of your royal father. He was slain at Waimano, and his head was placed upon a pole near Honouliuli for the birds to feed upon. He was of *akua* blood, and through a bird-god relative his spirit was given possession of the monster which the gods enabled me to slay."

The spirit of Hilo had been brought in with the head of the dead bird, and with the utterance of these words by the prince the eyes rolled, the ponderous jaws opened and closed, and with a noise like the scream of an *alae* the malignant spirit took its departure.

The truth of the dream of Kaululaau thus being verified, the king publicly thanked him for ridding the island of the monstrous scourge, and ordered especial honors to be paid him by all classes so long as it might be his pleasure to remain in the kingdom. In return the prince presented to the king the head, claws and feathers of the bird, the latter to be made into a mammoth *kahili*, and then made Kamakaua known to him, together with such other chiefs in his train as were entitled to royal recognition.

Kaululaau became at once the hero of the court as well as the idol of the people. He remained more than a month on Oahu, enjoying the unstinted hospitality of the king and his district chiefs. He was a favorite with the fairest women of the court; but he gave his heart to the beautiful Laiea-a-Ewa, sister of the wife of Kalona, and with her returned to Maui.

Landing at Lahaina after his long absence, he was joyfully welcomed home by his royal father, who had heard of his adventures and fully forgiven the faults of his youth. With grief he learned that his friend the high-priest, Waolani, had died some months before. Remembering his oath, he found the burial place of the priest, and with his remains secretly deposited the sacred spear-point of Lono, which had served him so effectively. He devoutly kissed the relic before he hid it for ever from view, and afterwards knelt and thanked Lono and the priest for its use.

Lands were given him in Kauaula, where he resided until the end of his days. Laiea was his only wife, and they were blessed with six children, whose names alone are mentioned by tradition.

KELEA, THE SURF-RIDER OF MAUI.

CHARACTERS.

KAWAO, king of Maui.
KELEA, sister of Kawao. .
PILIWALE, *alii-nui* of Oahu.
PAAKANILEA, wife of Piliwale.
LO-LALE, brother of Piliwale.
KALAMAKUA, a chief of Ewa, cousin of Lo-Lale.

KELEA, THE SURF-RIDER OF MAUI.

I.

KELEA, of whom in the past the bards of Oahu and Maui loved to sing, was the beautiful but capricious sister of Kawao, king of Maui, who in about A.D. 1445, at the age of twenty-five, succeeded to the sovereignty of that island. Their royal father was Kahekili I., the son of Kakae, who, with his brother, Kakaalaneo, was the joint ruler of the little realm from about 1380 to 1415. Kakae was the rightful heir to the *moiship*, and, as such, his son Kahekili succeeded him; but as an acci-lent in his youth had somewhat impaired his mental faculties, Kakaalaneo became, through the expressed will of the dying Kamaloohua, the joint ruler and virtual sovereign of the kingdom. He had sons and daughters of his own; but he loved his weak-minded brother, and respected the line of legitimate succession, and when the black *kapa* covered him, Kahekili became king of Maui and Lanai; for during that period the latter island was under the protection of the *mois* of Maui, while Molokai still maintained its independence.

Kakaalaneo was noted for his business energy and strict sense of justice. The court of the brothers was established at Lahaina —then known as Lele—and was one of the most respected in all the group. It was Kakaalaneo who introduced the bread-fruit there from Hawaii, and won the love of the people by continuous acts of mercy and benevolence. For some disrespect shown to his royal brother, whose mental weakness doubtless subjected him to unkind remarks, he banished his son Kaululaau to Lanai, which island, tradition avers, was at that time infested by powerful and malignant spirits. They killed pigs and fowls, uprooted cocoanut-trees and blighted *taro* patches, and a gigantic and mischievous gnome amused himself by gliding like a huge mole under the huts of his victims and almost upsetting them.

The priests tried in vain to quiet these malicious spirits. No sooner were they exorcised away from one locality than they appeared in another, and if they gave the *taro* patches a rest it was only to tear the unripe bananas from their stems, or rend the walls and embankments of artificial ponds, that their stores of fishes might escape to the sea. Aware of these grievances, Kaululaau took with him to Lanai a talisman of rare powers. It was the gift of his friend, the high-priest of his father, and consisted of a spear-point that had been dipped in the waters of *Po*, the land of death, and many generations before left by *Lono* on one of his altars.

Crowning a long spear with this sacred point, Kaululaau attacked the disturbing spirits, and in a short time succeeded either in bringing them to submission or driving them from the island. The gnome *Mooaleo* was the most difficult to vanquish. It avoided the prince, and for some time managed to keep beyond the influence of the charmed spear-point; but the monster was finally caught within the boundaries of a circular line scratched with the talisman upon the surface of the earth beneath which it was burrowing, and thereby brought to terms. It could not pass the line, no matter how far below the surface it essayed to do so. Heaving the earth in its strength and wrath, it chafed against the charmed restraint that held it captive, and finally plunged downward within the vertical walls of its prison. But there was no path of escape in that direction. It soon encountered a lake of fire, and was compelled to return to the surface, where it humbled itself before the prince, and promised, if liberated, to quit the island for ever. Kaululaau obliterated sixty paces of the line of imprisonment, to enable *Mooaleo* to pass to the sea, into which the hideous being plunged and disappeared, never to be seen again in Lanai.

In consideration of the great service of the exiled prince in restoring quiet and security to the island, his father permitted him to return to Maui, where he connected himself with the priesthood, and became noted for his supernatural powers. The charmed spear-point is referred to in later legends, and is thought to be still secreted with the bones of a high-priest in a mountain cave on the island of Maui, not far from the sacred burial-place of Iao.

But we have been straying two generations back of our story. The legendary accounts of the ruling families of the principal islands of the group are so threaded with romantic or fabulous incidents that, in referring to any of the prominent actors in the past, it is difficult to restrain the pen in its willingness to wander into the enchanted by-ways in which the *meles* of the period abound.

Having alluded to the immediate ancestors of Kelea, the sister of the young *moi* of Maui, we will now resume the thread of our legend by referring somewhat more particularly to the princess herself. Brought up in the royal court at Lahaina, with a brother only to divide the affections of her father, Kelea was humored, petted and spoiled as a child, and courted and flattered beyond measure as she grew to womanhood. The *meles* describe her as a maiden of uncommon beauty; but she was wayward, volatile and capricious, as might have been expected of one so schooled and favored, and no consideration of policy or persuasion of passion could move her to accept any one of the many high chiefs who sought her in marriage. She loved the water—possibly because she could see her fair face mirrored in it—and became the most graceful and daring surf-swimmer in the kingdom. Frequently, when the waters of Auau Channel surged wildly under the breath of the south wind, or *kona*, Kelea, laughing at the fears of her brother, would plunge into the sea with her *onini*, or surf-board, and so audaciously ride the waves that those who watched and applauded her were half-inclined to believe that she was the friend of some water-god, and could not be drowned.

No sport was to her so enticing as a battle with the waves, and when her brother spoke to her of marriage she gaily answered that the surf-board was her husband, and she would never embrace any other. The brother frowned at the answer, for he had hoped, by uniting his sister to the principal chief of Hana, to more thoroughly incorporate in his kingdom that portion of the island, then ruled by independent chiefs; but by other means during his reign, it may be remarked, the union of the two divisions was effected.

"Do not frown, Kawao," said Kelea, coaxingly; "a smile better becomes your handsome face. I may marry some day, just to please you; but remember what the voice said in the *anu* at the last feast of *Lono.*"

"Yes, I remember," replied Kawao; "but I have sometimes

believed that when the *kilo* declared that in riding the surf Kelea would find a husband, he was simply repeating an augury imparted to him by Kelea herself."

"You will anger the gods by speaking so lightly of their words," returned Kelea, reproachfully ; and Kawao smiled as the princess took her leave with a dignity quite unusual with her.

Kawao-loved his sister and was proud of her beauty ; and while he was anxious to see her suitably married, and felt no little annoyance at the importunities of her suitors, he nevertheless recognized her right, as the daughter of a king, to a voice in the selection of a husband.

But the voice from the *anu* was prophetic, whatever may have inspired it ; for while Kelea continued to ride the waves at Lahaina, a husband, of the family of Kalona-iki, of Oahu, was in search of her, and to that island we now request the reader to follow us.

There lived at that time at Lihue, in the district of Ewa, on the island of Oahu, a chief named Lo-Lale, son of Kalona-iki, and brother of Piliwale, the *alii-nui*, or nominal sovereign, of the island, whose court was established at Waialua. Kalona-iki had married Kikinui, and thus infused into the royal family the native and aristocratic blood of Maweke, of the ancient line of Nanaula.

Lo-Lale was an amiable and handsome prince, but for some cause had reached the age of thirty-five without marrying. The reason was traced to the death by drowning, some years before, of a chiefess of great beauty whom he was about to marry, and to whom he was greatly attached. As he was of a gentle and poetic nature, his disinclination to marriage may not be unreasonably attributed to that event, especially when supported by the relation that thereafter he abhorred the sea, and was content to remain at Lihue, beyond the sound of its ceaseless surges.

Piliwale had passed his fiftieth year, and, having but two daughters and no son, was more than ever desirous that his brother should marry, that the family authority might be strengthened and the line of Kalona perpetuated. And the friendly neighboring chiefs were equally anxious that Lo-Lale should become the head of a family, and, to inspire him with a disposition to marry, described with enthusiasm the beauty of many maidens of distinguished rank whom they had met on the other islands of the group.

To these importunities Lo-Lale finally yielded ; and as a suitable wife for so high a chief could not be found on Oahu, or, at least, one who would be personally acceptable to him, it was necessary to seek for her among the royal families of the other islands. Accordingly, a large *koa* canoe was fitted out at Waialua, and with trusty messengers of rank despatched to the windward islands in search of a wife for Lo-Lale. The messengers were instructed to quietly visit the several royal courts, and report upon the beauty, rank and eligibility of such marriageable chiefesses of distinguished families as they might be able to discover.

Among the chiefs selected for the delicate mission, and the one upon whose judgment the most reliance was placed, was Lo-Lale's cousin, Kalamakua, a noble of high rank, whose lands were on the coast of the Ewa district. He was bold, dashing and adventurous, and readily consented to assist in finding a wife for his royal and romantic relative.

Lo-Lale was at Waialua when the messengers embarked. He took an encouraging interest in the expedition, and when banteringly asked by his cousin if age would be any objection in a bride of unexceptionable birth, replied that he had promised to take a wife solely to please his royal brother, and any age under eighty would answer. But he did not mean it.

"Not so," replied Piliwale, more than half in earnest. "I will not become the uncle of a family of monsters. The bride must be as worthy in person as in blood."

"Do you hear, Kalamakua?" said Lo-Lale, addressing his cousin, who was standing beside the canoe, ready for departure ; "do you hear the words of Piliwale? She must be not only young but beautiful. If you bring or give promise to any other, she shall not live at Lihue ! "

"Do not fear," replied the cousin, gaily. "Whomsoever she may be, we will keep her in the family ; for if you refuse her, or she you, I will marry her myself ! "

"Fairly spoken ! " exclaimed the king ; "and I will see that he keeps his promise, Lo-Lale."

Although the object of the voyage was known to but few, hundreds gathered at the beach to witness the departure, for the canoe was decorated, and the embarking chiefs appeared in feather capes and other ornaments of their rank. Turning to the high-priest, who was present, Piliwale asked him if he had observed the auguries.

"I have," replied the priest. "They are more than favorable." Then turning his face northward, he continued : "There is peace in the clouds, and the listless winging of yonder bird betokens favoring winds."

Amid a chorus of *alohas !* the canoe dashed through the breakers and out into the open sea, holding a course in the direction of Molokai. Reaching that island early the next day, the party landed at Kalaupapa. The *alii-nui* received them well, but inquiry led to nothing satisfactory, and, proceeding around the island, the party next landed on Lanai. It is probable that they were driven there by unfavorable winds, as Lanai was a dependency of Maui at that time, and none but subject chiefs resided on the island. However, they remained there but one day, and the next proceeded to Hana, Maui, with the intention of crossing over to Hawaii and visiting the court of Kiha at Waipio. Inquiring for the *moi*, they learned that Kawao had removed his court from Lahaina, for the season, to Hamakuapoko, to enjoy the cool breezes of that locality and indulge in the pleasures of surf-bathing. They were further informed that a large number of chiefs had accompanied the *moi* to that attractive resort, and that Kelea, sister of the king, and the most beautiful woman on the island as well as the most daring and accomplished surf-swimmer, was also there as one of the greatest ornaments of the court.

This was agreeable information, and the party re-embarked and arrived the next morning off Hamakuapoko, just as the fair Kelea and her attendants had gone down to the beach to indulge in a buffet with the surf. Swimming out beyond the breakers, and oblivious of everything but her own enjoyment, Kelea suddenly found herself within a few yards of the canoe of the Oahuan chiefs. Presuming that it contained her own people, she swam still closer, when she discovered, to her amazement, that all the faces in the canoe were strange to her. Perceiving her embarrassment, Kalamakua rose to his feet, and, addressing her in a courtly and respectful manner, invited her to a seat in the canoe, offering to ride the surf with it to the beach—an exciting and sometimes dangerous sport, in which great skill and coolness are required.

The language of the chief was so gentle and suggestive of the manners of the court that the invitation was accepted, and the canoe mounted one of the great waves successively following two of lighter bulk and force, and was adroitly and safely beached. The achievement was greeted with applause on the shore, and when the proposal was made to repeat the performance Kelea willingly retained her seat. Again the canoe successfully rode the breakers ashore, and then, through her attendants, Kalamakua discovered that the fair and dashing swimmer was none other than Kelea, the sister of the *moi* of Maui.

With increased respect Kalamakua again invited his distinguished guest to join in the pleasure and excitement of a third ride over the breakers. She consented, and the canoe was once more pulled out beyond the surf, where it remained for a moment, awaiting a high, combing roller on which to be borne to the landing. One passed and was missed, and before another came a squall, or what was called a *mumuku*, suddenly struck the canoe, rendering it utterly unmanageable and driving it out upon the broad ocean.

When the canoe started Kelea would have leaped into the sea had she not been restrained ; but Kalamakua spoke so kindly to her—assuring her that they would safely ride out the storm and return to Hamakuapoko—that she became calmer, and consented to curl down beside him in the boat to escape the fury of the winds. Her shapely limbs and shoulders were bare, and her hair, braided and bound loosely back, was still wet, and grew chilling in the wind where it fell. Kalamakua took from a covered calabash a handsome *kihei*, or mantle, and wrapped it around her shoulders, and then seated her in the shelter of his own burly form. She smiled her thanks for these delicate attentions, and the chief was compelled to admit to himself that the reports of her great beauty had not been exaggerated. He could recall no maiden on Oahu who was her equal in grace and comeliness, and felt that, could she be secured for his eccentric cousin, his search would be at an end. He even grew indignant at the thought that she might not prove acceptable, but smiled the next moment at his promise to marry the girl himself should she be refused by his cousin.

But the fierce *mumuku* afforded him but little time to indulge such dreams. The sea surged in fury, and like a cockleshell the canoe was tossed from one huge wave to another. The spray was almost blinding, and, while Kalamakua kept the little craft squarely before the wind as a measure of first importance, his companions were earnestly employed in alternately baling and trimming as emergency suggested.

On, on sped the canoe, farther and farther out into the open sea, tossed like a feather by the crested waves and pelted by the driving spray. The scene was fearful. The southern skies had grown black with wrath, and long streamers sent from the clouds shot northward as if to surround and cut off the retreat of the flying craft. All crouched in the bottom of the boat, intent only on keeping it before the wind and preventing it from filling. A frailer craft would have been stove to pieces; but it was hewn from the trunk of a sound *koa* tree, and gallantly rode out the storm.

But when the wind ceased and the skies cleared, late in the afternoon, the canoe was far out at sea and beyond the sight of land. It was turned and headed back ; but as there was no wind to assist the paddles, and the waters were still rough and restless, slow progress toward land was made ; and when the sun went down Kalamakua was undecided which way to proceed, as he was not certain that the storm had not carried them so far from the coast of Maui that some point on Molokai or Oahu might be more speedily and safely reached than the place from which they started. Their supply of *poi* had been lost during the gale by the breaking of the vessel containing it ; but they had still left a small quantity of dried fish, raw potatoes and bananas, and a calabash of water, and ate their evening meal as cheerfully as if their supplies were exhaustless and the green hills of Waialua smiled upon them in the distance. Such was the Hawaiian of the past ; such is the Hawaiian of to-day. His joys and griefs are centred in the present, and he broods but little over the past, and borrows no trouble from the future.

The stars came out, and a light wind began to steal down upon them from the northwest. It was quite chilly, and felt like the breath of the returning trade-winds, which start from the frozen shores of northwestern America, and gradually grow warmer as they sweep down through the tropic seas. These winds, continuing, with intervals of cessation, eight or nine months in the year, are what give life, beauty and an endurable climate to the Hawaiian group.

As the breeze freshened sails were raised, and then the course to be taken remained to be determined. Kalamakua expressed his doubts to Kelea, as if inviting a suggestion from her ; but she was unable to offer any advice, declaring that she had not noticed the course of the wind that had driven them so far out upon the ocean.

"And I am equally in doubt," said the chief. "We may have been blown farther toward the rising of the sun than the headlands of Hana. If so, the course we are now sailing would take us to Hawaii, if not, indeed, beyond, while in following the evening star we might even pass Oahu. I therefore suggest a course between these two directions, which will certainly bring us to land some time to-morrow."

"Then, since we are all in doubt," replied Kelea, "and the winds are blowing landward, why not trust to the gods and follow them ?"

"Your words are an inspiration," returned the chief, delighted that she had suggested a course that would enable him to make Oahu direct ; for, as may be suspected, he was an accomplished navigator, and was really in little or no doubt concerning the direction of the several islands mentioned. "You have spoken wisely," he continued, as if yielding entirely to her judgment ; "we will follow the winds that are now cooling the shores of Hamakuapoko."

Thus adroitly was Kelea made a consenting party to her own abduction. Kalamakua took the helm, slightly changing the course of the canoe, and his companions made themselves comfortable for the evening. Their wet rolls of *kapa* had been dried during the afternoon, and there was room enough to spare to arrange a couch for Kelea in the bottom of the boat. But she was too much excited over the strange events of the day to sleep, or even attempt to rest, and therefore sat near Kalamakua in the stern of the canoe until past midnight, watching the stars and listening to the story, with which he knew she must sooner or later become acquainted, of his romantic expedition in search of a wife for his cousin.

It is needless to say that Kalea was surprised and interested in the relation ; and when Kalamakua referred to the high rank of his cousin, to his handsome person and large estates at Lihue, and begged her to regard with favor the proposal of marriage which he then made to her in behalf of Lo-Lale, she frankly replied that, if her royal brother did not object, she would give the proffer consideration.

As Kalamakua had concluded not to take the hazard of securing the consent of her brother, who doubtless had some other matrimonial project in view for her, he construed her answer into a modestly expressed willingness to become the wife of Lo-Lale, and the more resolutely bent his course toward Oahu. He watched the Pleiades—the great guide of the early Polynesian navigators—as they swept up into the heavens, and, bearing still farther to the northward to escape Molokai, announced that he would keep the steering-oar for the night, and advised his companions, now that the breeze was steady and the sea smoother, to betake themselves to rest. And Kelea at last curled down upon her couch of *kapa*, and Kalamakua was left alone with his thoughts to watch the wind and stars.

Although a long and steady run had been made during the night, no land was visible the next morning. Kelea scanned the horizon uneasily, and, without speaking, looked at Kalamakua for an explanation.

"Before the sun goes down we shall see land," said the chief.

"What land?" inquired Kelea.

"Oahu," was the reply, but the chief was not greeted with the look of surprise expected.

"I am not disappointed," returned the princess, quite indifferently. "You seem to have been sailing by the wandering stars last night, for before daylight I looked up and saw by *Kao* that your course was directly toward the place of sunset."

Five of the planets—Mercury, Mars, Venus, Jupiter and Saturn—were known to the ancient Hawaiians, and designated as *na hoku aea*, or wandering stars. The fixed stars were also grouped by them into constellations, and *Kao* was their name for Antares.

With a look of genuine surprise Kalamakua replied:

"I did not know before that so correct a knowledge of navigation was among the many accomplishments of the sister of Kawao."

"It required no great knowledge of the skies to discover last night that we were not bearing southward, and needs still less now to observe that we are sailing directly west," Kelea quietly remarked.

"I will not attempt to deceive one who seems to be able to instruct me in journeying over the blue waters," said Kalamakua, politely. "Your judgment is correct. We are sailing nearly westward, and the first land sighted will probably be the headlands of Kaawa."

"You have acted treacherously," resumed the princess, after a pause, as if suddenly struck with the propriety of protesting against the abduction.

"Possibly," was the brief reply.

"Yes," she continued, after another pause, "you have acted treacherously, and my brother will make war upon Oahu unless I am immediately returned to Hamakuapoko."

"He will find work for his spears," was the irritating response.

"Is it a habit with the chiefs of Oahu to steal their wives?" inquired Kelea, tauntingly.

"No," Kalamakua promptly replied; "but I would not eat from the same calabash with the chief who would throw back into the face of the generous winds the gift of the rarest flower that ever blossomed on Hawaiian soil!"

The pretty compliment of the chief moved Kelea to silence; yet he observed that there was a sparkle of pleasure in her eyes, and that the novelty and romance of the situation were not altogether distasteful to her.

Land was sighted late in the afternoon. It was Kaoio Point, on the western side of Oahu. Rounding it, they landed at Mahana, where they procured food and water and passed the night, and the next day had an easy voyage to Waialua.

Landing, Kalamakua at once communicated with Piliwale, giving the high rank of Kelea, as well as the strange circumstances under which she had been brought to Waialua. Queen Paakanilea promptly despatched attendants to the beach with appropriate apparel, and in due time the distinguished visitor was received at the royal mansion in a manner consistent with her rank.

The next day a message brought Lo-Lale from Lihue. He was dressed in his richest trappings, and brought with him, as an offering to Kelea, a rare necklace of shells and curiously-carved mother-of-pearl. He was conducted to the princess by Kalamakua. They seemed to be mutually pleased with each other. In fact, Lo-Lale was completely charmed by the fair stranger, and in his enthusiasm offered to divide his estates with his cousin as an evidence of his gratitude.

Kalamakua had himself become very much interested in Kelea, and secretly hoped that his cousin might find something in her blood or bearing to object to, in which case he felt that she might be induced to regard his own suit with favor ; but Lo-Lale declared her to be a model of perfection, and wooed her with so much earnestness that she finally consented to become his wife without waiting to hear from her brother.

Her rank was quite equal to that of Lo-Lale, and the king was so greatly pleased with the union that he added considerably to the estates of his brother at Lihue, and the nuptials were celebrated with games, feasting, dancing and the commencement of a new *heiau* near Waialua, which was in time completed and dedicated to *Lono*, with a large image of *Laamaomao*, the Hawaiian Æolus, at the inner entrance, in poetic commemoration of the winds that drove Kelea away from the coast of Maui.

At the conclusion of the festivities at Waialua, Kelea was borne all the way to Lihue in a richly-mounted *manele*, or native palanquin with four bearers. There were three hundred attendants in her train, exclusive of thirty-six chiefs as a guard of honor, wearing feather capes and helmets, and armed with javelins festooned with *leis* of flowers and tinted feathers. It was a right royal procession, and its entrance into Lihue was the beginning of another round of festivities continuing for many days. Portions of the *mele* recited by Lo-Lale in welcome of his wife to Lihue are still remembered and repeated, and the occasion was a popular theme of song and comment for a generation or more among the people of that district.

And thus Kelea, the beautiful sister of the *moi* of Maui, became the wife of Lo-Lale, brother of Piliwale, king of Oahu.

II.

It is now in order to return to Hamakuapoko, to note what transpired there on the sudden disappearance of Kelea before the strong breath of the *mumuku*. The king was profoundly grieved, and summoned the attendants of his sister to learn the particu-

lars of the misfortune. To all of them it was manifest that the
canoe had been blown out to sea in spite of the efforts of its occupants, and, as the gale continued to increase in violence during the day, it was feared that the entire party had perished. As
to the strangers, no one seemed to know anything of them or of
the island from which they came. They did not seem to belong
to the *makaainana*, or common people, and one of them, it was
believed from his bearing, was a high chief.

This was all the information the wailing attendants were able
to give. One man, who had noticed the canoe as it came and
went through the surf, thought it was from Hawaii, while another
was equally certain that it was from Oahu ; but as the general
structure of canoes on the several islands of the group differed
but little, their descriptions of the craft furnished no real clue to
the mystery.

With the cessation of the storm, late in the afternoon, came
a hope to Kawao that the missing canoe had safely ridden out
the gale, and would seek the nearest land favored by the changing winds. He therefore summoned the high-priest, and instructed him to put his diviners and magicians to the task of
discovering what had become of the princess Kelea. Pigs
and fowls were slain, prayers were said in the *heiau*, and late in
the evening information came through supernatural agencies that
Kelea was still living. But this was not satisfactory to the king.
He demanded something more specific, and a *kaula* of great
sanctity was prepared and placed in the *anu*, a wicker enclosure
within the inner court, and in due time, in answer to the questions of the high-priest, announced that the canoe containing the
princess was sailing in safety toward Oahu.

The words of the *kaula* were repeated to the king, and the
next day he despatched a well-manned canoe, in charge of one of
his plumed *halumanus*, or military aids, to find and bring back
the lost Kelea. Owing to unfavorable winds or bad management
the canoe did not reach Makapuu Point, Oahu, until the fourth
day. Proceeding along the northeastern coast of the island, and
landing wherever practicable to make inquiries, the easy-going
messenger did not arrive at Waialua until two days after the departure of Kelea for Lihue.

Learning that the princess had become the wife of Lo-Lale,
the disappointed *halumanu* did not deem it necessary to commu-

nicate with her, but briefly paid his respects to the king, to whom
he made known the nature of his errand to Oahu, and his resolution to return at once to Maui and acquaint his royal master with
the result of his mission.

Appreciating that, in his anxiety to see his brother properly
mated, he had countenanced a proceeding sufficiently discourte-
ous to the *moi* of Maui to warrant a hostile response, Piliwale
treated the *halumanu* with marked kindness and consideration,
and insisted upon sending an escort with him back to Maui, including the bearer of a friendly explanatory message from himself to Kawao.   For this delicate service no one could be found
so competent as the courtly Kalamakua, who was well versed in
the genealogy of the Kalona family, and would be able to satisfactorily, if not quite truthfully, explain why it was that the canoe
containing the princess, when driven out to sea, was headed for
Oahu instead of Maui when the storm abated.

Kalamakua was accordingly despatched on the mission.   Being a much better sailor than the *halumanu*, he found no difficulty either in parting company with him off the coast of eastern
Maui or in reaching Hamakuapoko three or four hours in advance of the party he was courteously escorting thither.   This
enabled the wily Oahuan to secure an audience with the king, and
deliver his message and explanation in full, before the *halumanu*
could land and give his version of the story.

Kalamakua's explanation of the impossibility, after the storm,
of reaching in safety any land other than Oahu or Molokai,
seemed to be satisfactory ; and when he dwelt upon the well-
known high rank of Lo-Lale, as recognized by the *aha-alii*, and
referred to his manly bearing, his amiable disposition and the
amplitude of his estates, Kawao answered sadly :

"Then so let it be.   It is perhaps the will of the gods.   I
would have had it otherwise ; but be to Kelea and her husband,
and to my royal brother the king of Oahu, my messenger of
peace."

Thanking the *moi* for his kindly words, Kalamakua took his
leave.   As he was about to re-embark in the afternoon for Oahu,
the discomfited *halumanu*, having but just then landed, passed
him on the beach.   Knowing that he had been outwitted, in his
wrath he reached for the handle of his knife.   But he did not
draw it.   Kalamakua stopped and promptly answered the chal-

lenge ; but the *halumanu* passed on, and with a smile he stepped into his canoe, and a few minutes later was on his way to Oahu with Kawao's welcome messages of peace.

As the years came and went in their quiet home at Lihue, Lo-Lale lost none of his affection for Kelea. No wars distracted the group. Liloa, the son of Kiha and father of Umi, had become the peaceful sovereign of Hawaii; Kahakuma, the ancestor of some of the most distinguished families of the islands, held gentle and intelligent sway in Kauai ; Kawao still ruled in Maui, and Piliwale in Oahu.

To gratify his wife, Lo-Lale surrounded her with every comfort. The choicest fruits of the island were at her command, and every day fresh fish and other delicacies of the sea were brought to her from the neighboring coasts. In short, everything not *tabu* to the sex was provided without stint. Summer-houses were constructed for her in the cool recesses of the Waianae Mountains, and a *manele*, with relays of stout bearers, was always at her service for the briefest journeys. The people of the district were proud of her rank and beauty, and at seasons of *hookupu*, or gift-making, she was fairly deluged with rare and valuable offerings.

Yet, with all this affluence of comfort and affection, Kelea became more and more restless and unhappy. Nor did the presence of her children, of whom she had three, seem to render her more contented. She longed for the sea ; for the bounding surf which had been the sport of her girlhood ; for the white-maned steeds of ocean, which she had so often mounted and fearlessly ridden to the shore ; for the thunder of the breakers against the cliffs ; for the murmur of the reef-bound wavelets timidly crawling up the beach to kiss and cool her feet ; and the more she yearned for her old-time pleasures, the greater became her dissatisfaction with the tamer life and surroundings of Lihue.

Knowing her love for the sea, Lo-Lale made occasional excursions with her to the coast, frequently remaining there for days together. Sometimes they visited the east and sometimes the south side of the island ; but the place which seemed to please her above all others was Ewa, where Kalamakua made his home. He, too, loved the sea, and during her visits there afforded her every opportunity to indulge her passion for it. Together they had charming sails around the Puuloa (Pearl River) lagoon, and gallant rides over the surf at the entrance. There, and there only, did she seem to recover her spirits ; there only did she seem to be happy.

This did not escape the notice of Lo-Lale, and a great grief filled his heart as he sometimes thought, in noting her brightened look in the presence of Kalamakua, that it was less the charms of the surf than of his cousin's handsome face that made the waters of Ewa so attractive to Kelea.

Life at Lihue finally became so irksome to her, and even the continued kindness of Lo-Lale so unwelcome, that she announced her determination to leave the home of her husband for ever. This resolution was not altogether unexpected by Lo-Lale, for he had not been blind to her growing restlessness and was prepared for the worst ; and as the prerogatives of her high rank gave her the undoubted privilege of separation if she desired it, he reluctantly consented to the divorcement. When asked where it was her purpose to go, she answered: "Probably to Maui, to rejoin my brother."

"More probably not beyond Ewa," was Lo-Lale's significant reply. "But, no matter where you may go," he continued, with dignity, "take your departure from Lihue in a manner consistent with your rank. You were received here as became the sister of a king and the wife of the son of Kalona-iki. So would I have you depart. I reproach you with nothing, myself with nothing ; therefore let us part in peace."

"We part in peace," was Kelea's only answer, and the next morning she quietly took her departure with four or five attendants. A chant expressive of Lo-Lale's grief at the separation was long after recited, but these lines are all of it that have been preserved :

> "Farewell, my partner on the lowland plains,
>   On the waters of Pohakeo,
>   Above Kanehoa,
>   On the dark mountain spur of Mauna-una !
>   O Lihue, she is gone !
>   Sniff the sweet scent of the grass,
>   The sweet scent of the wild vines
>   That are twisted by Waikoloa,
>   By the winds of Waiopua,
>   My flower !
>   As if a mote were in my eye,

The pupil of my eye is troubled ;
Dimness covers my eyes. Woe is me !"

Leaving Lihue, Kelea descended to Ewa, and, skirting the head of the lagoon by way of Halawa, on the afternoon of the second day arrived at the entrance, immediately opposite Puualoa. There she found a large number of nobles and retainers of Kalamakua, the high chief of the district, amusing themselves in the surf. As she had not seen the salt water for some months, Kelea could not resist the temptation to indulge in her old pastime, and, borrowing a surf-board from one of the bathers, plunged into the sea, and soon joined the party of surf-riders beyond the breakers.

Soon a huge roller made its appearance, and all mounted it and started for the shore. The race was exciting, for the most expert swimmers in the district were among the contestants ; but in grace, daring and skill Kelea very plainly excelled them all, and was loudly cheered as she touched the shore. Kalamakua was reposing in the shade, not far away, and, hearing the tumult of voices, inquired the cause. He was told that a beautiful woman from Lihue had beaten all the chiefs at surf-riding, and the people could not restrain their enthusiasm. Satisfied that there was but one Lihue woman who could perform such a feat, and that she must be Kelea, the wife of his cousin Lo-Lale, he proceeded to the beach just as a second trial had resulted in a triumph to the fair contestant quite as emphatic as the first. As she touched the shore Kalamakua threw his *kihei* (mantle) over her shoulders and respectfully greeted her. Kelea then informed him that she had formally separated from her husband and was about to embark for Maui.

"If that is the case," said Kalamakua, gently taking her by the arm, as if to restrain her, "you will go no farther than Ewa. When I went in search of a wife for Lo-Lale, I promised that if he objected to the woman I brought or recommended, or she to him, I would take her myself, if she so willed. You have objected to him. Is Kalamakua better to your liking ?"

"I will remain at Ewa," was the satisfactory answer.

"Yes, and you should have gone there instead of to Lihue, when you landed at Waialua years ago," continued Kalamakua, earnestly.

"My thought is the same," was Kelea's frank avowal ; and she beckoned to her attendants, and told Kalamakua that she was ready to follow him.

Did he expect her at the beach that morning? Tradition offers no direct answer to the question, but significantly mentions that Kalamakua spent one or two days at Lihue not long before, that houses were in readiness for her at Ewa, and that she was borne thither on a *manele*, escorted by the principal chiefs and nobles of the district.

Learning, not long after, that Kelea had become the wife of Kalamakua, the gentle-hearted Lo-Lale sent to her a present of fruits and a message of peace and forgiveness; but it was his request that they might never meet again, and he spent the remainder of his days in Lihue, caring for the welfare of his people and dreaming in the shadows of the hills of Kaala.

But little more need here be told. Kelea and Kalamakua lived happily together, and were blessed with a daughter, Laielohelohe, who inherited her mother's beauty, and became the wife of her cousin Piilani, son and successor of Kawao, *moi* of Maui; but it was not until after the betrothal of the cousins, which was agreed to in their childhood, that Kawao fully forgave his volatile sister for marrying a prince of Oahu without his consent.

Piikea, one of the daughters of Piilani and Laielohelohe, became in after-time the wife of the great Umi, of Hawaii, and through her great-grandson, I, the ancestress of Kalakaua, the present sovereign of the group. Lono-a-Pii, another of their children, succeeded his father as *moi* of Maui.

As a further example of the manner in which the blood of the reigning families of the several islands of the group was commingled in the early periods of their history, it may be mentioned that Kaholi, a son of Lo-Lale and Kelea, was united in marriage to Kohipa, one of the two daughters of Piliwale; while the other, Kukaniloko, who followed her father as sovereign of Oahu, became the wife of Luaia, grandson of Kakaalaneo, the joint ruler of Maui during the reign of the unfortunate Kakae.

Umi, the Peasant Prince of Hawaii.

CHARACTERS.

KIHA, king of Hawaii.

IKA, chief of a band of demi-demons.

PUAPUA-LENALENA, a demon dog.

LILOA, afterwards king of Hawaii.

PINEA, wife of Liloa.

HAKAU, son and successor of Liloa.

KAPUKINI, daughter of Liloa.

AKAHIA-KULEANA, a peasant girl loved by Liloa.

UMI, son of Akahia-kuleana.

MAAKAO, husband of Akahia-kuleana.

KUKULANI, wife of Hakau.

KULAMEA, the betrothed of Umi.

MAUKALEOLEO, the giant friend of Umi.

LAEANUI, the high-priest of Hawaii.

KAOLEIOKU, a warrior-priest.

NUNA and
KALOHE, } priests of Waipio.

OMAUKAMAU, brother of Kulamea, and
PIIMAIWAA, } lieutenants of Umi.

UMI, THE PEASANT PRINCE OF HA-
WAII.

THE HISTORIC LEGENDS OF LILOA, HAKAU, AND THE
"KIHA-PU."

I.

NOWHERE on the island of Hawaii do the palms grow
taller than in the valleys of Waipio, and nowhere is the
foliage greener, for every month in the year they are refreshed
with rains, and almost hourly cooled in the shadows of passing
clouds.

And sweet are the waters that sing through the valleys of
Waipio. They are fed by the tears of the trade-winds gathered
in the shaded gorges of the mountains where they find their
source, and are speeded to the ocean by hurrying and impatient
cascades through black channels fretted with bowlders and
fringed with everlasting green.

Tradition says the waters of Waipio, after their first descent
from the hills, at one time crawled quite sluggishly to the sea ;
but a great fish—larger than the island of Kaula—whose home
was in the depths off the coast of Hamakua, required more fresh
water than was furnished by the principal stream of the valley,
and *Kane*, who was friendly with the monster, increased the volume of the little river by creating new springs at its sources,
and accelerating the flow by raising the bed in places and providing additional riffles and cascades. The great fish no longer
frequents that part of the coast of Hamakua, but the cascades
and riffles remain, with the broad finger-marks of *Kane* upon the
rocks hurled into the gorge to create them.

Although but thinly populated now, Waipio was for many
generations in the past a place of great political and social im
portance, and the *tabus* of its great temple were the most sacred
in all Hawaii. For two hundred years or more it was the resi-

dence of the kings of that island, and was the scene of royal
pageants, priestly power and knightly adventure, as well as of
many sanguinary battles.

Waipio valley was first occupied as a royal residence by
Kahaimoelea, near the middle or close of the thirteenth century,
and so continued until after the death of Liloa, about the end of
the fifteenth century.   For some reason not clearly stated the
successor of Liloa removed his court from Waipio to the opposite coast of the island.   Although the glory of the old capital
departed with its abandonment as the royal residence, the *tabus*
of its great temple of *Paakalani* continued to command supreme
respect until as late as 1791, when the *heiau* was destroyed, with
all its sacred symbols and royal associations, by the confederated
forces of Maui and Kauai in their war with Kamehameha I.

Although the story about to be related opens in the reign of
Liloa, which closed with his death in about 1485, it is pertinent
to refer, as briefly as the strange circumstances of the time will
permit, to the father of that sovereign—the great Kiha—concerning whose career many curious traditions survive.   The reign
of Kiha was long and peaceful.   He was endowed not only with
marked abilities as a ruler, but with unusual physical strength
and skill in the use of arms.   In addition to these natural advantages and accomplishments, which gave him the respect and fear
of his subjects, it was popularly believed that he possessed supernatural resources, and could call to his aid, in an emergency,
weird forces in opposition to which mere human endeavor would
be weak and fruitless.   Under the circumstances, it is not strange
that the chiefs of the neighboring islands deemed it prudent to
court his friendship, and that no great wars distracted the kingdom during his reign.

Among the means at the command of Kiha for summoning to
his assistance the invisible forces subject to his call, the most
potential was a curious war-trumpet, the notes of which, when
blown by Kiha, could be heard a distance of ten miles, even
from Waipio to Waimea.   According to the character of the
blast, its voice was either a summons to unseen powers, a rally-
ing-cry to the people, or a dreadful challenge to battle.   This
trumpet was a large sea-shell.   It was a native of foreign waters,
and another like it could not be found in the Hawaiian group.
It was ornamented with rows of the teeth of distinguished chiefs

slain in battle, and could be so blown as to bring forth the dying groans or battle cries of all of them in dreadful diapason.

Many legends are related of the manner in which Kiha became possessed of this marvellous shell, but the most probable explanation is that it was brought from some one of the Samoan or Society Islands three or four centuries before, and had been retained in the reigning family of Hawaii as a charm against certain evils. In the hands of the crafty Kiha, however, it developed new powers and became an object of awe in the royal household. Whatever may have been the beneficent or diabolic virtues of this shell-clarion of Kiha—of the *Kiha-pu*, as it is called—its existence, at least, was a reality, since it is to-day one of the attractions of the Royal Hawaiian Museum of Honolulu, brought down by the Kamehameha branch of the Kiha line. When vigorously blown it still responds in sonorous voice, suggestive of the roar of breakers around the jutting cliffs of Hamakua; but *Lono* no longer heeds the mandate of its call, and brown-armed warriors come no more at its bidding. Of the many strange stories still retained of the *Kiha-pu*, one is here given, nearly in the language in which it has come down in Hawaiian chant and song.

A STORY OF THE KIHA-PU.

For a period of eight years, during the reign of Kiha, the *Kiha-pu* was missing from the cabinet of royal charms and treasures. A new temple was to be dedicated to *Lono*, not far from Waipio, and feathers of the *mamo*, *oo* and other birds were required to weave into royal mantles and redecorate *Kaili* and other gods of the king's household. But one of the *Kahu alii*, constituting the five classes of guardians of the royal person, was permitted to touch the *Kiha-pu*, nor did any other know of its depository in the king's chamber His name was Hiolo. He was the son of a distinguished chief, and his office was that of *ipukuha*, or spittoon-bearer—a position of peculiar responsibility, which could be filled only by persons of noble blood and undoubted attachment to their sovereign.

Desirous of hastily assembling and despatching to the neighboring sea-shores and mountains a large party of feather-hunters, the king, reclining in the shade of the palms in front of the

royal mansion, commanded Hiolo to bring to him the *Kiha-pu*,
that he might with a single blast summon his subjects throughout
the valleys of Waipio. Hiolo proceeded to the chamber of the
king, and a few minutes after returned pale and speechless, and
threw himself at the feet of Kiha, tearing his hair, lacerating his
flesh with his nails, and exhibiting other evidences of extreme
agony and desperation.

Nothing ever startled a sovereign of the line of Pili. Under
all circumstances he acted with apparent deliberation. It was a
natural trait, strengthened by example and education.

Kiha calmly regarded his *ipukuha* for a moment, and then
said :

"What spirit of evil possesses you ? Rise, Hiolo, and speak ! "

Hiolo rose to his feet, and, with a look of despair, exclaimed :

" It is no fault of mine ; but tear out the tongue that tells
you the *Kiha-pu* is gone ! "

Without replying, the king, with a terrible scowl upon his
face, rose and strode into his chamber. Parting the curtains
of *kapa* which secluded the back portion of the apartment, he
stepped to an elaborately carved and ornamented *ipu*, a container shaped and hollowed from the trunk of a *koa* tree. He found
the vessel open, and beside it on the matted floor the several
folds of *kapa* in which the *Kiha-pu* had been wrapped ; but instead of the sacred trumpet he discovered at the bottom of the
ipu a hideously-carved head and face of stone. The shell had
been adroitly abstracted, but the image that had been left in
its place saved the life of Hiolo, for by it Kiha discerned that
the theft and substitution had been achieved through supernatural agencies.

The loss of the *Kiha-pu* was a great grief to the king. But
he did not deem it prudent to admit that he no longer possessed the sacred talisman, and therefore announced to Hiolo
that the trumpet had been found. Under the pretence that it
had been carelessly misplaced by Hiolo, Kiha declared that he
would be its sole guardian thereafter.

There was great joy at the court when it was learned
from the lips of the king that the *Kiha-pu* had been found ;
yet it was observed that it was not used to summon the feather-hunters, and after the sun went down that evening many
thought they faintly heard the music of its voice coming in

from the sea. And the king detected the familiar sound, and, fearful that others might hear it as well, called together his poets and *hula* dancers, and permitted their boisterous merriment far into the night.

Early in the evening, while the palace grounds were a scene of revelry, the king repaired alone to the great temple of *Paakalani,* not far from the royal mansion, to consult with the high-priest and put in motion the weird forces of the *heiau* for the recovery of the *Kiha-pu.* He took with him the image left in the *ipu,* as a possible means of assistance, and enjoined a solemn secrecy upon every *kahuna* taken into the confidence of the high-priest.

The most noted *kilos,* seers and prophets of the temple were ordered to apply their arts, and a *kaula,* inspired by incantation, was questioned from within the *anu* of the inner sanctuary. The clouds were noted, the flights of birds observed, and the dreams of drugged priests interpreted, but nothing satisfactory was developed. Prayers were offered to the gods, sacrifices were laid upon the altar, and the vitals of freshly-slain pigs and fowls were carefully examined; but the only information obtained was that the *Kiha-pu* had been stolen by the chief of a band of demi-demons, or human beings controlled by evil spirits; that it was no longer on the island of Hawaii, but somewhere on the ocean beyond the eight Hawaiian seas; that it would one day be recovered by a being without hands and wearing neither mantle nor *maro,* but not until a cocoa-tree, planted in the next full of the moon, should yield its first fruit, to be eaten by the king.

So far as concerned the theft of the *Kiha-pu,* the seers of the temple had spoken correctly. For some months a dense forest in the mountains back of Waipio, interspersed with marshes and patches of rank undergrowth, had been inhabited by a small band of wild-looking men, who boldly helped themselves to the pigs, fowls and fruits of the neighboring farmers, and held noisy festivals almost nightly within the gloomy recesses of their mountain retreat. They were said to be only half-human, and capable of assuming other than their natural forms. They had occasionally visited Waipio in parties of from two to five, and entertained the people by telling fortunes and exhibiting strange feats of posturing and legerdemain. In the guise of an old woman the chief of the band had entered the royal mansion and stolen the *Kiha-pu*, leaving in its place the hideous stone image mentioned ; then, as if the object of their stay near Wai-pio had been attained, the entire band embarked the evening of the next day in stolen canoes for Kauai. When safely off the coast of Hamakua the demon-chief had defiantly wound a blast from the *Kiha-pu*, which the king had sought to drown in the tumult of the *hula*.

Kiha departed gloomily from the temple. The loss of the sacred trumpet afflicted him sorely. It had long been an heir-loom in the royal family of Hawaii, and its powers had been increased during his reign. In obedience to the revelation of a *kaula* of great sanctity, he had secretly deposited it in a cave near the summit of Mauna Kea and retired to a valley below. Near the middle of the following night a sound unearthly and terrible came echoing down the mountain-side, followed by a hurricane which uprooted trees and tore great rocks from their fastenings and hurled them into the gorges below. The earth trembled as if a volcano was about to burst forth, and a ruddy light hung about the summit. The sound ceased, the wind fell to a whisper, and Kiha rose to his feet in the dark-ness and said : "It is well. The great Lono has kept faith. He has blown the sacred trumpet, and henceforth it will have the voice of a god !" The next morning he repaired to the cave, and found the shell, not where he had left it, but on the top of a huge rock with which the entrance had been for ever closed. He raised the trumpet to his lips, and such sound as his heart desired came forth at the bidding of his breath. He breathed a simple call to his subjects, and it was heard the dis-tance of a day's journey. He gave a battle-blast, and his ears were stunned with the mingled cries and groans of conflict. He ventured an appeal to the unseen, and to a weird music around him rose gnomes, fairies and grinning monsters. He re-turned elated to the palace, and more and more, as its strange voices were heard, did the *Kiha-pu* become an object of awe and wonder.

Although he took every possible precaution to keep from the people all knowledge of the loss of the *Kiha-pu*, the king had little faith in the assurances of the seers of the great temple that it would in time be recovered. The conditions of its re-

Type of Scenery.

covery were too vague, distant and unsatisfactory to be entitled to serious consideration. However, within a few days, with his own hands he planted a cocoa-tree near the door of his chamber, and had a strong fence placed around it. He visited the spot daily and saw that the ground was kept moist, and in due time a healthy shoot came forth to reward his watchfulness. The members of the royal household wondered at the interest taken by the king in a simple cocoa sprout ; but when it was intimated that he was making a new experiment in planting, his care of the little tree ceased to attract remark.

And now, while the king is anxiously watching the growth of his cocoa-tree, and carefully guarding it from accident and blight, let us follow the travels of the *Kiha-pu*. Instead of sailing for Kauai through the island channels, the band of demi-demons took a northwest course, intending to reach their destination without touching at any intermediate point. The powers of the *Kiha-pu* were known to them, and their chief amused himself and his graceless companions by testing its virtues. When off the coast of Maui a blast of the trumpet brought near *Ukanipo*, a terrible shark-god, sent by *Kuula*, the powerful but exacting god of the fishermen of that island. On a jutting headland could be seen a *heiau* dedicated to him and his wife, *Hina*. Hundreds of sharks followed in the train of *Ukanipo*. They surrounded the canoes and lashed the sea into foam. Separating, they formed a great circle around the little fleet, and, swiftly approaching, drove a school of flying-fish across the canoes, many striking the sails and falling into the open boats and thus providing an opportune supply of favorite food.

Sighting Molokai, they thought of landing to replenish their water-calabashes ; but as the coast was rugged and the wind unfavorable, a blast of the trumpet was blown to *Kuluiau*, the goddess of rain. Instantly there was a commotion in the heavens. Black clouds began to gather around them, and they had barely time to arrange their *kapa* sheds and funnels before the rain poured down in torrents and filled their calabashes to overflowing.

Believing the *Kiha-pu* would bring them anything they desired, and returning thanks for nothing received, when off the northern coast of Molokai, near Kaulapapa, they sounded a call to *Laamaomao*, god of the winds, who since the days of Moikeha, more than two centuries before, had occupied a cave on that island.   Enraged at an appeal for favoring winds from such a source, *Laamaomao* opened the mouth of the *ipu* in which he kept the winds imprisoned, and turned it toward the sea.   A few minutes after a hot, fierce hurricane struck the canoes of the miscreants, upsetting two of them and tearing their sails in tatters.   The chief had sufficient presence of mind to call through the trumpet for *Maikahulipu*, the god who assists in righting upset canoes, and the foundered boats were soon restored to their proper positions and partially freed from water.   But there was no abatement in the violence of the wind.   For more than a day and a night the canoes were driven before it almost with the speed of a shark, until finally their drenched and wearied occupants heard before them through the darkness the sound of breakers against a rock-bound shore.   The danger was imminent, for paddles were useless.   Raising the trumpet to his lips, the chief called for *Uhumakaikai*, a powerful fish-god.   No response came, and the cliffs frowned before him as he hastily trumpeted for *Apukohai*, another fish-god of Kauai, whose acts were usually cruel and malicious.   The spray of shattered waves against the rocks began to wet the canoes, when they were seized by a force unseen, darwn away from the cliffs, swept around a northward point, and flung by the waves upon a sandy beach not far from Koloa.

Thus escaping with their lives, the party traveled overland and joined a band of congenial spirits in the mountains back of Waimea, where they remained until they were driven from the island for their misdemeanors.   Leaving Kauai, they crossed the channel, and, after moving from place to place for some years, finally took up their abode in a secluded spot near Waolani, on the island of Oahu.

In the possession of the *Kiha-pu*, Ika, the chief of the band, who claimed it as his individual property, became cruel and dictatorial to his companions.   He esteemed himself little less than a god, and demanded a full half of all the earnings and pilferings of his associates.   As the *Kiha-pu* was the cause of this exaction, one of the friends of Ika, not daring to destroy or purloin the shell, resolved to despoil it of its magic powers.   To this end, with great offerings of pigs and fowls, he consulted a priest of *Lono* at Waianae, and was told that a *tabu* mark, placed somewhere on the shell with the approval of *Lono*, would accomplish what was desired. As the priest alone could place the mark upon the shell, he consented to visit Waolani, and remain in the neighborhood until the trumpet could be brought to him. Everything having been arranged, one evening Ika, without great persuasion, was made drunk with *awa*, when the shell was stolen and conveyed to the priest, who, with a point of flint, hastily scratched near the outer rim a *pea* mark, or *tabu* cross, meantime burning incense and chanting a low prayer to *Lono*.

"Can its powers be restored?" inquired the friend of Ika, as the *tabued* trumpet was returned to him.

"Not while the *tabu* mark remains," replied the priest; "not until—but no matter; its magic voices are silent now."

Before Ika awoke from his drunken stupor the *Kiha-pu* had been restored to its usual place of deposit.

The next morning Ika partook of more *awa*, threw over his shoulders a cape of red—a color sacred to the gods—suspended the *Kiha-pu* from his neck with a cord of human hair, and went proudly forth to receive the homage of his companions. But they refused to accord him the honors to which he imagined he was entitled, and in his wrath he raised the trumpet to his lips to blast them with a proclamation of his superiority. A natural and monotonous sound issued from the shell. He regarded it for a moment with amazement, then replaced it to his lips and poured his breath into it with the full force of his lungs; but its many voices were silent; its thunder-tones had been hushed.

He hastily re-entered his hut to escape the comments of his companions, and discovered, after repeated trials, that the *Kiha-pu* had lost its magic powers, and in his hands was nothing more than a simple shell. Not doubting that it had been deprived of its virtues through supernatural agencies, Ika visited a renowned *kilo*, or wizard, living near Waialua, taking with him the *Kiha-pu*, which was enclosed in a pouch of *kapa*, that it might not be observed. The age of the *kilo* was a hundred and twenty-four years, and he was totally blind, subsisting upon the bounty of those who sought his counsel. Finding his hut after some difficulty, Ika presented him with a roll of *kapa* which he had brought with him from Waolani, and a pig which he had stolen in the valley below, and implored him to ascertain, if possible, the cause of the disenchantment of the *Kiha-pu*. Taking the trumpet from Ika, the *kilo* passed his wrinkled hands over it for some minutes, and then retired with it behind a screen of mats, leaving his visitor under the eye of an old crone, who had admitted him without a word and seated herself beside the opening.

It was a long time before the *kilo* reappeared, and it was then to inform Ika that little could be learned concerning the *Kiha-pu.* He had employed every means known to his art, and finally appealed to *Uli,* the supreme god of sorcery, when the reluctant answer came that the *Kiha-pu* had been silenced by a power greater than his. "I dare not inquire further," said the *kilo,* returning the trumpet.

"Will its voices ever return to it? Will your cowardice allow you to answer that question?" inquired Ika, in a sneering tone.

"Yes," replied the *kilo,* with an effort restraining his wrath and speaking calmly—"yes; its voices will be heard again in Hawaii, among the hills that have sent back their echoes."

Ika would have questioned the *kilo* farther, but the old woman rose and pointed toward the door, and with a look of disappointment he replaced the shell in its pouch of *kapa* and sullenly left the hut.

Returning to Waolani, Ika abandoned his lofty pretensions and mingled again with his companions on terms of comparative equality. This restored him to their friendship, and, remembering the words of the *kilo,* he prevailed upon a majority of them to accompany him to Hawaii. Stealing boats at Waikiki, the party set sail for Hawaii, and the fourth day landed at Kawaihae, in the district of Kohala. There they abandoned their canoes, or exchanged them for food, and in parties of four or five proceeded across the island by way of Waimea, and soon after took possession of their old quarters in the mountains back of Waipio, after an absence of eight years.

In all these years what had become of the cocoa-tree planted by Kiha, with the coming of the first-fruits of which the magic trumpet was to be restored by a being without hands and wearing neither mantle nor *maro?* For seven years he had watched and nurtured its growth, staying it against wind and storm, and guarding its every leaf and stem. It was a vigorous and shapely tree, and its leaves were above the touch of a battle-spear in the hands of the king. But no signs of fruit appeared, and the heart of Kiha was troubled with the thought that the tree might be barren, and that the gods had mocked him. The seventh year of its growth had come and was going, when one morning he descried among its branches three young cocoanuts, scarcely less in size than his clenched fist. He thought it strange that he had not seen them before, and then wondered that he had seen them at all, for they were closely hidden among the leaves. But there they were, to his great joy, and he watched them day by day until they attained an age and size at which they might be eaten. He then sent for the high-priest, and, pointing to the fruit, said:

"Behold the fruit of the tree planted by the hands of Kiha. At the rising of the sun to-morrow I shall eat of it. Will the gods fulfil their promise?"

"O chief!" replied the priest, "I do not see the means; but you planted the tree; the fruit is fit for food; eat of it to-morrow, if you will. The gods are all-powerful!"

At daylight the next morning the fruit was taken from the tree, and the king drank the milk of the three cocoanuts, and ate of the meat of all, first giving thanks to the gods. He then threw himself upon his *kapa-moe* until the sun was well up in the heavens, when he rose and went forth to meet his chief adviser, as was his daily custom, and learn from his spies and other confidential officers what of importance had transpired since the day before. The only information that seemed to interest him was that a lawless band of strange men—apparently the same who infested the neighborhood some years before—had reoccupied the marshy forest in the mountains back of Waipio, and would doubtless become a scourge to the planters in the upper part of the valley.

"It was through such a band that I was robbed of the *Kiha-pu*," thought the king. "It may be that the very same have returned and brought back with them the sacred trumpet. The ways of the gods are mysterious."

Communicating the thought to no one, Kiha despatched a discreet messenger to reconnoitre the camp of the marauders, and in the afternoon secretly visited the temple of *Paakalani*, where he learned through the *kaulas* that the *Kiha-pu* was somewhere on the island of Hawaii.

The sun was sinking in the west when the messenger returned, with the information that the chief of the demon band was Ika, who, with many of his followers, had been seen in and around Waipio many years before.

These tidings had scarcely reached the ears of the king when a tumult was discovered at the main gate of the palace enclosure, and a few minutes after an old man, with his arms bound behind his back, and followed by a strange-looking dog, was being dragged by a crowd of officers and others toward the royal mansion, in front of which Kiha was sitting, surrounded by a number of distinguished chiefs and titled retainers. The man was well advanced in years, and was clad in a *maro* and *kihei*, or short mantle of *kapa*, while from his neck was suspended an ivory charm rudely carved into the form of a dog's foot. He was above the average height, and around his stooped shoulders hung a tangled mass of grizzled hair. His beard was unshorn, and from beneath his shaggy brows peered a pair of small and malignant-looking eyes. He glowered savagely at his captors, and resented anything that seemed like unnecessary force in urging him along. The dog was a large, misshapen brute, with human-looking ears and a bluish coat of bristling hair. It had a long, swinish tail, and one of its eyes was white and the other green. The animal followed closely and sullenly at its master's heels, uttering an occasional low growl when too roughly jostled by the crowd.

When within a hundred paces of the mansion the officers halted with their prisoner, and an attendant was despatched by the king to ascertain the cause of the excitement. Learning that the officers were desirous of bringing before him a man suspected of pilfering from the royal estates, the king consented to listen to the accusation in person, and ordered the prisoner to appear in his presence. Approaching, the old man prostrated himself at the feet of Kiha, and the dog, giving voice to a dismal howl, crouched upon the earth, laid his nose between his paws, and bent his green eye upon the king. Kiha regarded both for a moment with an amused expression; but there was something demoniac in the appearance of the dog, and after catching a glimpse of it he could scarcely remove his gaze from the green eye that glared upon him.

Commanding one of the officers to speak for himself and the rest, that the matter might be briefly determined, the king was informed that the prisoner was a native of the island of Kauai, and some months before had landed with his dog in the district of Kau; that he was an *awa* thief and had trained his fiendish-looking dog to do his pilfering ; that the animal possessed the intelligence of a *kahuna* and the instincts of a demon, and could almost steal the mantle from a man's shoulders without detection ; that the prisoner had been driven for his thefts from Kau to Kona, and thence to Hamakua ; that he had been living for some months past at Kikaha, where his dog, *Puapua-lenalena,* as he was called, had become noted for his thefts ; that *awa* had been missed by the *luna* of one of the king's estates in the upper part of the valley ; that the night before a watch had been placed, and the demon dog had been detected in the act of leaving the royal plantation with a quantity of *awa* in his mouth ; that the animal had been followed to the hut of his master, who was found asleep under the influence of *awa,* which the dog had doubtless ground with his teeth into an intoxicating drink, since on being aroused the man denied that he had either stolen or chewed it ; and, finally, after some resistance, the prisoner had been brought to Waipio, followed by his dog, and was now before the king for examination and sentence.

After the officer had concluded his account of the misdemeanors of the prisoner, by permission of the king the old man rose to his feet, and was about to speak in his own defence when Kiha, turning his gaze with an effort from the green eye of the dog, abruptly inquired :

"What manner of animal is this, and how came he in your possession ? "

"O king ! " replied the prisoner, " the dog was given to me by my uncle, a distinguished *kaula* of Kauai, and it is believed that he was cast up from the sea."

"Enough ! " exclaimed the king, with a gesture of impatience. " Take them both to the temple of *Paakalani,*" he continued, addressing a chief with a yellow cape and helmet, " and there await my coming."

The prisoner and his green-eyed companion were removed to the temple, and in the dusk of the evening Kiha proceeded thither alone. Entering the royal retreat with which the *heiau* enclosure was provided, he sent for the high-priest, and soon after for the prisoner and his dog. They were conducted to the apartment, and the door was closed, a *kukui* torch held at another opening throwing a glare of light into the room.

The king sat for a few breaths in silence, while the priest was

scanning the prisoner and his strange companion.   Finally, pointing to the dog, Kiha turned to the priest and said :

"A wonderful animal—a being without hands, and wearing
neither mantle nor *maro !*"

"True," returned the priest, recalling the promise of the gods;
"and should he be the messenger, his services must not be
slighted."

"Listen," said the king, addressing the prisoner.   "I have
faith that this animal can do me a service.   In a marshy forest in
the mountains back of Waipio a band of conjuring outlaws have
lately found a retreat.   A magic shell of great power, stolen from
me many years ago, is now in the possession of some one of
them—probably of Ika, their chief.   Can you prompt this animal
to recover the *Kiha-pu ?* "

"Perhaps," replied the prisoner.

"Then do so," returned the king, "and I will not only give
you the life you have forfeited, but will see that you are provided
henceforth with all the *awa* you have an appetite to consume."

With these words of the king the dog rose to his feet, uttered a
growling sound which seemed to be half-human, and approached
the door.

"No instructions are required," said the old man ; "he under-
stands, and is ready to start upon his errand."

"Then send him forth at once," returned the king ; "the
night is dark and will favor him."

The door was opened, and like a flash the dog sprang from
the room, leaped the closed gate of the outer wall, and in the
darkness dashed up the valley toward the mountains.

"I will await his return here," said the king, looking inquiringly toward the prisoner.

"He will be back a little beyond the middle of the night," replied the old man.

"With the *Kiha-pu ?* " inquired the king.

"Either with or without it," was the answer.

Leaving the prisoner in the custody of the high-priest and his
attendants, Kiha walked out into the starlight.   His face was
feverish, and the kiss of the trade-winds was cool.   The *heiau* of
Paakalani was a *puhonua*, or sacred place of refuge—one of the
two on the island of Hawaii—and he wondered whether, under
any circumstances, he could properly demand the life of the pris-

oner were he to claim the protection of the temple. Had he voluntarily sought refuge in the *puhonua*, there would have been no doubt ; but as he was forcibly taken there by royal order, his right to exemption from seizure was a question of doubt.

Dismissing the subject with the reflection that the life or death of the prisoner was of little consequence, Kiha strolled toward the inner temple and reverently bowed before an image of *Lono* near the entrance. Remains of recent sacrifices still smelt rank upon the altar, and scores of gods of almost every grade and function looked grimly down upon him from the walls. Dim lights were seen in some of the quarters of the priests constructed against the outer wall of the enclosure, and a torch was burning at the main entrance.

As the evening wore on the silence of the *heiau* was broken only by the hooting of the sacred owls from the walls of the inner temple, and Kiha threw himself at the foot of a pepper-tree, and was soon wafted out into the boundless sea of dreams.

After leaping the gate of the *heiau* the dog started up the valley with the speed of the wind. As he swept past the thatched huts in his course, those who caught sight of him for an instant were sure that they beheld a demon, and the dogs that pursued speedily returned, to crouch whiningly behind their masters.

Reaching the upper end of the valley, the dog followed an ascending trail through a steep ravine coming down from the northward, and in a short time, considering the distance traveled, stood snuffing the air at the verge of the forest within which the outlaws had found a temporary refuge. Distant lights were seen flickering through occasional openings among the trees and tangled undergrowth, and at intervals strange voices, as if of song and merriment, were heard.

For some time the dog remained motionless, and then stealthily crept into the forest. What form he assumed, how he learned of the hiding-place of the *Kiha-pu*, and through what means he escaped discovery, are details which tradition has left to conjecture. It is told only that he succeeded in finding in the unguarded hut of Ika, seizing in his mouth, and escaping undiscovered from the forest with, the sacred trumpet.

So adroitly had the theft been committed that it seemed that the dog would surely escape without detection ; but in plunging down the steep ravine through which he had finally ascended to the forest, he dropped the *Kiha-pu*, breaking from the rim a piece embracing the small *pea* or *tabu* mark of silence placed upon it by the *kaula* of Waianae. In an instant the liberated voices of the trumpet poured forth in a blast which echoed through the hills and started the night-birds to screaming.

The sound was heard by the reveling demi-demons of the forest, and, ascertaining that the shell had been stolen, they poured down the mountain-side in pursuit of the plunderer. Their speed was something more than human, and the darkness did not seem to impede their steps. From time to time the voice of the trumpet came back to them ; but it grew fainter and fainter in the distance, until they finally abandoned the chase as hopeless, Ika himself suggesting that the *Kiha-pu*, with its voices in some manner restored to it, had taken wings and escaped.

The king slept under the pepper-tree until past the middle of the night, when the hooting of an owl almost at his ear awoke him, and he rose and re-entered the royal retreat, where he found the high-priest with a number of his attendants, and the prisoner intently listening at the half-open door.

Kiha was about to inquire the time of the night—for he had neglected to look at the stars before entering—when a noise was heard at the outer gate. The prisoner stepped forward and threw back the door, and the next moment the dog sprang into the room, laid the *Kiha-pu* at the feet of the king, and then dropped dead beside it.

The overjoyed king raised and placed the trumpet to his lips, and with a swelling heart roused the people of Waipio with a blast such as they had not heard for more than eight years. Liberating the prisoner, who was grief-stricken at the death of his dog, Kiha ordered that he henceforth be fed from the royal table.

Winding another blast upon the trumpet, the king returned to the palace, around which were congregated hundreds of excited people. Among them were chiefs in yellow capes and helmets, and warriors armed with spear and battle-axe. Summoning his *alii-koa*, or principal military leader, a brief council was held, followed by the sending forth of the plumed aids of the king, and the speedy concentration within the palace grounds of a picked body of three or four hundred warriors armed with short javelins and knives for close encounter.

The little army moved rapidly but noiselessly up the valley, and at early daylight surrounded and attacked the camp of the demon band. A desperate hand-to-hand conflict ensued ; but the miscreants were overpowered, and all slain with the exception of Ika and two others, who were reserved alive for the altar.

On the evening following, in the midst of great rejoicing, the *Kiha-pu* was rededicated to *Lono*, and Ika and his companions were slain without the walls and sacrificed, with a host of other offerings, in the temple of *Paakalani.*

II.

The reign of Liloa was as peaceful as that of Kiha, his distinguished father. He did not lack ability, either as a civil or military leader, however his pleasant and mirthful ways may have impressed to the contrary. He was fond of good living, fine apparel and comely women ; yet he held the sceptre firmly, and was prompt to punish wrong-doing in his chiefs or infringement of any of his prerogatives. Nevertheless, his heart was kind, and he frequently forgave the humble who had crossed his shadow, and the thoughtless who had violated the spirit of a royal *tabu.*

As he was distracted neither by domestic disturbance nor wars with neighboring kings, Liloa made frequent visits to the several districts of the island, sometimes with an imposing retinue of chiefs and retainers, but quite as often with no more than two or three trusty attendants. Sometimes he traveled *incognito*, visiting suspected district chiefs to observe their methods of government, and, when occasion for rebuke occurred, to their great confusion making himself known to them.

Near the close of the year 1460, before the annual festival of *Lono*, which inaugurated the beginning of a new year, Liloa went with a large and brilliant party, in gaily-decked double canoes carrying the royal colors, from Waipio to Koholalele, in Hamakua, to assist in the reconsecration of the old temple of *Manini*, the restoration and enlargement of which had just been completed. He took with him his high-priest, Laeanui, a band of musicians and dancers, and his chief navigator and astrologer, and the *heiau* was consecrated with unusual display. Laeanui recited the *kuawili*—the long prayer of consecration—and twenty-four human victims were laid upon the altar.

Ordering the party to return in the double canoes without

him, Liloa resolved to make the journey overland to Waipio with a single attendant; and it is quite probable that it was something more than accident that prompted the royal traveler to deviate from the shortest path to Waipio, and tarry for some hours in a pleasant grove of palms near Kealakaha, where dwelt with her old father one of the most beautiful maidens in all Hamakua.

The name of the girl was Akahia-kuleana. She was tall and slender, and her dark hair, which rippled down in wavelets, shrouded her bare shoulders like a veil. Her eyes were soft, and her voice was like the music of a mountain rivulet, and when her bosom was bedecked with *leis* of fragrant blossoms it seemed that they must have grown there, so much did she appear to be a part of them.

Although in humble life, Akahia was really of royal blood, since six generations back her paternal ancestor was Kalahua-moku, a half-brother to Kalapana, from whom Liloa drew his strain. She knew the rank of her royal visitor, and felt honored that he should praise her beauty; and when he kissed her lips at parting he left with her his *maro* and the ivory clasp of his neck-lace, at the same time whispering words in her ear which in a generation later transferred the sceptre of Hawaii from the di-rect line to humbler but worthier hands.

Before the trade-winds came and went again the gentle Akahia, unwedded, became a mother. At first her father frowned upon the child ; but it was a strong and healthy boy, who looked as if he might some day wield with uncommon vigor a *laau-palau* if not a battle-axe, and he soon became reconciled to the pre-sence of the little intruder. In those days, it is proper to men-tion, such events occasioned but little comment, and entailed upon the mother neither social ostracism nor especial reproach.

The child was named Umi, and, to give it a stronger pro-tector than herself, Akahia became the wife of her cousin Maa-kao, a strong, rough man, who had always shown great affection for her, and who felt honored in becoming the husband of one who might have taken her choice among many.

The father of Akahia cultivated a *kalo* patch larger than his necessities really required, and was abundantly supplied with pigs, poultry, yams, bananas, cocoanuts and breadfruit, which he was at all times enabled to exchange for fish, crabs, limpets and other products of the sea.

All land titles at that time vested either in the sovereign or the chiefs subject to him, and the producer was frequently required to return to his landlord a full third or half of all his labor yielded. Sometimes the land-owner was more liberal with his tenants ; but quite as often he took to the extent of his need or greed, with no one to challenge the injustice of his demands.

But the bit of land occupied by the father of Akahia was part of a large tract reserved for the benefit of the king, and because of the *alii* blood with which he was credited, but of which he made no boast, the rent he returned was merely nominal.

When Umi was about ten years of age the father of Akahia died, leaving his little estate to his daughter. She had two brothers living, both older than herself. But the cultivation of the soil was not congenial to them, and, as there had been no wars of moment in Hawaii for nearly two generations, one of them, who had been a dreamer from his youth, had been inducted into the service of the gods by the high-priest Laeanui, to whom Liloa had given in perpetuity the possession of Kekaha, in the district of Kona, and was otherwise influential ; while the second brother, on reaching manhood, had gone with spear and sling to Maui, and risen to distinction in the military service of the *moi* of that island.

So Akahia and her husband continued to occupy unmolested the old plantation. But the agents who collected the revenues of the king were less liberal with Maakao than they had been with the father of his wife, and he was compelled to make the same rent returns as other royal tenants. Nor this alone. A portion of their land had been given to another, embracing a little grove of *hawane* or cocoa-trees, some of which, it was averred, had been planted by the stewards of Pili nearly four centuries before, and their depleted stocks of pigs and fowls ceased to be the envy of their neighbors.

This harsh dealing with Akahia and her husband, it is needless to say, was done without the knowledge of the king; but they feared to complain, lest they might be despoiled of the little left them, and deemed it prudent to suffer in silence rather than arouse the wrath of an agent of whose powers they knew not the extent.

There were other little mouths to feed besides Umi's, and, as the years came and went with their scant harvests, Maakao became more and more discontented; but, with a hope in her heart of which Maakao knew nothing, Akahia toiled on without complaint. Year by year she saw Umi developing into manhood, and noted that in thought, habit and bearing he was different from others.

Umi loved his mother and was not unkind to Maakao; but he spent much of his time by the sea-shore where the great waves thundered against the cliffs, and in the hills where, among the *ohia* and sandal trees, the trade-winds whispered to him of the unknown. He would climb to the crown of the tallest cocoa-tree because there was danger in it, and buffet the fiercest waves in his frail canoe; but neither threat nor persuasion could ever induce him to delve in the slime of the *kalo* patch or plant a row of yams. He would bring fish from the sea and fruits from the mountains, but could not be prevailed upon to till the soil. He fashioned spears of cunning workmanship, and from the teeth of sharks made knives of double edge, but to the implements of husbandry he gave but little note.

At the age of sixteen Umi had reached almost the proportions of a man. His limbs were strong, his features manly and handsome, his eyes clear and full of expression, and in athletic sports and the use of arms he had no equal among his companions. His habits brought around him but few friends, yet his kindness to all left no pretext for enmity ; and while some said he absented himself from home in a spirit of idleness, others shook their heads and ventured the opinion that he visited the recesses of the wooded hills alone to converse with the *kini-akua* and learn wisdom from the gods. And his strange conduct, it may well be imagined, was made the subject of frequent discussion in the neighborhood, for Maakao complained continually of his idleness, and but for the intercessions of the mother, who alone was able to account for his peculiarities, would have closed his doors against him.

But Umi had a few friends to extol his goodness and defend him against unkind insinuation, and among them were Piimaiwaa and Omaukamau, youths of about his own age, and Kulamea, the younger and only sister of the latter. From childhood these friends had been his frequent companions, and as he grew to manhood, strong-limbed, resolute and gentle, they learned to regard him with a love prepared for any sacrifice.

Kulamea was a bright-eyed, dusky little fairy, who often accompanied Umi and her brother in their rambles. They petted her until she became an exacting little tyrant, and then Umi, at her command, made toys for her, climbed the tallest cocoa-trees, and scaled the steepest cliffs in search of flowers and berries that she liked ; and, in return for these kindnesses, what, at the age of fifteen, could Kulamea do but love almost to idolatry the brave and gentle companion who had developed into a splendid manhood ? And what could Umi do at twenty but return in kind the devotion of one now ripening into a charming womanhood, whose childish friendship was the brightest sunshine that had ever flecked the landscape of his dreamy life ?

With a feeling of uneasiness Akahia watched Umi's growing love for Kulamea, and when at twenty he would have married her, much to the gratification of Maakao, she kindly but firmly said to her son : " Be not in haste to fetter your free limbs. Be patient, as I have been for twenty years. Kulamea is worthy— but wait."

" Why wait ? " exclaimed Maakao, suddenly appearing. He had been listening without the door. " Why should he wait ? " he continued ; " he has all his life been idle, and it is time that he should have a house of his own."

" You have spoken well ! " replied Umi, drawing himself up to his full height, and looking scornfully down upon the husband of his mother—" you have spoken well, Maakao ! It is time, indeed, that I stopped this dreaming ! I will never eat food again under your roof. Now get you to your *kalo* patch ; you will find occupation there befitting you ! I will seek other means of living ! "

With these scornful words Umi strode haughtily from the house. Enraged at the insult, Maakao seized a *laau-palau*, or large *kalo*-knife, and sprang after him. Umi turned and reached for his *pahoa*. Maakao raised his weapon to strike, but it dropped to the earth as if a paralysis had seized his arm as Akahia sprang before him, exclaiming : " Do not dare to strike ! He is not your son; he is your chief! Down on your knees before him!"

To the dismay of Maakao and profound astonishment of Umi, Akahia then revealed the secret of Umi's birth, and, taking from their hiding-place the keepsakes left with her by Liloa, said, as she handed them to her son :

"Your father is king of Hawaii. Go to him in person and place these mementoes before him. Tell him Akahia-kuleana returns them to him by the hands of his and her son, who is worthy of him, and he will own you to be the child of his love. He is noble and will hold sacred his royal pledge. This should have been done long ago, but I could not bring my heart to part with you. Go, and may the gods be your protection and your guide !"

The strange revelation was soon known throughout the neighborhood, and Umi prepared for his journey to Waipio. How should he appear before Liloa, whose will was law and whose frown was death ? In what guise should he seek the presence of his royal father ?

"As an *alii-kapu !*" answered Akahia, proudly. Then from an *ipu* she brought forth a plumed helmet and cape of the feathers of the *oo*, which she had secretly fabricated with her own hands, and placed them upon the head and shoulders of her son.

To Kulamea alone was the news of what had befallen Umi unwelcome. She would have been more than content to share with him the common lot ; but now that he was about to be recognized as the son of the great Liloa, she felt that they were soon to part for ever. Other alliances would be found for him, and he would forget the humble playmate of his youth, who loved him, not because his father was a king, but because they had grown up together and neither of them could help it. So when, two days after, Umi started overland for Waipio, accompanied by his two trusty friends, Piimaiwaa and Omaukamau, Kulamea secreted herself to avoid the agony of a parting farewell from Umi ; but he found her, nevertheless, and made her happy by kissing and telling her that, whatever might be his future, she should share it ; and she believed him, for he had never deceived her.

Umi and his companions arrived in Waipio valley at nightfall. There they remained during the night, and the next morning crossed the little stream of Wailoa, near which was the royal mansion. There Umi left his companions and proceeded alone to the palace enclosure. His head was adorned with a helmet surmounted with white and scarlet plumes, and from his broad shoulders hung a cape of yellow feathers, such as an *alii* alone was permitted to wear, while around his loins was fastened the *maro* left with Akahia by the king, and the ivory clasp ornamented a necklace of rare and beautiful shells. In his hand he bore an *ihe*, or javelin, of unusual weight and exquisite finish, and many eyes followed him as he approached the palace ; for, although a stranger, it was manifest from his dress and bearing that he did not belong to the *makaainana*, or common people.

His mother had instructed him to seek the presence of the king in the most direct manner that occasion presented, and without asking the permission or assistance of any one, fearing, no doubt, that, to gain admission to the royal *hale*, he might exhibit and in some manner lose possession of the sole evidences of his paternity, and thus receive the punishment of an impostor. He therefore passed by, without seeking to enter, the gate of the enclosure, around which were lounging a score or more of sentinels and retainers, and, proceeding to the rear of the mansion, leaped over the high wall immediately back and within a hundred paces of the private apartments of the king.

Having thus violated a rule of royal etiquette, the penalty of which was death, unless mitigated by satisfactory explanation, Umi grasped his *ihe* firmly, determined, should he be opposed, to fight his way to the royal presence. It was a desperate resolution, but he had faith in himself, and was without fear.

His movements had been watched as he passed the gate of the enclosure without a word, and as he sprang over the wall he found a number of uplifted spears between him and the entrances to the mansion. Nerving himself for the worst, he strode past the interposing weapons, strongly hurling their points aside when too closely presented, and in a moment stood at the back entrance of the palace, through which no one but of the royal household was permitted to enter.

This audacity saved him from more determined opposition, since it seemed incredible that any one not possessing the confidence of the king would take such double hazard of his life. Stepping within the entrance, Umi turned, and, with a half-amused smile at the baffled guard now clamoring around the door, struck the handle of his javelin firmly into the ground, and walked unarmed into the presence of the king.

As Umi entered unannounced, the king had just finished his morning repast, and was lounging on a couch of many folds of *kapa*, unattended except by his spittoon-bearer and two half-grown boys with *kahilis*.

Astounded at the intrusion, the king rose to a sitting posture, and, with a frown upon his face, was about to speak, when Umi stepped to the couch and boldly seated himself in the lap of Liloa.

Although past sixty, the king still retained a goodly share of his earlier vigor, and, throwing Umi from his knees, angrily exclaimed :

"Audacious slave ! how dare you ! "

Umi rose to his feet, and, standing proudly before the king with folded arms, replied :

"The son of Liloa dare do anything ! "

For a moment the king did not speak. He looked into the face of the undaunted young stranger, and noted that it was noble ; and then his thoughts went back to Kealakaha, and to the fair young girl of better than common blood whom he had met there many years before while journeying to Waipio after consecrating the temple of *Manini*, and finally, almost as in a dream, to the pledge he had given and the tokens he had left with her. When all this came back to him he cast his eyes over the comely youth, and beheld his *maro* around the loins of Umi, and the ivory clasp of his necklace upon his breast. He could scarcely doubt, yet, as if he had recollected nothing, seen nothing, he calmly but kindly said :

"Young man, you claim to be my son. If so, tell me of your mother, and of the errand that brings you here."

Umi bowed and answered : "My mother, O king, is Akahia-kuleana, of Kealakaha, and my years were twenty at the last ripening of the *ohias*. For the first time, four days ago, she told me I was the son of the king of Hawaii, and to take to him this *maro* and this ivory clasp, and he would not disown me. You are Liloa, the honored sovereign of Hawaii. I am Umi, the humble son of Akahia-kuleana. From the hands of my mother I have brought to you this *maro* and this ornament of bone. If I am your son, seat me beside you on the *kapa ;* if not, order my body to the *heiau* as a sacrifice to the gods."

There was a struggle in the breast of the king, and his eyes were bent upon the bold youth with an expression of pride and tenderness as he said :

"How did you gain admission here alone and unannounced?"

"By leaping over the wall of the *pahale* and beating down the spears of your guards," replied Umi modestly.

"It was a dangerous undertaking," suggested the king, feigning a frown which wrinkled into a smile upon his lips; "had you no fear?"

"I am still young and have not yet learned to fear," returned Umi, with an air of self-reproach.

"Such words could come alone from a heart ennobled by the blood of Pilikaeae! You are indeed the son of Liloa!" exclaimed the king, with emotion, stretching forth his hand and seating Umi beside him. "Not these tokens alone but your face and bearing show it." And he put his arms around the neck of his son and kissed him, and ordered a repast, which they ate together, while Umi related to his royal father the simple events of his humble life.

As the strange entrance of Umi into the royal mansion had attracted much attention, many of the privileged retainers and officers of the court soon gathered in and around the palace; and the rank and possible purposes of the visitor were undergoing an earnest discussion—especially after it was learned that he was breakfasting with the king—when Hakau, the only recognized son of Liloa and heir-presumptive to the throne, suddenly appeared and sought the presence of his royal father.

There was a dark scowl on the face of Hakau on entering the room and observing a stranger in close conversation with the king and eating from the same vessels, nor did it disappear when Liloa presented Umi to him as his own son and Hakau's half-brother. Umi rose and frankly offered his brother the hand of friendship and affection; but the grasp and recognition of Hakau were cold, and when he was invited to sit down and partake of meat with his newly-found brother he excused himself with the falsehood that he had just risen from his morning meal. After a few words with the king, during which he closely scrutinized Umi's handsome face and manly form, Hakau withdrew, leaving no token in word or look of any feeling of joy at the meeting.

Although the kings of the Hawaiian group at that time usually had from two to six wives—either marriages of the heart or alliances with the families of neighboring kings to strengthen their dynasties—tradition has given to Liloa but one recognized wife. She was Pinea, a Maui chiefess of family distinction, who gave to Liloa a son and one daughter—Hakau and Kapukini. Hakau had reached his thirtieth year and had married the daughter of the chief and high-priest Pae. They had one child, a daughter, who had been given the name of her grandmother, Pinea. Kapukini had not quite reached womanhood, and was the idol of the court.

Hakau was a large, well-visaged man, but was haughty, selfish and cruel. Having been, until the sudden appearance of Umi at the court, the only recognized son of Liloa, his caprices had been humored until his heartlessness and tyranny had become almost a by-word in Hamakua. But the truth seems to be that he was naturally vicious and barbarous, and tradition speaks of no greater tyrant among all the rulers of Hawaii. Heedless of the rights of property, without return he took from others whatever he coveted, and in an insanity of pride and criminal envy caused to be secretly slain or disfigured such as were reputed to surpass him in personal beauty. Without giving note or credence to the many tales of barbarism with which tradition has connected his name, it is doubtless true that his cruelty and contempt for the rights of his subjects rendered him an unfit successor of the gentle and sagacious Liloa, under whose reign the humblest were protected, and peace and prosperity prevailed throughout the six districts of the island.

No further explanation of Hakau's freezing reception of Umi is required. He was envious of his handsome face and noble bearing, and hated him because of the love with which his father manifestly regarded him. But Hakau's feelings in the matter were not consulted, and the day following Umi was conducted to the temple of *Paakalani* in great pomp, where, to the solemn music of chant and sacred drum, the officiating priest with the newly-found son of the king went through the form of *oki-ka-piko*—a ceremony attending the birth of the children of royalty—and Umi was formally and publicly recognized as his son by the king of Hawaii.

Hakau was compelled, with great bitterness of heart, to witness this ceremony, but was too discreet to openly manifest his displeasure. Returning to the palace, Umi was formally presented to the royal household, and heralds proclaimed his rank and investiture of the *tabus* to which he was entitled.

Although the mother of Hakau, Pinea received him kindly, and Kapukini was more than delighted with her new and handsome brother. She clung to his hand, and artlessly declared that Hakau was cross with her and that she had prayed to the gods to send her another brother, just such a one as Umi, and they had done so.

Soon after a great feast was given by the king in honor of the new heir, and all the leading chiefs in the kingdom were invited to come and pay their respects to him. Twelve hundred chiefs were present, and the feasting and rejoicing continued for three days, interspersed with games and athletic sports, in which Umi shone with great splendor. In feats of strength and the skilful handling of arms he had few equals in all that great and distinguished gathering, and in conversations with the old he exhibited so much wisdom and prudence of speech that they wondered who had been his tutors ; and when they learned that he had been taught by no one and that the greater part of his young life had been passed in solitude, some of them thought the gods must have instructed him, and all admitted that he was a worthy son of Liloa and an honor to the royal line.

Umi was thus firmly established at the court of his royal father, and adequate revenues were set apart for his proper maintenance and that of a retinue befitting his high rank. His friends Piimaiwaa and Omaukamau, who were overjoyed at his good fortune, entered his service as his personal and confidential friends, and thenceforth became identified with his career, always appearing as the most faithful and self-sacrificing of his adherents.

In a week after his arrival at Waipio, Umi sent Omaukamau back to their old home with news of his recognition by the king. He also bore an order enlarging the area of Maakao and Akahia's possessions, and relieving them from rent and all other tenant charges. Nor did he forget Kulamea. He sent her a little present in token of his love, and word that, although it could not safely be so then, some day in the future she should be nearer to him, even though he might become the king of Hawaii. The token was dear to her, and dearer still his words, for she knew the heart of Umi and did not doubt; and thenceforth she lived and patiently waited for him, keeping her own secret, and firmly saying "no " to the many who sought her in marriage.

Umi's affability and intelligence soon made him a great favorite at the court and steadily endeared him to his father.   But in proportion as he grew in the favor of others Hakau's hatred for him increased, and but for the fear of his father would have manifested itself in open hostility ; but Liloa, who was growing old and feeble through a cureless malady, had not yet designated his successor, and Hakau deemed it prudent to make no outward showing of the intense envy and dislike of his brother which he was secretly nursing, and which he resolved should be gratified when the reins of government passed into his hands.

In a little less than two years after the recognition of Umi the black *kapa* covered Liloa.   When he felt the end approaching he called his two sons before him, and publicly gave the charge of the government and title of *moi* to Hakau, and the custody of the gods and temples to Umi.   "You are to be the ruler of Hawaii," he said to Hakau, "and Umi is to be your counselor."

There was grief all over the kingdom when the death of Liloa became known, for he was greatly beloved ; and, that his bones might never be desecrated, the high-priest Pae, whose daughter Hakau had married, secretly conveyed them to the Kona coast, and consigned them to the deep waters off Kekaha.

This was in accordance with the custom of the time—in fact, with the custom of earlier and later years, for the resting-place of the bones of Kamehameha I., who died in 1819, is unknown. A story survives that the remains of this eminent chief were entombed in the sea, but the more popular belief is that they were secretly conveyed to a cave or other place prepared for them in the hills back of Kailua, on the island of Hawaii, and there hidden for ever from mortal gaze.   In connection with this belief it is stated that just before daylight on the morning following the night of the death of Kamehameha, one of his nearest friends, while the guard had been removed to afford the opportunity, took the bones of his beloved chief upon his shoulders, and, alone and unseen, conveyed them to their secret sepulchre.   Returning, he encountered two natives who were preparing for the labors of the day.   Fearing that he had been followed, he inquired whether they had observed any one passing toward the hills that morning.   They declared that they had seen no one. Had they answered differently he would have slain them both on the spot, that their secret might have died with them.

The name of this chief was Hoolulu. He has been dead for many years ; and although he left children, to one of whom the secret may have been imparted, in accordance with native custom in such matters, it is now believed that all knowledge of the depository of the remains of the first Kamehameha is lost. In 1853, when the necessity of hiding the bones of distinguished chiefs was no longer recognized, Kamehameha III. visited Kailua and almost prevailed upon Hoolulu to point out the spot. They even started toward the hills for that purpose, but, as quite a number of persons were observed to be following, Hoolulu declined to proceed, and could never after be induced to divulge anything.

So fearful were the ancient chiefs of Hawaii that some indignity might be offered to their remains after death—for instance, that charmed fish-hooks or arrow-points for shooting mice might be made from their bones—that they were invariably hidden by their surviving friends, sometimes in the depths of the ocean, and quite as frequently, perhaps, in the dark recesses of volcanic caverns, with which the islands abound.

Immediately after Kamehameha I. had breathed his last his friend Kalaimoku assembled the principal chiefs around the body to consider what should be done with it. In his great admiration for the dead chief one of them solemnly said : " This is my thought : we will eat him raw ! " But the body was left to Liholiho, son and successor of the dead king who, with his queen, Kamamalu, died while on a visit to England in 1824.

The bones of no Hawaiian chief were ever more securely hidden than were those of the distinguished *alii-nui* Kualii, who ruled with a strong arm the turbulent factions of the island of Oahu some two centuries back. After the flesh had been stripped from the bones they were given in charge of a trusty friend to be secreted, and most effectually did he accomplish the delicate task assigned him. He had them pulverized to a fine powder, which he mixed with the *poi* to be served at the funeral feast to be given to the principal chiefs the day following. At the close of the repast, when asked if he had secreted the bones of the dead chief to his satisfaction, he grimly replied : " Hidden, indeed, are the bones of Kualii ! They have been deposited in a hundred living sepulchres. You have eaten them ! "

But we are wandering somewhat from our story. The day

after the death of Liloa, Hakau was ceremoniously invested with supreme authority, while the high-priest Laeanui gave formal recognition to Umi as guardian of the gods and temples. Both events were celebrated with display and sacrifice ; but it is said that the scream of the *alae*, a sacred bird of evil omen, was heard around the palace all through the night that Hakau first slept there as king, and that as Umi entered the temple of *Paakalani* to assume the guardianship of the gods the head of the great image of *Lono*, near the door of the inner temple, nodded approvingly.

Independently of Umi's position as prime minister or royal adviser, his authority as guardian of the gods and temples was second only to that of the king, and Hakau chafed under a bequest that had clothed his brother with a power little less than his own and placed him so near the throne. The consequence was that he seldom invited him to his councils, and secretly sought to cast discredit upon his acts as the nominal head of the priesthood. But Umi bore himself so nobly that Hakau's venom brought no poison to him, and the petty persecutions to which he was subjected not only failed to injure him, but actually added to his popularity with those who had felt the barbarity of his brother, whose first acts on coming to power were to dismiss, disrate and impoverish many of the old and faithful servants and counselors of his father, and surround himself with a party of unscrupulous retainers as cruel and treacherous as himself.

Enraged that his secret aud cowardly slanders of Umi failed to bring him into disrespect, Hakau's hostility began to assume a more open and brutal form. He publicly reviled his brother for his low birth, and assumed not only that Liloa was not his father, but that his mother was a woman without any distinction of blood.

Unable to bear these taunts, and not deeming it prudent to precipitate an open rupture with his brother, Umi quietly left Waipio with his two friends Piimaiwaa and Omaukamau, and, traveling through Hamakua without stopping at Kealakaha, where dwelt his mother and Kulamea, proceeded at once to Waipunalei, near Laupahoehoe, in the district of Hilo, where he concluded to remain for a time and await the development of events.

To support themselves Umi and his two friends devoted a portion of their time to fishing, bird-catching and the making of canoes, spears and other weapons ; and although the rank of Umi was studiously concealed, his intelligence, skilful use of arms and general bearing could not fail to attract attention and excite the curiosity of his humble associates. Not unfrequently strangers would prostrate themselves before him, so profoundly were they impressed with his appearance, but he declined to accept their homage and smilingly assured them that he was born and reared, like themselves, in humble life. As a further precaution against recognition, he carefully avoided the prominent chiefs of the district, deeming it probable that some of them had seen him in Waipio, or even witnessed the ceremonies attending his acceptance as the son of Liloa.

III.

It was not destined that Umi should remain long unknown among the hills of Hilo. His sudden disappearance and continued absence from the court had excited apprehensions of foul dealing, and Hakau himself, who had thus far failed in his efforts to discover the retreat of Umi, began to fear that he was somewhere secretly planning a deep scheme of retaliation. But Umi had as yet marked out for himself no definite plan of action. He smarted under the persecutions of Hakau, and did not doubt that, sooner or later, he would triumph over them and be restored to the rights and privileges bequeathed to him by his royal father ; but exactly when and how all this was to be accomplished were problems which he expected the future to assist him in solving.

And he was not disappointed. The future for which he had patiently waited was near at hand, and he was about to become the central figure of a struggle which would test to their utmost his courage and ability. One day, while strolling alone in the hills back of Waipunalei, there suddenly appeared before him a man of stupendous proportions. Umi regarded the object for a moment with amazement, and was about to speak when the monster dropped on his knees before him. In that position he was a head and shoulders above Umi, and the spear in his hand was of the measure in length of ten full steps. Although more than eleven feet in height, he was well proportioned, and the expression of his face was intelligent and gentle. He was young in years, yet his hair fell to his shoulders and was streaked with gray.

"Who are you, and why do you kneel to me?" said Umi, looking up into the face of the giant with a feeling of awe. "If I had your limbs I would kneel alone to the gods."

"I am Maukaleoleo, of Kona, and the most unfortunate of men," replied the monster in a ponderous but not unpleasant tone "My mother was Nuuheli; but she is now dead, and, having grown to the height of the trees, I live in the mountains among them, for men seem to fear and hate me, and women and children scream with fright at my approach."

"And who was your father?" inquired Umi, kindly.

"As he died when I was young," returned the giant, "and that was more than thirty years ago, I know not, except that his name was Mano, and that he claimed lineage from Kahaukapu, the grandfather of the great Liloa, whose unworthy son now rules in Hawaii."

"Hist!" exclaimed Umi, reaching up and placing his hand gently upon the shoulder of the monster. "There is death in such words, even to a man of Maukaleoleo's girth. The trees are listeners as well as myself."

"The trees will say nothing," was the reply, "for they often hear such words of Hakau. But why should I fear death? I was not born to be slain for speaking the truth. Listen, and then tell me why Maukaleoleo should fear anything that is human. When a boy a stranger met me one day on the cliffs overlooking the sea, where I was searching for the feathers of the *oo*. He was mighty in stature, and in fear I fell upon the ground and hid my face. He called me by name, and I looked up and saw that he held in his hand a small fish of the color of the skies at sunset. Handing the fish to me, he said: 'Eat this, and to see your face all men will look toward the stars.' I knew he was a god—*Kanaloa*, perhaps—and I feared to refuse. So I took the fish and ate it, and the stranger stepped over the cliffs with a smile on his face and disappeared. The fish was pleasant to the taste, and I could have eaten more. A strange sense of increasing strength seized me, and on my way home I lifted large rocks and felt that I could uproot trees. I said nothing to my mother of what had happened, but the next morning she looked at me with fright and wonder, for during the night I had grown an arm's length in height. Except upon my hands and knees I could no longer enter the door of the house where I was born, and everything with which I was familiar had a dwarfed and unnatural look. I was ashamed to meet my old associates, and only ventured from the house when it was too dark for me to be plainly seen. Larger and larger I grew, until at the age of fifteen I reached my present proportions, when my mother died, and I made my home in the mountains, where I have since spent the most of my time. What should one so treated by the gods fear from man?" And Maukaleoleo rose to his feet, towering like a cocoa-tree above his companion.

"A strange story, indeed! But if the trees, which are speechless, do not betray you, why should not I?" said Umi, curious to learn something farther of the strange being in whose veins possibly coursed the blood of kings.

"Because," answered the giant, slowly, "you are Umi, the son of Liloa, and Hakau is your enemy!"

Umi listened to these words in amazement, and then frankly said:

"You are right. I am Umi, the son of Liloa, and Hakau is not my friend. And now that you know so much, you cannot but also know that it is prudent for me to remain at present unknown. Let me ask in return that you will not betray me."

"I know all, and you may fear nothing," said Maukaleoleo. "Before the moon grows large again I shall be with you, spear in hand, on your way to Waipio. Meantime you may lose sight of me, but I shall be near you when my arm is needed. You have powerful friends. Be guided by them, and all will be well."

Umi held up his hand, and Maukaleoleo folded it in his mighty palm as he dropped upon his knees and exclaimed:

"Umi, son of Liloa! here in the hills, among the listening leaves, let Maukaleoleo be the first to hail you *moi* of Hawaii!"

Before Umi could rebuke the untimely utterance Maukaleoleo rose to his feet and with a low bow disappeared among the trees.

With whatever feeling of fear the *makaainana*, or laboring classes, of Waipunalei may have regarded Maukaleoleo, as he occasionally appeared among them like a moving tower, he was not without friends. He was well known to the priests and *kaulas* of the district, who believed that his huge proportions

were due to the special act of some god, and was always a welcome visitor at the home of Kaoleioku, a high-priest of great
influence both in Hilo and Hamakua. It is therefore probable
that this meeting with Umi was not entirely accidental, for the
day following Kaoleioku despatched a messenger to Umi, who
was found not without some difficulty, inviting him to a conference in a secluded spot near the head of a neighboring valley.

The object of the meeting was not stated, and Umi's first
thought was that the emissaries of his brother were seeking to
lure him to his death ; but no danger ever appalled him, and,
seizing his javelin and thrusting a *pahoa* into his girdle, he followed the messenger.

A brisk walk of an hour brought them to a small grass hut
partially hidden among the trees and undergrowth of an almost
dry ravine abruptly jutting into the valley. At that point the
valley was too narrow to admit of cultivation, although a broken
stone wall across the mouth of the ravine showed that at one
time three or four uneven acres behind it had been tilled. The
grass grew rank within the enclosure, and, in addition to several
varieties of forest trees that had taken root since the ground had
last been disturbed, a half-dozen or more cocoa-trees lifted their
heads above the surrounding foliage, and the broad leaves of as
many banana-stalks swayed lazily in the wind.

It was a lonesome-looking spot, and no sign of life in or
around the hut was visible as the messenger stopped at a gap in
the crumbling wall and awaited the approach of Umi. The chirp
of the crickets in the grass seemed to be a note of warning, and
the whistle of a solitary bird hidden among the leaves sounded
like a scream to Umi in that deserted and otherwise silent nook ;
but he grasped his *ihe* firmly and beckoned the messenger to proceed. As he stepped over the broken wall he caught a glimpse
of the ponderous form of Maukaleoleo through the branches of
a sandal-tree on the side of the hill overlooking the hut. Under
the eye of that mighty and friendly sentinel Umi dismissed all
thought of treachery or danger.

Reaching the door of the hut, he was met by the high-priest
Kaoleioku, who promptly extended his hand and invited him to
enter, while the messenger withdrew from the enclosure and took
a position where he commanded a view of the valley above and
below the mouth of the ravine.

There was no furniture in the hut beyond two or three rick-ety shelves, and on one side a raised platform of earth, which, with a *kapa* covering, might have been used either as a bed or seat. On entering the priest requested Umi to be seated, and then bowed low and said :

" I cannot doubt that I am standing before Umi, son of Liloa, and guardian of our sacred temples and our fathers' gods." To these words the priest silently awaited an answer.

Umi did not reply at once ; but after giving the face of the priest a searching glance, and recalling his meeting with Mauka-leoleo the day before, and the vision through the branches of the sandal-tree, he frankly answered :

" I cannot deny it."

" No ; you cannot, indeed ! " returned the priest, fervently ; " for so have the clouds told me, and so has it been whispered in my dreams. Word has come to me from Waipio that Hakau knows you are in Waipunalei, and his emissaries are already here with orders to assassinate you."

" Then further disguise would be useless, further delay cow-ardly ! " exclaimed Umi, rising from his seat and grasping his *ihe.* " His cruelty forces me at last to strike ! The time for action has come, and, spear in hand, as befits a son of Liloa, I will face the royal murderer in Waipio, and the black *kapa* shall be his or mine ! "

" Spoken like a king and a son of a king ! " returned the priest with enthusiasm, grasping Umi by the hand. " But you will not go alone. Come to me with your friends to-morrow—if possible to-night. Under my roof you will be safe, and there we will gather the spears that will make your journey to Waipio a triumphal march."

" Thanks are the only payment I can now make to your friendship," said Umi, in turn pressing the hand of the priest. " You may expect me and a few of my friends before another rising of the sun."

With a few hasty words of explanation Umi left the hut with his heart on fire, and the priest watched him with a smile until he passed the broken wall. There he was re-joined by the messenger, who silently preceded him down the valley.

As he started to return Umi looked toward the sandal-tree above the hut. Maukaleoleo was no longer there, but he frequently discerned a mighty form moving down the valley along the wooded hillside, and knew that his great friend was not far away.

The northeastern coast of the island of Hawaii presents an almost continuous succession of valleys, with intervening uplands rising gently for a few miles, and then more abruptly toward the snows of Mauna Kea and the clouds. The rains are abundant on that side of the island, and the fertile plateau, boldly fronting the sea with a line of cliffs from fifty to a hundred feet in height, is scored at intervals of one or two miles with deep and almost impassable gulches, whose waters reach the ocean either through rocky channels worn to the level of the waves, or in cascades leaping from the cliffs and streaking the coast from Hilo to Waipio with lines which seem to be of molten silver from the great crucible of Kilauea.

In the time of Liloa, and later, this plateau was thickly populated, and, requiring no irrigation, was cultivated from the sea upward to the line of frost. A few *kalo* patches are still seen, and bananas grow, as of old, in secluded spots and along the banks of the ravines; but the broad acres are green with cane, and the whistle of the sugar-mill is heard above the roar of the surf that beats against the rock-bound front of Hamakua.

In the first of these valleys south of Waipunalei was the estate of the high-priest Kaoleioku, which was thickly dotted with the huts of his tenants, and embraced some of the finest banana, cocoa and breadfruit groves in the district. For the accommodation of himself and family were two large mansions, constructed of heavy timbers and surrounded by a substantial stone wall. The priest was learned and hospitable, and his influence was second in the district only to that of the *alii-okane*.

Anticipating the arrival of Umi and his friends during the night, the priest had placed a watchman at the gate on retiring, with instructions to wake him should any one unknown to the sentinel apply for admission before morning. But Kaoleioku could not sleep, for his mind was filled with the shadows of coming events. He had discovered a son of

Liloa, the rightful guardian of the temples and his gods, secreted among the *makaainani* to escape the persecutions of
his tyrannical and heartless brother ; and as a reconciliation
between them did not seem to be possible, he had resolved
to urge Umi into open revolt at once, and to assist him to
the full extent of his power in organizing a force to contest
with Hakau the right to the sovereignty of Hawaii. This he
was moved to do, not more because Hakau was a tyrant,
than that he had sought to degrade the priesthood, of which
Umi was the nominal head, and in the dedication of a temple in Waimea had sacrilegiously usurped the powers and
privileges of the high-priest. Should the revolt prove unsuccessful, his life, he well knew, would be one of the forfeits
of the failure ; but the priest was a courageous man, and did
not hesitate to accept the hazard of the perilous undertaking.
Although reared in the priesthood, he could wield a spear with
the best, and when in arms his fifty years sat lightly upon him.

With his mind filled with the details of the dangerous labors before him, the priest tossed restlessly upon his couch of
kapa until past midnight, when he rose and strolled out among
the palms. Wearied with walking, he stretched himself upon the grass, and, fanned by the trade-winds and soothed
by the stars which seemed to smile upon him through the
branches of the trees, he followed his troubled thoughts into
the land of dreams ; and there a voice said to him thrice :
"Let the spears of Hakau be sent beyond the call of the
Kiha-pu, and the victory of Umi will be bloodless !"

A voice beside the sleeper awoke him, and he was informed by the watchman that a considerable number of
strangers were at the gate and desired admission. The priest
rose to his feet, and, with the mysterious words of the dream
still ringing in his ears, proceeded to the gate, where the tall
form of Umi loomed up in the darkness. Giving him his
hand with a warm word of welcome, the priest was about to
conduct him within when he was startled at the sudden appearance at the gate of a party of armed and resolute-looking men
—how many he was unable to distinguish.

The priest was about to speak when Umi laid his hand
upon his shoulder and said in a low voice: "All trusty
friends."

"Then all are welcome," replied the priest, and, giving an order to the watchman, he stepped aside with Umi, when two hundred warriors, appareled for battle, silently filed in double rank through the opening, following Omaukamau and Piimaiwaa to quarters evidently prepared for a much greater number.

"Truly, a good beginning!" exclaimed the priest, with enthusiasm, as the last of the little army passed the gate.

"A few that my good friends have been sounding since yesterday," said Umi, modestly. "They do not know me yet as Umi, but are inspired with a hatred for Hakau. The number could have been greatly increased, but I feared your ability to accommodate more without warning."

"It was thoughtful; but ten times their number can be secreted within these walls. But come," continued the priest, taking the arm of Umi and proceeding toward the larger mansion; "there is red in the east, and you must have rest and sleep. When you awake I will give you a dream to interpret. It relates to the business before us."

"Tell me of the dream before I sleep, good Kaoleioku," urged Umi, pleasantly, "and perhaps some god may whisper an answer to it in my slumbers."

"Well thought," replied the priest; and he related his dream to Umi as he conducted him to a room in the large *hale* and pointed to a pile of soft *kapa* on a low platform.

The priest bowed and retired, and Umi, who had rested but little for three days, threw himself upon the *kapa-moe* and slept soundly until the sun was high in the heavens.

The young chief awoke greatly refreshed, and, after his morning bath, sought the presence of the priest, who since daylight had been busily engaged in despatching messengers to his friends in various parts of the district, and even to Puna and Hamakua, and arranging for supplies of arms, provisions and other warlike stores. Against the walls of the enclosure a number of long sheds had been hastily constructed, under which, screened from observation from without, men were repointing spears and *ihes*, and repairing slings, daggers and other weapons. In fact, the enclosure began to assume the appearance of a military camp rather than the peaceful habitation of a priest; and as Umi looked around him he appreciated for the first time that a step had been taken which could not be retraced, and that the lives

of himself and many of his friends could be saved alone by destroying Hakau, in whose heart lived no feeling of mercy. But, as the
conflict had been forced upon him, he accepted it without fear or
regret, and his courage would not permit him to doubt the result.

Umi greeted and thanked the priest for the warlike preparations visible on all sides, and over their morning meal together
were discussed the resources and details of the coming struggle.
It was not believed that a sufficient force could be rallied in the
district to make head against the battalions of the king in open
fight, for news of the ripening rebellion was spreading in the
neighborhood and would soon reach Waipio.

"What we lack in spears must be made up in cunning," said
the priest, confidently. "The gods are with us, and the means
of victory will be pointed out."

"Perhaps," replied Umi, thoughtfully; "but sometimes the
direction is vague and we are apt to mistake it. Olopana failed
to interpret correctly the will of *Kane*, as sent to him through his
high-priest, and was driven by the floods from Waipio, and compelled to return to *Kahiki*, the land of his fathers."

"True," returned the priest, not a little astonished at Umi's
knowledge of the ancient chiefs of Hawaii, "and we must not
fall into the same error. The gods, perhaps, have already spoken.
'Let the spears of Hakau be sent beyond the call of the *Kiha-
pu*,' are the words that have come to me, but I can find no interpretation of them. We must make sacrifice at once, and consult
the *kaulas*."

"That would be well," said Umi; "yet it may be that a hint
of their meaning, if nothing more, has been sent to me. I slept
with the words this morning, you will remember, and now I recall that a whisper advised that we should take to our counsel
Nunu and Kakohe, of Waipio."

"You have made the way clear!" exclaimed the priest, earnestly. "I know the men well. They are priests of influence
and large learning. They were the advisers of Liloa, and are
now the enemies of Hakau."

"The same," said Umi; "I have met them both."

"Then will we despatch a discreet messenger for them at
once," returned the priest, rising abruptly. "Every moment is
precious, and their counsel may be the voice of the gods."

And now, while the messenger is on his way to Waipio, it may be in place to make some further mention of the two priests in search of whom he was sent, as they contributed in no small measure to Umi's final success, and were thereafter rated among his confidential counsellors.

Nunu and Kakohe were chiefs of distinction and belonged to the priesthood. They were both learned in the lore of the gods and the traditions of the people, and were so highly esteemed by Liloa that he frequently invited them to the royal mansion, and late in life spent one or more evenings with them in each month, when he listened to recitals of the traditions of his fathers, and mistier lines of demi-gods and heroes stretching backward in unbroken thread to the morning of creation. They were among the few who could recite the sacred genealogical *mele* of *Kumuhonua*, the Hawaiian Adam, and he loved to listen to the naming of the generations from the first man to *Nuu*, of the great flood, and thence to *Wakea*, and downward still nearly sixty generations to himself. Some differences existing between the genealogies of Hawaii and Maui, Liloa had sent them to the latter island to confer with its priests and historians, with the view of reconciling their disagreements. Their mission was successful, and what is known as the *Ulu* genealogy was the result of the learned conference.

These were among the friends of Liloa who, for the sake of the father and the honor of the royal line, had patiently and earnestly sought to divert Hakau from his barbarous practices. But he had scorned their kind offices, made light of their learning, and finally denied them admission to the palace. He hoped by his cruelty to drive them from Waipio; but in the prophetic flames they had read their future, and from within the sacred *anu* of the temple voices had come to them enjoining patience; so they sat down and waited.

Arriving at Waipio, the messenger of Kaoleioku had but little difficulty in finding the two priests of whom he was in search. It was some hours after nightfall, but on inquiry he was directed to their humble dwelling on the south side of the stream, and soon stood at their door. It was dark within, and on making his presence known two men appeared at the opening. The messenger saluted them politely, and, observing but a single person, they cautiously stepped from the door and inquired of the visitor his business with them.

By their garb and bearing he knew them to be priests, but that was not enough ; he could afford to make no mistake, so he dissembled and said :

"I have probably been misinformed ; this is not the house of Monana, the fisherman ?"

"My friend," said Nunu, "your words do not mislead us. Whether for good or evil I know not, but you are in search of Kakohe and Nunu, and they are here. If you have business with them, speak ; there are no listeners."

The messenger answered by unfolding from a piece of *kapa* an ivory talisman carved from a whale's tooth, which he handed to Nunu, with a request that he would examine it. Stepping to a fire still smouldering near the oven of the hut, the priest threw upon it a handful of dry bark, which in a moment burst into a flame and enabled him to inspect the *palaoa*. Returning and addressing a few words to his companion, the priest said to the messenger :

"You are from Kaoleioku, of Waipunalei."

"I am from Kaoleioku, of Waipunalei," repeated the messenger, bowing.

"How long since ?" inquired the priest.

"Late this morning," was the answer.

"You must have traveled swiftly, for the paths are rough and the distance is a long day's journey," suggested the priest, cautiously.

"My feet have known no rest," was the brief reply.

"What news bring you of Kaoleioku ?"

"None."

"Then why are you here with this *palaoa* ?"

"Because so commanded by Kaoleioku."

"There are rumors of coming troubles on the borders of Hamakua. Has Kaoleioku sent you to tell us of them ?"

"I am here to say nothing of Kaoleioku, but to say for him, and to say only, that he prays that Nunu and Kakohe will meet him under his own roof at Waipunalei without delay."

"And nothing more ?"

"Nothing more."

"You are discreet."

"I am simply the bearer of a message ; and now that I have delivered it, I am waiting for such answer as you may desire to send back with me to Kaoleioku."

"When will you return?"

"To-night."

"Then tell Kaoleioku that his friends Nunu and Kakohe will be with him by this time to-morrow. Now come," continued the priest, "there is meat in the *mua*, and you must eat, for there is a wearying journey before you."

The messenger was led into an adjoining hut, where meat and *poi* were set before him, and half an hour after he was scaling the hills east of the valley of Waipio.

Although the messenger was silent, the priests felt assured that there was a gathering of spears in the neighborhood of Waipunalei, and that Kaoleioku was secretly inciting a revolt. They knew that Umi was somewhere among the hills of Hilo, and felt strong in hoping that at the proper time he would be found at the head of the movement.

Hakau had very much underrated the power of the priesthood, and did not discover until too late that in seeking to persecute and degrade Umi, who had been given charge of the gods and temples by Liloa, he had provoked the hostility of a class which at that period of Hawaiian history no sovereign could safely defy. If the *tabus* of the *moi* were sacred, those of the high-priests were none the less inviolable, and the strongest chiefs in the group were those who held in greatest respect and enjoyed the largest friendship of the priesthood. Like the temporal rulers, the priests inherited their functions, and were as jealous of their prerogatives as royalty itself. It was through them that the civil as well as the religious traditions of the people had been brought down and perpetuated, and through their prayers and sacrifices only that the gods could be persuaded to accord success to important undertakings.

In the veins of some of the priests ran royal blood, and from time to time they left their *heiaus* and became distinguished as warriors ; but under no circumstances did they ever relinquish their sacred rights. They not unfrequently possessed large landed estates, the title to which remained inalienably in the family. Such, for example, was the Kekaha estate, in the district of Kona, Hawaii, which was the gift of Liloa to Laeanui, and which remained with the descendants of that eminent high-priest until the days of Kamehameha I.

Such a warrior-priest of goodly possessions was Kaoleioku, of

Waipunalei. He was the high-priest of the temple of *Manini*, at Koholalele, which was consecrated, as before related, in the time of Liloa. Although for some years he had seldom officiated, except on important occasions—preferring the quieter life of his estate at Waipunalei—he was greatly respected by the people of the district, and his influence proved a tower of strength to Umi.

IV.

True to the answer returned to Kaoleioku by his messenger, Nunu and Kakohe reached Waipunalei the following night ; and when they saw the warlike preparations, and learned that Umi was present and that the acclaim of revolt was to be raised in his name, they wept for joy. It was past midnight, and their limbs were weary, but they could not sleep. At their request the door of Umi's room was pointed out to them, and they went and sat down beside it. For an hour or more they did not speak. Then, when all was still within the walls, in a low tone they began the legendary chant of the kings of Hawaii. As they proceeded with a record which few on the island beside themselves could correctly repeat, their voices rose with their enthusiasm, and in a few minutes hundreds of half-naked men crept from their barrack lodgings and stood listening to the metric sentences of the learned historians. As they reached the name of Kiha, Umi stepped without the door. The priests recognized him and rose to their feet. Then, continuing the *mele*, they chanted the name of Kiha, of Liloa, of Hakau, and finally of Umi, represented as having wrested the sceptre from his unworthy brother, who was hated by his subjects and abandoned by the gods. With this they dropped on their knees before him and boldly saluted him as *moi* of Hawaii.

This acquainted many of the warriors present for the first time of Umi's rank, and the wildest enthusiasm seized them. They asked to be led at once to Waipio, and were only quieted when Kaoleioku appeared and assured them that their patriotic wishes would soon be gratified.

At first Kaoleioku deemed this early development of the purposes of the movement untimely, if not, indeed, unfortunate. Many preparations remained to be made. It had been a suggestion of Umi that a part of the rebel forces should be sent to Waipio by water ; but the canoes necessary for the expedition had not been secured, and not more than a thousand warriors had reported. Secrecy could no longer be maintained, and immediate and open action appeared to be now unavoidable. Yet it was through Nunu and Kakohe that his plans had been thwarted, and while he felt annoyed at what they had done, he retired, hoping they had acted advisedly in the matter.

The conduct of the priests was explained and approved the next morning. They urged immediate action. Hakau was not prepared for a sudden attack. For many years there had been no wars of consequence, and such of his supporters as the king could hastily summon to his assistance would be improperly armed and without discipline.

Their advice was for Umi to raise the standard of revolt at once. This news they would take to Waipio, with the further information that, although preparing for rebellion, Umi would not be strong enough to act for some time. Alarmed, Hakau would consult the high-priest Laeanui, who, notwithstanding their relations, was secretly his enemy, and a plan could be devised to induce the king to send his household guards and immediate followers to the mountains on some religious errand, when Umi, apprised of the situation by fires kindled at intervals on the hilltops between Waipio and Waipunalei, could swoop down with a few hundred resolute warriors and seize the king and the capital, and thus with a bold stroke achieve a bloodless triumph.

When the priests had developed this plan of action Kaoleioku rose to his feet and exclaimed with excitement :

" The gods have instructed you ! "

" You have spoken truly ; the gods have indeed instructed our friends ! " said Umi, impressively ; " for was it not said in your dreams that the victory would be bloodless if the spears of Hakau were sent beyond the call of the *Kiha-pu* ? "

" The meaning is now plain," returned the priest, reverentially. " The gods are with us, and we will be directed by them."

All the details were then carefully arranged, and the two priests returned to Waipio. It was soon rumored that they brought news of Umi, and Hakau sent for them, as had been expected. Fear had somewhat humbled him, and he greeted them with what seemed to be the greatest friendship and cordiality. He even chided them for absenting themselves so long from the royal mansion, where their visits, he assured them, would always be welcome. They assumed to be greatly gratified at his protestations of good-will, but secretly despised him for his shallow hypocrisy.

When questioned by the king the priests frankly informed him that they had left Umi and Kaoleioku together no longer than the day before, and advised him to lose no time in despatching to the mountains all the men he could summon, to gather fresh feathers of rare birds with which to redecorate his god of war.

Hakau was startled by this advice, for the ceremony of *kauilaakua* was never performed except in times of war or other imminent peril.

"What!" he exclaimed, with assumed astonishment, "shall this be done because Umi lives, and you have seen him with the high-priest of *Manini?*"

"No; not because Umi lives," replied Nunu quietly, "but because he is preparing for rebellion."

"Rebellion!" repeated Hakau, angrily. "Does he expect to be able to maintain himself in Hilo?"

"His aims reach beyond Hilo," ventured the priest.

"To Puna?"

"Beyond Puna."

"To Kau?"

"Beyond Kau."

"Then he must aim at the whole island," exclaimed Hakau, savagely.

"At the whole island," repeated the priest, maliciously.

"He shall have land enough to bury him, and no more!" hissed the king. "But you are croakers, both of you. Before considering your advice I shall consult Laeanui and the seers of *Paakalani*, and hear what the gods say of this wide-spread conspiracy, as your fears and cowardice tell the story."

Hakau abruptly dismissed the priests, and despatched a messenger for the high-priest Laeanui, but it was late in the afternoon before he could be found. He was old and venerable in appearance, and his hair, white as the snows of Mauna Kea, fell to his knees, covering his shoulders like a veil.

They had met but rarely since the death of Liloa, for the old priest seldom left the temple grounds, and Hakau as seldom visited them ; and as the bearded and white-haired prophet entered the royal mansion, all bent respectfully before him, and a feeling of awe crept over the king as the priest stood silently and with folded arms before him.

"My greeting to you, venerable servant of the gods!" said the king.

The priest bowed, but remained silent, and Hakau resumed abruptly :

"I have learned that Umi and a priest named Kaoleioku are plotting treason together in Hilo, near the borders of Hamakua. What know you of Kaoleioku?"

"A man to be feared if he is in earnest," replied the priest curtly.

"Have auguries of the movement been invoked?" inquired the king.

With a gesture the priest replied in the negative.

"And why not?" continued Hakau, impetuously. "What are priests and temples for, if not to guard the kingdom against coming dangers?"

"If it so please them, the gods answer when they are asked through sacrifice," replied the priest ; and then, with rising anger, he continued: "Your father respected the gods, and came to the temple when he would consult them, and his son must do the same."

"Well, then," said Hakau, discovering that the priest neither loved nor feared him, "I will be at the temple to-night, some time after sunset, and have you there the best of your diviners."

"I shall await your coming," replied Laeanui, briefly, as he bowed low and retired.

"Although he gave me his daughter," muttered Hakau, as Laeanui left the room, "he has no love for me, and I as little for him. But no matter ; I must not quarrel with him now. Wait until I have dealt with Umi and his confederates, and then—" But he did not finish the sentence, for he suddenly recollected that the high-priesthood was an inherited position, like his own, and its bestowal was not a royal prerogative. There were bloody means of creating vacancies, however, and these flashed through the wicked brain of Hakau.

Small Temple on Kauai, 1793.

The night that followed was dark, with a steady wind from the northwest and occasional showers. It was some time after sunset before the king entered the outer gate of the *heiau* of *Paakalani*. He was accompanied by four attendants, two of whom bore a muzzled pig and two fowls; the others were trusty friends. A *kukui* torch was kept burning in front of the house of the high-priest, another between the altar and inner court, and a third near the entrance of the royal retreat, with which that *heiau*, like many others, was provided. Toward the latter Hakau and his party proceeded, and were soon joined by Laeanui and a number of officiating priests and *kilos*.

Entering the royal *hale*, a few words passed between the king and Laeanui, when the attendants of Hakau were relieved of their burdens and sent without the enclosure. The *kaika*, or large sacrificial drum, was then sounded with three measured strokes, and in a few minutes six officiating priests, three of them with knives in their hands and the others bearing torches, made their appearance. To them the pig and fowls were entrusted, and, preceded by the torch-bearers, the king and high-priest, followed by the attendants of the temple, with measured pace moved toward the altar.

Reaching the place of sacrifice, the high-priest uttered a prayer to the godhead, and separate supplications to *Kane*, *Ku* and *Lono*, intoned by the assisting priests, when the fowls were decapitated and their headless bodies placed upon the altar. The priest watched them until they were motionless, and then opened them and carefully examined the heart, liver and entrails of each.

The king glanced anxiously at the priest, but the latter made no response. The pig was then ordered to be slain. The throat of the animal was cut and its bleeding body was also placed upon the altar. The flow of the blood was scrupulously noted, and, after the respirations had been counted and the animal ceased to breathe, the body was hastily opened. The spleen was removed and held above the head of the priest while another prayer was spoken, and then the other organs were separately examined.

Completing the inspection, Laeanui stepped back from the altar.

"Well," said the king, impatiently, "what say the gods?"

"The gods are angry, and the portents are evil," replied the priest.

"Then promise them a hundred human sacrifices," exclaimed Hakau. "If their favor is to be purchased with blood, I will drown the *heiau* with an ocean of it. But," he continued, "I am not satisfied with these auguries. Let me hear from the *anu*."

Immediately behind the altar was the entrance to the inner court of the temple. Within, and about three paces back from the door, which was covered with a wide breadth of *kapa*, was placed the *anu*, a wicker enclosure four or five feet in diameter, in which stood the oracle. On each side of the entrance were carved images of *Kane, Ku, Lono* and other Hawaiian deities, while at intervals of three or four feet along the walls a score or more of gods of lesser potency stood guard above the sacred spot.

To the last request of Hakau the priest replied: "The king shall hear from the *anu*."

The lights were then extinguished, and all except the king and high-priest retired some distance from the altar, that no whisper of the oracle might reach them. Hakau was nervous as he stepped with the priest in front of the entrance to the inner temple. A prayer was uttered by the priest; the *kapa* screen was drawn aside by hands unseen, and the king stood looking into the intense darkness of the *sanctum sanctorum* of the temple.

"Speak!" said the priest, withdrawing behind the altar, and leaving the king alone before the *anu*.

"Speak!" repeated a hollow voice from within the sacred enclosure.

For some minutes Hakau remained awed and silent; then, in a voice which scarcely seemed to be his own, he said:

"Great power, I hear that dangers threaten."

"Dangers threaten!" came like an echo from within.

"How may they be averted?" inquired the king.

For a time there was no answer. Finally a voice from the *anu* replied:

"Do homage to *Kane;* make glad the war-god of Liloa!"

"So do I promise," answered the king; "but will that give me victory?"

"Victory!" was repeated from the *anu*.

Elated at what he had heard, Hakau continued:

"Now tell me, mighty spirit, whether Umi—"

"Nothing more!" interrupted the voice from within, as the *kapa* suddenly dropped before the entrance.

"Well, thanks for so much," said Hakau, turning and joining the priest at the altar, and repeating to him, with some favorable additions, the words that he had heard. Darkness hid the smile upon the lips of Laeanui.

"The day after to-morrow we will hold here a festival to *Kane,* and the altar shall be heaped with offerings," said the king. "To-morrow I will send my people to the mountains to gather feathers of sacred and royal colors, and *Kaili,* the neglected war-god of Liloa, shall be made glorious in new plumage and glad with abundant sacrifice."

"It is well," replied the priest.

"Now let the conspirators marshal their spears!" continued Hakau, confidently, "and we will make short work of them. They cannot be punished in the hills of Hilo. With a showing of weakness we will lure them to Waipio, and not one of them shall escape. We will cut off their retreat, and close in their faces the gates of the *puhonui!*"

As already mentioned, of the two *puhonuis,* or places of refuge, on Hawaii at that time, one was an adjunct of the *heiau* of *Paakalani,* at Waipio. In times of war their gates, with white flags to mark them, were always open, and those who succeeded in passing into the enclosure were safe from assault, even though pursued by the king himself.

This savage proposal to close the gates of the *puhonui* was promptly resented by Laeanui. He would as soon have thought of tumbling the gods from their pedestals and consigning them to the flames.

"You suggest what is impossible," said the priest. "Since the days of Wakea the *puhonui* has been sacred. Its gates cannot be closed to the defenceless, and the gods have said that he who shuts them against the weak shall seek in vain their shelter from the arm of the strong."

"Well, then, keep them open!" retorted the king, sharply. "They will run swiftly who enter them!"

Torches were relighted, and the king and his attendants left the *heiau.* They had not passed beyond the outer wall before Nunu emerged from the inner court. His was the voice that had answered the king from the *anu.* Thus in the temple of

Paakalani was shaped the destruction of Hakau, and the priests whom he had insulted and defied opened broadly and surely the way to his death.

The next morning an unusual commotion was observed in and around the royal mansion, and as party after party left the inclosure—some proceeding toward the sea-coast, and others up the valley and into the mountains beyond—the villagers wondered at the proceeding, and predicted that a strict *tabu* would soon follow, whatever might be the occasion. But when they learned that the war-god was to be redecorated, and an imposing religious festival was to follow the day after, they knew that trouble of some kind was anticipated by the king, and soon found a correct explanation of the movement in the rumors which they, too, had heard concerning Umi and his friends in Hilo and eastern Hamakua. The possibility of an uprising against Hakau gave them no uneasiness, however, for his cruelties had secured for him their hatred, while the name of Umi was to all classes a synonym of strength and gentleness.

The king was not indifferent to the danger with which he was about to be confronted, and promptly despatched *lunapais* to the district chiefs of Kohala, Kona, and Hamakua, ordering them to report without delay at Waipio with two thousand warriors each, while the governor of Hilo was commanded by a special *lunapai* to march at once with a body of warriors to Waipunalei, with the view of precipitating the movement of Umi upon Waipio, where, it was not doubted, he would be overwhelmed and crushed.

All these were proper precautions, but they were taken too late ; for at the time the feather-hunters and *lunapais* were leaving on their respective missions, Umi, at the head of over two thousand well-armed and resolute warriors, had reached a point within a two hours' march of Waipio, and was awaiting a signal to swoop down upon the valley.

And now let us return to Waipunalei, and note what had been occurring there during the preceding forty-eight hours. As soon as the priests left for Waipio, two days before, trusty and intelligent sentinels followed and took their respective stations, designated by Maukaleoleo, on the summits of seven different hill-tops discernible from each other from Waipunalei to Waipio. The first, coming eastward from Waipio, was three miles, perhaps, from the temple of *Paakalani ;* the last was a rocky pinnacle about four miles from Waipunalei. This was the station of Maukaleoleo.

The sentinels were instructed to gather large heaps of dry grass and bark ; to keep small fires smouldering and ready for use ; to vigilantly watch the peaks in the direction of Waipio ; to apply the torch the instant a signal-fire was seen, and keep the pile burning until it was plainly answered by the next station toward Waipunalei.

All that day and through the following night armed men were arriving at the rendezvous at Kaoleioku's, until something more than two thousand warriors had reported, and every spare moment of the next day was devoted to forming them into companies and battalions, giving them leaders and preparing them for a rapid march.

Many of the warriors were accompanied by their wives, daughters or sisters ; for in those days, and later, women not unfrequently followed their fathers, brothers and husbands to battle, generally keeping in the rear to furnish them with food and water, but sometimes, in a close and desperate conflict, mingling bravely in the fight. In such cases they gave and received blows, and expected and were accorded no consideration because of their sex.

Instances are given in Hawaiian tradition of the tide of battle being turned, on more than one occasion, by desperate women transformed from camp-followers into warriors ; and as late as ·1819 we behold Manona, wife of Kekuokalani, the last sturdy champion of the gods of his fathers, falling lifeless in battle upon the body of her dead husband at Kuamoo, while Kaahumanu and Kalakau, widows of the great Kamehameha, commanded the fleet of canoes operating with the land forces under Kalaimoku.

After the visit of the priests from Waipio the purpose of the revolt was no longer disguised, and whenever Umi made his appearance among the assembled and assembling warriors he was greeted with the wildest enthusiasm. His romantic history was known to them, and had been made the theme of song. His many triumphs at the festival given by Liloa in honor of his formal recognition were recited by those who had witnessed them, and his grand proportions and noble bearing stamped him as of chiefly blood ; and when his friends Piimaiwaa and Omau-kamau spoke of the great learning displayed by him when questioned by the priests, and intimated that he had been instructed by the gods and was under their care, every doubt of success vanished, and the order for an advance upon Waipio was awaited with impatience.

Maukaleoleo mysteriously came and went, but always at night, and seldom remaining longer than a few minutes. He was known to all within the enclosure, and allowed to pass unchallenged, as he could be mistaken for no one else. As he strode through the gateway, bearing a spear scarcely less than thirty feet in length, the sentinels regarded him with awe ; and when they saw him converse with Umi and then silently depart, they shook their heads and said, " Perhaps he is *Lono !* "

The temple of *Manini*, dedicated by Liloa just before his meeting with the mother of Umi, and of which Kaoleioku was the high-priest, was a reconstruction and enlargement of an old *heiau* which was in existence certainly as early as the time of the warlike Kalaunuiohua, who reigned between the years 1260 and 1300. With a large army and proportionate fleet of canoes he invaded Maui, Molokai and Oahu, and, taking their captured sovereigns with him, made a descent upon Kauai. But his triumphs ended there. After an obstinate battle he was defeated and taken prisoner, but was subsequently released and permitted to return to his own kingdom.

It was during the reign of this sovereign that the prophetess Waahia lived. She accompanied him in his expeditions as far as Oahu, but refused to proceed with him to Kauai. She declared that the gods would bring calamity upon him if he invaded that island, and sought to persuade him to consolidate his conquests and return to Hawaii. But the warrior-king cared but little for priests or temples, and was in the habit of destroying · both when they failed to subserve his purposes. Enraged at the unfavorable auguries of Waahia, and fearful that they might come to the ears of and demoralize his warriors, the king induced her to return to Hawaii. One tradition says she voluntarily abandoned Kalaunuiohua, while another relates that she consented to return only on condition that the war-god of the king be sent back with her. This god had been in the reigning family of Hawaii since the days of Paao, and had been sanctified by that father of the priesthood. To distinguish it from other war-gods it was known as *Akuapaao*, and was held in great veneration. When asked for an explanation of the strange request, the prophetess boldly declared that, if the god was taken to Kauai, it would never return except at the head of a conquering army that would make of Hawaii a tributary kingdom.

" Then take it with you!" exclaimed the king, savagely, " and if I return to Hawaii alive I will burn you both together ! "

" You will burn neither," said Waahia. " When you return to Hawaii you will think better of the gods and their servants ; and in generations to come, when angry spears shall be crossed in the *hale* of the kings of Hawaii, the hand will be stronger that places the fresh *lei* upon the shoulders of *Akuapaao*."

The prophetess prepared to embark. The god, wrapped in a fold of *kapa*, so that it might not be recognized, was brought to the beach and delivered to the departing seeress. The canoe, which was large enough to accommodate thirty persons, was shoved into the surf. It was provided with food and a calabash of water. Declining all assistance or companionship in her journey, Waahia stepped into the canoe with the image in her arms, and, after carefully depositing it in the bow of the boat, returned and seated herself near the stern. Half a dozen men were waiting for the word to launch the canoe from the sands upon which the stern was lightly resting. But the seeress raised no sail, touched no oar. For some minutes she sat, silent and motionless, with bent head and clasped hands, as if in prayer, while hundreds of curious eyes watched her in amazement, wondering what would become of her, even should the unmanned craft be successful in passing the breakers. Then she slowly rose to her feet, and the canoe began to glide toward the reef. Faster and faster it moved, until, mounting a retreating wave, it was borne swiftly out into the calmer waters; then, slightly turning in its course, it dashed southward with the speed of the wind, and was soon lost to the view of the awe-stricken beholders.

Waahia looked beneath the waves and smiled, for *Ukanipo*, the shark-god, with scores of assistants, was bearing her onward; and then from his *ipu Laamaomao*, the Hawaiian Æolus, let loose the imprisoned winds, and refreshing zephyrs cooled the face of the prophetess and accelerated the speed of the canoe, until it seemed to leap from wave to wave; and great sea-birds screamed with fright as it dashed past and awoke them from their billowy slumbers, leaving behind it a long trail of troubled waters.

Passing to the southward of the intervening islands, the canoe was borne with undiminished speed through the channel of Alenuihaha to the northeastern coast of Hawaii, and before sunset was beached at Koholalele. The prophetess knew the meaning of this. Near by was the old *heiau* of *Manini*, and thither, as she felt instructed, was taken and deposited the war-g d *Akuapaao*, with the solemn injunction to the high-priest in charge that it was never to be removed from the inner court unless the life of the *moi* was in peril or the kingdom was invaded by a foreign foe.

The old *heiau* had given place to a more imposing structure during the reign of Liloa. Its outer walls had been enlarged, raised and repaired, and its inner belongings improved and redecorated; but its sacred relics had not been disturbed, and its many gods remained where they had been for generations.

Among the most sacred idols of the temple, even after the death of Liloa, was the *Akuapaao*. Its name indicated alike its age and sanctity; and while the legends connected with it had become vague and distorted in their transmission through a long line of priests, the prophecy of Waahia still clung to it, and it was especially reverenced by the few to whom was entrusted the secret of its functions.

Hakau had learned of this god from his royal father, and the same morning that his retainers were sent to the hills for feathers two priests were despatched to Koholalele, with orders to bring to Waipio, in the king's name and without delay, the war-god *Akuapaao*. Should the priests of the temple refuse to surrender the idol, then the messengers were instructed to call upon the district chiefs for assistance, and take it by force, no matter at what cost of life.

But the king was too late for at early daylight of the morning of the day before his messengers left Waipio, Maukaleoleo strode into the rebel headquarters with the *Akuapaao* in his arms. Kaoleioku had, of course, instructed the giant where and how to secure the image, for in years past he had been its custodian, and his orders continued to be obeyed by the priests of *Manini*. The idol, completely wrapped in *kapa*, was deposited in the private *heiau* of the high-priest, and Maukaleoleo left the enclosure

as quietly as he had entered it a few minutes before. The sentinels wondered, as usual, but bowed in silence as he came and
went.

The priest rose with the sun, and learned that Maukaleoleo
had already been a visitor that morning. He hastened to the
heiau, and there found the *Akuapaao*. He was overjoyed. He
removed the *kapa* covering from the idol, placed it upon a ped-
estal between the images of *Ku* and *Lono*, and then found Umi
and brought him to the *heiau*. Entering, Kaoleioku closed the
door and pointed to the *Akuapaao*. Umi bowed reverently before it.

"Listen, O Umi!" said the priest; "listen, O son of Liloa!
Behold the war-god of your fathers! It was sanctified by the
touch of Paao, and for generations, in the inner chamber of
Manini, has awaited your coming. From Waahia, the prophetess,
have come down, through the chief priests of the *heiau*, these
words: 'When angry spears shall be crossed in the *hale* of the
kings of Hawaii, the hand will be the stronger that places the
fresh *lei* upon the shoulders of *Akuapaao*.' The spears are about
to be crossed; the god is here; let yours be the hand, and not
Hakau's, to place the *lei-ai* upon the shoulders of *Akuapaao!*"

The words of the prophecy came to Umi as a dream. Overwhelmed with their significance, he fell upon his knees and exclaimed:

"God of my fathers! be you my guide until I prove unworthy of your protection!"

"Your realm is yet small," said the priest, "and is enclosed
within these walls. Let us pay respect to the gods, that its
boundaries may be enlarged."

Thereupon a strict *tabu* was ordered to all within the walls, to
begin at midday and continue until the setting of the sun. The
time was brief, but events were pressing, and it could not safely
be extended.

The *tabu*, or *kapu*, as it is sometimes written, was strictly a
prerogative of the high chiefs and priests of olden Hawaii.
There were fixed *tabus* of custom, and declared *tabus* of limited
duration by the temporal and spiritual rulers. The penalty for
the violation of all *tabus* was death. It was *tabu* of custom for
men and women to eat together, or for women to eat of the flesh
of swine, fowls, turtle and many kinds of fish. Everything

belonging to the kings, priests and temples was *tabu,* or sacred, and springs, paths, fishing-grounds, water-courses, etc., were fre-- quently thus kept from the use of the people. Declared general *tabus,* for the propitiation of the gods or the amelioration of a public evil, were either strict or common, according to the emergency. During the time of a common *tabu* the people were required to abstain from their usual avocations and attend at the *heiau,* where morning and evening prayers were offered. A strict *tabu* was more sacred. While it continued—generally one or two days—all, with the exception of the *alii-nui* and priests, were compelled to remain within doors. Every fire and every light was extinguished ; no canoe was launched ; all noises ceased ; the pigs and dogs were muzzled, and fowls were placed under calabashes. These *tabus* were proclaimed by heralds, and their wanton violation was an unpardonable offence.

In preparation for the *tabu* to be declared by Umi, flowers and feathers were brought, and *leis* of both were woven. Everything being in readiness, heralds proclaimed the *tabu* and its duration, with the further announcement that the occasion was the arrival of the mighty war-god *Akuapaao* and its coming decoration by Umi.

As the sun touched the mark of meridian, the gates of the enclosure were barred and guarded by the religious attendants of the priest ; the fires were everywhere extinguished ; the few animals within the walls were either muzzled or hidden ; men, women and children suddenly disappeared within their dwellings or quarters, and mats were hung at the openings ; Umi and the priest retired alone to the *heiau* and closed the door, and silence, disturbed only by low whispers and the muffled footfalls of the watching priests, reigned over the twenty-five hundred persons gathered within the enclosure.

In the *heiau,* or apartment of the gods, to which Umi and the high-priest retired, were a number of images and sacred relics. Near the centre of the room was a small altar, upon which had been deposited the *leis* provided for the decoration of *Akuapaao.* They sat down beside it, and for an hour or more nothing was heard but the whispered prayers of the priest, addressed in turn to the several gods before him. Then, rising and leading Umi by the hand to the *Akuapaao,* in a low voice he formally presented him to the god as the son of Liloa and rightful ruler of the Hawaiian people. Another prayer was uttered, and then Umi, with the words, "Accept this, O *Akuapaao*, with the homage of Umi!" proceeded reverently to place around the head and neck of the image a number of fragrant *leis* of flowers and wreaths of brilliant feathers.

The priest watched the act intently. As the last wreath of feathers, resembling a crown in appearance—the *lei-hula-alii*—was placed upon the head of the image, a sunbeam flashed through what seemed to be a small rent in the thatched roof, and for a moment haloed the heads of Umi and the god. The priest read the answer and smiled. He felt as assured of the favor of the gods as if it had been pledged in a voice of thunder, and Umi bent low in acknowledgment of the joyful revelation.

The sun dropped behind the hills; twilight turned to bronze the gold of the valleys, and the *tabu* was at an end. It was proclaimed that the auguries were highly favorable, and the silence of the *tabu* was broken by wild strains of music and shouts of rejoicing.

V.

As darkness settled upon the camp of the insurgents Umi felt that the hour for action was closely at hand. He therefore gave orders that preparations for instant departure be maintained throughout the night. The moon was waning, with a promise of rising some time before morning, and the night set in dark and cloudy, with occasional showers.

About two hours before midnight Maukaleoleo suddenly and silently strode past the sentinels. Seeking Umi, he found him in council with his friends Omaukamau, Piimaiwaa and the high-priest. They were arranging the order of march by the four narrow paths at that time leading to Waipio.

The giant stooped low and looked in upon the council through the doorway. He could scarcely distinguish the faces within by the light of the flambeau kept burning near the entrance. He did not attempt to enter, but stood silent and motionless, with his hands upon his knees, peering into the room as if to attract attention. Umi smiled as he recognized the huge object, and stepped to the door. The giant rose until his head was above the ridge-pole, and then bowed like the bending of a tree before the wind.

"Well, my good friend," said Umi, "after thanking you for your last night's work, let me ask what word you bring."

"None," replied the giant. "There is no light yet, but I am impressed that it will be seen before morning."

"And so am I, good Maukaleoleo," returned the chief, "and your signal will find us prepared."

"That is what I came to learn," answered the giant, bowing and turning to depart.

"But do not mistake for a signal the rising moon, which will soon set its torch upon the hill-tops," suggested Umi, pleasantly.

"Unless the moon should rise in the west, which it has not done since the days of Maui, the mistake would scarcely be possible," replied Maukaleoleo, with a smile upon his great face, and then, with a few long strides, disappearing in the darkness.

It must have been at about the time of this interview that Hakau was leaving the *heiau* at Waipio, after having invoked the auguries of sacrifice and listened to the voice of Nunu from the darkness of the inner temple. The king had scarcely passed the gate of the temple leading to the sacred pavement of Liloa, which connected the *heiau* with the royal mansion, and which privileged feet alone could tread, when Nunu, after exchanging a few words with the high-priest, also left the enclosure, but neither over the sacred pavement nor toward the palace. Taking a path which did not seem to be new to him, from the facility with which he traveled it by the light of the stars, he crossed the valley and mounted the high ridge of hills enclosing it on the southeast. Ascending the ridge for some distance, and until the lights of the valley could no longer be seen, he proceeded slowly upward, at intervals striking together two stones and listening for a response. At length it came, like an echo of his own signal, and a few minutes' walk brought him to a large heap of dry leaves and limbs, from behind which Kakohe rose and greeted him.

"Fire it at once!" said Nunu. "I will explain all when the signal is answered."

Behind a rock, a few paces away, a small fire was smouldering. Kakohe sprang and seized a burning brand, which he applied to the heap, and in a moment the red flames reached heavenward, throwing a lurid light upon the surrounding hills.

With their backs to the fire the two priests looked anxiously toward the south and east, and in a few minutes far in the distance gleamed an answering flame. Satisfied that their signal had been seen and responded to, they permitted the fire to die out, and then returned to the valley to await the important events of the morrow.

Leaving the rendezvous of the rebels, Maukaleoleo slowly returned to his station, for even his mighty limbs at times grew weary, and the path leading up the mountain was obscure and narrow. Reaching the summit, he examined a small fire hidden among the rocks, and was about to stretch himself upon the ground, with his face turned eastward, when he discerned a strange, star-like speck upon the horizon. For a moment it paled, and then grew brighter and brighter. He stepped to a tree near a huge pile of combustibles, and, glancing along a horizontal limb that had been previously trimmed for the purpose, discovered that it pointed directly toward the light. All doubt at once disappeared. He knew it was the signal. Springing for a brand, the heap was lighted, and by its wild glare in the darkness Maukaleoleo rapidly descended to the valley. His fatigue had vanished, for the signal of Hakau's death had been lighted by his own hands, and his great heart was in arms.

The signal was at once discerned by the watchmen at Umi's quarters, and in a few minutes all was quiet commotion within the walls. Torches were lighted, armed warriors sprang with alacrity into line, and half an hour after Umi, in feather mantle and helmet plumed with royal colors, and preceded by the war-god *Akuapaao*, borne upon a *manele*, or palanquin, resting upon the shoulders of *kahunas*, with Kaoleioku as high-priest, marched out of the enclosure, followed by two thousand well-armed and devoted supporters. His address to his warriors was brief. "The moments are precious," said Umi, "and must not be wasted in words. Let our spears speak, and at sunset to-morrow we will eat meat in peace in Waipio !"

As a measure of precaution, in case of disaster, a force sufficient to hold the premises of the high-priest was left within the walls. The advancing army was formed into three divisions, the right commanded by Omaukamau and the left by Piimaiwaa, while Umi remained with the centre. Their orders were to move rapidly, but as quietly as possible, by three different routes, and form a junction at their intersection with the *alanui*, or great path, leading from the coast to the inland village of Waimea. This junction it was expected the left division, traveling a difficult mountain-path, would be able to reach two or three hours after sunrise.

It was, perhaps, an hour short of midnight when the last of the little army left the enclosure, followed by two or three hundred women bearing food, water, extra weapons and a variety of camp necessaries. The warriors were full of enthusiasm, and when Maukaleoleo stepped in among them from the mountains like a protecting deity their shouts could scarcely be restrained. His appearance was most welcome to Umi, who thanked him warmly for what he had done, and expressed a desire that he would remain near him during the march, as his familiarity with the mountains and their paths would render his advice valuable.

"But I see another mighty friend has opportunely reported," said Umi, pleasantly, as he pointed toward the east. "As the moon is about to look over the hills, the torches may soon be extinguished, for the paths will be plainer without them."

The divisions separated, and, dispensing with their torches, soon swarmed the several paths leading to Waipio. Each division was preceded some distance in its march by a party of scouts, with instructions to let no one pass to their front, lest he might be a messenger of warning.

The paths were rough and in places almost choked with undergrowth, and the advance was exceedingly laborious; but no word of complaint was heard, and about the middle of the forenoon the left division, and the last to arrive, reached the Waimea trail at a point leaving the entire force but a short march to Waipio. A brief halt was ordered, and the food and water brought by the women were served to their relatives, and to others if any remained.

Taking no thought of himself, Umi advised his attendants to eat if they could find food, declaring that he required nothing, and then threw himself under the shade of a tree for a few minutes of much-needed rest. A cool breeze fanned his heated face, on which the beard had as yet grown but lightly, and his heavy eyelids closed, dropping him gently into the land of shadows, where he bathed in cool waters and partook of food that was delicious—more delicious, it seemed, because it was served by Kulamea.

Something awoke him—he scarcely knew what—and his eyes caught the form of a woman as it vanished behind the tree under which he was lying. He smiled, and, partially rising, discovered on the ground beside him a calabash of *poi*, reduced with water to the consistency of thick gruel. His mouth and throat were parched, and, without stopping to learn who had provided it, he raised the vessel to his lips and drained it to the bottom. It was a goodly draught, and refreshed him greatly.

Holding the empty calabash in his hand, he began to examine it, at first carelessly, and then with greater interest, for it was not a common vessel. Nor was it the first time that he had seen it. It was the calabash he had carved with images of birds and flowers for Kulamea before he went to Waipio to become the son of a king.

He beckoned to Maukaleoleo, who was leaning against a tree a few paces distant, with his head among the branches. The giant smiled as he approached, as if divining the question Umi was about to ask.

"Did you see the person who left this calabash?" inquired Umi, exhibiting the vessel.

"I saw her," replied the giant.

"Then it was left by a woman?"

"By a woman."

"Did you observe her?"

"As closely as I ever observe any woman."

"What was her appearance?"

"Ordinary men would describe her, I presume, as being young, graceful and attractive."

"And you?"

"I would call her a plaything, as I would any other woman whose head did not touch my beard."

"True," said Umi, smiling as his fancy pictured a becoming mate for the giant; "you can know but little of women. But would you recognize the plaything who left this calabash, were you to see her again?"

The giant intimated that he would probably recognize her.

"Then seek among the women of the camp, and, if found,

say to her for Umi that if she prizes the calabash he will return it to her, if she will claim it after the sun sets to-day and show that she is the rightful owner."

Maukaleoleo bowed and departed on his errand, and Umi hung the calabash at his girdle.

Another advance was ordered, and in an hour or less the little army lay hidden along the brow of the ragged hills overlooking the valley of Waipio on the south and east and extending to the sea. A fleet messenger was despatched over the hills to a waterfall, the sound of which could be heard dropping into the valley from a great height in an unbroken cataract. He returned, bringing with him a strangely-marked piece of *kapa* which he had found suspended from a limb near the verge of the fall.

It was the final signal of Nunu, and implied that the king's attendants had been sent to the mountains and sea-shore, and the palace was defenceless. Preparations were made for an immediate descent into the valley. As the paths leading down were tortuous and narrow, the warriors were ordered to break ranks and make the descent as rapidly and as best they could, and promptly re-form on reaching the valley.

The word was given, and the advance began. First the summit bristled with spears, then down the hillsides swept a swarm of armed men. In their rapid descent they seemed to be hopelessly scattered, but they re-formed on reaching the valley, and in good order advanced toward the little stream, across which was the royal mansion, and not far from it the temple of *Paakalani*.

The wildest excitement prevailed in the village. Some seized their arms, and others ran toward the hills, but no opposition was offered. At the head of the little army marched Umi, himself almost a giant, and by his side the mighty Maukaleoleo, naked but for the *maro* about his loins, and bearing a ponderous spear, the ivory point of which could be seen above the tree-tops.

Plunging into and crossing the stream, detachments were despatched at a running pace to surround the royal enclosure and cut off all escape, especially to the *puhonui*, while with the main force Umi advanced to the great gate of the outer wall, which had been hastily closed and fastened, and demanded admission. No reply being made, although a confusion of voices could be heard from within, Umi was about to order up a force to beat down the gate when Maukaleoleo leaned his spear against the wall, and, laying hold of a rock which no two other men could lift, hurled it against the gate, and it was torn from its fastenings as if struck by a missile from Kilauea. He then seized the broken obstruction and flung it from the entrance as if it had been a screen of matting, and Umi and his followers poured into the enclosure. Driving before them a score or two of hastily-armed attendants of the king, they raised a wild battle-shout and rushed toward the palace.

So secret had been the movement of the insurgents, and so rapid was their advance after reaching the valley, that Hakau was not made aware of their presence until they began to cross the stream near the royal mansion. The first information bewildered him. Recovering, he ordered the gates to be closed and barred, and every one to arm within the grounds. A messenger was sent to mount the walls and report the probable number of the assail-ants ; but the most of them were in the stream at the moment of observation, and the king was relieved with the assurance that the force did not number more than one or two hundred.

"Then we can beat them off until assistance comes," said Hakau, confidently. "Hold the gates with your lives !" he shouted ; then, hastily entering the *mua*, he took from the *ipu* in which it was deposited the *Kiha-pu*, the sacred war-trumpet of the Hawaiian kings, and sprang to the front of the palace. He placed the shell to his lips to sound a blast of alarm, which with the breath of Liloa was wont to swell throughout a radius of ten or twelve miles. Filling his lungs for a mighty effort, which he doubted not would bring to his assistance the villagers and feather-hunters despatched to the hills, he wound a blast through the shell. But no such voice ever issued before from the mys-terious chambers of the *Kiha-pu*. Instead of a note of alarm swelling over the hills in wild and warlike cadence, they gave forth a dreadful discord of torture-wrung screams and groans, horrifying all within the walls, but scarcely audible beyond them.

Hakau dropped the shell to the earth as if his lips had been burned with its kiss, and with a feeling of desperation seized a javelin and grimly awaited the onset at the gate. His suspense was brief. The gate went down with a crash ; and when he saw his handful of defenders retire before the incoming flood of war-riors led by Umi, Hakau retreated to the *mua* with three or four of his attendants, where he resolved to defend himself to the death.

The door of the *mua* was scarcely barred before Umi reached it. A hundred warriors pressed forward, but he waved them back. He looked at Maukaleoleo, and the next moment the door was a mass of splinters. Umi resolutely stepped within, Kaoleioku, the warrior-priest, at his side. As he entered, with a hiss Hakau made a thrust at him with his javelin. Umi caught and wrenched the weapon from his grasp, and was about to strike when Kaoleioku stayed every uplifted hand by exclaiming :

"Hold ! Let this be a sacrifice, and not a murder ! In the name of the gods I slay him ! "

With these words the high-priest drove his *ihe* through the heart of Hakau, and he fell dying at the feet of Umi.

Hakau strove to speak, but his words were bitter and choked him.

"Bear him with respect to a couch," said Umi. " He is the son of a king, and so let him die."

His orders were obeyed, and Hakau, the tyrant king of Hawaii, breathed his last as Umi turned and left the *mua*.

The palace was now in the possession of Umi, with its gods, its sacred emblems, its royal regalia and all the paraphernalia of supreme authority ; but he appreciated that much remained to be done, and that, too, without delay. The feather-hunters would soon return from the hills and sea-shore ; but they could be dealt with in detail as they arrived in small parties, and were, therefore, not greatly to be feared. The distant chiefs summoned by the *lunapais* of the dead king were the principal cause of anxiety. Some time during the next day they would begin to arrive with their quotas of warriors, and Umi was not quite confident that they would accept the situation peacefully.

To be prepared for any emergency, he ordered his entire force to quarters within the palace grounds, despatched parties to procure supplies of food, received the allegiance of the attendants and guards found in and around the royal mansion, and sent out heralds to proclaim the death of Hakau by the will of the gods, and the assumption of sovereign authority by Umi, the son of Liloa.

The *Kiha-pu* was discovered near the door, where it had been dropped by Hakau. No one dared to touch it. It was recognized by a chief who had seen it before, and who guarded it until Umi appeared. The chief pointed to the sacred shell, and with an exclamation of joy Umi raised it to his lips and sounded a vigorous blast, which swept over the valleys and echoed through the hills with its old-time voice of thunder.

All within the walls were startled. Kaoleioku approached, and Umi raised the shell and repeated the sonorous blast. "It is not the breath of Umi," said the priest, impressively; "it is the voice of the gods proclaiming their approval of the work of this day !"

The body of Hakau was removed to a small structure within the enclosure, where it was given in charge of his wife and mother, Kukukalani and Pinea, and their attendants, to be prepared for burial. And Kapukini, the sister of Hakau and half-sister of Umi, mourned with them ; but her grief was not great, for Hakau had been unkind even to her.

Before nightfall the feather-hunters began to come in ; but the situation was made known to them on reaching the valley, and such of them as were not deterred by fear proceeded to the palace and gave their adherence to Umi, thus relieving him of some slight cause of apprehension, and considerably augmenting the strength of his little army.

Umi's promise to his warriors was made good, for that night they ate their meat in peace within the palace-walls at Waipio. All needed rest, but not one of them more than Umi himself. The night was dark, but the air was cool without, and after his evening meal Umi strolled out and threw himself down on a fold of *kapa* under the palms in front of the mansion. He was soon joined by Kaoleioku, his trusty lieutenants Omaukamau and Piimaiwaa, and several chiefs of distinction.

The events of the day were being discussed, and the possibilities of the morrow, when Maukaleoleo loomed up in the darkness like the shadow of a palm, and requested permission to approach the group. It was granted, of course, for the giant had proven himself to be one of the stanchest and most valuable of Umi's friends. But he was not alone. Behind him, and almost hidden by his burly form, walked Kulamea. She wore a *pau* of five folds, and over her shoulders a light *kihei* of ornamented *kapa*. Her black hair fell below her waist, and a woven band of blossoms encircled her head.

"By your instruction," said the giant, bowing before Umi, "I sought out the woman who left with you beyond the hills to-day a curiously-carved calabash, and acquainted her with your wish that she should come to you and claim it. But she feared to do so, because you are now the king of Hawaii."

"Were I the king of the eight Hawaiian seas she should not fear," replied Umi. "Seek and say to her— "

"Let Umi speak the words himself," interrupted the giant; saying which, he advanced a few paces into a better light, and, stepping aside, Kulamea stood revealed before the group.

"Kulamea!" exclaimed Umi, rising.

"Kulamea!" repeated Omaukamau, in astonishment, for he did not know before that his sister was in Waipio. "What evil spirit prompted you to venture here at such a time as this?"

"Do not chide her, Omaukamau," said Umi, placing his hand tenderly upon the shoulder of the fair playmate of his youth. "The triumph of to-day is as much to her as it is to her brave brother, and no one could be more welcome."

Omaukamau was silent, and Kulamea sank on her knees before Umi. He raised her to her feet and kissed her; then, taking from his girdle and placing in her hands the calabash she had come to claim, he said:

"In the presence of all here Umi returns this calabash to Kulamea, his wife!" Then, leading her to her brother, he continued: "Give her attendants, and see that she is provided with all else that befits her station." Omaukamau kissed his sister, and led her into the mansion.

During this scene Maukaleoleo stood looking down upon the group with folded arms and an amused expression upon his face.

"Perhaps I should have asked your consent," said Umi, smiling and looking up into the face of the giant.

"Umi is now in a condition to take from his subjects without asking," pertinently replied the monster; "but in this instance there seems to be no other claimant, and the title is unquestioned."

"And have I your approval as well?" inquired Umi, more seriously, addressing Kaoleioku.

"Better than mine," replied the priest, warmly: "you have the approval of the gods; for in fulfilling your pledge to a simple and confiding woman you have kept faith with them."

The rest of the prominent events leading to, and connected with, the accession of Umi to the moiship of Hawaii, will be very briefly referred to. As the district chiefs and their warriors arrived at Waipio in response to the call of the dead king, they accepted the changed conditions without protest, and promptly tendered their allegiance to Umi.

The second day after his death Hakau's remains were quietly and without display taken to the hills and entombed, and the day following Umi was publicly anointed king of Hawaii in the presence of nearly ten thousand warriors. The games and festivities of the occasion continued for ten days.

The *Akuapaao* was placed in the temple of *Paakalani*, and at the death of the venerable Laeanui, which occurred shortly after, Kaoleioku, who was of the family of Paao, was created high-priest.

Omaukamau and Piimaiwaa became the confidential advisers of Umi, as well as his favorite military captains, and Maukaleoleo served in his many campaigns, his strength and prowess furnishing subjects for numerous strange stories still living in Hawaiian tradition.

Eng.d by H.B Hall's Sons New York.

Kapiolani

LONO AND KAIKILANI.

CHARACTERS.

KEAWENUI, king of Hawaii.

KANALOA-KUAANA,
LONOIKAMAKAHIKI and } sons of Keawenui by different mothers.
PUPUAKEA,

KUKAILANI, nephew of Keawenui.

KAIKILANI, daughter of Kukailani.

KAKUHIHEWA, king of Oahu.

LANAHUIMIHAKU, a chief of Oahu.

OHAIKAWILIULA, a chiefess of Kauai.

HEAKEKOA, a man of Molokai.

KAIKINANE, a woman of Molokai.

LONO AND KAIKILANI.

A ROMANTIC EPISODE IN THE ROYAL ANNALS.

I.

WHAT a hustling and barbaric little world in themselves were the eight habitable islands of the Hawaiian archipelago before the white man came to rouse the simple but warlike islanders from the dream they had for centuries been living! Up to that time their national life had been a long romance, abundant in strife and deeds of chivalry, and scarcely less bountiful in episodes of love, friendship and self-sacrifice. Situated in mid-ocean, their knowledge of the great world, of which their island dots on the bosom of the Pacific formed but an infinitesimal portion, did not reach beyond a misty Kahiki, from which their fathers came some centuries before, and the bare names of other lands marking the migratory course of their ancestors thither.

The Hawaiians were barbarous, certainly, since they slew their prisoners of war, and to their gods made sacrifice of their enemies; since no tie of consanguinity save that of mother and son was a bar to wedlock; since murder was scarcely a crime, and the will of the *alii-nui* on every island was the supreme law; since the masses were in physical bondage to their chiefs and in mental slavery to the priesthood. Yet, with all this, they were a brave, hospitable and unselfish people. The kings of the islands of Hawaii, Maui, Oahu and Kauai were in almost continual warfare with each other until brought under one government by Kamehameha I.; but the fear of foreign invasion never disturbed them, and the people, who feared their gods, reverenced their rulers and possessed an easy and unfailing means of sustenance and personal comfort, were content with a condition which had been theirs for generations and was hopeless of amelioration; for the high chiefs in authority claimed a lineage distinct from that of the masses, and between them frowned a gulf socially and politically impassable.

The Hawaiians were never cannibals. The most conspicuous of their barbarisms was the sacrifice of human beings to their gods; but did not the temples of early Gaul and Saxon flow with the blood of men? and did not one of the fathers of Israel sharpen his knife to slay the body of his son upon the altar of the God of Abraham? They knew but little of the arts as we know them now, and the useful and precious metals were all unknown to them; yet they made highways over the precipices, reared massive walls of stone around their temples, carried effective weapons into battle, and constructed capacious single and double canoes and barges, which they navigated by the light of the stars. They had no language either of letters or symbolism, but so accurately were their legends preserved and transmitted that the great chiefs were able to trace their ancestry back, generation by generation, to something like a kinship with the children of Jacob, and even beyond in the same manner to Noah, and thence to Adam. What wonder, then, that under their old kings the islands of Hawaii should have been the home of romance, and that the south wind should have sighed in numbers through the caves of Kona?

And now, borne by the soft breath of the tropics, let us be wafted to the island of Hawaii, and backward over a misty bridge of historic *meles* to the reign of Kealiiokoʻloa, a son of Umi and grandson of the famed Liloa. It was during his brief reign—extending, perhaps, from 1520 to 1530—that for a second time a white face was seen by the Hawaiians. A Spanish vessel from the Moluccas was driven upon the reefs of Keei, in the district of Kona, and completely destroyed. But two persons were saved from the wreck—the captain and his sister. They were first thought to be gods by the simple islanders; but as their first request was for food, which they ate with avidity, and their next for rest, which seemed to be as necessary to them as to other mortals, they were soon relieved of their celestial attributes and conducted to the king, who received them graciously and took them under his protection. The captain—named by the natives Kukanaloa—wedded a dusky maiden of good family, and the sister became the wife of a chief in whose veins ran royal blood.

On the death of Kealiiokoloa his younger brother, Keawenui, assumed the sceptre in defiance of the right of Kukailani, his nephew and son of the dead king, who was too young to assert his authority. This he was the better enabled to do in consequence of the sudden death of the king, possibly by poison, before his successor had been formally named. Keawenui's usurpation, however, was resisted by the leading chiefs of the island, who refused to recognize his authority and rose in arms against him. But he inherited something of the martial prowess of his father, Umi, and, meeting the revolted chiefs before they had time to properly organize their forces, destroyed them in detail, and thereafter reigned in peace. Nor could it well have been otherwise, for the bones of the rebellious chiefs of Kohala, Hamakua, Hilo, Puna, Kau and Kona were among the trophies of his household, and Kukailani, lacking ambition, was content with the lot of idleness and luxury which the crafty uncle placed at his command.

And thus, while Keawenui continued in the *moiship* of Hawaii, Kukailani, the rightful ruler, grew to manhood around the court of his uncle. In due time the prince married, and among the children born to him was Kaikilani, the heroine of this little story. At the age of fifteen she was the most lovely of the maidens of Hawaii. Her face was fairer than any other in Hilo, to which place Keawenui had removed his court ; and that is saying much, for the king was noted for his gallantries, and the handsomest women in the kingdom were among his retainers. If her complexion was a shade lighter than that of others, it was because of the Castilian blood that had come to her through her grandmother, the sister of Kukanaloa, and brighter eyes than hers never peered through the lattices of the Guadalquivir.

Kaikilani became the wife of the king's eldest son, Kanaloa-kuaana, and, in further atonement of the wrong he had done her father, on his death-bed Keawenui formally conferred upon her the *moiship* of Hawaii. Among the other sons left by Keawenui at his death was Lono. His full name was Lonoikamakahiki. His mother was Haokalani, in whose veins ran the best blood of Oahu.

Early in life Lono exhibited remarkable intelligence, and as he grew to manhood, after the death of his father, in athletic and warlike exercises and other manly accomplishments he had not a peer in all Hawaii. So greatly was he admired by the people, and so manifestly was he born to rule, that his brother, the hus-

band and adviser of the queen, recommended that he be elevated to the *moiship*, in equal power and dignity with Kaikilani.

What followed could have occurred only in Hawaii. A day
was appointed for a public trial of Lono's abilities before the
assembled chiefs of the kingdom. Although but twenty-three
years of age, his knowledge of warfare, of government, of the
unwritten laws of the island and the prerogatives of the *tabu*
was found to be complete ; and Kawaamaukele, the venerable
high-priest of Hilo, whose white hairs swept his knees, and who
had foretold Lono's future when a boy, bore testimony to his
thorough mastery of the legendary annals of the people and his
zeal in the worship of the gods.

So much for his mental acquirements. To test his physical
accomplishments the chiefs most noted for their skill, strength
and endurance were summoned from all parts of the kingdom.
It was a tournament in which one man threw down the glove to
every chief in Hawaii. The various contests continued for ten
consecutive days, in the presence of thousands of people, and
between the many trials of strength and skill were interspersed
feasting, music and dancing. The scene was brilliant. More
than a hundred distinguished chiefs, in yellow mantles and helmets, presented themselves to test the prowess of Lono in
exercises in which they individually excelled. But the mighty
grandson of Umi vanquished them all. He outran the fleetest,
as well on the plain as in bringing a ball of snow from the top
of Mauna Kea. On a level he leaped the length of two long
war-spears, and in *uli-maita*, *holua* and other athletic games he
found no rival. In a canoe contest he distanced twelve competitors, and then plunged into the sea with a *pahoa* in his hand,
and slew and brought to the surface the body of a large shark.
He caught in his hands twenty spears hurled at him in rapid succession by as many strong arms, and in the *moku-moku*, or wrestling contests, he broke the limbs of three of his adversaries.

Among the witnesses of these contests was the still young
and comely Kaikilani. It is true that she had frequently met
the young hero, and regarded him with such favor as she might
the brother of her husband ; but now, at the end of his victories,
he appeared to her almost as a god, with whom it would be an
honor to share the sovereignty of the kingdom; and when,
amidst the plaudits of thousands, she threw the royal *mamo* over

his shoulders with her own hands, and in doing so kissed his cheek, her husband saw that she loved Lono better than she had ever loved him. "The gods have decreed it," said Kanaloa, in sorrow, but with no feeling of bitterness, "and so shall it be!"

He consulted with the chiefs and high-priest, and at the conclusion of a feast the same evening, given in honor of Lono, he took his brother by the hand and led him to the apartment of the queen. As they entered, Kaikilani rose from a soft couch of *kapa*, and waited to hear the purpose of their visit; for it was near the middle of the night, and but a single *kukui* torch was burning in front of the door. The heart of Kanaloa fluttered in his throat, but he finally said, with apparent calmness:

"My good Kaikilani, what I am about to say is in sorrow to myself and in affection for you. Of all the sons of our father, Lono seems most to have the favor of the gods. Is it strange, then, that he should have yours as well? It is therefore deemed best by the gods, the chiefs and myself that you accept Lono as your husband, and share with him henceforth the government of Hawaii. Is it your will that this be done?"

Kaikilani was almost dazed with the abrupt announcement; but she understood its full meaning, and, after gazing for a moment into the face of Lono and reading no objection there, she found the courage to answer:

"Since it is the will of the gods, it is also mine."

"So shall it be made known by the heralds," said Kanaloa, bowing to hide his grief, and leaving Lono and the queen together.

Thus it was that Lono, of whom tradition relates so. many romantic stories, became the *moi* of Hawaii and the husband of the most attractive woman of her time, Queen Kaikilani.

II.

Peace and prosperity followed the elevation of Lono to the throne of Hawaii. His fame as an able and sagacious ruler soon spread to the other islands of the group, and his court as well as his person commanded the highest respect of his subjects. Weary of inaction, and having no desire to embroil the kingdom in a foreign war, he at length concluded to visit some of the neighboring islands with his queen, and particularly Kauai, which he had once seen when a boy.

Leaving the government in charge of his brother Kanaloa, Lono embarked on his journey of pleasure with a number of large double canoes and a brilliant retinue. He took with him *pololous, kahilis* and other emblems of state, and the *hokeo*, or large calabash, containing the bones of the six rebellious chiefs slain by his royal father at the beginning of his reign.

The double canoe provided for Kaikilani and her personal attendants was fitted out in a manner becoming the rank of its royal occupant. It was eighty feet in length, and the two together were seven feet in width. Midway between stem and stern a continuous flooring covered both canoes, which was enclosed to a height of six feet, thus providing the queen with a room seven feet broad and twenty feet in length. The apartment was abundantly supplied with cloths and mats of brilliant colors, and the walls were decorated with festoons of shells and *leis* of flowers and feathers. In front of the entrance stood two *kahilis*, and behind a *kapa* screen was a carved image of *Ku*, surrounded by a number of charms and sacred relics. The canoes were brightly painted in alternate lines of black and yellow, while above their ornamented prows towered the carved and feathered forms of two gigantic birds with human heads. Forty oarsmen comprised the crew, and sails of mats were ready to lift into every favoring breeze.

The double canoe of the king was smaller and less elaborately ornamented ; and as it moved out of the harbor of Hilo, bearing the royal ensign and followed by the sumptuous barge of the queen and the humbler crafts of servants and retainers, the shores were lined with people, and hundred in canoes paddled after them to give them their parting *alohas* beyond the reef. The auguries had not been favorable. So said the high-priest, and so had the people whispered to each other. But, after preparing for the journey, Lono could not be persuaded to relinquish it. It was therefore with misgivings that he was seen to depart ; and for many days thereafter sacrifices were offered for him in the temples, and a strict *tabu* was ordered for a period of three days, during which time no labor was performed and a solemn silence prevailed over all the land embraced in the dread edict. Swine were confined, fires were extinguished, dogs were muzzled, fowls were hidden under calabashes, and the priests alone were seen and heard, and they but sparingly. Such was the strict *tabu* for the propitiation of the gods in case of emergency or peril, and death was the certain penalty of its violation.

The weather was fair, and the royal party first stopped at Lahaina. It had been Lono's purpose to spend a week or more at the court of Kamalalawalu, but the *moi* was absent at the time, and the squadron left Maui the next day for Oahu. A fair wind wafted the party through Pailolo channel to the western point of Molokai. The sky was clear, and Lono began to discern the tops of the mountains of eastern Oahu, when one of his nephews threw his spear into and wounded a large shark which for some time had been slowly moving around the bows of the canoe. In an instant the weapon was thrown back with a violence which drove the point through the rim of the boat. Blood tinged the waves, but the shark disappeared.

Before Lono could recover from his astonishment a furious wind rose from the south and west, and the fleet was driven around to the north side of Molokai, and finally succeeded in effecting a landing at Kalaupapa. Two of the canoes were destroyed during the gale, and the thoughtless young chief who cast the spear was washed into the sea and devoured by a school of black sharks before assistance could reach him. Landing with his party, Lono learned from a priest the cause of the disaster that had overtaken him. It was the god *Moaalii*, who had taken his characteristic form of a shark and was guiding the fleet to Oahu, that had been wounded by Lono's nephew.

The weather continued boisterous for some days, and Lono and his party became the guests of the chiefs of Kalaupapa. It was not a very inviting spot, and to beguile the time Lono and Kaikilani amused themselves with the game of *konane*, played upon a checkered board and closely resembling the game of draughts. One day, when thus occupied in the shade of a palm near the foot of an abrupt hill, Lono heard a voice above them. He gave but little attention to it until the name of Kaikilani was pronounced. He listened without raising his head, and soon heard the voice repeat :

"Ho, Kaikilani ! Your lover, Heakekoa, is waiting for you ! "

Lono looked up, but could see no one above them. He inquired the meaning of such words addressed to the wife of the *moi* of Hawaii ; but the queen, seemingly confused, was either unable or unwilling to offer any explanation.   Enraged at what he hastily conceived to be an evidence of her infidelity, Lono seized the *konane* board and struck her senseless and bleeding to the earth. Without waiting to learn the result of his barbarous blow, Lono strode to the beach, and, ordering his canoe launched, set sail at once for Oahu, without leaving any orders for the remainder of the fleet.

As he shoved from the shore Kaikilani approached, and, holding out her blood-stained hands, pitifully implored him to remain or take her with him ; but he waved her back in anger and resolutely put out to sea.   She watched the canoe of her impetuous husband until it became a speck in the distance, and then with a despairing moan sank senseless upon the sands.

Kaikilani was tenderly borne to her domicile by her attendants, and for nine days struggled with a fever which threatened her life.   During all that time she tasted neither fish nor *poi*, but in her delirium appealed continually to Lono, declaring that no one had called to her from the cliffs.   On the tenth day her mind was clear and she partook of food, and then on her hands and knees a young woman crawled to the side of her *kapa-moe*, and, having permission to speak, said :

"O queen, I am the innocent cause of your misery, and my heart breaks for you.   I am the daughter of the chief Keeokane, and he has sent me to you.   Heakekoa loves me, and it was my name, Kaikinane, that he called from the cliffs, and not yours. It is better that confusion should come to me than shame and grief to the queen of Hawaii."

Kaikilani admonished her attendants to remember the words of the girl, that they might be able, if necessary, to repeat them to Lono, and then dismissed her with presents and a promise to speak kindly of her to her father, who was greatly annoyed at the distress which the indiscretion of his daughter had brought to their distinguished guest.

As soon as she had sufficiently recovered, Kaikilani, not knowing what had become of her husband, sorrowfully returned to Hawaii in the hope of finding him there and explaining away the cause of his anger.   But the news of Lono's assault upon her and his sudden departure from Molokai had preceded her, probably through the return of some of the canoes of the fleet, and when she arrived at Kohala she found the kingdom in a state of rebel-lion.

With the avowed intent of slaying Lono, should he return to Hawaii, Kanaloa had assumed the regency, supported by the principal chiefs of the island, the relatives of the queen, and all the brothers of Lono with the exception of Pupuakea, a stalwart and warlike son of Keawenui by an humble mother unnamed in the royal annals, and who had large possessions in the district of Kau.

But Kaikilani still loved her hot-headed but instinctively gen-erous husband, and refused to give countenance to the revolt raised in her behalf. She therefore hastily left Kohala at night, and, so sailing as to escape the observation of the rebels, sudden-ly appeared off the coast of Kau and placed herself in communi-cation with Pupuakea, the only chief of note that still adhered to the fortunes of Lono. He had succeeded in rallying to the sup-port of his cause a very considerable force, but he knew that it would avail him little against the united armies of the opposition, and after a full consideration of the situation it was decided that Pupuakea should remain on the defensive until the return of Lono, of whom Kaikilani resolved to go at once in search.

With this understanding Kaikilani, inspired by the hope of winning back her husband's love, after a few preparations started on her errand ; but not before she had made sacrifices to the gods and implored their assistance, and Pupuakea brought word to her from the temple that the auguries of her journey showed a line of dark clouds ending in sunshine. But what cared she for clouds, if the sunshine of Lono's presence was to come at last ? But where was Lono ? Perhaps in the bottom of the sea ; but, if alive, she resolved to find him, even though the search took her through all the group to the barren rocks of Kaula.

Rounding the capes of Kau and sailing nearly northward, Kaikilani first stopped at Lahaina ; but a week spent there con-vinced her that Lono was not on the island of Maui. The *moi* treated her with great respect and kindness, and offered to assist in the search for her husband on the other islands ; but she de-clined his services, and next visited Lanai. Causing a thorough search to be made of that island, and despatching a party to the windy wastes of Kahoolawe, the queen proceeded to Molokai, to assure herself that Lono had not returned to Kalaupapa, and then set sail for Oahu. She first landed at Waikiki, on that island, but, learning that the king had established his court at Kailua, departed for that place the next day, and reached it without difficulty, for the captain of her crew was the distinguished old navigator, Kukupea, who for a wager, in the reign of Keawenui, had made the direct passage in a canoe between the Hawaiian bay of Kealakeakua and the island of Niihau without sighting intermediate land.

III.

Leaving Kaikilani entering the bay of Kailua, it will be in order to briefly refer to the adventures of Lono after his sudden departure from Kalaupapa. Half-crazed at what had occurred, to divert his thoughts from his cruelty he seized a paddle, and vigorously used it hour after hour until he was compelled to cease through exhaustion. The wind was fair, but, inspired by his example, twenty others plied the paddle ceaselessly in turns of ten, and in a few hours the royal canoe was hauled up on the beach of Kailua, on the northwestern coast of Oahu, where, as before stated, Kakuhihewa, the *moi* of the island, had temporarily established his court.

As Lono approached the shore his state attracted attention. A chief and priest, who had at one time been in the service of Lono's father, recognized the sail and insignia of the craft, and informed the king that it must be that some one nearly connected with the royal family of Hawaii had come to visit him. This secured to Lono a cordial and royal welcome. Houses were set apart for his accommodation, and food in abundance was provided for him and his attendants. Although he scrupulously concealed his name and rank, and in that respect enjoined the closest secrecy upon his attendants under penalty of death, his commanding presence and personal equipment rendered it apparent that he was either one of the sons of Keawenui or a chief of the highest rank below the throne.

Pleading fatigue, and courteously desiring to be left to himself until the day following, Lono partook of his evening meal, sent from the table of the king, alone and in silence, and at an early hour retired to rest. But the heat was oppressive, and thoughts of Kaikilani disturbed his slumbers, and near midnight he strolled down to his canoe on the beach to catch the cool breeze of the sea. While there another double canoe arrived from Kauai, having on board a high chiefess, who was on her way to Hawaii and had touched at Kailua for fresh water.

To pass the time Lono engaged in conversation with the fair stranger, and so interested her that she repeated to him twice a new *mele* that had just been composed in honor of her name—Ohaikawiliula—and which was known only to a few of the highest chiefs of Kauai. Portions of the celebrated chant are still retained by old Hawaiians.

The *mele* diverted his mind from bitter thoughts, and when he returned to his couch he enjoyed a refreshing sleep. At daylight the next morning the king, without disturbing his royal guest, repaired to the sea-shore for his customary bath just as the Kauai chiefess was preparing to depart. Making himself known to her, she recited to him until he was able to repeat the new *mele*, and then made sail for Hawaii. As she had arrived after midnight, and the *mele* was new, the king was pleased at the thought of being able to surprise Lono by reciting it to him ; but his amazement was great and his discomfiture complete when, on meeting his guest after breakfast and bantering him to repeat the latest Kauaian *mele*, Lono recited in full the poem he had so quickly and correctly committed to memory the night before. This incident is related by tradition in evidence of Lono's mental capacity.

Notwithstanding the mystery which surrounded him at the court of Oahu, Lono soon became a great favorite there. No one could throw a spear so far or so accurately, and in all games and exercises of strength or skill he found no equal. He was generous and fearless, and in his pastimes reckless of his life. Although he was beset with their smiles and blandishments, women seemed to have no charm for him, and he politely but firmly declined to avail himself of that feature of early Hawaiian hospitality which held a host to be remiss in courtesy if he failed to provide his guest with female companionship. He preferred the sturdier contests of men, and introduced to the Oahuans a number of new games of skill and muscle.

While the most of the chiefs were generous admirers of the accomplishments of their unknown visitor, a few were jealous of his popularity, among them the grand counselor of the king, Lanahuimihaku, who on one occasion sneeringly referred to him as "a nameless chief." To this taunt Lono, towering above his traducer with a menace of death in his face, replied that he would flay him alive if he ever met him beyond the protection of his king; and then he brought from his canoe the great calabash of bones, and, exhibiting the trophies of his father's prowess, chanted the names of the slain. This apprised them all that he was indeed a son of Keawenui, but which one they did not know.

But Lono's stay in Kailua was drawing to a close, for one day, while he was playing *konane* with the king within the enclosure of the palace grounds, Kaikilani's canoe was being drawn up on the beach below. She saw, to her great joy, the canoe of her husband, and ascertained where he might be found. Proceeding alone toward the royal mansion, with a fluttering heart she approached the enclosure, and through an opening in the wall discerned the stalwart form of Lono. Stepping aside to avoid his gaze, she began to chant his *mele inoa*—the song of his own name. He was startled at hearing his name mentioned in a place where he supposed it to be unknown. He raised his head and listened, and, as the words of the *mele* floated to him, he recognized the voice of Kaikilani. Rising to his feet, with dignity he now addressed the king:

"My royal brother, disguise is no longer necessary or fitting. I am Lonoikamakahiki, son of Keawenui and *moi* of Hawaii, and the gods have sent to me Kaikilani, my wife. It is her voice that we now hear."

Then, turning and approaching the wall behind which Kaikilani was standing, Lono began to chant her name, coupled with words of tenderness and reconciliation; then, springing over the obstruction, he clasped his faithful wife in his arms, and the past was forgiven and forgotten.

The rank of his guests now being known, Kakuhihewa was anxious to give them a befitting recognition; but, learning of the revolt in Hawaii and the peril of Pupuakea, Lono embarked for his kingdom at once. Reaching and passing Kohala, where he learned the rebels were in force, he landed at Kealakeakua, and immediately despatched a messenger to Pupuakea, in Kau, with information of his arrival in Puna. The brother responded promptly, and, leading his forces over a mountain path to avoid the coast villages, joined Lono at Puuanahulu. Meantime, Lono's name had brought thousands to his standard, and on the arrival of Pupuakea he boldly attacked and defeated the insurgents at Wailea. They were followed and again defeated at Kaunooa.

Reinforcements reaching the rebels from Kohala, two other battles were fought in rapid succession, both resulting in their defeat. In these engagements two of Lono's brothers were slain, and the body of one of them was offered as a sacrifice at the *heiau* of Puukohola.

The last of the rebels were defeated at Pololu, and the island returned to its allegiance to Lono and Kaikilani. Kanaloa-kuaa-na, who originated the revolt, also submitted, and was forgiven and restored to favor through the intercession of the queen.

The legends relate many subsequent romantic adventures of Lono ; but he and Kaikilani both lived to good old ages, and when they died were succeeded in the sovereignty of Hawaii by lineal blood.

THE ADVENTURES OF IWIKAUIKAUA.

CHARACTERS.

KAIKILANI, queen of Hawaii.

MAKAKAUALII, brother of Kaikilani.

IWIKAUIKAUA, son of Makakaualii.

KANALOA-KUAANA and
KANALOA-KAKULEHU, } princes of Hawaii.

KEALIIOKALANI, daughter of Kaikilani.

KEAKEALANIKANE, son of Kanaloa-kuaana.

KEAKAMAHANA, daughter of Kealiiokalani.

KAIHIKAPU, king of southern Oahu.

KAUAKAHI, daughter of Kaihikapu.

KAUHIAKAMA, *moi* of Maui.

KAPUKINI, queen of Maui and sister of Iwikauikaua.

MAHIA, chief of Kahakuloa, Maui.

THE ADVENTURES OF IWIKAUIKAUA.

A STORY OF ROYAL KNIGHT-ERRANTRY IN THE SIXTEENTH
CENTURY.

I.

ONE of the most interesting characters distinctly observed
among the misty forms and dimly outlined events of the
remaining Hawaiian traditions of the sixteenth century is Iwikauikaua. In him the knight-errantry of the period found a distinguished exponent and representative, and his deeds add a bold
tint to the glow of romance and chivalry lighting up the life and
reign of the great Lono, and lend a lustre to the names and
events with which they are associated. Of royal lineage, but
without estates or following beyond his personal attendants, he
sought his fortune with spear and battle-axe, and in the end
became the husband of a queen and one of the ancestors of a
long line of kings.

As he was the nephew of Queen Kaikilani—whose reign in
Hawaii, including that of her husband, Lono, embraced, it may
be presumed, the period between the years A.D. 1565 and 1595—
and was a stout friend and supporter of the ruling family, a proper understanding of the rank, position and aspirations of Iwikauikaua necessitates a brief reference to the strange political
events which surrounded his youth and conspired to shape his
romantic career.

When Kealiiokoloa, the son of Umi, suddenly died, in about
A.D. 1535, after a reign of perhaps not more than ten years, he
left as his heir a young son named Kukailani. His right to the
throne was unquestioned, but, as he had not been formally designated by his father as his successor, Keawenui, the younger
brother of the dead king, assumed the sceptre, and maintained
his claim to it by meeting in battle and slaying the six principal
chiefs of the island who rebelled against the usurpation.

Kukailani seems to have possessed but little force or spirit, and was content during his life with such maintenance as his uncle was willing to provide. In due time he married, and became the father of Kaikilani and Makakaualii. The former became the wife of Kanaloa-kuaana, the eldest son of Keawenui, and subsequently the wife of his brother Lono, as related in the legend of "*Lono and Kaikilani.*" As if desirous of atoning for the injustice done to his nephew, Kukailani, on his death-bed Keawenui named as his successor Kaikilani, daughter of the deposed prince, and wife of Kanaloa-kuaana, his own son. Why Keawenui restored the sceptre to his brother's family through Kaikilani instead of her brother, Makakaualii, finds ready explanation in the fact that Kaikilani was the wife of his eldest son, through which union both families would thereafter share in the sovereignty.

Makakaualii, whose claims to the *moiship* were thus overlooked or disregarded by Keawenui, was the father of our hero, Iwikauikaua. But, if wrong was done in the matter, it was never openly resented by either father or son, and Iwikauikaua always remained the steadfast friend of his royal aunt, Kaikilani.

The position of Kukailani, on the death of his father, was such as could have been patiently borne only by one entirely destitute of ambition. Custom would have accorded him ample estates and a following consistent with his rank ; but his crafty uncle did not deem it prudent to tempt him to rebellion by according him even the powers of a district chief. It was safer for him to remain at court, living upon the bounty and under the watchful eye of Keawenui. He was doubtless a high officer of the royal household, retaining the *tabus* and *meles* of his family, and receiving the respect due to his rank ; but no lands were set apart for him, and he had no retainers beyond his personal attendants.

But Kukailani seemed to be content with his situation, and so utterly indifferent to the rights of his family that it does not appear that he ever demanded a more befitting recognition of the claims of the children born to him. Hence, like their father, Makakaualii and Kaikilani were compelled to live upon the bounty of the king until the latter was chosen to the succession.

And this was also the inheritance of Iwikauikaua, the son of Makakaualii. He was a landless chief of royal blood, and circumstances indicate that he was quite a youth when Keawenui died and Kaikilani assumed the sceptre. He grew to manhood around the court of his royal aunt, and was among the many who rejoiced when Lono became her husband and, with her, the joint ruler of Hawaii.

In person he was handsome and imposing, and his accomplishments befitted his rank. Through Kaikilani the *moiship* had been restored to the Kealiiokoloa branch of the royal family, but the previous usurpation had left him without estates, and less near than was his due to the throne, and he chafed under his hard fortune and resolved to retrieve it—not by rebellion or trespass upon the rights of others, but through the channels of bold and legitimate endeavor. When a boy a *kaula* told him that he would die either a king or the husband of a queen, and he never forgot the prophecy. In fact, it seems to have taken possession of him and to have become the guiding star of his early life.

Iwikauikaua makes his first appearance as a striking and consequential figure of Hawaiian tradition in the midst of the revolt of Kanaloa-kuaana and other chiefs of Hawaii against Lono. The revolt was organized during the absence of Lono and Kaikilani on a friendly visit to the other islands of the group, and embraced nearly every prominent chief in the kingdom. They had resolved to kill Lono should he return to the island, and the conspiracy seemed to be as formidable as time and determination could make it. With a single exception, all the brothers of Lono were arrayed against him, and his cause was considered almost hopeless.

The rebellion had its origin, avowedly, in a report that Lono had in a fit of jealousy killed Kaikilani on the island of Molokai; but other motives must have existed, for the return of Kaikilani with her husband to Hawaii did not put an end to the uprising, but rather stimulated the conspirators in their resolution to wrest the sovereignty of the island from Lono at all hazards.

The only brother of Lono who refused to join in the conspiracy was Pupuakea. He was the sturdy and warlike son of Keawenui by a mother whose name is not mentioned by tradition, and was endowed with lands in the district of Kau. Removing in early manhood to his estates in that district, he sel-

dom visited the court and took no part in its bickerings. As
his mother was doubtless of an humble family, he was not considered the equal in rank of the other sons of Keawenui, and
therefore preferred to reside where he would not be continually
reminded of his inferiority. When the revolt against Lono was
organized he was invited by Kanaloa-kuaana to give it his support ; but no promises of lands were made to him, as to other
distinguished chiefs, nor was he deemed to be of sufficient consequence to entitle him to a voice in the councils of the rebels.
This slight of Pupuakea led to the defeat and ruin of the conspirators. The chief of whom they thought so little had developed into a leader of influence and ability in his distant home, and
it was around him that was gathered the nucleus of the force
which in the end gave victory to Lono.

When Kaikilani returned alone from Molokai, and found the
kingdom on the verge of revolution, she secretly consulted with
Pupuakea, as almost the only chief of consequence to be relied
upon ; and when she next returned with Lono, Pupuakea was at
the head of a force large enough to overawe the rebels of Kau,
but too small to venture beyond that district without support.

The main rebel army was concentrated in the district of Kohala, which Lono avoided on his return from Oahu, landing at
Kealakeakua, on the coast of Kona. It was early in the morning
when the canoes of Lono, bearing a small party of attendants,
were drawn up on the beach. No one was there to oppose him :
but the rebels were in possession of all the machinery of the
government, as well as five of the six divisions of the island,
and the outlook would have been gloomy to any one less resolute and daring than Lono. He had less than a hundred followers, and, taking from his canoe the *hokeo*, or calabash, containing
the bones of the six rebellious district chiefs slain by his father,
placed it within a sanctuary of mats on the beach, and beside it
raised the royal standard and *kahilis*. This done, he summoned
the people to arms, started a courier to Pupuakea, and despatched
lunapais to the neighboring chiefs, commanding them to march
to his assistance at once.

But the people were timid. The revolt was not popular, but
the cause of Lono seemed to be hopeless, and the masses hesitated. The hesitation was brief, however. Late in the afternoon a force of five or six hundred warriors was observed ap-

proaching from the northward. Lono hastily prepared for the best defence possible, and for retreat to his canoes should he be unable to hold his ground. Nearer and nearer came the threatening column. It was finally halted within two hundred paces of Lono's position, when from the front rank emerged a tall young chief in feather cape and helmet. At the end of his spear was displayed a large *ti* leaf as a token of peace. Accompanied by two aids bearing weapons similarly bedecked, he boldly strode past the lines of Lono and asked for the king. He was conducted to his presence, and, observing Kaikilani beside her husband, was about to kneel when Lono stepped forward and grasped him by the hand, exclaiming :

"Welcome, Iwikauikaua, for I know you come as a friend ! "

"Yes, I come as a friend," replied the chief, "and have with me a few brave warriors, whose services I now tender."

"But are you not afraid to be the friend of Lono at such a time as this ? " inquired the king, glancing admiringly at the bold front of the young chief. "The whole island seems to be in arms against me."

Lono knew he was exaggerating the danger, but desired to learn the worst.

"No, not the whole island," promptly replied the chief. "Pupuakea will soon join us with three thousand spears or more, and it will not be long that Lono will lack warriors."

"You are right," returned the king, hopefully ; "we will find spears and axes enough in the end to clear a way to Kohala."

Kaikilani joined Lono in thanking her nephew for his timely assistance, and Iwikauikaua retired to find quarters for his followers and arouse others to the defence of the king.

The appearance of the young chief with his few hundreds of warriors was indeed most opportune. It inspired the people with confidence in the success of Lono, and they began to rally to his support in large numbers ; and, observing that the tide was turning in his favor, the neighboring chiefs came to his assistance with their followers, thus swelling his force within three days to as many thousands of warriors of all arms.

Hastily organizing his little army, Lono boldly pushed on toward Kohala, steadily recruiting his ranks as he moved, and at Puuanahulu was joined by Pupuakea with nearly three thousand additional spears from Kau. Thus enabled to operate on the offensive, he attacked and defeated the rebel army at Wailea, and again at Puako, or at some point not far north of that place.

After the second engagement the rebels retreated northward, and, receiving reinforcements from Kohala, made another stand at Puupa, where they were again defeated, but through some mishap Iwikauikaua was taken prisoner. They then fell back to Puukohola, near which place a large *heiau* was maintained at that time. There Kanaloa-kakulehu, one of the brothers of Lono, resolved to sacrifice the distinguished prisoner.

Iwikauikaua received the announcement stoically. He was conducted to the altar within the *heiau*. The assistants were in readiness to take him beyond the walls for execution, and the priests were in attendance to offer the sacrifice in due form to Kanaloa-kakulehu's god of war. Ascending the steps of the altar, the young chief turned to the high-priest and said:

"I am ready, but it is not the will of the gods that I should be offered."

"What know you of the will of the gods?" answered the priest, sternly.

"And what know you," returned the chief, "since you have not inquired?"

Such questioning was not common at the altar, and for a moment the priest was disconcerted. Finally he said:

"You say it is not the will of the gods. Make it so appear, and your life shall be spared; but if you fail your right eye shall see the left in my hand, and you will be slain with torture."

"So let it be!" exclaimed the chief; and, lifting his face upward, he addressed an audible prayer to *Ku*, *Uli* and *Kama*. As he proceeded with the solemn invocation not an unfavorable omen appeared. The winds died away and the birds in the neighboring trees remained silent. Concluding the prayer, he folded his arms and stepped down from the altar. By an unseen hand the cords that bound his limbs had been cut, and he approached the high-priest and bowed before him. This manifestation of the will of the gods could not be mistaken, and Iwikauikaua was conducted to a hut within the *heiau*, where he was advised to remain until he could leave the place in safety. No hostile hand could be laid upon him within the walls of the temple. There he was under the protection of the high-priest, and beyond the reach of the highest temporal authority.

But Iwikauikaua did not long require the protection of the *heiau*. At daylight the next morning Lono attacked the rebels at Puukohola, and after an obstinate battle defeated them, taking prisoner his brother Kanaloa-kakulehu, whom he promptly ordered to be sacrificed at the *heiau*. As he was brought to the altar for that purpose, his last moments were embittered by the farewell which Iwikauikaua waved to him with simulated grief as he left the enclosure to join the victorious army. Although Lono had directed the sacrifice of his brother in retaliation for the supposed death of Iwikauikaua, he did not countermand the order, as he might have done in time, when he found the latter had miraculously escaped.

Several other battles were fought, in all of which Iwikauikaua took a distinguished part, and the island returned to its allegiance to Lono and Kaikilani. The services of Papuakea were rewarded with such additional lands of deceased rebel chiefs as he chose to accept, and Iwikauikaua was offered possessions either in Kona or Hamakua, or a military charge in the royal household. But in the end he decided to accept neither. They presented to him no opportunity for such advancement as the gods had promised, and which now, since their manifestation in his favor at Puukohola, seemed to be almost assured to him.

He had fixed his eye upon his pretty cousin Kealiiokalani, the daughter of Kaikilani. She stood close to the throne, and evinced a decided partiality for the dashing young chief. The gossip of the court was that the princess loved Iwikauikaua and would be more than content to become his wife. But royal marriages in all ages and in every clime have been less a suggestion of hearts than of state considerations ; and so it was in this instance. Unknown to all but himself, it was the fair face of the princess that had prompted him to espouse the cause of Lono when it seemed to be almost hopeless, and his services certainly entitled him to almost any reward ; but Keakealanikane, the son of Kaikilani by her first husband, Kanaloa-kuaana, had been named as successor to the *moiship*, and Kealiiokalani was selected to become his wife. Such marriages of close kinship were not uncommon among the chiefly families of ancient Hawaii, and the children born to them were accorded the very highest rank.

This arrangement for the succession left Iwikauikaua little to hope for on Hawaii, and he determined to seek his fortune among the other islands of the group. Tempting inducements were held out to him to remain, but he declined them all. To the princess alone he whispered that her betrothal to Keakealanikane had rendered his departure advisable, and she grieved that circumstances had decreed their separation. Ambition doubtless first attracted him to his fair cousin ; but her nature was gentle and loving, and he finally regarded her with a sincere and romantic attachment, which she seems to have fully reciprocated.

II.

In a large double canoe, painted red, and at its masthead flying the pennon of an *aha-alii*, Iwikauikaua, with a score or more of attendants, set sail from Kohala in quest of adventure. Passing Maui, he spent some time in visiting the small island of Lanai, where he was entertained in a princely manner by the leading chiefs. Proceeding thence to Molokai, he remained a week or more in the neighborhood of Kalaupapa, and then sailed for Oahu.

He landed at Waikiki, on that island, and was well received by Kaihikapu, one of the three principal chiefs of Oahu. His father was the noted Kakuhihewa, who had entertained Lono during his voluntary exile, and who at his death, a short time before, had divided the island among his three oldest sons, leaving the dignity of *moi* to Kanekapu. Harmony existed among the brothers, and all of them followed the example of their father in maintaining attractive petty courts and imposing establishments. The *moi* retained possession of the royal mansion at Kailua, which was two hundred and forty feet in length and ninety in breadth, and adorned with all the taste and skill of the period.

Kaihikapu had a princely mansion at Ewa, but his court was at Waikiki at the time of the arrival of Iwikauikaua. The young chief, whose rank was at once recognized, was provided with quarters for himself and attendants near the court, and soon became a favorite with the nobility. The part he had taken in the battles of Lono, together with his miraculous escape at the temple of Puukohola, became the talk of the court, and he was treated as a hero.

In the pleasure of the courts of Oahu, Iwikauikaua spent a

number of years on the island, and finally became the husband
of Kauakahi, daughter of Kaihikapu. It was not a love-match,
at least so far as Iwikauikaua was concerned, for after his marriage he squandered the most of his time for some years in roaming from district to district and giving little heed to the future.
At length he began to crave a more active life, and was about to
seek it on some other island when the noted war of the Kawelos,
of Kauai, gave employment to his spear.

Kawelo had been driven from Kauai by his cousin, and,
finding refuge in Oahu, had been given lands in the Waianae
Mountains by Kaihikapu. Instead of settling there in peace, he
began to construct canoes and prepare for a return to Kauai with
a force sufficient to maintain himself on that island. Kaihikapu
was finally induced to assist him, and so substantially that he invaded Kauai, deposed and killed his cousin, and assumed the
moiship. Iwikauikaua took part in the expedition, but became
disgusted with the jealousies of the Kauai chiefs and returned to
Oahu at the close of the war, without attempting to avail himself
of the opportunities afforded by the rebellion.

His marriage with Kauakahi promised him no advancement.
His hair began to be tinged with gray, and the future presented
to him no sign of the fulfilment of the prophecy of his youth.
He consulted the *kaulas,* but they gave him no satisfaction. One
of them told him, however, that his fortunes lay to the windward,
and he provisioned a double canoe, and, with a competent crew
and a few retainers, set sail in that direction without taking leave
of any one. He stopped for a few days on Molokai, and a *kaula*
there advised him to go to Maui. He accordingly set sail for
that island, where resided two of his sisters, whom he had not
seen for many years. One of them, Kapukini, was the wife of
Kauhiakama, the *moi* of Maui ; and the other, Pueopokii, of
Kaaoao, a prominent chief of Kaupo.

He landed at Lahaina, and made himself known to Kapukini.
Their greeting was affectionate, and they had much to relate of
their past lives. She was the only wife of Kauhiakama, and he
was astounded to hear that the aged *moi* had started two days
before with a hostile army for Oahu. The object of the invasion
was not clear, but Iwikauikaua felt satisfied that it would end
disastrously, and impatiently awaited the result. The only son
of Kapukini had reached his manhood, and Iwikauikaua advised

his sister to prepare for his installation as *moi*, expressing the opinion that Kauhiakama would never return. His surmises proved to be correct. Within ten days a mere handful of the force with which the *moi* had embarked for Oahu returned, bringing news of the defeat and death of Kauhiakama.

The *moi* had landed at Waikiki, where he was met and defeated by the united chiefs of Oahu. He was slain during the battle, and his body was taken to the *heiau* of Apuakehau, where it was treated with unusual indignity—so unusual, in fact, that Kahekili, the *moi* of Maui, many generations after remembered the act, and retaliated in kind upon the chiefs captured by him in his conquest of Oahu.

Kauhiakama had always been a rash and visionary leader, and his tragical end did not surprise Iwikauikaua. It was on his report that his warlike father, Kamalalawalu, had invaded Hawaii, and met defeat and death at the hands of Lono, and with equal thoughtlessness he had thrown a small invading force into the most thickly populated district of Oahu, and led it to slaughter.

But, whatever may have been the weaknesses of Kauhiakama, a lack of courage was certainly not one of them, and the news of his death, together with that of the indignity visited upon his remains, created a wild excitement among the chiefs of Maui. His son was installed as *moi* without opposition, and a general demand for revenge went up from the whole island. Large quotas of warriors were offered from every district, and the young *moi* was implored to baptize the beginning of his reign with the best blood of Oahu.

But Iwikauikaua advised the excited chiefs to act with discretion. No one more than himself felt like avenging the death of Kauhiakama, who was the husband of his sister; "but," he said to them, "the chiefs of Oahu are united, and a war upon one of them means a conflict with the whole island. Their spears are as long and as many as ours, and their knives are as sharp; therefore let not the chiefs of Maui be hasty."

Many of the chiefs agreed with Iwikauikaua that an invasion of Oahu in revenge for the death of their *moi* would not be advisable, and the newly-anointed king was of the same opinion; but others, especially those who had lost friends or relatives in the late expedition, clamored for war, and not a few of them intimated that the advice of Iwikauikaua was inspired either by friendship for the Oahuans or personal cowardice.

These insinuations reached the ear of Iwikauikaua, and the manner in which he repelled them was bold and effective. Three hundred chiefs of the higher grades had gathered to take part in the installation of the new *moi*, and such of them as were entitled to a voice in the national councils were assembled to discuss the project of war and such other matters as they might be requested to consider. As a near relative of the royal family, Iwikauikaua had been invited to participate in the deliberations, but he had modestly refrained from urging his opinions, and had thus far spoken only when directly appealed to. Several remarks of a sneering character had been dropped within his hearing, and finally a chief from Wailuku, glancing insultingly toward him, declared that the chiefs of Maui were "not afraid to use their spears."

Iwikauikaua could no longer bear these taunts in silence. With a dark scowl upon his handsome face, he rose to his feet and impetuously replied :

" Nor am I afraid to use mine, either in defence of the *moi* of Maui or in challenge to any chief here who presumes to doubt my courage ! I scorn to defend myself with words ! Without these walls, with spear and battle-axe, I am prepared to answer one and all !"

Several chiefs sprang to their feet, as if to accept the bold challenge, and confusion for a time prevailed ; but order was restored when Mahia, the venerable chief of Kahakuloa, rose and, commanding silence, said :

" Chiefs of Maui, hear my words and be calm. We have invited Iwikauikaua to advise with us, and by insulting him we degrade ourselves. He is high in rank and distinguished for his courage. He was the friend of the great Lono, of Hawaii, and a leader in his battles. He is the brother of Kapukini, and our respect is his due. Some of you have spoken words which seem to hold his valor lightly, and he has answered, as I would have answered had the complaint been mine, by inviting you to test the courage you doubt with spear and battle-axe No other answer could have been made by a brave man, and we should respect the nobility that prompted it. We should say to Iwikauikaua, whose body is scarred with the teeth of many battles : ' We have spoken hastily ; let us now be friends !' "

The effects of the eloquent words of the old warrior were magical. Those who had offended made prompt retraction, and looks and expressions of courtesy and kindness came to Iwikaui-kaua from all parts of the council. By reputation he was known to many of the older chiefs, and when they recounted to the younger his chivalrous services in the wars of Hawaii he was overwhelmed with manifestations of respect and kindly feeling.

The demand for an invasion of Oahu with a large force steadily abated with discussion and a better understanding of the danger and uncertainty of the project, and was entirely abandoned with the sudden appearance of a fleet of hostile canoes off the coast of Honuaula. It was a strong predatory expedition from Hawaii. Several villages had been plundered on the southern coast, and Wailuku was now threatened.

Lono, the warlike king of Hawaii, had been dead for some years, and under the reign of Keakealanikane several of the more powerful of the district chiefs had assumed an attitude of comparative independence. The most noted of these were the I family, of Hilo, and the Mahi chiefs, of Kohala. Each could muster some thousands of warriors, and occasional plundering or retaliatory expeditions were undertaken to the other islands without the knowledge or countenance of the sovereign authority.

The fleet discovered off the coast of Honuaula, and reported by runners to the *moi*, was from Kohala and under the command of one of the Mahi chiefs in person. As the young *moi* was unused to war, Iwikauikaua offered his services, and with fifty chiefs and two thousand warriors crossed the mountains and drove the plunderers from the coast. As it was surmised that other expeditions of a similar or more aggressive character might follow, the chiefs found employment for some time in repairing canoes, establishing signals, and placing their coast settlements in better conditions of defence.

Returning to Lahaina, Iwikauikaua learned from a Hilo chief on a visit to relatives in Kauaula that Keakealanikane, king of Hawaii, had recently died, and that Kealiiokalani, his wife, could not long survive a cancerous ailment of the stomach with which she was afflicted. The mention of the name of that princess brought back a flood of tender and romantic memories, and Iwikauikaua resolved to revisit his native island. He was begged by the young *moi* to remain as his *mahana* and chief counsellor, a position to which his rank entitled him ; but he seemed to hear the voice of the dying princess calling to him from Hawaii, and with becoming state set sail at once for Hilo, where the royal court had been temporarily established.

It was past midnight of the second day of his departure from Lahaina when Iwikauikaua reached Hilo. He landed quietly, making himself known to no one. He found the place still in mourning for the deceased *moi*, and learned that Keakamahana, the elder of the two daughters and only children of Kealiioka-lani, had been formally installed as *moi*, or queen, the day before, with the royal mother as chief adviser or premier.

Early next morning Iwikauikaua, clad in a feather cape and other insignia of rank, and accompanied by a number of attendants, proceeded to the royal mansion. Being a chief of unquestioned rank, he was admitted to the *pahale*, but, on applying for an audience with the queen or her first counsellor, was told that the former was still in mourning and could not be seen, and the latter was too ill to receive visitors ; but a proffer was made to carry any message he desired to either.

"Then take to Kealiiokalani the words that her cousin, Iwikauikaua, is at her door," said the chief.

At the mention of his name the *kahu* in attendance, a venerable chief, regarded the visitor for a moment with amazement. He had fought by his side in the wars of Lono, and in his face recognized the dashing young chief who a generation before had been saved by the gods from sacrifice at Puukohola.

"Iwikauikaua, indeed !" exclaimed the *kahu*, with emotion. "I know you well. Years ago our spears drank blood together, from the shores of Kona to the high lands of Pololu !"

Iwikauikaua was pleased at the recognition, and, after exchanging a few pleasant words with the old *kahu*, the latter conveyed his brief message to Kealiiokalani. She was in her own apartment at the time, reclining on a soft couch of *kapa*, and surrounded by a group of silent and sad-eyed attendants. Near her sat Keakamahana, the fair young *moi*, who was doing all that affection could suggest to soothe and strengthen her suffering mother. Prayers had been said, offerings to the gods had been made, and renowned *kahunas* had resorted to the most potent herbs, charms and incantations known to them in behalf of the royal sufferer. But nothing could stay the dreadful malady that was eating away her life, and all hope of her recovery had been abandoned. The cancerous gnawing was declared by the priests to be the work of an evil spirit, which prayer and sacrifice could not dislodge.

The *kahu* delivered the message of Iwikauikaua with some hesitation, for the condition of the patient had become more critical since the death of her husband. But when she heard the name of the visitor, and learned that he was without, her eyes assumed something of the brightness of her girlhood, and she ordered him to be admitted at once.

As Iwikauikaua entered he was silently conducted to the couch of Kealiiokalani. For a moment he gazed at her wan face ; for a moment she glanced at the gray hairs which the years had brought to him since he said farewell to her in Kohala. He knelt beside the couch. He took her hand and held it to his heart, and the silence that followed best interpreted the thoughts of both.

Rising, and learning to his embarrassment that the young woman whom he had scarcely noticed was Keakamahana, daughter of Kealiiokalani and queen of Hawaii, Iwikauikaua knelt respectfully before her, and gallantly kissed the hand with which she gave him welcome. A low order was given to an attendant by the mother, and in a moment she was alone with the queen and Iwikauikaua. Casting her eyes around and observing no others present, she beckoned them closer, and in broken sentences said :

"The black *kapa* will soon cover me. Listen, Iwikauikaua ! Early in life it was in our hearts to be the husband and wife of each other. It was the fault of neither that we were denied that hope. It was not my fault that you left Hawaii. It was not your fault that I grieved when you went to other lands. But you have returned at last. The gods have directed you back to Hawaii. They will give to me in death what they refused to my youth. In Keakamahana I will be your wife ! "

She paused for a moment, her listeners bending over her in silence, and then continued :

"Take him as your husband, Keakamahana. He is the gift of your mother. He is brave and noble, and you will need his counsel when I am gone."

Overcome by these words of affection, the chief knelt beside the couch, and the eyes of Keakamahana were filled with tears.

" Do you promise ? " inquired the mother.

" I promise," replied the queen, giving her hand to the kneeling chief.

" I promise," repeated Iwikauikaua, as he clasped and kissed the proffered pledge.

" I am content," returned the sufferer, as a smile of happiness lighted up her face.

The attendants were recalled, wondering what had occurred, and Iwikauikaua, almost bewildered, took his leave.

Tradition plainly recites the brief remainder of the career of this distinguished chief. Kealiiokalani died a few days after the strange betrothal just noted, and Iwikauikaua became the husband of Queen Keakamahana, thus romantically fulfilling the aspiration and prophecy of his youth.

Their daughter, Keakealani, succeeded her mother as queen of Hawaii, and one of her husbands was the son of Iwikauikaua by the wife left by him in Oahu.

With this adventurous and erratic chief originated, it is claimed, the custom of burning *kukui* torches by daylight on state occasions, especially in connection with the obsequies of persons of royal lineage ; and it was within the present generation that the exclusive right to the ceremonial was contested by the two royal families claiming the prerogative through descent from Iwikauikaua. Certain customs, like chants and *meles*, are matters of inheritance, and remain exclusively in the families with which they originate.

THE PROPHECIES OF KEAULUMOKU.

CHARACTERS.

KAHEKILI, *moi* of Maui.
KALANIOPUU, king of Hawaii.
NAMAHANA, widow of Kamehamehanui.
KEEAUMOKU, a royal chief of Hawaii.
KAHANANA, a warrior of Waihee.
MAHIHELELIMA, governor of Hana, Maui.
KAAHUMANU, daughter of Keeaumoku.
KAMEEIAMOKU and
KAMANAWA, } brothers of Keeaumoku.
KIWALAO, son of Kalaniopuu.
KEAULUMOKU, the poet-prophet of Hawaii.
KAMEHAMEHA I., the conqueror of the group.
KEOUA, half-brother of Kiwalao.
KEAWEMAUHILI, a royal chief of Hawaii.

THE PROPHECIES OF KEAULUMOKU.

THE CAREER OF KEEAUMOKU, THE PRINCE-SLAYER AND KING-MAKER.

I.

THE days had just begun to lengthen after the summer solstice of 1765 when a great grief fell upon the royal court of the island of Maui. Kamehamehanui, the king, had died very suddenly at Wailuku, which had been his favorite place of residence, and his brother and successor, Kahekili, had removed his court to Lahaina. The bones of the dead king had been carefully secreted, the customary mourning excesses had been indulged in, and many new apportionments of lands had been made in accordance with the bequests of the deceased *moi* and the will of his successor.

Kamehamehanui was an amiable sovereign, but his reign was not as successful as that of his father, Kekaulike. His right to the sceptre had been contested by his brother, Kauhia, and he was secured in it only through the efforts of Alapainui, the king of Hawaii. Subsequently Kalaniopuu, the successor of Alapainui, wrested from him the district of Hana and the celebrated fortress of Kauwiki, and retained possession of both at the time of Kamehamehanui's death. The lands of the district might have been recaptured, perhaps, but the fortress commanding them was well-nigh impregnable, and Hana remained a dependency of Hawaii.

Kamehamehanui's political wife was his half-sister Namahana, with whom he had two children; but as both of them died in their infancy. his brother, Kahekili, succeeded him as *moi* of the island by common consent. After the death of his brother, Kahekili at once removed his court to Lahaina, where the customary period of mourning was concluded.

It was while the members of the royal family were still in mourning at Lahaina that a distinguished stranger suddenly landed, with a number of personal attendants, and presented himself at court. His double canoe bore the ensign of an *alii*, and his garb and bearing showed him to be of the higher nobility. His age was perhaps thirty years, although he looked somewhat older. He was over six feet in height, and well proportioned. His face was handsome, and his hair and beard were closely cropped. He was clad in a *maro* and short feather mantle, and around his head was bound a single fold of yellow *kapa*. By a cord of hair was suspended from his neck a *palaoa*, or carved whale's tooth, and his left wrist was ornamented with a bracelet of curious shells. He was courageous, courtly, and in his best moods agreeable and captivating, and was a splendid representative of the rude chivalry of his time.

As he stepped ashore and proceeded to the royal mansion, way was respectfully made for him, even as a stranger of distinguished bearing, and his name secured him admission at once to the presence of Kahekili, who welcomed him to Lahaina, and set apart ample accommodations for himself and lodgings for his attendants.

Who was this stranger? He was no common chief who would have thus presumed to present himself at the court of the *moi* of Maui and expect the courtesy of royal entertainment. Two generations before Lonoikahaupu, who had peacefully inherited the sovereignty of the western side of the island of Kauai, while the noted Kualii, of Oahu, retained possession of the remainder, paid a royal visit of state to the windward islands of the group. His blood was of the best in the archipelago, and his equipment and retinue were brilliant and imposing. He embarked with a number of large double canoes, the royal *kaulua* being over eighty feet in length, and was attended by a company of skilled musicians and dancers. He also took with him his chief navigator, priest and astrologer, and a corps of personal attendants in keeping with his rank.

In turn he visited Oahu, Maui and Molokai, where he was entertained with distinguished honors, and then set sail for Hawaii, of which Keawe was then king. Touching at Hilo, he found that the royal court had been temporarily established in Kau, and thither he proceeded, to pay his respects to Keawe and his beautiful but volatile wife and half-sister, Kalani-kau-leleiaiwi. He was becomingly received and entertained by the royal couple, and spent some weeks in the enjoyment of the festivities arranged for his amusement. The result was that the queen became enamored of the handsome Kauaian king, who was duly recognized at once as one of her husbands.

From this union a son was born, who was named Keawepoe-poe, when the father returned to Kauai and there remained. This son grew to manhood, and by marriage with Kumaiku, of the royal line of Maui, became the father of the three distinguished chiefs who, with Keawe-a-Heulu, were the leading captains of Kamehameha in the conquest of the group at the close of the eighteenth century. One of these sons of Keawepoepoe was Keeaumoku, the Warwick of his time, the slayer and maker of kings.

Keeaumoku's first effort in king-making occurred in 1754. On the death, in that year, of his uncle Alapainui, and the succession of his cousin Keaweopala to the Hawaiian throne, he became dissatisfied with his allotment of lands and raised the standard of revolt in Kekaha. Defeated, he fled in his canoes to Kau, where Kalaniopuu had for some years maintained himself in independence of Alapainui. Joining their forces, they marched northward, defeated and slew Keaweopala in Kona, and Kalaniopuu, who was the grandson of Keawe and had a valid claim to the sovereignty, was proclaimed *moi* of Hawaii.

It is probable that Keeaumoku's services were substantially rewarded by Kalaniopuu; but in his early years he was turbulent and hot-tempered, and in 1765 he found a pretext for hurling defiance at the king and fortifying himself in the northern part of Kohala. Kalaniopuu promptly placed himself at the head of an adequate force, took the fort by assault, and crushed the rebellion with a single blow. But Keeaumoku escaped over the *pali* alone, reached the beach, secured a canoe and paddled out to sea. Night coming on and the skies being clouded, he lost his way and nearly perished through thirst and hunger; but he finally reached Lanai, where he found friends, and not long after sailed for Maui in a well-equipped double canoe and a respectable retinue of attendants. He landed at Lahaina, and the reader need not be told that the distinguished stranger who so suddenly presented himself at the court of Kahekili, as already mentioned, was Keeaumoku.

The occupation of the district of Hana by the king of Hawaii was a source of irritation to Kahekili, and he welcomed Keeaumoku, not more as an enemy of Kalaniopuu than as a chief who might be useful to him in the war which he then meditated for the recovery of the captured territory.

But Keeaumoku was not content to subsist upon the favor of Kahekili. In his veins ran the blood of kings, and his pride rebelled against a life of dependence, however attractive it might be made for him. But he was without available lands or revenues, for his rebellion against Kalaniopuu had deprived him of both, notwithstanding his inalienable landed rights in South Kona, and he began to cast about for the means of raising himself again to the dignity of a landed chief.

His eyes soon fell upon the comely Namahana, widow of Kamehamehanui. To her belonged the fair and fertile lands of Waihee. But she was the inheritance of Kahekili, whose purpose it was to accept her as a wife at the end of her period of mourning. This must have been known to Keeaumoku, who was thoroughly acquainted with royal customs of his time ; yet he paid such court to the sorrowing dowager, and so sweetly mingled his protestations of love with her sighs of grief, that she became his wife without consulting with the *moi*.

Kahekili was naturally enraged at the union, and was about to manifest his displeasure in a manner dangerous to Keeaumoku, when Namahana retired with her new husband to her estates at Waihee. Kahekili's first impulse was to follow and slay them both ; but as Namahana was popular with the nobility, and Kahekili had not been in power long enough to be quite sure of the fealty of the chiefs, he discreetly concluded to leave to the future the punishment of the offending couple.

Taking up his residence at Waihee, Keeaumoku enlarged and beautified his grounds and buildings, and established a petty court of princely etiquette and appointments. He was fond of display, and soon attracted to Waihee many of the more accomplished young chiefs of the island. The mother and two of the brothers of Namahana attached themselves to the household, and a number of Molokai chiefs, despoiled of their lands by the king of Oahu, became his retainers. He had carefully trained bands of musicians and dancers, and his entertainments were frequent and bountiful.

In the midst of this semi-royal gayety and splendor Kahekili quietly crossed the mountains and temporarily established his

court at Wailuku, but a few miles from Waihee. He had heard
of Keeaumoku's royal style of living, and desired to learn from
personal observation whether it was inspired by an innocent love
of display or designs more ambitious. As Keeaumoku had rebelled against two successive Hawaiian sovereigns, and boldly
seized the widow of a king in the very household of her royal
claimant and protector, Kahekili had reason to regard him with
suspicion, and a week's stay at Wailuku, during which reserved
courtesies had been exchanged between them, convinced him
that Keeaumoku was a dangerous subject. But how was he to
be dealt with? He had committed no act of treason, and an assault upon him would not be sustained by the chiefs.

In this dilemma Kahekili resorted to strategy. He induced
Kahanana, a resolute warrior and subordinate land-holder of
Waihee, to embroil Keeaumoku in a difficulty with his own people. To this end Kahanana complained—probably without
cause—that he had been frequently neglected by the servants of
Keeaumoku in the distribution of fish after fortunate catches,
and urged his grievance with so good a showing of sincerity that
many of his friends stood prepared to espouse his quarrel. This
done, he armed himself for battle, and, the following night, killed
three of Keeaumoku's laborers. Being attacked in return, he
was at once supported by a party of warriors secretly detailed
for that purpose by Kahekili, and a general fight resulted, which
lasted in a desultory way for three or four days. In the end,
however, Keeaumoku and his party were overpowered and compelled to seek safety in flight.

Keeaumoku and Namahana, with her mother and two brothers, and a considerable following of chiefs and retainers, escaped over the Eka mountains and embarked for Molokai. But
Kahekili was not content with the escape of Keeaumoku from
Maui. He resolved to destroy him, and soon after invaded
Molokai with a large force. Keeaumoku and his allies met the
invaders in war-canoes as they approached the shore. A desperate sea-fight followed, which was continued long into the night
by torchlight; but Keeaumoku was again defeated, and with difficulty escaped to Hana with Namahana and her relatives.

This placed Keeaumoku beyond the reach of Kahekili, for
that district of Maui was still under Hawaiian control; but in escaping from one enemy he was compelled to throw himself upon

the mercy of another. He was hospitably received, however, by Mahihelelima, the governor of the district, and was so far forgiven by Kalaniopuu as to be permitted to remain under the protection of the fortress of Kauwiki, where for some time, in the shaded valleys at the base of Haleakala, he found a respite new to his turbulent life.

II.

In a secluded valley within sight of the fortress of Kauwiki, with a few devoted friends and attendants, Keeaumoku and his family lived unmolested and almost unnoticed for several years. It was a season of peace between Hawaii and Maui, and Keeaumoku spent his days in dreaming of wars to come, and political changes that would place him again in a position more consistent with his rank. He made spears and battle-axes, and laid them away ; he constructed canoes and housed them near the neighboring beach.

He loved his wife, who was content to share his exile, and when, in 1768, a daughter was born to him, Keeaumoku felt that the gods were smiling upon him once more, and took courage. It is said that the child was born with a yellow feather in her hand—a symbol of royalty—and she was named Kaahumanu and tenderly cared for.

In 1775 Kalaniopuu, king of Hawaii, suddenly appeared in the district of Hana with a considerable force, and began to ravage the neighboring lands of Kaupo. Kahekili promptly met and repulsed him, however, and he returned to Hana and abandoned the campaign by re-embarking with his shattered army for Hawaii. Keeaumoku took no part in the brief struggle, and was disappointed that nothing decisive had been accomplished. The death of either of the two sovereigns engaged would have been to him a signal of deliverance. But he was not disheartened. He knew the war would soon be resumed on a grander scale, and found partial contentment in the hope that it would result in changes favorable to his fortunes.

Exasperated at his defeat, Kalaniopuu spent nearly two years in preparing for a crushing invasion of Maui. In honor of his war-god, *Kaili,* he repaired and put in order two *heiaus,* and instructed his high-priest, Holoae, to maintain continuous religious services, and exert his highest powers to accomplish the defeat and death of Kahekili. He landed with six heavy divisions of warriors on the southern coast of Maui, but was defeated with great slaughter in the neighborhood of Wailuku, and compelled to sue for peace. With him were the two brothers of Keeaumoku, Kameeiamoku and Kamanawa, who attended the young Prince Kiwalao in his visit of conciliation to Kahekili after the battle.

Kalaniopuu returned to Hawaii with what remained of his army, and the next year again invaded Maui, and for several months carried on a desultory warfare with Kahekili in the several districts of the island. He was assisted by the governor of Hana, and was able for some time to maintain a foothold in Hamakualoa and elsewhere.

Keeaumoku offered his services to neither side, but remained a quiet and almost unobserved spectator of the hostile movements which at intervals convulsed the island, and sometimes swept past the very door of his exile home in Hana. The proper time for him to act had not yet arrived, and years of solitude had schooled him to patience.

It was during this campaign that Captain Cook, the celebrated English explorer, arrived off the coast of Maui with the two vessels under his command, exhibiting faces that were new to the natives, and ships which seemed to be the ocean palaces of their gods. This was in November, 1778. In January of that year Cook had touched the group for the first time. He had landed at Kauai and Niihau, and had now returned from the Arctic seas to winter among the Hawaiian Islands.

Abandoning the fruitless war, Kalaniopuu returned to Hawaii with his invading army. During the campaign of the year before he had been assisted to the extent of a battalion of warriors by Kahahana, king of Oahu. Among the followers of the Oahuan *moi* at that time was the celebrated poet and prophet Keaulumoku. He was a native of Naohaku, in the Hamakua district of Hawaii, and was distantly related to Kahekili, being a son of a cousin of Kekaulike, the father of Kahekili. From his youth he was dreamy and psychologic, and spent his time in roaming among the hills, watching the stars and listening to the music of the ocean. Some years before he had become attached to the court of Kahahana, and had followed that sovereign to Maui in

1777. He remained on the island after the return of Kahahana to Oahu, and the year following, when Kalaniopuu again invaded Maui, the poet was found among his household.

Although but sixty-two years of age, in appearance Keaulu- moku was much older. His eyes were bright, but his form was bent, and his white hair and beard swept his shoulders. When he sang all listened, and his wild utterances were treasured up and re- peated as inspirations from the gods. He was known on all the islands of the group, and it was safe for him to travel anywhere. He had been a friend of Keeaumoku, many years before, on Hawaii, and when he learned, during the campaign of 1778, that the unfor- tunate chief was an exile in Hana and had ceased to be accounted among the leaders of the time, he resolved to visit and console him.

Without making his purpose known to any one, Keaulumoku crossed the mountains, and, the third day, stood before his friend in Hana. Their greeting was affectionate, and after eating they sat down and wailed over Keeaumoku's misfortunes. Then Namahana came with stately grace to welcome the old poet, bringing with her Kaahumanu, who was then a bright-eyed child of ten. He kissed the hand of Namahana, advising her to be of good cheer, and, embracing the child and looking into her eyes, told her that his dreams that night should be of her. And so they were, for the next morning he solemnly sang in the shade of the palms that Kaahumanu would be loved by a chief of renown and become the wife of a king.

"And what of her father?" inquired Keeaumoku. "Is he to rot with his spears in Hana?"

"No," replied the poet, promptly. "The great work of Kee- aumoku's life is still before him. He will become the slayer of princes and maker of kings."

"One have I already helped to royal honors," returned the chief, doubtingly, "and by his favor I am stifling here in Hana."

"Another and a greater is still to follow, in whose service Keeaumoku will die in peace," answered the poet.

"Who is the coming hero?" inquired the chief.

"You will not mistake him when you meet," was the evasive reply.

"And when will that be?" ventured Keeaumoku.

No reply being made, the chief continued :

"Well, no matter when ; I have learned to be patient !"

Conveying the Body of Kalaniopuu to Honaunau.

(FROM A PAINTING IN THE ROYAL PALACE.)

The predictions of the poet extended no farther ; but his words cheered the heart of Keeaumoku, and when he left for Lahaina the next day, grateful eyes followed his footsteps far into the mountains.

Returning to Hawaii after his unsuccessful campaign of 1778, Kalaniopuu remained for a time in Kona, and after the death of Captain Cook, in February, 1779, removed his court to Kohala, taking with him the poet Keaulumoku. The next year, feeling his end approaching—for he was nearly eighty years of age—Kalaniopuu set his kingdom in order by proclaiming his son Kiwalao as his successor, and naming his nephew, Kamehameha, as the custodian of his war-god. He then put down the rebellion of Imakakaloa in Kau, and, after changing residences two or three times for his health, finally died at Kailikii, in January, 1782.

A few months before the death of Kalaniopuu, Kahekili, learning of the failing health of his old opponent, prepared for the recovery of the district of Hana, which had been for nearly forty years under Hawaiian rule. Marching into the district and investing the fortress of Kauwiki, he finally reduced it by cutting off its water-supply, and Eastern Maui again became a part of the dominions of the *moi* of Maui. This occurred about the time of the death of Kalaniopuu.

But what became of Keeaumoku and his family, whose home for years had been among the hills of Hana? Learning of the meditated invasion of the district, and unwilling to trust himself to the mercy of Kahekili, Keeaumoku fled with his family to the almost barren island of Kahoolawe, where he lived in seclusion until after the fall of Kauwiki and death of Kalaniopuu, when he boldly returned to Hawaii, quietly settled on his old and in-alienable estates at Kapalilua, in South Kona, and awaited the development of events, which he plainly perceived were rapidly and irresistibly tending toward wide-spread revolution and disor-der. For more than fifteen years he had heard the clash of arms only at a distance, and he yearned for the shouts of battle and the music of marching columns.

The mourning for Kalaniopuu continued for many weeks, and rumors unsatisfactory to the Kona chiefs were afloat con-cerning the new *moi's* proposed division of the lands subject to royal apportionment. Preparations for the burial of the bones of the deceased king were finally completed. In double canoes, one of them bearing the corpse of his royal father, Kiwalao set sail with a large party of chiefs, warriors and retainers for Honaunau. There it was his purpose to deposit the remains in the neighboring burial-place of *Hale-a-Keawe*, sacred to the ashes of Hawaiian kings, and then proceed with the redivision of such of the lands of the kingdom as were at his disposal.

When off Honokua the second day, Keeaumoku came down from Kapalilua and boarded the fleet. His avowed purpose was to wail over the body of Kalaniopuu. His return to Hawaii had become generally known, and Kiwalao regarded with a curiosity not unmixed with suspicion the warring and impetuous chief, who had been first the friend and then the enemy of his father, and who had suddenly emerged at a critical moment full-armed from the obscurity of years.

What was the object of Keeaumoku's visit to the mourning fleet? Was he anxious, on the eve of stirring events, to behold the face of the young king, remembering the words of Keaulumoku, "You will know him when you meet"? Perhaps. But, whatever may have been his original purpose in visiting the fleet, when he left, in keeping with the turbulent instincts of his life, his thoughts were aglow with projects of rebellion.

Hastening to Kehaha, where his brothers, Kameeiamoku and Kamanawa, with Kamehameha, Kekuhaupio and other chiefs, were in council, Keeaumoku informed them that the destination of Kiwalao was Kailua, which place he would proceed to occupy after depositing the royal remains at Honaunau. This information, he declared, was given to him by one of Kiwalao's attendants.

Not doubting the truth of Keeaumoku's story, and believing it to be the purpose of Kiwalao to occupy the entire district of Kona, which embraced lands not subject to royal disposal, the assembled chiefs moved with their followers and occupied quarters in the neighborhood of Honaunau.

Keeaumoku now became a leading spirit in the events which rapidly followed. The funeral cortége landed at Honaunau, the remains of the dead king were ceremoniously entombed at *Hale-a-Keawe*, and Kiwalao ascended a platform, and to the assembled chiefs proclaimed the will of his father. In the divisions of lands that followed the Kona chiefs were not consulted; nor does it appear that they were additionally provided for, and Keeaumoku had little difficulty in persuading them that they had been treated with intended disrespect and hostility.

In an interview with Kiwalao, Kamehameha was coolly received, and the disaffected chiefs began to prepare for battle. They selected Kamehameha as their leader, and for some days there was a vigorous mustering of forces on both sides. An attack was finally made by the rebellious chiefs, and a battle of some magnitude ensued. Keeaumoku was again in his element. His voice was heard above the din of battle, and his famished weapons drank their fill of blood. Entangled with his spear, he fell upon the rocky ground. Several warriors rushed upon him. Two of them attacked him with daggers, while a third struck him in the back with a spear, exclaiming, " The spear has pierced the yellow-backed crab ! "

Kiwalao, not far distant, witnessed the encounter, and called to the assailants of Keeaumoku to secure his *palaoa*, or ivory neck ornament. The attention of Kamanawa was attracted to the struggle, and he sprang with a few followers to the assistance of his brother, driving back his assailants. At that moment Kiwalao was struck in the temple with a stone, and fell stunned to the ground. Observing the circumstance, Keeaumoku crawled to the fallen king, and, with a knife edged with sharks' teeth, cut his throat.

With the death of Kiwalao the rout of his army became general. The victory made Kamehameha master of the districts of Kona, Kohala and Hamakua, while Keoua, the brother of Kiwalao, held possession of Kau and Puna, and Keawemauhili declared himself independent of both in Hilo.

Keeaumoku's brilliant part in this first of the battles of the period for the sovereignty of Hawaii established him at once in the favor of Kamehameha, and raised him high in the esteem of the distinguished chiefs whose valor ennobled the closing years of barbaric supremacy in the group.

III.

War soon occurred between Kamehameha and the independent chiefs of Hilo and Kau, but, as no marked advantages to either side resulted, Kamehameha established his court at Ha-

laula, in Kohala, and occupied himself in improving the condition of his people.   During the campaign he had met with some
reverses, but Keeaumoku's faith in the final triumph of his great
leader remained unshaken through every disaster.   He thought
he saw in him that captain, greater than Kalaniopuu, of whom
the poet dreamed in Hana, and was soon after confirmed in the
belief by the definite prophecy of Keaulumoku.

Restlessly roaming from place to place, the old singer finally
selected a temporary abode near Halaula, shortly after the removal of the court of Kamehameha to that village.   There he
was frequently visited by Keeaumoku, sometimes accompanied by
Kaahumanu, who was budding into an attractive womanhood, and
sometimes by Namahana, who regarded him with a reverence due
to one whose utterances seemed to be inspired by the gods.

Since the death of Kalaniopuu the voice of Keaulumoku had
been silent.   He mourned over the distracted condition of the
island, and sympathized with the people in their enforced warfare with each other.   Vainly had he sought to penetrate the
mists of desolation and disorder, and catch a glimpse of what
was beyond.   No light had come to him through the clouds ; to
his prayers no answering voice had whispered in his dreams.

But the curtain was raised for him at last, and, as the shades
of the future trooped before him in awful pantomime, in a voice
wild as the winds sweeping through the gorge of Nuuanu he
chanted the prophetic *mele* of *Hau-i-Kalani*.   After describing
the horrors of the civil war then desolating the island, he concluded by predicting that Kamehameha would triumph over his
enemies, and in the end be hailed as the greatest of Hawaiian
conquerors.

The chant created great enthusiasm among the followers of
Kamehameha.   Keeaumoku listened to it with rapt attention,
and at its conclusion stooped over the old poet and said :

"I asked you a question in Hana, which you did not answer then.   Is it answered now ? "

Keaulumoku looked into the face of the chief for a moment
as if to collect his thoughts, and then dreamily replied :

"It is answered ! "

"Such was my thought," returned the chief.   "I have some
rare dainties from the sea.   Come and eat with me to-night, and
I will ask to be taught the *mele* you have just chanted."

Keaulumoku made no reply, and Keeaumoku walked slowly toward the palace, trying to remember the words of the poet which had so thrilled his listeners.

What occurred between Keeaumoku and the old poet during their repast that evening will never be known ; but certain it is that henceforth Keeaumoku never doubted the final success of Kamehameha, and when, in the summer of 1785, the latter retired discomfited from an invasion of Hilo, Keeaumoku smiled as he said to his chief: " Thus far you have only skirmished with your enemies ; you will win when you fight battles ! "

In 1784 Keaulumoku died. For months the old poet had lived alone in a hut near Kauhola. He avoided company and seldom spoke to any one. Feeling his end approaching, he one day announced that the evening following he would chant his last *mele*. Hundreds collected around his hut at the time appointed. They did not enter, but sat down, conversing in whispers, and respectfully waited.

An hour passed, and another, but the old singer did not make his appearance. Finally the mat which served as a door was drawn aside, and Keaulumoku's white head and bent form were seen in the opening. Seating himself within view of all, he began to chant a *mele* in tremulous tones. As he proceeded his voice became louder, and every word was breathlessly listened to. He spoke of the coming conquest of the group by Kamehameha, whom he designated as the son of Kahekili, and also as "the lone one." He also predicted the early extinction of the Kamehameha dynasty, the domination of the white race, the destruction of the temples, and finally the gradual death of the Hawaiian people. Concluding his chant, the old seer raised his hands as if to bless his listeners, and fell back dead. A great wail went up from the people, and they tenderly bore the body of the dead poet to the *heiau*, where it was accorded the burial rites of a prophet.

Much of the last prophecy of Keaulumoku was preserved and repeated, and by conversing with the many who listened to it Keeaumoku managed to secure a satisfactory version of the final song of the dying poet.

From the first of Kamehameha's battles Keeaumoku had not doubted the triumph of that chief over all adversaries in the end, and eagerly grasped at every circumstance calculated to strengthen the conviction.   So believing, his way seemed to be clear.

But what of Kaahumanu, whose promised lover was to be a chief of renown, and whose husband was to be a king ?   She was an attractive maiden of seventeen, and a few months after the death of Keaulumoku, and while Kamehameha was engaged in peaceful pursuits at Halaula, her father suddenly brought her to court.   Fresh, sparkling and graceful, and related to the royal lines of Maui and Hawaii, she attracted the immediate attention of Kamehameha, and he disposed of the claims of her many suitors at once by making her his wife.

There was little in the appearance of the great chief to please the eye of a girl of seventeen.   His features were rugged and irregular, and he held in contempt the courtly graces which imparted a charm to the intercourse with each other of the nobility of the time.   He was already the husband of two recognized wives ; but Kaahumanu was ambitious, and, with admiration but no affection for him, she consented to become his wife.

Keeaumoku was now persistent in inspiring Kamehameha with the thought of becoming the master of the group.   He recited to him the prophetic chants of Keaulumoku, and brought to him the favoring auguries of the *kaulas*.

An unsuccessful attempt to recover the district of Hana in 1786 was followed in 1790 by another invasion of Maui, when Kamehameha completely subjugated the island, and then turned his attention to Keoua, the independent chief of Kau, who had slain the chief of Hilo and assumed the sovereignty of the southern districts of Hawaii.

The war with Keoua continued for more than a year, and every effort of Kamehameha to crush this last of his rivals on Hawaii was successfully resisted.   For nine years Keoua had maintained himself against the power of Kamehameha, and still remained master of Kau and the most of Puna.   Treachery was finally resorted to, and Keoua fell.

The old temple of Puukohola had been partially rebuilt, and a noted seer had predicted that its completion would give to Kamehameha the undisputed sovereignty of Hawaii.   The temple was hastily finished, and Keoua was invited to a conference with his opponent at Kawaihae, with the view, he was led to believe, of peacefully settling their differences.   Nearing the shore of the place of meeting, where he saw and exchanged greetings with Kamehameha, he was about to land when Keeaumoku met him in a canoe and treacherously assassinated him, and his body was taken to the newly-completed temple and sacrificed to the war-god of his betrayer.

Keoua was a brave, noble, and magnanimous chief, and the apologists of Kamehameha have not succeeded in relieving him from the odium of Keeaumoku's cowardly act. He was the half-brother of Kiwalao, and his death left Kamehameha the master of Hawaii.

Truly, as predicted by the seer, had Keeaumoku become the slayer of princes and the maker of kings. But his work was not yet completed. Kamehameha was the sovereign of Hawaii, but the conquest of the group was still before him. Every circumstance, however, conspired in his favor. Kahekili, the warlike king of Maui and conqueror of Oahu, died in 1794, and a rupture had occurred between his successor and Kaeo, the *moi* of Kauai.

Everything being in readiness, early in 1795 Kamehameha invaded Oahu with a mighty army, defeated and subsequently captured and sacrificed to his war-god King Kalanikupule, and shortly after received the submission of the *moi* of Kauai—thus becoming the acknowledged master of, and for the first time in their history consolidating under one government, the several islands of the Hawaiian group.

The prophecies of Keaulumoku have all been fulfilled. Keeaumoku, the slayer of princes and maker of kings, died peacefully as governor of the windward islands in 1804. Kaahumanu became the wife of a king, and died as chief counsellor of the islands in 1832. The temples of the Hawaiian gods were destroyed immediately after the death of Kamehameha, in 1819, and but a tenth of the number of natives found on the islands at the close of the last century are now left to sing of the achievements of their ancestors, who first made their home in the group when the Roman Empire was falling to pieces under the assaults of Northern barbarism.

THE CANNIBALS OF HALEMANU.

CHARACTERS.

KALO AIKANAKA, or KOKOA, a cannibal chief.
KAAOKEEWE, or LOTU, a lieutenant of Kokoa.
PALUA, daughter of Kokoa.
KAHOLEKUA, wife of Lotu.
NAPOPO, brother of Kaholekua.

THE CANNIBALS OF HALEMANU.

I.

ALTHOUGH barbarous to the extent to which a brave, warm-hearted and hospitable people were capable of becoming, every social, political and religious circumstance preserved by tradition tends to show that at no period of their history did the Polynesians proper—or the Hawaiian branch of the race, at least—practise cannibalism. In their migrations from the southern coasts of Asia to their final homes in the Pacific, stopping, as they did, at various groups of islands in their voluntary or compulsory journeyings, the Polynesians must have been brought in contact with cannibal tribes.; but no example ever persuaded them into the habit of eating human flesh, or of regarding the appetite for it with a feeling other than that of aversion and disgust. In offering a human sacrifice it was customary for the officiating priest to remove the left eye of the victim after the lifeless body had been deposited upon the altar, and present it to the chief, who made a semblance of eating it. Even as learned and conscientious an inquirer as Judge Fornander has suggested that this custom was possibly the relic of a cannibal propensity existing among the Polynesian people far back in the past. The assumption is quite as reasonable that the rite was either a simple exhibition of bravado, or the expression of a desire on the part of the chief to thereby more strictly identify himself with the offering in the eyes of the gods.

Several traditions have come down the centuries referring to the existence of cannibal tribes or bands at one time or another in the Hawaiian archipelago, particularly on the islands of Oahu and Kauai, and harrowing stories of their exploits are a part of the folk-lore of the group. But in every instance the man-eaters are spoken of as foreigners, who came from a land unknown, maintained local footholds for brief seasons in mountain fastnesses, and in the end were either exterminated or driven from the islands by the people for their barbarous practices. It is difficult to fix, even approximately, the period of the earlier of these occurrences, as they are mentioned in connection with ruling chiefs whose names do not appear in the chronological *meles* surviving the destruction of the ancient priesthood. Instead of being foreigners, it is not improbable that the cannibals referred to in some of the traditions were the remnants of a race of savages found on one or more of the islands of the group when the first of the Polynesians landed there. This, it may be presumed, was somewhere near the middle of the fifth century of the Christian era.

It has generally been assumed by native historians that the ancestors of the Hawaiian people found the entire group uninhabited at the time of their arrival there. The bird, the lizard and the mouse, with an insect life confined to few varieties, were the sole occupants of that ocean paradise, with its beautiful streams, its inviting hills, its sandal forests, its cocoa and *ohia* groves, its flowering plains, its smiling valleys of everlasting green. But the interval between the fifth century and the eleventh—between the first and second periods of Polynesian arrival—is a broad blank in the legendary annals of Hawaii, and the absence of any record of the circumstance cannot be satisfactorily accepted as evidence that, on arriving at the group from the southern islands, the Polynesians of the fifth century did not find it sparsely occupied by an inferior and less capable people, whom they either affiliated with or destroyed. In some of the *meles* vague references are made to such a people, and ruins of temples are still pointed out as the work of the *Menehunes*—a half-mythical race or tribe, either from whom the Hawaiians descended, or with whom they were in some manner connected in the remote past.

To whatever period, however, many of these stories of cannibalism may refer, circumstances tend to show that the legends connected with the man-eaters of Halemanu are based upon events of comparatively recent centuries. The natives, who still relate fragments of these legends to those whom curiosity prompts to visit the cannibals' retreat near the northern coast of Oahu, generally refer the adventures described to the early part or middle of the eighteenth century, and a half-caste of intelligence informed the writer that his grandfather had personal knowledge of the cannibal band. Although the sharpness of the details preserved indicates that their beginning could not have been very many generations back, the occupation of Halemanu by Aikanaka and his savage followers could have occurred scarcely later than the latter part of the seventeenth century—probably during the reign of Kualii or his immediate successor, somewhere between the years 1660 and 1695. At that time Oahu was governed by a number of practically independent chiefs, whose nominal head was the governing *alii-nui* of the line of Kakuhihewa, of whom Kualii was the great-grandson.

It will therefore be assumed that it was near the close of the seventeenth century that Kalo Aikanaka, with two or three hundred followers, including women and children, landed at Waialua, on the northern coast of Oahu, and temporarily established himself on the sea-shore not far from that place. Ten years before, more or less, he had arrived with a considerable party at Kauai from one of the southern islands—which one tradition does not mention. The strangers came in double canoes, and, as they were in a starving condition, it was thought that they had been blown thither by adverse winds while journeying to some other islands. They were hospitably received and cared for by the people of Kauai, and for their support were given lands near the foot of the mountains back of Waimea. In complexion they were somewhat darker than the Kauaians, but otherwise did not differ greatly from them either in dress, manners, modes of living or appearance. They knew how to weave mats, construct houses of timber and thatch, make spears and knives, and hollow out canoes of all dimensions. They were familiar with the cocoanut and its uses, and required no instruction in the cultivation of *kalo* or *taro*. They were expert fishermen, and handled their weapons with dexterity. Their language, however, was entirely different from that of the Kauaians; but they soon acquired a knowledge of the latter, and in a short time could scarcely be distinguished from the natives of the island.

Although known as Kalo Aikanaka by the natives, the real name of the chief of the strangers was Kokoa. The name of his principal lieutenant or adviser, which is given as Kaaokeewe by tradition, was Lotu, or Lotua. Kokoa was of chiefly proportions, and his muscular limbs were tattooed with rude representations of

birds, sharks and other fishes.   His features were rather of the
Papuan cast, but his hair was straight, and the expression of his
face was not unpleasant.   The appearance of Lotu, on the contrary, was savage and forbidding.   His strength was prodigious,
and he made but little disguise of his lawless instincts.   The wife
of Kokoa had died during the passage to Kauai, leaving with him
a daughter of marriageable age named Palua.   Tradition says she
was very beautiful, and wore necklaces and anklets of pearls.
Her eyes were bright, her teeth were white, and the ends of her
braided hair touched her brown ankles as she walked.   Lotu was
married, but without children.   He did not like them, and more
than one, it is said, had been taken from the breast of Kaholekua
and strangled.

The strangers brought with them two or three gods, and made
others after their arrival.   They knew nothing of the gods of the
Kauaians, and preferred to worship their own.   To this the natives did not object ; but in the course of time they discovered
that their *tabu* customs, even the most sacred, were not observed
by the strangers.   Their women were permitted to eat cocoanuts, bananas, and all kinds of flesh and fish, including the varieties of which native females were not allowed to partake.
Fearing the wrath of the gods, the chief of the district visited
Kokoa and requested him to put a stop to these pernicious practices among his people.   He promised to do so, and for a time
they ceased ; but the offenders soon fell back into their old habit
of indiscriminate eating, and the chief again visited Kokoa, prepared to put his previous request into the form of an order.   The
order was given, but not with the emphasis designed by the chief
in making the visit, for he then met Palua for the first time, and
found it difficult to speak harshly to the father of such a daughter.   In fact, before he left the chief thought it well to leave the
matter open for further explanation, and the next day returned
to make it, and to ask Kokoa, as well, to give him the beautiful
Palua for a wife.   Father and daughter both consented, and
within a few days Palua accompanied the chief home as his wife.
There, at least, it was expected that Palua would respect the *tabus*
she had violated before her coming, and the chief appointed a
woman to instruct her thoroughly in the regulations applicable to
her changed condition.   She promised everything, but secretly
complied with no requirement.   The chief implored her to obey

the mandates of the gods, and sought to screen her acts from the eyes of others ; but her misdemeanors became so flagrant that they at last came to the knowledge of the high-priest, and her life was demanded. Her husband would have returned Palua to her father, but the priest declared that her offences had been so wanton and persistent that the gods would be satisfied with nothing short of her death, and she was therefore strangled and thrown into the sea.

Learning of the death of his daughter, Kokoa in his rage slew a near kinsman of the chief and made a feast of his body, to the great delight of his followers. They were cannibals, but the fact was not known to their neighbors, as they had thus far restrained their appetites for human flesh, and avoided all mention to others of their propensity for such food. Their relish for it, however, was revived by the feast provided by the wrath of Kokoa, and they were not sorry to leave the lands they had been for some time cultivating back of Waimea, and find a home in the neighboring mountains, where they could indulge their savage tastes without restraint.

Locating in a secluded valley in the mountains of Haupu, Kokoa and his people remained there for several years. They cultivated *taro* and other vegetables, and for their meat depended upon such natives as they were able to capture in out-of-the-way places and drag to their ovens. Suspected of cannibalism, they were finally detected in the act of roasting a victim. Great indignation and excitement followed this discovery, and the chief of the district called for warriors to assist him in exterminating the man-eaters. But Kokoa did not wait for a hostile visit. His spies informed him of what was occurring in the valleys below, and he hastily dropped down to the opposite coast, seized a number of canoes at night, and with his followers immediately set sail for Oahu. The party first landed at Kawailoa ; but a Kauaian on a visit to that place recognized one of their canoes as the property of his brother, and was about to appeal to the local chief, when they suddenly re-embarked and coasted around the island to Waialua, where they found a convenient landing and concluded to remain.

II.

We now come to the final exploits of Kokoa and his clan in Oahu. It is probable that they did not remain long in the immediate neighborhood of Waialua, where the people were numerous and unoccupied lands were scarce. Sending their scouts into the mountains in search of a safe and uninhabited retreat, one of exceptional advantages was found in the range east of Waialua, some eight or ten miles from the coast, and thither they removed. The spot selected has since been known as Halemanu. Before that time it was probably without any particular name. It is a crescent-shaped plateau of two or three hundred acres, completely surrounded by deep and almost precipitous ravines, with the exception of a narrow isthmus, scarcely wide enough for a carriage-way, connecting it with a broad area of timberless table-land stretching downward toward the sea.

Nature could scarcely have devised a place better fitted for defence, and Kokoa resolved to permanently locate there. Near the middle of the plateau he erected a temple, with stone walls two hundred feet by sixty, and twenty feet in height. This structure was also designed as a citadel, to be used in emergencies. About fifty paces from the temple was the *hale* of the chief—a stone building of the dimensions of perhaps fifty feet by forty. It was divided into three rooms by wicker partitions, and roofed with stout poles and thatch. Between this building and the temple was a large excavated oven, with a capacity for roasting four or five human bodies at the same time, and a few paces to the westward was the great carving-platter of Kokoa. This was a slightly basin-shaped stone rising a foot or more above the surface, and having a superfice of perhaps six by four feet. A little hewing here and there transformed it into a convenient carving-table, from which hundreds of human bodies were apportioned to his followers by Kokoa, who reserved for himself the hearts and livers, as delicacies to which his rank entitled him. The lines of the buildings described may still be traced among the tall grass, and the oily-appearing surface of the carving-table, known as " Kalo's *ipukai*," bears testimony to this day to the use made of it by the cannibals of Halemanu. The platter is now almost level with the surface of the ground, and its rim has been chipped down by relic-hunters, but time and the spoliations of the curious have not materially changed its shape.

Having provided the plateau with these conveniences and the huts necessary to accommodate his people, Kokoa next put the place in a condition for defence by cutting the tops of the exposed slopes leading to it into perpendicular declivities, and erecting a strong building covering the width and almost entire length of the narrow back-bone connecting it with the plain below. There was then no means of reaching the plateau except by a path zigzagging down the upper side to the timbered gulches beyond, or by the trail passing directly through the building occupying the apex of the isthmus.

Of this entrance Lotu, the savage lieutenant of Kokoa, was made the custodian. And there he sat in all weather, watching for passers, the most of whom, if acceptable, he found a pretext for slaying and sending to the great oven of his companions. His almost sleepless watchfulness was due less to a disposition to serve others than to his merciless instincts, which found gratification in blood-letting and torture. Tradition says there was a hideous humor in the manner in which he dealt with many of his victims. In allowing them to pass he inquired the objects of their visits either to the plateau or the gulches beyond. They informed him, perhaps, that they were in quest of *hala* leaves, of poles for huts, of wood for surf-boards, of small trees for spears, or of flints for cutting implements, as the case may have been. When they returned he examined their burdens closely, and if aught was found beyond the thing of which they were specifically in search—even though so trifling an object as a walking-staff, or a twig or flower gathered by the way—he denounced them as thieves and liars, and slew them on the spot.

In this manner many hundreds of people were slain and eaten ; but as no one ever returned to tell the story of what was transpiring at Halemanu, the cannibals remained for some time undisturbed. But if their real character was not known, their isolation and strange conduct gradually gained for them the reputation of being an evil-minded and dangerous community, and visitors became so scarce at length that Lotu found it necessary to drop down into the valleys occasionally in search of victims. Nor were these expeditions, which demanded great caution, always successful ; and when they failed, Lotu sometimes secretly killed and sent to the oven one of his own people, with faces mutilated beyond recognition. Among these were all of his own relatives and two of the three brothers of his wife. To escape the fate of the others, the surviving brother, whose name was Napopo, fled to Kauai.

In physical strength Napopo was scarcely less formidable than Lotu ; but he was young in years, and lacked both skill and confidence in his powers. To supply these deficiencies, and prepare himself for a successful encounter with Lotu, which he resolved to undertake in revenge for the death of his brothers, he sought the most expert wrestlers and boxers on Kauai, and learned from them the secrets of their prowess. He trained himself in running, swimming, leaping, climbing, and lifting and casting great rocks, until his muscles became like hard wood, and his equal in strength and agility could with difficulty be found on all the island. And he skilled himself, also, in the use of arms. He learned to catch and parry flying spears, and hurl them with incredible force and precision. From the sling he could throw a stone larger than a cocoanut, and the battle-axe he readily wielded with one hand few men were able to swing with two. Having thus accomplished himself, and still distrustful of his powers, he made the offer of a canoe nine paces in length to any one who in a trial should prove to be his master either in feats of strength or the handling of warlike weapons. Many contested for the prize, but Napopo found a superior in no one.

During the contests a strong man, with large jaws and a thick neck, came forward and challenged Napopo to compete with him in lifting heavy burdens with the teeth. The bystanders were amused at the proposal, and Napopo was compelled by their remarks and laughter to accept it, although he regarded it as frivolous. Fastening around his middle a girdle of cords, he cast himself on the ground and said to the man : " Now with your teeth lift me to the level of your breast." Stooping and seizing the girdle in his teeth, the man with a great effort lifted Napopo to the height demanded. The other was then girded in the same manner. He seemed to be confident of victory, and said to Napopo, as he threw himself at his feet : " You will do well if you raise me to the level of your knees." Napopo made no reply, but bent and gathered the girdle well between his teeth, and raised the body to the height of his loins. " Higher ! " exclaimed the man, thinking the strength of his antagonist was even then taxed to its utmost ; " my body is scarcely free from the ground ! " He had scarcely uttered these words before Napopo rose erect, and with a quick motion threw him completely over his head. Bruised and half-stunned by the fall, the man struggled to his feet, and, with a look of wonder at Napopo, hurriedly left the place to escape the jeers of the shouting witnesses of his defeat.

Now confident of his strength and satisfied with his skill, Napopo returned to Oahu in the canoe which so many had failed to win. Landing at Waialua, he by some means learned that his sister, Kaholekua, the wife of Lotu, had been killed by her husband. Arming himself with a spear and knife of sharks' teeth, Napopo proceeded to Halemanu. Arriving at the house barring the entrance to the stronghold, he was met at the door by Lotu. Their recognition was cold. The eyes of Lotu gleamed with satisfaction. No longer intimidated, as in the past, Napopo paid back the look with a bearing of defiance.

" Leave your spear and enter," said Lotu, curtly.

Napopo leaned his spear against the house and stepped within, observing, as he did so, that Lotu in his movements kept within reach of an axe and javelin lying near the door.

" Where is Kaholekua ? " inquired Napopo.

" There, " replied Lotu, sullenly, pointing toward a curtain of mats stretched across a corner of the room.

Without a word Napopo stepped to the curtain and drew it aside. He expected to find his sister dead, if at all, but she was still living, although lying insensible from wounds which seemed to be mortal. With a heart swelling with rage and anguish, he closed the curtain and returned to the door. He could not trust himself to speak, and therefore silently stepped without, in the hope that Lotu would leave his weapons and follow him. To this end he stood for a few minutes near the entrance, as if overwhelmed with grief, when Lotu cautiously approached the door. Advancing a step farther, Napopo suddenly turned and seized him before he could reach his weapons, and a desperate barehanded struggle followed. Both were giants, and the conflict was ferocious and deadly. From one side to the other of the narrow isthmus they battled, biting, tearing, pulling, breaking, with no decided advantage to either ; but the endurance of Napopo was greater than that of his older antagonist, and in the end he was able to inflict injury without receiving dangerous punishment in return. Both of them were covered with blood, and their *maros* had been rent away in the struggle, leaving them perfectly nude.

Although Napopo had in a measure overpowered his mighty adversary, he found it difficult to kill him with his naked hands. He could tear and disfigure his flesh, but was unable to strangle him or break his spine. He therefore resolved to drag him to the verge of the precipice, and hurl him over it into the rocky abyss below. Struggling and fighting, the edge of the gulf was reached, when Lotu suddenly fastened his arms around his antagonist, and with a howl of desperation plunged over the brink. Dropping downward to destruction together, Lotu's head was caught in the fork of a tree near the bottom of the declivity and torn from the body, and Napopo, clasped in the embrace of the lifeless but rigid trunk, fell dead and mangled among the rocks of the ravine still farther down.

Recovering her consciousness during the battle, Kaholekua dragged herself from the house just in time to witness the descent of the desperate combatants over the precipice. Approaching the verge, she uttered a feeble wail of anguish and plunged headlong down the declivity, her mangled remains lodging within a few paces of those of her husband and brother.

The conclusion of these tragical scenes was observed by a party from the plateau above—one tradition says by Kokoa himself. However this may be, the cannibal chief concluded that Halemanu was no longer a desirable retreat, and a few days after crossed the mountains to Waianae with his remaining followers, and soon thereafter set sail with them for other lands. What became of the party is not known; but with their departure ends the latest and most vivid of the several legends of cannibalism in the Hawaiian archipelago.

KAIANA, THE LAST OF THE HAWAIIAN KNIGHTS.

CHARACTERS.

KALANIOPUU, king of Hawaii.

KOLALE, wife of Kalaniopuu.

KIWALAO, son of Kalaniopuu, and his successor.

LILIHA, wife of Kiwalao.

KEOPUOLANI, daughter of Kiwalao.

KEOUA, half-brother of Kiwalao.

KEAWEMAUHILI, uncle of Kiwalao.

KAMEHAMEHA I., successor of Kiwalao.

KEEAUMOKU,
KAMEEIAMOKU and } brothers and chiefs of Hawaii.
KAMANAWA,

KAAHUMANU, one of the wives of Kamehameha I.

KAHEKILI, king of Maui.

KALANIKUPULE, king of Oahu, son of Kahekili.

KAEO, king of Kauai.

KAMAKAHELEI, queen of Kauai.

IMAKAKALOA, chief of Puna.

KALAIMOKU, a distinguished chief.

KAKUHAUPIO, a counsellor of Kamehameha I.

KAIANA, one of the captains of Kamehameha I.

KEPUPUOHI, wife of Kaiana.

NAHIOLEA, brother of Kaiana.

KAIANA, THE LAST OF THE HAWAIIAN KNIGHTS.

KAMEHAMEHA, KAAHUMANU, CAPTAIN COOK, AND THE FINAL CONQUEST.

I.

AMONG the distinguished Hawaiian chiefs connected with the final conquest and consolidation of the group by Kamehameha the Great, and standing in the gray dawn of the close of the eighteenth century, when the islands were rediscovered by Captain Cook and tradition began to give place to recorded history, was Kaiana-a-Ahaula. He was one of Kamehameha's greatest captains, and the events of his life, which closed with his death in the last battle of the conquest, embrace one of the most interesting periods in Hawaiian history. After giving to the conqueror his best energies for years, and faithfully assisting in cementing the foundations of his greatness, he turned against him on the very eve of final triumph, and perished in attempting to destroy by a single blow the power he had helped to create.

What was it that caused Kaiana to turn his spear in hopeless desperation against his victorious chief, to whom the gods and their prophets had promised everything? Had not *Pele* destroyed his enemies with fire and smoke? and had not Keaulumoku, the inspired bard of Naohaku, chanted the fadeless glory of his triumphs? The war-god of Liloa—the fateful *Kaili*—led the van of his conquering columns, and *Kalaipahoa*, the poison god of Molokai, was among the deities of his household. The high-priest Hewahewa, who traced his sacerdotal line back to Paao, was his mediator in the temples, and every voice from the *anu* was a note of encouragement and promise of victory. The great chiefs of Hawaii were his friends, and his war-canoes cruised almost unopposed throughout the eight Hawaiian seas. Musket and cannon had been added to his weapons of war, and white men had enlisted to some extent in his service. But, with all these advantages and assurances of success, Kaiana suddenly threw defiance in his face and became his open enemy.

By some the defection of Kaiana has been attributed to cold-blooded and unprovoked treachery ; by others to an assumption by Kaiana that by blood Kamehameha was not entitled to the sovereignty of the group, and that his defeat in Oahu would dispose of his pretensions in that direction, and possibly open to himself a way to supreme power ; and by still others to the jealousies of Kamehameha, which rendered the life of Kaiana no longer safe in his service. By these it is claimed that Kamehameha was jealous, not only of the growing military fame of Kaiana, but of a suspected regard of his favorite wife, Kaahumanu, for the handsome and distinguished chief. And this, indeed, as shown by native and other testimony, seems to have been the leading if not sole cause of the estrangement between Kamehameha and his great captain.

In the council of chiefs on the island of Molokai, to which Kaiana was not invited, and which he had reason to believe had decreed his death, ambition was the crime which Kamehameha imputed to him, when in truth the real and unmentioned offence was his suspected intimacy with Kaahumanu. And so it will appear that women's eyes in Hawaii, as elsewhere, have in all ages swayed the hearts and nerved the arms of the greatest, and not unfrequently changed the current of vital political events.

But, before bringing Kaiana full into the light, it is proper that some reference should be made to the great chief under whose banners he so stubbornly fought, and against whose authority he finally rebelled ; and in doing so it will be interesting, perhaps, to glance briefly at certain prominent events connected with the rediscovery of the islands by Captain Cook, the assumption of the sovereign authority of Hawaii by Kamehameha, and the final consolidation of the several islands of the group under one central government.

Kamehameha was a man of tremendous physical and intellectual strength. In any land and in any age he would have been a leader. The impress of his mind remains with his crude and vigorous laws, and wherever he stepped is seen an imperishable track. He was so strong of limb that ordinary men were but children in his grasp, and in council the wisest yielded to his judgment. He seems to have been born a man and to have had no boyhood. He was always sedate and thoughtful, and from his earliest years cared for no sport or pastime that was not manly. He had a harsh and rugged face, less given to smiles than frowns, but strongly marked with lines indicative of self-reliance and changeless purpose. He was barbarous, unforgiving and merciless to his enemies, but just, sagacious and considerate in dealing with his subjects. He was more feared and admired than loved and respected; but his strength of arm and force of character well fitted him for the supreme chieftaincy of the group, and he accomplished what no one else could have done in his day.

Kamehameha was born at Kohala, Hawaii, in November, 1740. His father was Keoua, half-brother of Kalaniopuu, and nephew of Alapainui, who was at that time king of Hawaii. His mother was Kekuiapoiwa, a granddaughter of Kalanikauleleiaiwi, who was a sister of Keawe, the previous *moi* of the island. This sister was the mother of Alapainui by a chief of the Mahi family of Kohala. With another husband—Lonoikahaupu, a *tabu* chief of Kauai—she became the mother of Keawepoepoe, who was the father of Keeaumoku, Kameeiamoku and Kamanawa, who, with Keawe-a-Heulu, were the principal chiefs and supporters of Kamehameha in his conquest of the group. By a Kauai wife Lonoikahaupu became the grandfather of Kaumualii, the last independent sovereign of Kauai, and grandfather of Kapiolani, the present queen of the islands.

Keawe, the previous king of Hawaii, had four recognized wives, and two others whose names have not been preserved by tradition. One of them was the mother of Ahaula, who was the father of Kaiana. On the death of Keawe his two elder sons lost their lives in a struggle for the mastery, and Alapainui, the son of the sister of Keawe, and who through his father was chief of Kohala, assumed the *moiship*, and, after a few battles, peacefully maintained his claim to it. Having secured the sovereignty of the island, he invited to court the elder sons of his two deceased half-brothers, and there maintained them until one of them died and the other rose in rebellion against him. These two sons were Kalaniopuu, who was king of the island at the time of the arrival of Captain Cook in 1778, and Keoua, the

father of Kamehameha. The mother of these wards of Alapainui was Kamakaimoku, a chiefess of Oahu. Their fathers having been brothers, and Kamakaimoku being the mother of both,
they bore to each other the mixed relationship of half-brother
and cousin. She also became the wife of Alapainui, and by him
the mother of Manoua, who was the grandmother of Kekuaokalani, the last distinguished champion of idolatry in 1819.

To this record of the tangled relationships of the chiefly families of the group at that period may be added the intimations of
tradition that Peleioholani, a chief of Kauai, was the actual
father of Kalaniopuu, and that Kahekili, the *moi* of Maui, was
the real father of Kamehameha; and in proof of the latter the acts
and admissions of Kahekili are cited. But these scandals may
very properly be dismissed as the offspring of the hatred and
jealousies of later years.

Kamehameha was born at Kohala while Alapainui was there
with his court, superintending the collection of a mighty fleet for
the invasion of Maui. It was a stormy night, and the first sounds
that greeted the ears of the infant chief were the howling of the
winds and the din of warlike preparations. On the night of its
birth the child was stolen from its mother's side and carried away
by Naeole, the chief of Halawa, and for some days nothing was
heard of it. The father searched and the mother wailed, but the
infant could not be found. It was finally discovered, however,
and Naeole, instead of being punished for the theft, was allowed
to keep possession of the child until it was five years old, when it
was taken to the court of Alapainui and there reared as became
a prince. Tradition assigns no reason for the theft of the child,
or for the retention of it for five years by the kidnapper ; but,
whatever may have been the reason, it is manifest that Naeole's
offence was considered neither flagrant nor unusual.

When Kamehameha reached the age of twelve or fourteen
years, his father, Keoua, suddenly died, and a suspicion became
current that he had been either poisoned or prayed to death
through the instrumentality of Alapainui. This suspicion seems
to have been shared by Kalaniopuu, and believing, or assuming
to believe, that his own life was in danger, he withdrew from the
court and attempted to take with him Kamehameha ; but in this
he was frustrated. A fight occurred at Piopio while the body of
Keoua was lying there in state, and Kalaniopuu was driven to

his war-canoe, in which he escaped. This act placed him in open revolt against his royal uncle, and he prepared to sustain it. Forces were hastily gathered on both sides, and after a few battles, in which Kalaniopuu was generally unsuccessful, he retired to the district of Kau, and declared himself the independent sovereign of the southern portion of the island. For some reason Alapainui did not disturb his rebellious nephew farther, but spent the two remaining years of his life in Hilo and Waipio, the residence of many of the ancient *mois*.

When Alapainui died he was succeeded by his son Keaweopala. Dissatisfied with his allotment of lands, Keeaumoku, a nephew of the dead king, rebelled against the new *moi*, but was defeated and compelled to seek safety with Kalaniopuu, whom he found already in the field, intent upon contesting the sovereignty of the island with Keaweopala. The two joined forces, and met and defeated the royal army in Kona. Keaweopala was slain in battle, and Kalaniopuu was declared *moi* of Hawaii. Young Kamehameha was taken to the court of his royal uncle, and educated in all the princely accomplishments of the period.

Although it is probable that Kamehameha took part in some of the earlier wars of Kalaniopuu, he makes his first prominent appearance in tradition as a military leader in about 1775, in a battle on Maui, between Kalaniopuu and Kahekili, the *moi* of that island, or of the greater portion of it. Kalaniopuu was defeated, but the conduct of Kamehameha was notably cool and sagacious. It is reasonable to believe that he also took part in the disastrous campaign of the following year, when the army of Kalaniopuu was almost annihilated on the lowlands near Wailuku.

This battle was one of the most sanguinary spoken of in Hawaiian tradition. Kalaniopuu invaded the island with six heavy divisions of warriors of all arms. The members of the royal family were formed into a life-guard called *Keawe*, while the nobles entitled to the privilege of eating at the same table with the king composed two distinct brigades, known as *Alapa* and *Piipii*. A landing was effected on the southern side of the island. The headquarters of Kahekili were at Wailuku, between which and the coast stretched a slightly elevated sandy plain.

The *Alapa* took the advance, and, without waiting for support, pushed boldly on toward Wailuku. This brigade was the flower of the Hawaiian army. It was composed of eight hundred men, each one of whom was of noble blood. They were all large men of nearly equal stature, and their spears were of equal length. Marching shoulder to shoulder, with feather capes and plumed helmets, tradition describes their advance as a spectacle such as had never before been witnessed. But Kahekili was not appalled at the sight. He permitted them to approach within a mile or more of Wailuku, when he suddenly precipitated upon them a force of four or five thousand spears. The battle was a slaughter. The *Alapa* refused to yield or retreat, and of the eight hundred helmeted chiefs but two escaped to tell the tale of the slaughter of their comrades. But a single prisoner was taken, and he died of his wounds before he could be despatched in form and offered in sacrifice. It was historic ground. On the sandy plain many battles had before been fought, and near and above it was the sacred burial-place of Iao, where had been deposited the bones of many of the ancestors of the battling chiefs.

The next day a general battle was fought on the same ground, and Kalaniopuu was defeated. But he was not crushed. The loss of life had been great on both sides, and a temporary peace was established on the condition that the Hawaiian army should at once be withdrawn from Maui. The suspension of hostilities was secured partly through the instrumentality of the wife of Kalaniopuu, Kalola, who was the full sister of Kahekili.

But this peace was of short duration. Scarcely a year elapsed before Kalaniopuu again invaded Maui, where he continued to hold a fortified possession in Hana, and began to ravage its coasts. Without decisive results, the campaign extended into months, Kalaniopuu maintaining a foothold in Hamakualoa, but being unable to extend his conquests greatly beyond it.

II.

It was during the indecisive campaign just referred to that Captain Cook—having a few months before touched at Kauai and Niihau—returned to the Hawaiian group from the Arctic Ocean, and anchored off the coast of Maui, where he freely communicated with the wondering natives, and exchanged courtesies with Kalaniopuu and his principal chiefs, including Kamehameha.

It is now admitted that the Hawaiian group was first discovered by Juan Gaetano, a Spanish navigator, in 1555, while on a voyage from the western coast of Mexico to the Moluccas, or Spice Islands ; but the secret was kept from the world, and the first European to touch at the islands, to communicate with the natives and make his discovery known, was Captain Cook.

In the hydrographic bureau of the naval department of the Spanish government exists an old manuscript chart pretty correctly locating the group and crediting Gaetano with the discovery. He named the islands *Islas de Mesa*, or Table Islands. It is probable that he made a landing on one of the islands with a few of his crew, since tradition refers to the sudden appearance of white men at about that period ; but if he did land he left no record of the circumstance, and it is not shown that he ever returned to the group, or that any of his countrymen profited by the discovery. It has been claimed that Captain Cook was directed to the islands by an old Spanish chart of which he had in some manner become possessed ; but his own evidence, as well as that of his officers, favors the assumption that the rediscovery of the islands by him was accidental.

Early in December, 1777, Captain Cook, with the British national ships *Resolution* and *Discovery*, left the Society group for the northwest coast of America. On inquiry the natives of Bolabola Island informed him that they knew of no lands north or northwest of them, and it is not probable that he expected to meet with any ; but after a voyage of sixteen days he discovered Christmas Island, and on the 18th of January, 1778, sighted Oahu, of the Hawaiian group, and to the northward of it Kauai. He first landed at the latter island, where he was well received by the natives. He was believed to be their god *Lono*, whose return to the group had been promised, and divine honors were accorded him. His ships were provided with everything they required, and the fairest women of the island, including the daughter of the queen, were sent to greet and welcome him.

He next visited Niihau, where he was received in the same hospitable manner, and on the 2d of February, without visiting the other islands of the group, proceeded on his voyage toward Behring's Strait in search of a northwest passage to the Atlantic. The approach of winter putting an end to further explorations in the north, he returned to the islands, and on the 26th of November, 1778, sighted Maui, and the next day his ships were visited by hundreds of natives. The news of his previous visit to Kauai and Niihau had spread throughout the group, and he was treated with the greatest friendship and hospitality.

Three days later, when off the northwest coast of Maui, he was ceremoniously visited by Kalaniopuu, and six or eight chiefs, Kamehameha among them, accompanied him almost to Hawaii, when they left in their canoes, which had been taken in tow, and returned to Maui, to the great relief of their friends.

Beating around the coasts of Hawaii, it was not until the 17th of January, 1779, that the vessels came to anchor in Kealakeakua Bay, on the western side of the island. They were at once crowded with natives, and the high-priest came aboard, recognized Cook as the god *Lono*, and threw over his shoulders the sacred mantle of red. In the afternoon Cook went ashore, and in a neighboring temple permitted himself to be publicly and ceremoniously worshipped. Meantime the vessels were abundantly and gratuitously supplied with pigs, poultry, fruits and vegetables, and the officers and crews were treated with the greatest kindness.

On the 24th of January Kalaniopuu returned from Maui, and on the 26th paid the ships a formal visit. The visit was returned, and Cook, as before, was received on shore with divine honors, against which he offered no protest. He was placed among the gods in the temple, and sacrifices were offered to him as one of the Hawaiian Trinity.

How were the devotion and kindness of the simple natives requited? By eating out the substance of the people, violating the *tabus* of the priests and trampling upon the edicts of the king. Cook became exacting, dictatorial and greedy, and from his conduct it almost seemed that he began to consider himself in reality the god for whom he was mistaken by the superstitious natives.

Under the circumstances, his departure for the leeward islands of the group, on the 4th of February, was regarded with satisfaction by the natives ; but the vessels encountered a storm, and on the 11th returned to Kealakeakua Bay for repairs. Their reception was much less jubilant than before, and not a canoe went off to greet their return. However, Kalaniopuu visited the ships the next day, and permitted the natives to resume intercourse with them.

But it was plain that the feelings of the people had undergone a change. They found that the white strangers had appetites like themselves, and were just as subject to bodily ills. They also discovered that they were selfish, unjust and overbearing, and were not entitled to the consideration with which they had been treated. Petty bickerings began to occur, and finally a young chief named Palea was knocked down with a paddle by an English sailor while attempting to save his canoe from wanton damage.

In retaliation Palea stole a boat from one of the ships. Cook demanded its restoration, but, as it had been hastily broken up for its iron nails and fastenings, Kalaniopuu could not, of course, return it. Thereupon Cook ordered a blockade of the harbor, resulting in the killing of a prominent chief who attempted to enter it, and then landed with an armed boat's crew with the view of seizing and holding the king as security for the return of the missing boat.

Kalaniopuu was in the act of peacefully accompanying Cook to one of his vessels in the harbor, and had reached a point not far from the landing, when the brother of the chief who had been killed in attempting to enter the harbor angrily approached to demand an explanation. By this time a large crowd of natives had surrounded the king, and believing, no doubt, that the intentions of the chief were hostile, Cook drew a pistol and fired upon him, and the next moment shot and killed a native who had assaulted him with a stone. He also struck with his sword a chief named Kanaina. The latter seized and held him.

Believing Cook to be a god, it was not thought that he could be killed. Struggling to free himself, he must have received a wound from some quarter, for he sank to the earth with a groan. The groan was fatal to him. "He is not a god! he groans!" exclaimed the people, and without hesitation they slew him at once.

Fire was immediately opened upon the natives from the boat, and shortly after with cannon from the vessels in the harbor. Consternation seized the people huddled on the beach. Many were killed, and the most of the remainder fled to the hills, taking with them the body of Cook. A party of carpenters and sail-makers, at work some distance away, became involved in the struggle, but the most of them escaped to the ships through the kind offices of friendly chiefs.

The bones of the unfortunate captain were stripped of their flesh, as was then the custom, and divided among a few prominent chiefs. Kamehameha, it is said, received the hair. A few days after, in response to the request of Captain King, such of the bones as could be recovered were brought on board the *Resolution*, by order of Kalaniopuu, and committed to the deep with military honors. The ships then left Kealakeakua Bay, and after touching at Oahu, Kauai and Niihau, finally sailed northward on the 15th of March, leaving behind them a train of evils which a full century of time has failed to eradicate.

III.

Abandoning his campaign in Maui, Kalaniopuu, who was nearly eighty years of age and quite feeble, removed his court to Kohala after the death of Captain Cook, and subsequently to Waipio, where he remained for some months. Desiring to settle the succession while he lived, he called his high chiefs together and proclaimed his son Kiwalao as his heir and successor in the government and the supervision of the *tabus*, and Kamehameha as the custodian of his war-god *Kaili*, to which duty the *heiau* of Moaula, in Waipio, was formally dedicated after extensive repairs. A temple was also consecrated to the same god in Hilo.

Shortly after Imakakaloa, who had raised the standard of revolt in Puna, was captured after a stubborn war, and condemned to be sacrificed at the temple of Pakini. In the absence of Kalaniopuu the performance of the ceremonies devolved upon Kiwalao. First in order came the offerings of pigs and fruits, to be followed by the body of the rebel chief ; but while Kiwalao was making the first of the offerings, Kamehameha seized the body of the chief, offered it in sacrifice and then dismissed the assembly.

As the sacrifice was to the war-god *Kaili*, of which he was the custodian, Kamehameha doubtless claimed and boldly assumed the right to conduct the ceremonies himself. But the daring act of insubordination created an intense excitement at the royal court, many regarding it as little less than rebellion, and Kalaniopuu advised Kamehameha to retire to Kohala for a season, as he could not answer for his safety in Waipio. He accepted the advice of his uncle, and, taking with him his wife

Kalola, his brother Kalaimamahu and the war-god *Kaili*, removed to his patrimonial estates at Halawa, in Kohala, where he remained until the death of Kalaniopuu, which shortly occurred.

Early in 1782 Kalaniopuu died, and his body was brought to Honaunau for interment in the sacred burial-place of *Hale-a-Keawe*. Fearful that the division of lands which usually followed the installation of a new *moi* would not be satisfactory, several prominent chiefs, among them Kamehameha, repaired to Honaunau to assist in the interment of the dead king and listen to the proclamation of Kiwalao. After the body had been deposited Kiwalao ascended a platform and informed the assembled chiefs that, by the will of his royal father, the sovereignty of Hawaii had been bequeathed to him, and the custody of the war-god *Kaili* to Kamehameha. No other chief was mentioned as having been provided for, and profound dissatisfaction followed.

At an *awa* party in the evening Kiwalao declined to drink of the *awa* prepared by Kamehameha, as custom rendered it proper that he should do. By Kekuhaupio, the aged counsellor of Kamehameha, the bowl was struck from the hand of another to whom it had been passed untasted by Kiwalao, and Kamehameha and his friend abruptly left the house. An open rupture followed the division of lands soon after made, and Kamehameha was forced to take up arms against Kiwalao by the disaffected chiefs. He was made their leader, and around him rallied the chiefs of Kona, Kohala and Hamakua, while Kiwalao was generally sustained by the chiefs of Hilo, Puna and Kau.

After hasty preparations on both sides a battle was fought at Hauiki, in which Kiwalao was slain. The royal army was routed, and Keoua, the half-brother of Kiwalao, fled to Kau, where he declared himself king of Hawaii, while Keawemauhili, the uncle of the dead king, who was allowed to escape owing to his extremely high rank, retired to Hilo and set up an independent government of his own. After the death of Kiwalao, Keopuolani, his infant daughter, whose mother had fled with her to Kahekili, *moi* of Maui, was the only one whom Keawemauhili was willing to recognize, and three distinct factions began to struggle for the mastery of the island.

While a desultory warfare was being carried on by the three rival chiefs of Hawaii, during which Kamehameha was steadily growing in strength, a new element of military and naval power made its appearance in the group, and became an important factor in the political changes that speedily followed. In 1786 the first foreign vessels, after the departure of the *Resolution* and *Discovery*, touched at the islands, and during the year following American, English, French, Spanish and Portuguese merchantmen in considerable numbers visited the group, and the people began to supply themselves with knives, axes, cloths, beads and other articles of foreign manufacture, and the chiefs with swords, guns, powder and lead and other warlike materials. Payment for these articles was made to some extent in pigs, fowls, fruits and vegetables, but principally in sandal-wood, in which the mountainous districts of the islands abounded, and which found a ready market in China. Many deserting sailors entered the service of the chiefs of Oahu and Hawaii, and to a less extent of the other islands, and became the instructors of the natives in the use of fire-arms; and Kamehameha was especially fortunate in securing the services of Isaac Davis and John Young, who took an active part in the campaigns of the final conquest. Young married into a native family of consequence, and became the grandfather of the late queen-dowager Emma, widow of Kamehameha IV.

In 1790 Kamehameha, during a temporary cessation of hostilities on Hawaii, invaded Maui with a large force. To the expedition Keawemauhili had been in some manner induced to contribute a battalion of warriors. In retaliation for this showing of friendship for Kamehameha, Keoua invaded Hilo, defeated and killed Keawemauhili, and assumed the sovereignty of that district. Nor did he stop there. During the absence of Kamehameha he overran the districts of Hamakua and Kohala, and was in the act of possessing himself of the whole island when Kamehameha abruptly left Maui, which he had completely subjugated, and returned to Hawaii.

Kaiana had been left to guard the district of Kona during the absence of Kamehameha, and that was the only division left unoccupied by Keoua. Kamehameha landed with his forces at Kawaihae, and Keoua fell back with his army to Paauhau. There and at Koapapa a two days' battle was fought, when Keoua retreated to Hilo, and Kamehameha retired to Waipio to recruit his losses.

Stopping for a few days to divide the lands of the district

among his chiefs, Keoua started on his return to Kau. His path led by the crater of Kilauea. His army, marching in three divisions, encamped on the mountains, the central division finding quarters not far from the crater. Before morning an eruption occurred, and four hundred warriors were suffocated. This was considered a special visitation of the wrath of *Pele*, the goddess of the volcano, and she was thereafter deemed to be the friend of Kamehameha.

For a year or more continuous efforts to crush the power of Keoua were made by Kamehameha. Kaiana operated against him in Kau, and Keeaumoku in Hilo, but he stubbornly and successfully resisted. Availing himself of this condition of affairs, Kahekili, *moi* of Maui, assisted by Kaeo, king of Kauai, invaded Hawaii, probably for the purpose of creating a diversion in favor of Keoua, but the combined armies were driven from the island by Kamehameha.

Keoua, however, remained unsubdued, and Kamehameha resolved at every sacrifice to crush him, as a preliminary step toward the conquest of the entire group, which at that time he began to meditate. Some time before he had sent the grandmother of Kaahumanu to Kauai to consult the prophets of that island, and word was brought back to him from the renowned Kapoukahi that if he would rebuild the *heiau* of Puukohola and dedicate it to his war-god, he would become the master of Hawaii. Some work had been done on the temple, and Kamehameha determined to complete it at once. He therefore ordered large relays of people from the surrounding districts to repair to Kawaihae and assist in the building of the *heiau*. Many thousands responded. With the exception of Keliimaikai, a brother of Kamehameha, who was left uncontaminated for the consecration, every chief took part in the labor, and the temple was soon completed, with sacrifices embracing a large number of human beings as the work progressed.

Thus was the temple of Puukohola completed, but, pending its formal consecration, Keawe-a-Heulu and Kamanawa, two of the principal counselors of Kamehameha, were despatched to Kau under a flag of truce, to invite Keoua to visit Kamehameha, with the view of arranging terms of peace. Keoua received the ambassadors kindly, and consented to the conference. His actions show that he suspected the motives of Kamehameha, but he resolutely accepted the hazard of placing himself at the mercy of his enemies.

Proceeding in state in a double canoe, Keoua arrived at the landing of Mailekini, in Kawaihae. Observing Kamehameha on the beach, Keoua called to him, and was invited to land. Several canoes were around him, and as he leaped ashore Keeaumoku, from one of them, treacherously drove a spear through his body, killing him at once. An attack was then made upon his attendants, and all but two of them were slain. As this, and many other events noted in this chapter, are briefly referred to in the legend of "The Prophecies of Keaulumoku," it will be sufficient to mention that the body of Keoua was taken to the temple of Puukohola, and there sacrificed to *Kaili* with ample pomp and ceremony. The possessions of the unfortunate chief passed into the hands of Kamehameha, who at once became the acknowledged sovereign of the entire island. This was in 1792.

In Kamehameha's previous campaign against Maui, from which he had been recalled by the successes of Keoua at home, that island, as already stated, had been completely subjugated. At the time of the invasion, Maui, Oahu, Molokai and Lanai were all in the possession of Kahekili, who had taken up his residence in Oahu, leaving his son Kalanikupule in charge of Maui. In a single mighty battle on the plains between East and West Maui, Kamehameha had destroyed the army of Kalanikupule, who had escaped to Oahu and joined his father, while the most of the chiefs of Maui had sought refuge on the other islands.

After this victory Kamehameha despatched a messenger to Kahekili, informing him of his intention to invade Oahu, and the old king returned to him this answer: "Tell Kamehameha to return to Hawaii, and when the black *kapa* covers the body of Kahekili the whole group shall be his." This answer seems to have been hardly honest, however, for, soon after Kamehameha returned to Hawaii, Kahekili entered into a combination with Kaeo, king of Kauai, and made war upon Kamehameha in his own home, with the disastrous results to the confederates already mentioned.

In 1794 Kahekili died, leaving Kalanikupule as his successor, and a claimant to the sovereignty of Oahu, Maui, Molokai and

Lanai. Kaeo, the younger brother and ally of Kahekili, and who had become the king of Kauai by marrying Queen Kamakahelei, and had shared in the government of Maui after the withdrawal of the forces of Kamehameha, concluded to return temporarily to Kauai after the death of Kahekili. Taking with him a portion of his army, he first touched at Molokai to collect tribute, and then landed on Oahu for further supplies. Although his visit was friendly, he met with opposition from Kalanikupule, and a battle followed, in which Kaeo was slain.

The Oahu king was assisted by the seamen of two English vessels lying in the harbor of Honolulu, the *Jackal* and *Prince Leboo*. After the victory a feast was given on board the vessels, to which the king and a number of his chiefs were invited. Some of the boats of the vessels, returning from the shore with their crews, grounded on the reef. Perceiving this, Kalanikupule and his chiefs seized the vessels, killing their captains and a number of others. Elated with the possession of these vessels and their armaments, the king resolved to invade Hawaii. Embarking his army in canoes, he took passage in one of the vessels, on board of which had been stored the most of his guns and war materials.

The crews of the vessels had been retained to manage them, and Kalanikupule sailed out of the harbor in high glee. But he did not proceed far. After reaching deep water the foreigners sent him and his attendants back to Waikiki in a boat, and then sailed for Hawaii, where they delivered Kalanikupule's war supplies to Kamehameha, who was even then preparing for a descent upon Oahu and the final conquest and consolidation of the group. This was in the latter part of 1794. The amount of war material delivered to Kamehameha was not large, but all of it proved of service to him.

IV.

With this somewhat extended reference to Kamehameha and the prominent chiefs of his time, which brings the tracings of public events down to the eve of the concluding struggle of the conquest, we will now return to Kaiana, through whose relations with Kamehameha some curious glimpses of the domestic life of the latter are brought to view. We have thus far seen him as a warrior. We will now observe him as a husband, whose peace was disturbed by jealousies, and whose heart, stern in all things else, was not proof against the tender influences of love.

At the close of his unsuccessful campaign against the chiefs of Hilo and Kau, in 1785, Kamehameha took up his residence at Kauhola, where he devoted himself for a time to more peaceful pursuits. To stimulate his people to industry he gave his personal attention to agriculture, and the piece of ground cultivated with his own hands is still pointed out. Continuous wars had impoverished his possessions, and he was anxious to restore to productiveness his neglected lands.

Up to this time Kamehameha had two recognized wives, Kalola and Peleuli. This Kalola was not the widow of Kalaniopuu, although bearing a similar name. She was a granddaughter of Keawe, king of Hawaii. Peleuli was the daughter of Kamanawa, brother of Keeaumoku, and one of his stanchest supporters.

For some months Kamehameha lived quietly at Kauhola. The inspired song of Keaulumoku, who had died the year before, predicting that he would become the sovereign of the group, still rang in his ears, and in the midst of their labors his people were encouraged in the practice of the manly games and pastimes which added to their strength, skill and endurance in war. Sham fights on land and sea, and swimming, diving, wrestling, running and leaping contests, were frequent ; and during the annual feast of *Lono*, beginning with the winter solstice and continuing for five days, a tournament was given which brought to Kauhola the leading chiefs of Hamakua, Kohala and Kona. Among them was the famous Keeaumoku, who had charge of the district of Kona. He was accompanied by his family, of which his daughter, Kaahumanu, was the most attractive feature.

Twenty years before Keeaumoku, who was of the royal line, rebelled against Kalaniopuu, and was defeated and forced to find refuge on Maui, whose *moi*, Kamehamehanui, had died but a few days before, leaving the government to his brother Kahekili. Keeaumoku, whose fortunes were desperate, succeeded in captivating and marrying Namahana, the widow of the deceased king, very much to the chagrin and disappointment of Kahekili, whose claim to the dowager was sustained by the royal custom of the time. A difficulty followed, and Keeaumoku and his wife took up their residence on the northern side of the island. But they were not permitted to remain there in peace. Through the hostility of Kahekili they were driven to Molokai, and thence to the district of Hana, in eastern Maui, which was then held by the king of Hawaii, and there, through the mercy of Kalaniopuu, they were allowed for some years to reside ; and there, in 1768, Kaahumanu was born. On the death of Kalaniopuu, in 1782, Keeaumoku returned to Hawaii, and in the war for the succession espoused the cause of Kamehameha and became one of his chief counselors and captains.

Kaahumanu was one of the most attractive women of her time, and inherited something of the restless and independent spirit of her warlike father. She was in her eighteenth year when she made her appearance at the court of Kamehameha, during the festival of *Lono,* in 1785. The wives of Kamehameha were well along in years, Peleuli being the mother of a full-grown son, and Kaahumanu charmed the great chief with her freshness and independence. His warlike soul yielded to the fascination, and to win her smile he took part in the contests of the festival and overcame all competitors. He then proposed to make her his wife. Keeaumoku readily consented, but Kaahumanu could only be won by the promise that her children should become the political heirs of Kamehameha. This promise was given, and Kaahumanu became the wife of Kamehameha. It is probable that he intended to observe the compact at that time, but as Kaahumanu died childless he was in the end left to dispose of the succession through other and more distinguished channels.

Kaahumanu became the wife of Kamehameha's heart. He loved her as well as he was capable of loving any woman, and she was the only one whose indiscretions were regarded by him with feelings of jealousy. His other wives were not restricted by him to his sole attentions, and even the blue-blooded Keopuolani, whom he subsequently married, and who became the mother of his heirs to the throne, had a joint husband in Hoapili.

But in the affections of Kaahumanu Kamehameha would brook no joint occupant or rival. She doubtless sought to avail herself of the privileges of the times, but Kamehameha objected with a frown which would have meant death to another, and for years their relations were the reverse of harmonious.

Kaiana's father was Ahaula, who was the son of Keawe, king of Hawaii, by a mother whose name is now unknown. The mother of Kaiana was Kaupekamoku, a granddaughter of Ahia, of the I family of Hilo, from whom the present sovereign of the islands draws his strain. The birthplace of Kaiana is not recorded, but he was probably reared in the neighborhood of Hilo, and thoroughly instructed in all the chiefly accomplishments of the period. He grew to a splendid manhood. He was nearly six and a half feet in height, was well proportioned, and possessed a strikingly handsome face. This is the testimony of Captain Meares, with whom he made a voyage to China in 1787.

Kaiana was of high rank and boundless ambition, and in early manhood cast his fortunes with Kahekili, the warlike *moi* of Maui, to whom he was related. He was among the prominent chiefs who assisted Kahekili in his conquest of Oahu in 1783, and took a distinguished part in the decisive battle of Kaheiki. Kahahana, the unfortunate king of Oahu, escaped to the hills, where he remained secreted for nearly two years, when he was betrayed by the brother of his wife and slain by order of Kahekili.

This cruel treatment of Kahahana, together with the rapacity of the invaders, created a revulsion of feeling among the Oahu chiefs, and a wide-spread conspiracy was organized by the father of Kahahana and others against Kahekili and the Maui chiefs to whom had been assigned lands in the several districts of the island. The plan was to rise in concert and kill them all in one night, including Kahekili. But the murderous project miscarried. By some means it became known to Kahekili, and he despatched messengers to the threatened chiefs, warning them of their danger. All but one of them were notified. The messenger failed to reach Hueu, who was at Waialua, and he was killed. But fearfully was his death avenged. Kahekili collected his forces for a war for blood. Men, women and children were butchered without mercy, and the native Oahu chiefs were almost extirpated. So great was the slaughter that one of the Maui chiefs built a house at Lapakea, the walls of which were laid up with the bones of the slain.

In this rebellion a number of Kahekili's own chiefs turned

The God "Kumauna," Four Miles above Hilea, Hawaii.
(HUGE FACE DELINEATED IN THE CLIFF.)

against him, among whom were Kaiana and Kaneoneo, the latter being the first husband of Kamakahelei, queen of Kauai. What incited the defection of Kaiana is not known, but he was probably dissatisfied with the lands apportioned to him by Kahekili, and hoped to profit by the restoration of the island to native rule.

Kaneoneo was killed, but Kaiana managed to escape to Kauai. Kaneoneo was of the royal line of Kauai, and, as already stated, the first husband of the queen of that island. How he came to be a supporter of Kahekili in his conquest of Oahu, or what prompted his subsequent espousal of the cause of the Oahu chiefs, are matters which tradition has left to conjecture.

Kamakahelei's second husband, whom she had selected some years before while her first was living, as was then the custom, was the gallant Kaeo, or Kaeokulani, the younger brother of Kahekili. He was commended to her not more through his princely blood than his many accomplishments and graces of person, and she appears to have been greatly attached to him.

She had two daughters with Kaneoneo, both of whom were of marriageable age when she became the wife of Kaeo. She was the granddaughter, it may be mentioned, of Lonoikahaupu, a prince of Kauai, who in his younger years visited Hawaii, was accepted as the temporary husband of Kalani, the sister of Keawe, and through her became the grandfather of Keeaumoku and his two distinguished brothers. The daughters of the queen were Lelemahoalani and Kapuaamohu, the latter of whom, in marriage with Kaumualii, the last independent king of Kauai, became the grandmother of the present queen, Kapiolani.

Kaeo took no part in the conquest of Oahu by his brother, but remained at Kauai, assisting the queen in her government, while Kaneoneo found occupation first in aiding and then in opposing Kahekili. Escaping from Oahu after the defeat of the rebellious chiefs and death of Kaneoneo, Kaiana presented himself before the queen of Kauai, who was a distant relative, and Kaeo, who was of closer kinship, and related to them the story of Kahekili's merciless operations on Oahu. He sought to create an active sympathy in favor of the unfortunate Oahuans, but Kaeo was too sagacious to place himself in hostility to his warlike brother, who had extended his sway over all the islands between Kauai and Hawaii.

However, Kaiana was kindly received at the court of Kauai, and given lands for his proper maintenance. But he could not remain quiet. While the clash of arms was heard on the other islands, he chafed under the restraints of his exile, and attempted to organize a force of warriors for a descent upon Oahu. Kaeo prevented the departure of the expedition, however, and a mutual feeling of suspicion and antagonism was soon developed between him and his reckless and restless cousin.

As the avenues to advancement through the chances of war seemed to be temporarily closed to him, Kaiana donned his best attire, gave entertainments and began vigorously to play the courtier. He first sought to supplant Kaeo in the affections of the queen. Failing in that, he next paid court to her daughter Kapuaamohu. The latter was disposed to regard his suit with favor, but Kaeo, through the pretended advice of a *kaula*, objected to the alliance, and in a spirit of recklessness Kaiana embarked in the ship *Nootka* for China late in 1787. That vessel, in the course of trade, touched at Kauai just as the fortunes of Kaiana seemed to be the most desperate, and Captain Meares was easily prevailed upon to permit the handsome Hawaiian to accompany him to the Asiatic coast.

Arriving in Canton, Kaiana spent some months in studying the arts of war and mingling with the people of strange races, and in the latter part of 1788 returned in the *Iphigenia* to Kauai, bringing with him a very considerable supply of muskets, powder, lead and other munitions of war. As the manner in which he secured these supplies is not stated, we are constrained to believe that he must have taken with him to China a quantity of sandal-wood, which was readily marketable in that country.

But Kaeo would not permit him to land on Kauai. The clouds had indicated approaching danger the day before, and Kaiana was told that he would be slain and sacrificed if his foot touched the shore. The vessel, therefore, sailed for Hawaii, where Kaiana landed and offered his services to Kamehameha. They were promptly accepted. His supply of arms and knowledge of other lands rendered him a valuable ally at the time, and Kamehameha gave him an important command and took him into his fullest confidence. This was early in 1789, and, in the succeeding wars with Keoua, Kaiana became an active leader, as already mentioned. The knives, hatchets, axes and swords brought by him from China were found to be useful, but the fire-arms were generally of old patterns, and the most of them were soon rendered entirely unserviceable through the inability of the natives to keep them in repair.

V.

Very soon after her marriage Kaahumanu was detected in flagrant flirtations with certain chiefs whose business brought them to the court of her husband, and Kamehameha set a close watch upon her actions. This led to bitter words between them, and in time it became a matter of gossip that Kamehameha was jealous of his young wife. The arrival of Kaiana added another to the list of Kaahumanu's admirers, and in time another wrinkle to the stern face of her warrior-husband. Kaiana was one of the handsomest chiefs of his day, and Kaahumanu could not disguise her infatuation for him. But, whatever may have been the temptation, he was too discreet to awaken the jealousy of Kamehameha, and was not displeased when he was despatched with an army against Keoua in the distant district of Kau.

After the death of Kalaniopuu, in 1782, and the defeat and death of Kiwalao, the widow of the former, whose name was Kalola, left for Maui, taking with her the widow and infant daughter of Kiwalao. Kahekili, brother of Kalola, provided for the family and gave them his protection. After the conquest of Oahu by Kahekili he removed his court to that island, taking with him his sister and her family. In 1785 they returned to Maui with Kalanikupule, the son of Kahekili, who had been appointed viceroy of the island, and there remained, principally at Olowalu, until 1790, when Kalanikupule was driven from Maui by Kamehameha, and they sought refuge at Kalamaula, on the island of Molokai.

Seeing his way clear to the conquest of the group, and anxious to ally himself to the superior blood which came through Kalola and Kiwalao, Kamehameha despatched a messenger to Molokai, requesting· Kalola not to return to Oahu, but to place herself and family under his protection. Following the messenger to Molokai, and learning that Kalola was ill and not expected to recover, Kamehameha paid her a visit in person, and received the assurance of the dying dowager that, when she passed away, her daughter and granddaughter should be his.

The granddaughter was Keopuolani, then a girl of fourteen. She subsequently became the wife of Kamehameha and the mother of the ruling princes of his dynasty. In recognition of her superior rank Kamehameha always approached her on his knees, even after she had become his wife and he the undisputed sovereign of the group. Such was the deference invariably paid to rank at that time and earlier.

Kalola did not live but a few days after her meeting with Kamehameha. At her death he manifested his sorrow by knocking out two of his front teeth, and then formally took charge of and removed to Hawaii her daughter and granddaughter, not only as a sacred legacy from Kalola, but as a token of reconciliation and alliance between himself and the elder branch of the Keawe dynasty.

Kaahumanu well understood the meaning of this reconciliation, and it was with little pleasure that she welcomed Liliha and her daughter to Hawaii. She knew it was the purpose of Kamehameha to marry Keopuolani as soon as she reached a proper age ; but she was childless and could urge no valid objection to the union. The thought of it, however, did not sweeten her temper or quicken her sense of propriety. She became more reckless, and her husband more and more suspicious, until they finally separated, when Kaahumanu returned to her father, where she remained for more than a year, and where, it is said, Kaiana frequently visited her.

Of these visits Kamehameha was apprised by Kepupuohi, the wife of Kaiana, of whom tradition makes but spare mention. She was jealous of her husband's attentions to Kaahumanu, and it was through her that Kamehameha became aware of their secret meetings. His spies had overlooked what the jealous eyes of the wife had discovered, and it is intimated that they retaliated in kind upon the recreant couple. Be that as it may, Kamehameha sent for Kaahumanu, and through the offices of Captain Vancouver, whose vessel was at that time anchored in Kealakeakua Bay, a reconciliation was effected between them.

But Kamehameha did not forgive Kaiana. His thoughts were bent upon the conquest of Oahu, and he needed his assistance in that important enterprise ; but he determind to crush him whenever he could do so without injury to himself. Kaiana felt the coldness of his chief, and had observed unmistakable evidences of his hatred ; but he neglected no duty, and resolved that, if an open rupture could not be avoided, Kamehameha should not be in a position to urge a reason for it that would command the respect and approval of his supporting chiefs.

Summoning his district chiefs to muster their quotas of canoes and armed men, Kamehameha prepared for the conquest of Oahu and a final struggle for the mastery of the group. It is said that his army numbered sixteen thousand warriors, some of them armed with muskets, and that so great was the number of his canoes that they almost blackened the channels through which they passed.

The army embarked from Hawaii early in 1795, and, after touching at Lahaina for refreshments, landed for final preparation on Molokai, the fleet of canoes being distributed for miles along the coast. Kaiana had promptly responded to the call of his chief, and was there with a heavy quota of warriors and canoes.

A council of war was called at Kaunakakai to discuss the plans of the campaign, but Kaiana was not invited to participate in its proceedings. His exclusion from the council alarmed Kaiana, and he suspected that he was the principal subject of discussion. He left his quarters, and calling at the house of Namahana, the mother of Kaahumanu, learned from her that the council was discussing some private matter, the nature of which she did not know. He next visited Kalaimoku, after the adjournment of the council, and endeavored to ascertain what had been done, but the answers of the chief were evasive and unsatisfactory. He did not dare to tell Kaiana, who was allied to him in blood, that Kamehameha had charged Kaiana before the council with meditated treason, which implied his death, and that his advisers had prevailed upon him to allow the matter to rest until after the conquest of Oahu.

On his way back to Hamiloloa, where his warriors were encamped, Kaiana again passed the house of Namahana. It was past sunset, and he was striding through the dying twilight, his thoughts a tumult of doubt and indignation, when from behind a clump of bushes he heard his name pronounced in a low tone.

He stopped and listened, and " Kaiana ! " again came to him in a soft voice.

Fearful of treachery, he hesitated for a moment, then drew a knife from a scabbard hanging from his neck, and cautiously walked around the screening undergrowth.

"Who calls?" inquired Kaiana, observing a crouching figure among the bushes.

"Your friend," was the answer; and Kaahumanu rose and stood before him.

What passed between them can only be conjectured; but Kaahumanu must have satisfied Kaiana of Kamehameha's hostile purposes concerning him, for when he reached his quarters he promptly informed his brother Nahiolea of the danger awaiting both of them, and apprised him of his resolution to abandon Kamehameha on the passage to Oahu and join forces with Kalanikupule. "The movement is hazardous," explained Kaiana, "but it will enable us, at least, to die like chiefs, with arms in our hands, instead of being slain like dogs."

As the several divisions were preparing to embark for Oahu the next morning, Kaiana visited the squadron of canoes set apart for the accommodation of the wives and daughters of Kamehameha and his principal chiefs, and secretly informed his wife of his purpose to join Kalanikupule. She expressed surprise at the announcement, but declined to follow him, declaring that she preferred to cast her fortunes with Kamehameha. "But," she continued, bitterly, "perhaps Kaahumanu would follow you, if asked to do so !" Kaiana made no reply to this cutting suggestion, but waved his wife a hasty farewell, and joined his embarking warriors.

The other divisions of the invading army were well out to sea before Kaiana's sails were set, and he found no difficulty in making his way unobserved to Kailua, on the northern side of the island, while Kamehameha landed with the main body of his forces in the neighborhood of Honolulu, his canoes extending along the beach from Waialae to Waikiki.

Disembarking his warriors at Kailua, to the number of perhaps fifteen hundred, Kaiana offered his services to Kalanikupule, whose army was rapidly occupying positions in the valleys back of Honolulu. The *moi* received him with open arms, promising him the sovereignty of Maui should they succeed in destroying

Kamehameha; and the united armies, climbing over the Nuuanu and Kalihi passes, confronted the advancing lines of Kamehameha.

Learning of the desertion of Kaiana and the warriors under his command, Kamehameha exhibited but little surprise. He did not doubt his ability to defeat the combined armies of his opponents, for the auguries had been favorable and he had faith in his gods; nor did he regret that through his defection Kaiana had at last placed himself in a position to be dealt with as an open enemy.

With his war-god *Kaili* in the van, Kamehameha, at the head of a mighty force, marched up Nuuanu Valley, where, three miles back of Honolulu, behind a stone wall stretching from one hill to the other of the narrowing gorge, was entrenched the main body of the allied armies. And behind the wall stood Kaiana, grim, silent and desperate, with a musket in his hand, awaiting the approach of Kamehameha.

Nearer and nearer advanced the attacking column, with shouts that were repaid by yells of defiance from behind the defences. A few volleys of musketry were exchanged by the hundred or more of warriors in possession of fire-arms on each side, but Kaiana took no part in the noisy conflict. He was watching for the approach of one whose life he longed for more than all the rest, and for which he was willing to exchange his own.

But he watched in vain. A field-piece, under the direction of John Young, was brought to bear upon the wall, and Kaiana fell with the first shot, mortally wounded. After a few more shots the Hawaiians charged up the hill, their shouts drowning the roar of the breakers against the reef below. Kaiana drew himself up against the wall. His heart had been laid almost bare, and his eyes were growing dim. With an effort he raised his musket, fired it at random in the direction of the storming column, hoping the bullet might by chance find the heart of Kamehameha, and then fell dead.

The rout of the Oahuans and their allies was complete. They broke and fled in all directions. Some were driven over the *pali*, a precipice six or seven hundred feet in height at the head of the valley, and others escaped over the hills. Kalanikupule found refuge for a time in the mountains, but he was finally captured, slain and offered as a sacrifice to Kamehameha's war-god at Waikiki.

This was the last battle of the conquest, and the victory gave to Kamehameha the sovereignty of the group, for the king of Kauai, recognizing his power, soon after yielded to him his peaceful allegiance. But it brought to a close the career of one of the most noted of modern Hawaiian chiefs—Kaiana-a-Ahaula—over whose death Kamehameha rejoiced, and Kaahumanu mourned in silence. Her love proved fatal to more than one, but he was the grandest and brightest of all who perished by the sweet poison of her smiles.

Kaala, the Flower of Lanai.

CHARACTERS.

KAMEHAMEHA I., king of Hawaii.
OPONUI, a chief of Lanai.
KAALA, daughter of Oponui.
KALANI, mother of Kaala.
KAAIALII, a lieutenant of the king.
MILOU, the bone-breaker.
UA, a friend of Kaala.
PAPAKUA, a priest.

KAALA, THE FLOWER OF LANAI.

A STORY OF THE SPOUTING CAVE OF PALIKAHOLO.

I.

BENEATH one of the boldest of the rocky bluffs against which dash the breakers of Kaumalapau Bay, on the little island of Lanai, is the *Puhio-Kaala*, or "Spouting Cave of Kaala." The only entrance to it is through the vortex of a whirlpool, which marks the place where, at intervals, the receding waters rise in a column of foam above the surface. Within, the floor of the cave gradually rises from the opening beneath the waters until a landing is reached above the level of the tides, and to the right and left, farther than the eye can penetrate by the dim light struggling through the surging waves, stretch dank and shelly shores, where crabs, polypii, sting-rays and other noisome creatures of the deep find protection against their larger enemies.

This cavern was once a favorite resort of *Mooalii*, the great lizard-god; but as the emissaries of *Ukanipo*, the shark-god, annoyed him greatly and threatened to imprison him within it by piling a mountain of rocks against the opening, he abandoned it and found a home in a cave near Kaulapapa, in the neighboring island of Molokai, where many rude temples were erected to him by the fishermen.

Before the days of Kamehameha I. resolute divers frequently visited the Spouting Cave, and on one occasion fire, enclosed in a small calabash, was taken down through the whirlpool, with the view of making a light and exploring its mysterious chambers; but the fire was scattered and extinguished by an unseen hand, and those who brought it hastily retreated to escape a shower of rocks sent down upon them from the roof of the cavern. The existence of the cave is still known, and the whirlpool and spouting column marking the entrance to it are pointed out; but longer and longer have grown the intervals between the visits of divers to its sunless depths, until the present generation can point to not more than one, perhaps, who has ventured to enter them.

Tradition has brought down the outlines of a number of supernatural and romantic stories connected with the Spouting Cave, but the nearest complete and most recent of these *mookaaos* is the legend of Kaala, the flower of Lanai, which is here given at considerably less length than native narration accords it.

It was during an interval of comparative quiet, if not of peace, in the stormy career of Kamehameha I., near the close of the last century, and after the battle of Maunalei, that he went with his court to the island of Lanai for a brief season of recreation. The visit was not made for the purpose of worshipping at the great *heiau* of *Kaunola*, which was then half in ruins, or at any of the lesser temples scattered here and there over the little island, and dedicated, in most instances, to fish-gods. He went to Kealia simply to enjoy a few days of rest away from the scenes of his many conflicts, and feast for a time upon the affluent fishing-grounds of that locality.

He made the journey with six double canoes, all striped with yellow, and his own bearing the royal ensign. He took with him his war-god, *Kaili*, and a small army of attendants, consisting of priests, *kahunas*, *kahili* and spittoon-bearers, stewards, cooks and other household servants, as well as a retinue of distinguished chiefs with their personal retainers in their own canoes, and a hundred warriors in the capacity of a royal guard.

Landing, the victorious chief was received with enthusiasm by the five or six thousand people then inhabiting the island. He took up his residence in the largest of the several cottages provided for him and his personal attendants. Provisions were brought in abundance, and flowers and sweet-scented herbs and vines were contributed without stint. The chief and his titled attendants were garlanded with them. They were strewn in his path, cast at his door and thrown upon his dwelling, until their fragrance seemed to fill all the air.

Among the many who brought offerings of flowers was the beautiful Kaala, "the sweet-scented flower of Lanai," as she was called. She was a girl of fifteen, and in grace and beauty had no peer on the island. She was the daughter of Oponui, a chief of one of the lower grades, and her admirers were counted by the hundreds. Of the many who sought her as a wife was Mailou, "the bone-breaker." He was a huge, muscular savage, capable of crushing almost any ordinary man in an angry embrace; and while Kaala hated, feared and took every occasion to avoid him, her father favored his suit, doubtless pleased at the thought of securing in a son-in-law a friend and champion so distinguished for his strength and ferocity.

As Kaala scattered flowers before the chief her graceful movements and modesty were noted by Kaaialii, and when he saw her face he was enraptured with its beauty. Although young in years, he was one of Kamehameha's most valued lieutenants, and had distinguished himself in many battles. He was of chiefly blood and bearing, with sinewy limbs and a handsome face, and when he stopped to look into the eyes of Kaala and tell her that she was beautiful, she thought the words, although they had been frequently spoken to her by others, had never sounded so sweetly to her before. He asked her for a simple flower, and she twined a *lei* for his neck. He asked her for a smile, and she looked up into his face and gave him her heart.

They saw each other the next day, and the next, and then Kaaialii went to his chief and said:

"I love the beautiful Kaala, daughter of Oponui. Your will is law. Give her to me for a wife."

For a moment Kamehameha smiled without speaking, and then replied:

"The girl is not mine to give. We must be just. I will send for her father. Come to-morrow."

Kaaialii had hoped for a different answer; but neither protest nor further explanation was admissible, and all he could do was to thank the king and retire.

A messenger brought Oponui to the presence of Kamehameha. He was received kindly, and told that Kaaialii loved Kaala and desired to make her his wife. The information kindled the wrath of Oponui. He hated Kaaialii, but did not dare to exhibit his animosity before the king. He was in the battle of Maunalei, where he narrowly escaped death at the hands of Kaaialii, after his spear had found the heart of one of his dearest friends, and he felt that he would rather give his daughter to the sharks than to one who had sought his life and slain his friend. But he pretended to regard the proposal with favor, and, in answer to the king, expressed regret that he had promised his

daughter to Mailou, the bone-breaker. "However," he continued, "in respect to the interest which it has pleased you, great
chief, to take in the matter, I am content that the girl shall fall
to the victor in a contest with bare hands between Mailou and
Kaaialii."

The proposal seemed to be fair, and, not doubting that Kaaialii
would promptly accept it, the king gave it his approval, and the
contest was fixed for the day following. Oponui received the
announcement with satisfaction, not doubting that Mailou would
crush Kaaialii in his rugged embrace as easily as he had broken
the bones of many an adversary.

News of the coming contest spread rapidly, and the next day
thousands of persons assembled at Kealia to witness it. Kaala
was in an agony of fear. The thought of becoming the wife of
the bone-breaker almost distracted her, for it was said that
he had had many wives, all of whom had disappeared one after
another as he tired of them, and the whisper was that he had
crushed and thrown them into the sea. And, besides, she loved
Kaaialii, and deemed it scarcely possible that he should be able
to meet and successfully combat the prodigious strength and
ferocity of one who had never been subdued.

As Kaaialii was approaching the spot where the contest was
to take place, in the presence of Kamehameha and his court and
a large concourse of less distinguished spectators, Kaala sprang
from the side of her father, and, seizing the young chief by the
hand, exclaimed :

"You have indeed slain my people in war, but rescue me
from the horrible embrace of the bone-breaker, and I will catch
the squid and beat the *kapa* for you all my days ! "

With a dark frown upon his face, Oponui tore the girl from
her lover before he could reply. Kaaialii followed her with his
eyes until she disappeared among the spectators, and then
pressed forward through the crowd and stepped within the circle
reserved for the combatants. Mailou was already there. He
was indeed a muscular brute, with long arms, broad shoulders
and mighty limbs tattooed with figures of sharks and birds of
prey. He was naked to the loins, and, as Kaaialii approached,
his fingers opened and closed, as if impatient to clutch and tear
his adversary in pieces.

Although less bulky than the bone-breaker, Kaaialii was large and perfectly proportioned, with well-knit muscles and loins and shoulders suggestive of unusual strength. Nude, with the exception of a *maro*, he was a splendid specimen of vigorous manhood ; but, in comparison with those of the bone-breaker, his limbs appeared to be frail and feminine, and a general expression of sympathy for the young chief was observed in the faces of the large assemblage as they turned from him to the sturdy giant he was about to encounter.

The contest was to be one of strength, courage, agility and skill combined. Blows with the clenched fist, grappling, strangling, tearing, breaking and every other injury which it was possible to inflict were permitted. In *hakoko* (wrestling) and *moko* (boxing) contests certain rules were usually observed, in order that fatal injuries might be avoided ; but in the combat between Kaaialii and Mailou no rule or custom was to govern. It was to be a savage struggle to the death.

Taunt and boasting are the usual prelude to personal conflicts among the uncivilized ; nor was it deemed unworthy the Saxon knight to meet his adversary with insult and bravado. The object was not more to unnerve his opponent than to steel his own courage. With the bone-breaker, however, there was little fear or doubt concerning the result. He knew the measure of his own prodigious strength, and, with a malignant smile that laid bare his shark-like teeth, he glared with satisfaction upon his rival.

"Ha ! ha !" laughed the bone-breaker, taking a stride toward Kaaialii ; "so *you* are the insane youth who has dared to meet Mailou in combat ! Do you know who I am ? I am the bone-breaker ! In my hands the limbs of men are like tender cane. Come, and with one hand let me strangle you !"

"You will need both !" replied Kaaialii. "I know you. You are a breaker of the bones of women, not of men ! You speak brave words, but have the heart of a coward. Let the word be given, and if you do not run from me to save your life, as I half-suspect you will, I will put my foot upon your broken neck before you find time to cry for mercy !"

Before Mailou could retort the word was given, and with an exclamation of rage he sprang at the throat of Kaaialii. Feigning as if to meet the shock, the latter waited until the hands of Mailou were almost at his throat, when with a quick movement he struck them up, swayed his body to the left, and with his right foot adroitly tripped his over-confident assailant. The momentum of Mailou was so great that he fell headlong to the earth. Springing upon him before he could rise, Kaaialii seized his right arm, and with a vigorous blow of the foot broke the bone below the elbow. Rising and finding his right arm useless, Mailou attempted to grapple his adversary with the left, but a well-delivered blow felled him again to the earth, and Kaaialii broke his left arm as he had broken the right. Regaining his feet, and unable to use either hand, with a wild howl of despair the bone-breaker rushed upon Kaaialii, with the view of dealing him a blow with his bent head ; but the young chief again tripped him as he passed, and, seizing him by the hair as he fell, placed his knees against the back of his prostrate foe and broke his spine.

This, of course, ended the struggle, and Kaaialii was declared the victor, amidst the plaudits of the spectators and the congratulations of Kamehameha and the court. Breaking from her father, who was grievously disappointed at the unlooked-for result, and who sought to detain her, Kaala sprang through the crowd and threw herself into the arms of Kaaialii. Oponui would have protested, and asked that his daughter might be permitted to visit her mother before becoming the wife of Kaaialii ; but the king put an end to his hopes by placing the hand of Kaala in that of the victorious chief, and saying to him :

"You have won her nobly. She is now your wife. Take her with you."

Although silenced by the voice of the king, and compelled to submit to the conditions of a contest which he had himself proposed, Oponui's hatred of Kaaialii knew no abatement, and all that day and the night following he sat alone by the sea-shore, devising a means by which Kaala and her husband might be separated. He finally settled upon a plan.

The morning after her marriage Oponui visited Kaala, as if he had just returned from Mahana, where her mother was supposed to be then living. He greeted her with apparent affection, and was profuse in his expressions of friendship for Kaaialii. He embraced them both, and said : "I now see that you love each other ; my prayer is that you may live long and happily together." He then told Kaala that Kalani, her mother, was lying dangerously ill at Mahana, and, believing that she would not recover, desired to see and bless her daughter before she died. Kaala believed the story, for her father wept when he told it, and moaned as if for the dead, and beat his breast ; and, with many protestations of love, Kaaialii allowed her to depart with Oponui, with the promise from both of them that she would speedily return to the arms of her husband.

With some misgivings, Kaaialii watched her from the top of the hill above Kealia until she descended into the valley of Palawai. There leaving the path that led to Mahana, they journeyed toward the bay of Kaumalapau. Satisfied that her father was for some purpose deceiving her, Kaala protested and was about to return, when he acknowledged that her mother was not ill at Mahana, as he had represented to Kaaialii in order to secure his consent to her departure, but at the sea-shore, where she had gathered crabs, shrimps, limpets and other delicacies, and prepared a feast in celebration of her marriage.

Reassured by the plausible story, and half-disposed to pardon the deception admitted by her father, Kaala proceeded with him to the sea-shore. She saw that her mother was not there, and heard no sound but the beating of the waves against the rocks. She looked up into the face of her father for an explanation ; but his eyes were cold, and a cruel smile upon his lips told her better than words that she had been betrayed.

"Where is my mother?" she inquired ; and then bitterly added : "I do not see her fire by the shore. Must we search for her among the sharks ?"

Oponui no longer sought to disguise his real purpose. "Hear the truth !" he said, with a wild glare in his eyes that whitened the lips of Kaala. "The shark shall be your mate, but he will not harm you. You shall go to his home, but he will not devour you. Down among the gods of the sea I will leave you until Kaaialii, hated by me above all things that breathe, shall have left Lanai, and then I will bring you back to earth !"

Terrified at these words, Kaala screamed and sought to fly ; but her heartless father seized her by the hand and dragged her along the shore until they reached a bench of the rocky bluff overlooking the opening to the Spouting Cave. Oponui was among the few who had entered the cavern through its gate of circling waters, and he did not for a moment doubt that within its gloomy walls, where he was about to place her, Kaala would remain securely hidden until such time as he might choose to restore her to the light.

Standing upon the narrow ledge above the entrance to the cave, marked by alternate whirlpool and receding column, Kaala divined the barbarous purpose of her father, and implored him to give her body to the sharks at once rather than leave her living in the damp and darkness of the Spouting Cave, to be tortured by the slimy and venomous creatures of the sea.

Deaf to her entreaties, Oponui watched until the settling column went down into the throat of the whirlpool, when he gathered the frantic and struggling girl in his arms and sprang into the circling abyss. Sinking a fathom or more below the surface, and impelled by a strong current setting toward the mouth of the cave, he soon found and was swept through the entrance, and in a few moments stood upon a rocky beach in the dim twilight of the cavern, with the half-unconscious Kaala clinging to his neck.

The only light penetrating the cave was the little refracted through the waters, and every object that was not too dark to be seen looked greenish and ghostly. Crabs, eels, sting-rays and other noisome creatures of the deep were crawling stealthily among the rocks, and the dull thunder of the battling waves was the only sound that could be distinguished.

Disengaging her arms, he placed her upon the beach above the reach of the waters, and then sat down beside her to recover his breath and wait for a retreating current to bear him to the surface. Reviving, Kaala looked around her with horror, and piteously implored her father not to leave her in that dreadful place beneath the waters.

For some time he made no reply, and then it was to tell her harshly that she might return with him if she would promise to accept the love of the chief of Olowalu, in the valley of Palawai, and allow Kaaialii to see her in the embrace of another. This she refused to do, declaring that she would perish in the cave, or the attempt to leave it, rather than be liberated on such monstrous conditions.

"Then here you will remain," said Oponui, savagely, "until I return, or the chief of Olowalu comes to bear you off to his home in Maui!" Then, rising to his feet, he continued hastily, as he noted a turn in the current at the opening : "You cannot escape without assistance. If you attempt it you will be dashed against the rocks and become the food of sharks."

With this warning Oponui turned and plunged into the water. Diving and passing with the current through the entrance, he was borne swiftly to the surface and to his full length up into the spouting column ; but he coolly precipitated himself into the surrounding waters, and with a few strokes of the arms reached the shore.

II.

Kaaialii watched the departure of Kaala and her father until they disappeared in the valley of Palawai, and then gloomily returned to his hut. His fears troubled him. He thought of his beautiful Kaala, and his heart ached for her warm embrace. Then he thought of the looks and words of Oponui, and recalled in both a suggestion of deceit. Thus harassed with his thoughts, he spent the day in roaming alone among the hills, and the following night in restless slumber, with dreams of death and torture. The portentous cry of an *alae* roused him from his *kapamoe* before daylight, and until the sun rose he sat watching the stars. Then he climbed the hill overlooking the valley of Palawai to watch for the return of Kaala, and wonder what could have detained her so long. He watched until the sun was well up in the heavens, feeling neither thirst nor hunger, and at length saw a *pau* fluttering in the wind far down the valley.

A woman was rapidly approaching, and his heart beat with joy, for he thought she was Kaala. Nearer and nearer she came, and Kaaialii, still hopeful, ran down to the path to meet her. Her step was light and her air graceful, and it was not until he had opened his arms to receive her that he saw that the girl was not Kaala. She was Ua, the friend of Kaala, and almost her equal in beauty. They had been reared together, and in their love for each other were like sisters. They loved the same flowers, the same wild songs of the birds, the same paths among the hills, and, now that Kaala loved Kaaialii, Ua loved him also.

Recognizing Kaaialii as she approached, Ua stopped before him, and bent her eyes to the ground without speaking.

"Where is Kaala?" inquired Kaaialii, raising the face of Ua and staring eagerly into it. "Have you seen her? Has any ill come to her? Speak!"

"I have not seen her, and know of no ill that has befallen her," replied the girl; "but I have come to tell you that Kaala has not yet reached the hut of Kalani, her mother; and as Oponui, with a dark look in his face, was seen to lead her through the forest of Kumoku, it is feared that she has been betrayed and will not be allowed to return to Kealia."

"And that, too, has been my fear since the moment I lost sight of her in the valley of Palawai," said Kaaialii. "I should not have trusted her father, for I knew him to be treacherous and unforgiving. May the wrath of the gods follow him if harm has come to her through his cruelty! But I will find her if she is on the island! The gods have given her to me, and in life or death she shall be mine!"

Terrified at the wild looks and words of Kaaialii, Ua clasped her hands in silence.

"Hark!" he continued, bending his ear toward the valley. "It seems that I hear her calling for me now!" And with an exclamation of rage and despair Kaaialii started at a swift pace down the path taken by Kaala the day before. As he hurried onward, he saw, at intervals, the footprints of Kaala in the dust, and every imprint seemed to increase his speed.

Reaching the point where the Mahana path diverged from the somewhat broader *ala* of the valley, he followed it for some distance hoping that Ua had been misinformed, and that Kaala had really visited her mother and might be found with her; but when he looked for and failed to find the marks of her feet where in reason they should have been seen had she gone to Mahana with her father, he returned and continued his course down the valley.

Suddenly he stopped. The footprints for which he was watching had now disappeared from the Palawai path, and for a moment he stood looking irresolutely around, as if in doubt concerning the direction next to be pursued. In his uncertainty several plans of action presented themselves. One was, to see what information could be gathered from Kaala's mother at Mahana, another to follow the Palawai valley to the sea, and a third to return to Kealia and consult a *kaula*. While these various suggestions were being rapidly canvassed, and before any conclusion could be reached, the figure of a man was seen approaching from the valley below.

Kaaialii secreted himself behind a rock, where he could watch the path without being seen. The man drew nearer and nearer, until at last Kaaialii was enabled to distinguish the features of Oponui, of all men the one whom he most desired to meet. His muscles grew rigid with wrath, and his hot breath burned the rock behind which he was crouching. He buried his fingers in the earth to teach them patience, and clenched his teeth to keep down a struggling exclamation of vengeance. And so he waited until Oponui reached a curve in the path which brought him, in passing, within a few paces of the eyes that were savagely glaring upon him, and the next moment the two men stood facing each other.

Startled at the unexpected appearance of Kaaialii, Oponui betrayed his guilt at once by attempting to fly; but, with the cry of "Give me Kaala!" Kaaialii sprang forward and endeavored to seize him by the throat.

A momentary struggle followed; but Oponui was scarcely less powerful than his adversary, and, his shoulders being bare, he succeeded in breaking from the grasp of Kaaialii and seeking safety in flight toward Kealia.

With a cry of disappointment, Kaaialii started in pursuit. Both were swift of foot, and the race was like that of a hungry shark following his prey. One was inspired by fear and the other with rage, and every muscle of the runners was strained. Leaving the valley path, Oponui struck for Kealia by a shorter course across the hills. He hoped the roughness of the route and his better knowledge of it would give him an advantage; but Kaaialii kept closely at his heels. On they sped, up and down hills, across ravines and along rocky ridges, until they reached Kealia, when Oponui suddenly turned to the left and made a dash for the temple and *puhonua* not far distant. Kaaialii divined his purpose, and with a last supreme effort sought to thwart it. Gaining ground with every step, he made a desperate grasp at the shoulder of Oponui just as the latter sprang through the entrance and dropped to the earth exhausted within the protecting walls of the *puhonua*. Kaaialii attempted to follow, but two priests promptly stepped into the portal and refused to allow him to pass.

"Stand out of the way, or I will strangle you both!" exclaimed Kaaialii, fiercely, as he threw himself against the guards.

"Are you insane?" said another long-haired priest, stepping forward with a *tabu* staff in his hand. "Do you not know that this is a *puhonua*, sacred to all who seek its protection? Would you bring down upon yourself the wrath of the gods by shedding blood within its walls?"

"If I may not enter, then drive him forth!" replied Kaaialii, pointing toward Oponui, who was lying upon the ground a few paces within, intently regarding the proceedings at the gate.

"That cannot be," returned the priest. "Should he will to leave, the way will not be closed to him; otherwise he may remain in safety."

"Coward!" cried Kaaialii, addressing Oponui in a taunting tone. "Is it thus that you seek protection from the anger of an unarmed man? A *pau* would better become you than a *maro*. You should twine *leis* and beat *kapa* with women, and think no more of the business of men. Come without the walls, if your trembling limbs will bear you, and I will serve you as I did your friend, the breaker of women's bones. Come, and I will tear from your throat the tongue that lied to Kaala, and feed it to the dogs!"

A malignant smile wrinkled the face of Oponui, as he thought of Kaala in her hiding-place under the sea, but he made no reply.

"Do you fear me?" continued Kaaialii. "Then arm yourself with spear and battle-axe, and with bare hands I will meet and strangle you!"

Oponui remained silent, and in a paroxysm of rage and disappointment Kaaialii threw himself upon the ground and cursed the *tabu* that barred him from his enemy.

His friends found and bore him to his hut, and Ua, with gentle arts and loving hands, sought to soothe and comfort him. But he would not be consoled. He talked and thought alone of Kaala, and, hastily partaking of food that he might retain his strength, started again in search of her. Pitying his distress, Ua followed him—not closely, but so that she might not lose sight of him altogether.

He traveled in every direction, stopping neither for food nor rest. Of every one he met he inquired for Kaala, and called her name in the deep valleys and on the hill-tops. Wandering near the sacred spring at the head of the waters of Kealia, he met a white-haired priest bearing from the fountain a calabash of water for ceremonial use in one of the temples. The priest knew and feared him, for his looks were wild, and humbly offered him water.

"I ask not for food or water, old man," said Kaaialii. "You are a priest—perhaps a *kaula*. Tell me where I can find Kaala, the daughter of Oponui, and I will pile your altars with sacrifices!"

"Son of the long spear," replied the priest, "I know you seek the sweet-smelling flower of Palawai. Her father alone knows of her hiding-place. But it is not here in the hills, nor is it in the valleys. Oponui loves and frequents the sea. He hunts for the squid in dark places, and dives for the great fish in deep waters. He knows of cliffs that are hollow, and of caves with entrances below the waves. He goes alone to the rocky shore, and sleeps with the fish-gods, who are his friends. He—"

"No more of him!" interrupted the chief, impatiently. "Tell me what has become of Kaala!"

"Be patient, and you shall hear," resumed the priest. "In one of the caverns of the sea, known to Oponui and others, has Kaala been hidden. So I see her now. The place is dark and her heart is full of terror. Hasten to her. Be vigilant, and you will find her; but sleep not, or she will be the food of the creatures of the sea."

Thanking the priest, Kaaialii started toward the bay of Kaumalapau, followed by the faithful Ua, and did not rest until he stood upon the bluff of Palikaholo, overlooking the sea. Wildly the waves beat against the rocks. Looking around, he could discern no hiding-place along the shore, and the thunder of the breakers and the screams of the sea-gulls were the only sounds to be heard. In despair he raised his voice and wildly exclaimed:

"Kaala! O Kaala! where are you? Do you sleep with the fish-gods, and must I seek you in their homes among the sunken shores?"

The bluff where he was standing overlooked and was immediately above the Spouting Cave, from the submerged entrance to which a column of water was rising above the surface and breaking into spray. In the mist of the upheaval he thought he saw the shadowy face and form of Kaala, and in the tumult of the rushing waters fancied that he heard her voice calling him to come to her.

"Kaala, I come!" he exclaimed, and with a wild leap sprang from the cliff to clasp the misty form of his bride.

He sank below the surface, and, as the column disappeared with him and he returned no more, Ua wailed upon the winds a requiem of love and grief in words like these :

> " Oh ! dead is Kaaialii, the young chief of Hawaii,
>   The chief of few years and many battles !
>   His limbs were strong and his heart was gentle ;
>   His face was like the sun, and he was without fear.
>   Dead is the slayer of the bone-breaker ;
>   Dead is the chief who crushed the bones of Mailou ;
>   Dead is the lover of Kaala and the loved of Ua.
>   For his love he plunged into the deep waters ;
>   For his love he gave his life. Who is like Kaaialii ?
>   Kaala is hidden away, and I am lonely ;
>   Kaaialii is dead, and the black *kapa* is over my heart :
>   Now let the gods take the life of Ua !"

With a last look at the spot where Kaaialii had disappeared, Ua hastened to Kealia, and at the feet of Kamehameha told of the rash act of the despairing husband of Kaala. The king was greatly grieved at the story of Ua, for he loved the young chief almost as if he had been his son. " It is useless to search for the body of Kaaialii," he said, "for the sharks have eaten it." Then, turning to one of his chiefs, he continued : "No pile can be raised over his bones. Send for Ualua, the poet, that a chant may be made in praise of Kaaialii."

Approaching nearer, Papakua, a priest, requested permission to speak. It was granted, and he said :

"Let me hope that my words may be of comfort. I have heard the story of Ua, and cannot believe that the young chief is dead. The spouting waters into which Kaaialii leaped mark the entrance to the cave of Paiikaholo. Following downward the current, has he not been drawn into the cavern, where he has found Kaala, and may still be living? Such, at least, is my thought, great chief."

"A wild thought, indeed !" replied the king ; "yet there is

some comfort in it, and we will see how much of truth it may reveal."

Preparations were hastily made, and with four of his sturdiest oarsmen Kamehameha started around the shore for the Spouting Cave under the bluff of Palikaholo, preceded by Ua in a canoe with Keawe, her brother.

III.

When Kaaialii plunged into the sea he had little thought of anything but death. Grasping at the spouting column as he descended, it seemed to sink with him to the surface, and even below it, and in a moment he felt himself being propelled downward and toward the cliff by a strong current. Recklessly yielding to the action of the waters, he soon discerned an opening in the submerged base of the bluff, and without an effort was drawn swiftly into it. The force of the current subsided, and to his surprise his head rose above the surface and he was able to breathe. His feet touched a rocky bottom, and he rose and looked around with a feeling of bewilderment. His first thought was that he was dead and had reached the dark shores of *Po*, where *Milu*, prince of death, sits enthroned in a grove of *kou* trees ; but he smote his breast, and by the smart knew that he was living, and had been borne by the waters into a cave beneath the cliff from which he had leaped to grasp the misty form of Kaala.

Emerging from the water, Kaaialii found himself standing on the shore of a dimly-lighted cavern. The air was chilly, and slimy objects touched his feet, and others fell splashing into the water from the rocks. He wondered whether it would be possible for him to escape from the gloomy place, and began to watch the movements of the waters near the opening, when a low moan reached his ear.

It was the voice of Kaala. She was lying near him in the darkness on the slimy shore. Her limbs were bruised and lacerated with her fruitless attempts to leave the cave, and she no longer possessed the strength to repel the crabs and other loathsome creatures that were drinking her blood and feeding upon her quivering flesh.

"It is the wailing of the wind, or perhaps of some demon of

the sea who makes this horrible place his home," thought Kaai-alii.

He feared neither death nor its ministers ; yet something like a shudder possessed him as he held his breath and listened, but he heard nothing but the thunder of the breakers against the cavern walls.

"Who speaks ?" he exclaimed, advancing a pace or two back into the darkness.

A feeble moan, almost at his feet, was the response.

Stooping and peering intently before him, he distinguished what seemed to be the outlines of a human form. Approaching and bending over it, he caught the murmur of his own name.

"It is Kaala ! Kaaialii is here !" he cried, as he tenderly folded her in his arms and bore her toward the opening. Seating himself in the dim light, he pushed back the hair from her cold face, and sought to revive her with caresses and words of endearment. She opened her eyes, and, nestling closer to his breast, whispered to the ear that was bent to her lips :

"I am dying, but I am happy, for you are here."

He sought to encourage her. He told her that he had come to save her ; that the gods, who loved her and would not let her die, had told him where to find her ; that he would take her to his home in Kohala, and always love her as he loved her then.

She made no response. There was a sad smile upon her cold lips. He placed his hand upon her heart, and found that it had ceased to beat. She was dead, but he still held the precious burden in his arms ; and hour after hour he sat there on the gloomy shore of the cavern, seeing only the pallid face of Kaala, and feeling only that he was desolate.

At length he was aroused by the splashing of water within the cave. He looked up, and Ua, the gentle and unselfish friend of Kaala, stood before him, followed a moment after by Kamehameha. The method of entering and leaving the cave was known to Keawe, and he imparted the information to his sister. Ua first leaped into the whirlpool, and the dauntless Kamehameha did not hesitate in following.

As the king approached, Kaaialii rose to his feet and stood sadly before him. He uttered no word, but with bent head pointed to the body of Kaala.

"I see," said the king, softly ; "the poor girl is dead. She could have no better burial-place. Come, Kaaialii, let us leave it."

Kaaialii did not move. It was the first time that he had ever hesitated in obeying the orders of his chief.

"What! would you remain here?" said the king. "Would you throw your life away for a girl? There are others as fair. Here is Ua; she shall be your wife, and I will give you the valley of Palawai. Come, let us leave here at once, lest some angry god close the entrance against us!"

"Great chief," replied Kaaialii, "you have always been kind and generous to me, and never more so than now. But hear me. My life and strength are gone. Kaala was my life, and she is dead. How can I live without her? You are my chief. You have asked me to leave this place and live. It is the first request of yours that I have ever disobeyed. It shall be the last!"

Then seizing a stone, with a swift, strong blow he crushed in brow and brain, and fell dead upon the body of Kaala.

A wail of anguish went up from Ua. Kamehameha spoke not, moved not. Long he gazed upon the bodies before him; and his eye was moist and his strong lip quivered as, turning away at last, he said: "He loved her indeed!"

Wrapped in *kapa*, the bodies were laid side by side and left in the cavern; and there to-day may be seen the bones of Kaala, the flower of Lanai, and of Kaaialii, her knightly lover, by such as dare to seek the passage to them through the whirlpool of Palikaholo.

Meles of the story of the tragedy were composed and chanted before Kamehameha and his court at Kealia, and since then the cavern has been known as *Puhio-kaala,* or "Spouting Cave of Kaala."

THE DESTRUCTION OF THE TEMPLES.

CHARACTERS.

LIHOLIHO (Kamehameha II.), king of the Hawaiian Islands.

KEOPUOLANI, the queen-mother,
KAAHUMANU, chief counselor, and } widows of Kamehameha I.
KALAKUA,

KALAIMOKU, prime minister.

KEKUAOKALANI, the defender of the gods.

MANONO, wife of Kekuaokalani.

HEWAHEWA, high-priest of Hawaii.

HOAPILI, guardian of the Princess Nahienaena.

NAIHE, counselor and orator.

KEKUANAOA, treasurer of the king.

KAPIHE, commander of the national vessels.

LAANUI, a companion of the king.

THE DESTRUCTION OF THE TEMPLES.

THE LAST GREAT DEFENDER OF THE HAWAIIAN GODS.

I.

ON the 1st of October, 1819, a fleet of four canoes bearing the royal colors set sail from Kawaihae, in the district of Kohala, on the northwestern coast of Hawaii. The canoes were large and commodious, and were occupied by between sixty and seventy persons, a portion of whom were females. The most of the men were large, muscular and over six feet in height, while the dress and bearing of many of the women indicated that they were of the *tabu* and chiefly classes.

The costumes of a number of those of both sexes who seemed to be of rank were a strange admixture of native and foreign fabric and fashion. American and European manufactures were beginning to find a market in the islands, and the persons of many were adorned with rich cloths, jewelry and other tokens of civilization. Their weapons and utensils were largely of metal, and a squad of ten warriors armed with muskets, in one of the canoes, showed that the white man's methods of warfare had received the early and earnest attention of the Hawaiian chiefs and leaders.

The canoe leading the little squadron was double, with covered apartments extending into and across the united decks of both, and the persons occupying it, with the exception of soldiers, sailors and servants, were distinguished alike for their gaudy trappings and a boisterous merriment infusing a feeling of jollity throughout the fleet. In this canoe was Liholiho, who, on the death of his distinguished father, Kamehameha I., something less than five months before, had become sole monarch of the Hawaiian group. In addition to two of his queens, he was accompanied by Kapihe, the commander of the royal vessels ; Kekuanaoa, the royal treasurer, and a retinue of chiefly friends and personal attendants.

On the 8th of the previous May his royal father had died at Kailua, leaving to Liholiho the kingdom his arms had won, with Kaahumanu as second in authority and guardian of the realm. The morning following the death of his father Liholiho left Kailua for Kohala to avoid defilement, and there remained for ten days, when he returned to Kailua and formally assumed the sceptre. At the end of the season of mourning, for superstitious reasons the young king again left for Kohala, and took up his residence for a time at Kawaihae. Remaining there until the 1st of October, on the advice of Kaahumanu he had started on his return to Kailua.

During the brief residence of Liholiho at Kawaihae, Kaahumanu inaugurated a vigorous conspiracy against the priesthood, and resolved to persuade the young king to repudiate the religion and *tabus* of his fathers. In this scheme she was assisted by Keopuolani, the mother of Liholiho ; Kalaimoku, the prime minister, and Hewahewa, the high-priest, who claimed descent from the renowned Paao.

In the latter part of the reign of the first Kamehameha the gods and *tabus* of the priesthood began to lose something of their sanctity in the estimation of the masses. Although the first Christian missionaries to the islands did not arrive until nearly a year after the death of Kamehameha I., many trading and war vessels had touched at Hawaiian ports during the two preceding decades. No very clear idea of the Christian religion had been imparted to the natives by the sailors and traders with whom they had been brought in contact ; but it could not have escaped their observation that the foreigner's disregard of the *tabu* brought with it no punishment, and they very naturally began to question the divinity of a religious code limited in its scope to the Hawaiian people.

The results of this growing scepticism were frequent violations of the *tabu*. To check this seditious tendency summary punishments were inflicted. A woman was put to death for entering the eating apartment of her husband, and Jarvis relates that three men were sacrificed at Kealakeakua, a short time before the death of Kamehameha—one of them for putting on the *maro* of a chief, another for eating a forbidden article, and the third for leaving a house that was *tabu* and entering one that was not. Kamehameha had learned something of the religion of the

Interior of an Ancient Temple.

foreigners, but not enough to impress him greatly in its favor; and when questioned concerning it during his last illness he replied that he should die in the faith of his fathers, although he thought it well that his successor should give the subject attention.

Different motives influenced the leaders in this conspiracy against the religion and *tabus* of the group. Kaahumanu, the favorite wife of Kamehameha I., but the mother of none of his children, was bold, ambitious and unscrupulous. Left second in authority under the young king, she chafed at the restraints imposed by the *tabu* upon her sex. Many of the most palatable foods were denied her by custom, and in her intercourse with foreigners acts of courtesy were chilled and hampered by numerous and irksome *tabu* interdictions. To enable her to eat and drink of whatever her appetites craved, and to do so in the presence of males, Kaahumanu was prepared to strike at the roots of a religious system which had maintained her ancestors in place and power, even though she had no definite knowledge of the new faith with which she hoped to supplant it.

Although the uncle of one of the wives of Liholiho—Kekau-onohi—Kalaimoku was not of distinguished rank. He was a chief of decided ability, however, and had been by degrees advanced under the first Kamehameha, until he became the prime minister of the second. Not being a *tabu* chief by birth, he was easily persuaded by Kaahumanu to lend his assistance in depriving those of higher rank of their *tabu* prerogatives, and to this end he and his brother Boki were baptized by the Roman Catholic chaplain of the French corvette *L'Uranie* shortly after the assumption of the government by Liholiho. This was done while the young king was residing at Kawaihae, and without his knowledge.

Keopuolani, the political wife of Kamehameha I., and the mother of Liholiho, Kauikeaouli and Nahienaena, was the daughter of Kiwalao, and of supreme *tabu* rank. So well was this recognized that her distinguished husband, it is related, always approached her with his face to the earth. She lacked decision of character, however, and her adhesion to the conspiracy against the *tabu* was doubtless due to the influence over her of the crafty Kaahumanu.

Whatever may have been the motives of others, the apostasy

of Hewahewa seems to have been the result of conviction. Being the high-priest of Hawaii, he had everything to lose and nothing to profit by the destruction of the religious system of which he was the supreme and honored head. Of an inquiring mind, the little knowledge he had gained of the new creed had convinced him of the inconsistency of his own, and when the time came to strike he acted boldly. His hand was the first to apply the torch to the temples. Had he hesitated the conspiracy would have failed, for the influence of the high-priest with the masses at that time was second only to that of the king.

Liholiho was strong only in his attachments. Born in 1797, when the group had been consolidated under one government and further wars were not apprehended, he had not been given that austere and solid training in civil and military life imparted to the princes of the previous generation. He was attracted by the vices rather than the virtues of the foreigners at intervals visiting the islands, and, realizing that his future was secure, had devoted almost exclusively to pleasure the ripening years of his youth. Light-hearted, affectionate and gentle, he had shown so little taste for public affairs at the age of twenty-two that his dying father, in bequeathing to him the sceptre, deemed it prudent to accompany it with the condition that, should he wield it unworthily, the supreme power should devolve upon Kaahumanu.

These were the prominent actors in the scheme for the destruction of the priesthood, and this the character of the young king who had been tarrying for some months at Kawaihae, and to whom a message had been sent by Kaahumanu, informing him that, on his return to Kailua, she would openly set the gods at defiance and declare against the *tabu*. This information did not greatly astonish Liholiho. He knew of the growing hostility to the *tabu;* had talked with Hewahewa on the subject; had learned that his mother had failed to respect it on late occasions, and had himself seen it violated without harm to the offender. Yet he feared the consequences of an open declaration against the priesthood. He remembered the fate of Hua, whose bones whitened in the sun. He knew that his arrival at Kailua would precipitate the crisis, and compel him either to renounce or defend the gods of his fathers ; and after leaving Kawaihae, as we have seen, with a party occupying four canoes, he pursued his way very leisurely toward Kailua, seemingly in no haste to reach his destination.

Moving southward, and passing the rocky point immediately north of Puako, sail was shortened in the royal fleet, and the canoes drifted slowly along the coast, taking just wind enough to hold their course. Carousings were heard in the royal quarters. Liholiho appeared, and, waving his hand to a group of men and women forward, a wild *hula* dance was soon in progress, to the accompaniment of drums and rattling calabashes. The king watched the dancers for some time with a vacant air, and then began to mark the drum-beats with his feet. The emphasis of the movement increased, until, dismissing his dignity, his voice finally rose above the rude music, and he began to dance with an enthusiasm which seemed to be almost frenzied. Others of the royal party joined in the revelry, and for half an hour or more the vessel was the scene of tumultuous merriment. Bottles and calabashes of intoxicating liquors were then passed from one to another of the companions of the king, and the *hula* was continued, followed by chants, *meles* and other methods of enjoyment. Drinking was frequent, and the humbler members of the party were sparingly supplied with gin, whiskey and other stimulants. Similar scenes were transpiring in the canoes following, and the debauch was the wildest ever witnessed on any one of the eight Hawaiian seas.

"Let us make drunk the water-gods!" exclaimed the king. "Here, Kuula, is a taste for you; and here, Ukanipo, is your share!" And he tossed into the ocean two bottles of liquor.

"Let us hope the gods may not be angered by the unusual sacrifice," said Laanui, one of the favorite companions of the king. He spoke seriously, and Liholiho's face wore a troubled expression for a moment as he replied:

"Then you have not yet lost faith in the gods, Laanui?"

"No," was the prompt answer of Laanui.

The king did not continue the conversation. Turning and beckoning to a servant, more liquor was brought, after which the revelry was continued all through the day and far into the night. Meanwhile, so little progress had been made that at noon the next day the fleet was off Kiholo.

For another twenty-four hours the feasting, drinking and dancing continued, when the revelers were met by a double canoe sent by Kaahumanu from Kailua in search of the royal party. The messengers of his chief counselor were courteously received by Liholiho, and, hoisting all sail, he was escorted by them to Kailua, where he was warmly welcomed by Kaahumanu and the members of the royal family.

Appearances of dissipation were plainly visible in the language and bearing of the king, and Kaahumanu regarded the moment as auspicious for committing him to some flagrant and public act of hostility to the *tabu*. Both she and Keopuolani, the queen-mother, had been secretly violating it, since the death of Kamehameha I., by eating of foods interdicted to their sex, and to screen themselves from exposure it was necessary that the religious system should be destroyed of which the *tabu* was the vital force. This could be accomplished only through the united efforts of the king and high-priest. Hewahewa was prepared to do his part as the religious head of the kingdom, but the young king, notwithstanding the pressure that had been brought to bear upon him by Kaahumanu and a few of the leading chiefs of his court, was still undecided.

A feast was prepared in honor of the king's return to Kailua. In accordance with native custom, separate tables for the sexes were spread, and a number of foreigners were present as the invited guests of Kaahumanu. During the afternoon Liholiho, in response to well-devised banters, had been induced to drink and smoke with the female members of his family. This was a favorable beginning, and, farther emboldened by his mother, who deliberately ate a banana in his presence and drank the milk of a cocoanut, he declared that he would openly set the *tabu* at defiance during the approaching feast.

It was feared that his courage would fail, and he was not left to himself for a moment until he led the way to the feast. His step was unsteady, and his face wore a troubled expression as he proceeded to the pavilion, accompanied by Kaahumanu, Keopuolani and other members of the royal household. As they separated to take seats at their respective tables, the queen-mother gave Liholiho a look of encouragement, and Kaahumanu said to him in a low tone :

" If you have the courage of your father, this will be a great day for Hawaii."

The king made no reply, for at that moment his eyes fell upon

wooden images of Ku and Lono, on opposite sides of the entrance, and he stepped briskly past them and seated himself at
the head of one of the tables. The sight of the idols almost unnerved him, and some of the guests observed that his hand trembled as he raised to his lips and drained a vessel of what seemed
to be strong liquor.

The guests were all seated. Hewahewa rose, and, glancing at
the troubled face of the king, lifted his hands and said with firm-
ness : " One and all, may we eat in peace, and in our hearts give
thanks to the one and only god of all."

The words of the high-priest restored the sinking courage of
the king. He rose from his seat, deliberately walked to one of
the tables reserved for the women, and seated himself beside his
mother. During the strange proceeding not a word was spoken,
not a morsel touched. Some believed him to be intoxicated ;
others were sure that he was insane. Since the age of Wakea no
one had so defied the gods and lived. Many natives rose from
the tables, and horror took the place of astonishment when Liholiho, encouraged by his mother, began to freely partake of the
food prepared for the women. Interdicted fish, meats and fruits
were then brought to the tables of the women by order of the
king, who ate from their plates and drank from their vessels.

Now satisfied that the king was acting deliberately and with
the approval of the most influential dignitaries of the kingdom,
including the supreme high-priest, a majority of the chiefs present promptly followed the example of their sovereign, and an
indescribable scene ensued. " The *tabu* is broken ! the *tabu* is
broken !" passed from lip to lip, swelling louder and louder as it
went, until it reached beyond the pavilion. There it was taken
up in shouts by the multitude, and was soon wafted on the winds
to the remotest corners of Kona. Feasts were at once provided,
and men and women ate together indiscriminately. The *tabu*
foods of palace and temple were voraciously eaten by the masses,
and thousands of women for the first time learned the taste of
flesh and fruits which had tempted their mothers for centuries.

At the conclusion of the royal feast a still greater surprise bewildered the people. " We have made a bold beginning," said
Hewahewa to the king, thus adroitly assuming a part of the responsibility ; " but the gods and *heiaus* cannot survive the death
of the *tabu*."

"Then let them perish with it!" exclaimed Liholiho, now nerved to desperation at what he had done. "If the gods can punish, we have done too much already to hope for grace. They can but kill, and we will test their powers by inviting the full measure of their wrath."

To this resolution the high-priest gave his ready assent, and orders were issued at once for the destruction of the gods and temples throughout the kingdom. Resigning his office, Hewahewa was the first to apply the torch, and in the smoke of burning *heiaus*, images and other sacred property, beginning on Hawaii and ending at Niihau, suddenly passed away a religious system which for fifteen hundred years or more had shaped the faith, commanded the respect and received the profoundest reverence of the Hawaiian people. No creed was offered by the iconoclasts in lieu of the system destroyed by royal edict, and until the arrival of the first Christian missionaries, in March of the year following, the people of the archipelago were left without a shadow of religious restraint or guidance.

II.

While the abolition of the *tabu* system received the universal approval of the masses, the destruction of the gods and temples met with very considerable remonstrance and opposition. It was believed by many that the priesthood might be preserved without the *tabu*, and that the king had transcended his sovereign power in striking down both at a single blow. Hence many gods were saved from the burning temples, and thousands refused to relinquish the faith in which they had been reared. Deprived of their occupations, the priests denounced the destruction of the *heiaus*, and it was not long before a formidable conspiracy against the government was organized on Hawaii, under the leadership of Kekuaokalani, a chief of rare accomplishments and a cousin of the king. Defection appeared at the court, and several chiefs of distinction gave their support to the revolutionary movement.

However it may be regarded in the light of its results, on the part of Kekuaokalani the rebellion was a brave and conscientious defence of the religion of his fathers. He raised the standard of revolt within a day's march of Kailua, and invited to its support all who condemned the action of Liholiho in decreeing the de-

Ancient Temple by the Sea-Shore, 1793.

struction of the national religion. He scorned all compromises
and concessions, and but for the firearms of the whites would
doubtless have wrested the sceptre from his royal cousin.

It has been asserted that Kekuaokalani was ambitious and
availed himself of the discontent created by the anti-religious decrees of Liholiho as a possible means of seizing the reins of government. This assumption is not sustained either by the words
or acts of the unfortunate chief. The ambassadors sent to him
after the first skirmish of the conflict reported that he declined
all terms of peaceful settlement. This, however, was not the case.
What he demanded was that Liholiho should withdraw his edicts
against the priesthood, permit the rebuilding of the temples, and
dismiss Kalaimoku as prime minister and Kaahumanu as chief
counselor of the government. These conditions were declined,
and the ambassadors returned with the story that they had offered
to leave the question of religion entirely with the people, but that
Kekuaokalani would have nothing but war. A correct statement
of what occurred at the interview would doubtless have weakened
the royal cause, and was therefore withheld. After the resigna-
tion of Hewahewa as high-priest the position devolved upon Kekuaokalani by right of precedence, and, believing in the sanctity
of his gods, as a brave man he could not do less than take up
arms in their defence.

No characters in Hawaiian history stand forth with a sadder
prominence, or add a richer tint to the vanishing chivalry of the
race, than Kekuaokalani and his courageous and devoted wife,
Manono, the last defenders in arms of the Hawaiian gods. They
saw all that the light around them presented, but the only gods
known to them were those of their fathers, and they died in a
futile effort to protect them. They were brave, noble and conscientious, and the cause in which they perished cannot detract
from the grandeur or dim the glory of the sacrifice.

In the veins of Kekuaokalani ran the best blood both of Hawaii
and Oahu. He was a nephew of Kamehameha I., and his strain
was even superior in rank to that of his distinguished uncle. His
great-grandmother was Kamakaimoku, a princess of Oahu, who
became the wife of Kalaninuiamamao, one of the sons of Keawe,
king of Hawaii, and the mother of Kalaniopuu, grandfather of
Keopuolani, mother of Liholiho. One of the full sisters of Kalaniopuu was Manona, the grandmother of Kekuaokalani.

One of the early wives of Kamehameha I. was Kalola, a chiefess of Hawaii. She subsequently became the wife of Kekuamanoha, a younger brother of Kahekili, king of Maui, and the mother of Manono, wife of Kekuaokalani. As the mother of Manono was a daughter of Kumukoa, one of the sons of Keawe, king of Hawaii, and her father was a prince of Maui, she was not only of high rank, but was related in blood both to her husband and the reigning family.

Kekuaokalani is referred to by tradition as one of the most imposing chiefs of his day. He was more than six and a half feet in height, perfect in form, handsome in feature and noble in bearing. Brave, sagacious and magnetic, he possessed the requirements of a successful military leader ; but as war had practically ceased with the conquest of the group by Kamehameha I., and he had little taste for the frivolities of the court, where he might have worn out his life in honored idleness, he turned his attention to the priesthood. Beginning at the bottom, with patient application he passed through the intervening degrees until he stood beside the high-priest, fully his equal in learning, and more than his peer in devotion to his calling. He mastered the chronological *meles* of the higher priesthood and the esoteric lore and secret symbols of the temple, and with the death of Hewahewa it was the universal expectation that the duties of the high-priesthood would devolve upon him. In disposition he was humane, charitable and unselfish, and, appreciating the nobility of his character, his wife worshipped him almost as a god. In return he bestowed upon her the full measure of his affection, and the waters of their lives flowed peacefully on together until the grave engulfed them both.

This was the character of the sturdy chief around whom the friends of the dethroned gods of Hawaii began to rally. He counseled peace and submission so long as he could find listeners among the disaffected, but in the end he was forced into the revolt and became the leader of the movement.

He was present at the royal feast at Kailua when Liholiho publicly violated the *tabu* and decreed the destruction of the temples. He saw Hewahewa, the venerable high-priest, who had been to an extent his religious guide and instructor, cast the first brand upon the *heiau* where they had so often worshipped together and sought the counsels of the gods. At first all this seemed to be a horrible dream, but the burning temples and frantic rejoicings of the populace soon convinced him that it was a bewildering reality, and he threw himself to the earth and prayed that his sight might be blasted, that he might witness no farther the sacrilegious acts of the people.

"Liholiho's brain is on fire with strong drink, and he may be urged to do anything," thought Kekuaokalani; "but Hewahewa —it must be that he is insane, and it is my duty to speak with him."

He sought and found the high-priest, and learned to his great grief that Hewahewa was not only sound in mind, but was in thorough accord with the king in his determination to destroy the temples and repudiate the priesthood.

"And you, a high-priest of the blood of Paao, advise this!" said Kekuaokalani, bitterly.

"I advise it," was the calm reply of Hewahewa; "but I am no longer the high-priest of Hawaii; the king has been so notified."

"Then here and now do I assume the vacant place," returned Kekuaokalani, promptly.

"By whose appointment?" inquired Hewahewa.

"By the will of the outraged gods whose temples are turning to ashes around us!" replied Kekuaokalani, with energy. "They will teach me my duty, even should they fail to visit vengeance upon their betrayers!"

With these words Kekuaokalani turned and walked away. His heart was filled with anguish, and the shouts of the people drove him almost to despair. Reaching the pavilion, he lifted and placed upon his shoulder the prostrate and mutilated image of Lono that had stood beside the entrance, and with the precious burden strode gloomily and defiantly past the palace and disappeared.

For a month or more nothing was heard of Kekuaokalani at the court. Meantime, the work of destruction continued, and the smoke of burning temples rose everywhere throughout the group. At length word reached Kailua that some of the priesthood, sustained by a number of influential chiefs, were inciting a revolt in South Kono. Little attention was paid to the report until it was learned that Kekuaokalani had accepted the leadership of the movement. This alarmed the court, and a council of

chiefs was called.   Discussion developed the prevailing opinion
that the threatened uprising was merely a local disturbance that
could be quelled without difficulty, and Liholiho's apprehensions
were further relieved by the assurance of one of the chiefs that,
with the assistance of forty warriors, he would undertake to bring
Kekuaokalani a prisoner to Kailua within three days.

" Not with forty times forty ! " said Hewahewa, earnestly.
Better than any one else he understood and appreciated the lofty
courage of Kekuaokalani, and was too generous to listen to its
disparagement without protest.   " No, not with forty times
forty ! " he continued.   " Without Kekuaokalani the revolt will
amount to nothing ; with him, it means war."

" Then war let it be, since he invites it ! " exclaimed Kalaimoku.

" But may he not be persuaded to peace ? " inquired the
king, addressing the question, apparently, to Hewahewa.

" Undoubtedly," replied the latter, " if we are prepared to
accept his conditions."

" What, think you, would be the conditions ? " returned the
king.

" The restoration of the *tabu* and the rebuilding of the temples," was the deliberate answer of Hewahewa.

The king was silent ; but before the council dissolved it was
understood that a force would be sent against the rebels at once,
and for a week or more preparations for the campaign were in
progress, under the supervision of Kalaimoku.   Everything at
length being in readiness, the royal army, numbering, it is presumed, not less than fifteen hundred warriors, some of them
bearing firearms, moved southward from Kailua in the direction
of Kaawaloa, where had been established the rebel headquarters.

Having accepted the leadership of the rebellion, and regarding himself as a champion selected by the gods for their defence,
Kekuaokalani vitalized the movement with an energy and enthusiasm which soon brought the people to its support in large
numbers, and the winter solstice found him in command of an
army large enough to inspire him with a reasonable hope of
success.

The five intercalated days between the winter solstice and
the beginning of the new year had from time immemorial been
set apart as a season of *tabu*, dedicated to festivities in honor of

Lono, one of the Hawaiian trinity. In the midst of the general religious demoralization Kekuaokalani devoted to the season its customary observances—the last yearly festival ever authoritatively given to Lono in the group.

The movements of the government were regularly and rapidly reported to Kekuaokalani, and when the royal troops left Kailua he was prepared to meet them. Through his efforts a *heiau* near Kaawaloa had escaped destruction. Thither he repaired, and, offering sacrifices to the gods, prayed that they would manifest their power by giving him victory.

He did not await the assault of the royal forces. Leaving Kaawaloa, he attacked and defeated their advance not far north of that place, throwing the entire army into confusion. Satisfied with the success, he returned to Kaawaloa.

News of the repulse reaching Kailua, a consultation was called by the king, and Kalaimoku urged the prompt advance of reinforcements by land and sea, and an immediate and overwhelming attack upon the rebels at Kaawaloa, rightly claiming that every day would add to the strength of the insurgents under the inspiration of the slight victory they had achieved.

This advice was accepted, and every available force was immediately sent to the front, including a squadron of double canoes under the command of Kaahumanu and Kalakua, one of them carrying a mounted swivel in charge of a foreigner.

Uncertain as to the strength of the rebels, and by no means confident of the results of a struggle which had opened in favor of his enemies, Liholiho advised a resort to peaceful negotiations before staking everything on the chances of battle. Hoapili, who stood in the capacity of husband to the queen-mother, and Naihe, hereditary national counselor and orator, were selected as ambassadors to confer with Kekuaokalani, and Keopuolani volunteered to accompany them.

Reaching the camp of the insurgents, the ambassadors were graciously received by Kekuaokalani, and used every means to effect an amicable settlement of the difficulties that had brought two hostile armies face to face; but nothing satisfactory could be accomplished. They were not authorized to offer such terms as Kekuaokalani felt that he could consistently accept, inasmuch as they failed to embrace either the restoration of the *tabu* or the rebuilding of the temples. Naihe offered to leave the question of religion optional with the insurgents.　To this proposal Ke-kuaokalani bitterly replied :

"You offer the scales of the fish after you have picked the bones.　As they are without temples, where would they worship ?　As they are without altars, where would they sacrifice ?　As they are without the *tabu*, what to them would be sacred and acceptable to the gods ? "

"Then must we take back the word that Kekuaokalani will have nothing but war ? " said Keopuolani, sadly.

"No, honored mother of princes," replied Kekuaokalani, in a tone so solemn and impressive that his listeners stood awed in his presence.　"Say, rather, that Kekuaokalani, the last high-priest, it may be, of Hawaii, is prepared to die in defence of the gods to whose service he has devoted his life.　If they are omnipotent, as he believes them to be, their temples will rise again ; if not, he is more than willing to hide his disappointment in the grave ! "

Naihe was his uncle ; Kamakaimoku was the great-grand-mother both of Keopuolani and himself, and the king was his cousin.　As a condition of peace he demanded the recall of the edicts against the *tabu* and the temples.　As this could not be conceded, the ambassadors appealed to his relationship with themselves and the royal family ; but he could not be moved.　"We are proud of our blood," he said to Keopuolani, "but who but the gods made kings of our ancestors ? "

Finding that nothing could be effected, the ambassadors withdrew with tokens of mutual regret, and were safely and respectfully escorted beyond the rebel lines.　The reports they allowed to be circulated on their return, that Kekuaokalani had refused to consider any terms of peace, and that they had narrowly escaped with their lives, were inventions employed to mislead and exasperate the royal army.

With the departure of the ambassadors Manono sought her husband to learn the results of the conference.　The information that no agreement had been reached did not surprise her. For weeks past all the auguries had indicated blood, and the night before the *alae* had screamed in the palms behind her hut.

"Thank the gods for the omen ! " said Kekuaokalani.

"But the voice of the *alae* is a presage of evil," suggested Manono.

" Only to those who do evil," replied the chief. " The fate of the gods, whose battles we fight, is shaped by themselves."

" Have you no fear of the result ? " inquired Manono.

" I fear nothing," was the reply ; " but the thought has sometimes come to me of late that the gods are reserving for Liholiho and his advisers a punishment greater than I may be able to inflict. Should that be so, I am obstructing with spears the path of their vengeance, and will be sacrificed."

" The will of the gods be done ! " said Manono, devoutly. " But, whatever may be the fate of Kekuaokalani, Manono will share it."

" Brave Manono ! " exclaimed the husband, with emotion. " If the gods so will it we will die together ! "

That night Kekuaokalani took up his line of march for Kailua, determined to give battle to the royal forces wherever he might encounter them. He moved near the coast, and the next morning the hostile armies met at Kuamoo. Arranging his forces in order of battle, Kekuaokalani sent to the front a number of newly-decorated gods in the charge of priests, and, in turn addressing the several divisions, conjured them in impassioned language to defend the gods of their fathers.

Kalaimoku commanded the royal army in person. The battle opened in favor of the rebels, and with them would have been the victory but for the great superiority of the royalists in firearms. At a critical juncture a battalion of musketeers, some of whom were foreigners, charged the rebel centre, when the division gave way in something of a panic, and soon the entire rebel forces were in retreat. Retiring to the adjacent seaside, under cover of a stone wall they made a successful resistance for some time ; but the squadron of double canoes already referred to, under the command of Kaahumanu and Kalakua, enfiladed the position with musketry and a mounted swivel, and the insurgents abandoned the unequal struggle, the most of them scattering and seeking shelter in the neighboring hills.

Although wounded early in the action, Kekuaokalani gallantly kept the field. Everywhere was his tall form seen moving throughout the conflict, rallying and cheering his followers, while at his side fought the brave Manono. He finally fell with a musket-ball through his heart. With a wild scream of despair Manono sprang to his assistance, and the next moment a bullet

pierced her temple, and she fell dead across the body of her dying husband. Kalaimoku was the first to approach, and gazing
long upon the noble features of Kekuaokalani, grand even in
death, turned to his followers and said : " Truly, since the days
of Keawe a grander Hawaiian has not lived ! "

Thus died the last great defenders of the Hawaiian gods.
They died as nobly as they had lived, and were buried together
where they fell on the field of Kuamoo.

Small bodies of religious malcontents were subdued at Waimea and one or two other points, but the hopes and struggles of
the priesthood virtually ended with the death of Kekuaokalani.

THE TOMB OF PUUPEHE.

CHARACTERS.

Makakehau, a chief of Lanai.
Puupehe, daughter of a chief of Maui.

THE TOMB OF PUUPEHE.

A LEGEND OF THE ISLAND OF LANAI.

SAILING along the lee-shore or southwest coast of Lanai, a huge block of red lava, sixty feet in diameter and eighty or more feet in height, is discerned standing out in the sea, and detached from the mainland some fifty or sixty fathoms. The sides are precipitous, offering no possible means of ascent, and against it the waves dash in fury, and in the niches of its storm-worn angles the birds of ocean build their nests. Observed from the overhanging bluff of the neighboring shore, on the summit of the lonely column is seen a small enclosure formed by a low but well-defined stone wall. This is known as "The tomb of Puupehe"—the last resting-place of one of the most beautiful of the daughters of Maui, whose body was buried there by her distracted husband and lover, Makakehau, a warrior of Lanai. How the summit was reached by the lover with his precious burden is a mystery, but the wall is still there to show that the ascent was made in some manner, and tradition assumes that it was through the agency of supernatural forces.

Puupehe was the daughter of Uaua, a petty chief of Maui, and Makakehau won her, it is related without detail, as the joint prize of love and war. How this could have occurred it is difficult to imagine, since Lanai was always a dependency of Maui in the past, and no direct wars between the two islands are mentioned by tradition. It may therefore be inferred that she was the spoil of some private predatory expedition, and that the efforts of the young warrior to jealously seclude her from the gaze of men were prompted not more by the infatuations of her beauty than the fear that she might be recaptured.

However this may have been, they are described in the *Kanikau*, or "Lamentation of Puupehe," as mutually captive to each other in the bonds of love. The maiden was a sweet flower of Hawaiian beauty. Her glossy brown and spotless

body " shone like the clear sun rising out of Heleakala." Her
flowing hair, bound by wreaths of *pikaki* blossoms, streamed
forth as she ran "like the surf-crests scudding before the
wind," and the starry eyes of the daughter of Uaua so dazzled the youthful brave that he was called Makakehau, or " Misty
Eyes."

Fearing that the radiant beauty of his captive might cause
her to be coveted by some of the chiefs of the land, he said to
her : " We love each other well. Let us go to the clear waters
of Kalulu. There we will fish together for the *kala* and *bonita*,
and there will I spear the turtle. I will hide you, O light of my
heart ! in the cave of Malauea. Or we will dwell together in
the great ravine of Palawai, where we will eat the young of the
uwau, and bake them in the *ti* leaf with the sweet *pala* root.
The *ohelo* berries of the Kuahiwa will refresh us, and we will
drink of the cool waters of Maunalei. I will thatch a hut in
the thicket of Kaohai, and we will love on till the stars die."

The *meles* tell of their loves in the Pulou Ravine, where they
caught the bright *iwi* birds and scarlet *apapani*. How sweet
were their joys in the *maia* groves of Waiakeakua, where the
lovers saw naught so beautiful as themselves! But the misty eyes
were soon to be made dimmer by weeping, and dimmer till the
drowning brine should shut out their light for ever.

Makakehau left his love one day in the cave of Malauea,
while he went to the mountain to fill the *huawai* with sweet water. This cavern yawns at the base of the cliff overlooking the
rock of Puupehe. The sea surges far within, but there is an
inner space or chamber which the expert swimmer can reach,
and where Puupehe had often found seclusion, and baked the
honu, or sea-turtle, for her absent lover.

This was the season for the *kona*, the terrific storm that comes
up from the equator, and hurls the billows of ocean with increased violence against the southern shores of the Hawaiian Islands.

Makakehau beheld from the rocky springs of Pulou the
vanguard of an approaching *kona*—scuds of rain and thick
mist rushing with a howling wind across the round valley of
Palawai. He knew the storm would fill the cave with a wild
and sudden rush of waters, and destroy the life of his beautiful
Puupehe.

Every moment was precious. He flung aside his calabashes

of water, and at the top of his speed started down the mountain. With mighty and rapid strides he crossed the great valley, where he met the coming storm in its fury. Over the rim he dashed with an agonized heart, and down the ragged slope of the *kula* to the shore, which the waves were already lashing in a voice of thunder.

The sea was up, indeed! The yeasty foam of surging, wind-rent billows whitened the cliffs, and the tempest chorussed the mad anthem of the battling waves. Oh! where should Misty Eyes seek for his love in the blinding storm?

A rushing mountain of sea fills the mouth of the cave of Ma-lauea, and the pent air within hurls back the invading torrent with a stubborn roar, blowing outward great streams of spray. It is a savage war of the elements—a battle of the forces of nature well calculated to thrill with pleasure the hearts of strong men. But a lover looking into the seething gulf of the whirlpool —what would be to him the sublime conflict? what to see amid the boiling brine the upturned face and tender body of the idol of his heart?

Others might agonize on the brink, but Misty Eyes sprang into the dreadful caldron and snatched his lifeless love from the jaws of an ocean grave.

The next day fishermen heard the lamentation of Makakehau, and the women of the valley came down and wailed over Puu-pehe. They wrapped her body in bright, new *kapa*, and covered it with garlands of fragrant *nauu*. They prepared it for inter-ment, and were about to place it in the burial ground of Manele; but Makakehau prayed that he might be left alone one night more with his lost love, and the request was not refused.

When the women returned the morning following they found neither corpse nor wailing lover. At length, looking toward the rock of Puupehe, they discovered Makakehau at work on the lofty apex of the lone sea-tower. The wondering people of the island watched him with amazement from the neighboring cliffs, but, heedless of their observation, he continued his labors. Some sailed around the base of the column in their canoes, but could discover no means of ascent. Every face of the rock was either perpendicular or overhanging.

The conviction then became general—since there seemed to be no other possible explanation—that some sympathizing *akua,* or spirit, had responded to the prayer of Makakehau, and assisted him in reaching the summit of the tower with the body of his dead bride ; and in this form has tradition brought down the touching story.

Makakehau finished his labors. He laid his love in a grave prepared by his own hands, placed the last stone upon it, and then stretched out his arms and thus wailed for Puupehe :

> ' Where are you, O Puupehe ?
> Are you in the cave of Malauea ?
> Shall I bring you sweet water,
> The water of the fountain ?
> Shall I bring the *uwau*,
> The *pala* and *ohelo ?*
> Are you baking the *honu?*
> And the red, sweet *hala ?*
> Shall I pound the *kalo* of Maui ?
> Shall we dip in the gourd together ?
> The bird and the fish are bitter,
> And the mountain water is sour.
> I shall drink it no more ;
> I shall drink with Aipuhi,
> The great shark of Manele."

Ceasing his sad wail, Makakehau gazed for a moment upon the grave where were buried the light and hope of his life, and then leaped from the rock into the boiling surge at its base. His body was crushed in the breakers. The witnesses of the sacrifice secured the mangled remains of the dead lover, and interred them with respect in the *kupapau* of Manele.

This is the story told by the old bards of Lanai of the lonely rock of Puupehe, and the still inaccessible summit, with the marks of a grave upon it, attests with reasonable certainty that the *mele* has something of a foundation in fact.

The Story of Laieikawai.

CHARACTERS.

LAIEIKAWAI, the heroine, called also *Ka wahine o ka liula*, "the lady of the twilight," daughter of a chief of Oahu.

LAIELOHELOHE, twin-sister of Laieikawai.

WAKA, their grandmother, a powerful sorceress.

KAPUKAIHAOA, a priest of Kukaniloko, Oahu.

HULUMANIANI, a prophet of Kauai.

AIWOHIKUPUA, a chief of Wailua, Kauai, of *kupua* or supernatural birth, and from a foreign country.

MOANALIHAIKAWAOKELE, Aiwohikupua's father, and

LAUKIELEULA, his mother, both mysterious beings, and inhabitants of the Moon.

KAONOHIOKALA, brother of Aiwohikupua, and a demi-god living in the Sun.

MAILE-HAIWALE,
MAILE-KALUHEA,
MAILE-LAULII, } sisters of Aiwohikupua.
MAILE-PAKAHA, and
KAHALAOMAPUANA the youngest,

KEKALUKALUOKEWA, king of Kauai after Kauakahialii.

HAUAILIKI, a petty chief of Mana, Kauai.

HALAANIANI, a petty chief of Puna, Hawaii, and

MALIO, his sister, a sorceress.

HINAIKAMALAMA, a chiefess of Hana, Maui.

POLIAHU, a goddess of Mauna Kea, Hawaii.

KIHANUILULUMOKU, a gigantic *moo*, or lizard god.

THE STORY OF LAIEIKAWAI.

A SUPERNATURAL FOLK-LORE LEGEND OF THE FOURTEENTH CENTURY.

PREFATORY.

EARLY in the spring of 1885 a party of six or eight ladies and gentlemen—the writer being of the number—made a carriage circuit of the island of Oahu. Ample preparations for the little journey had been made by the governor of the island, and the marshal of the kingdom acted in the double capacity of guide and escort. A score of attending natives accompanied the party on horseback, and a delightful week or more was consumed in skirting the breezy beaches of Koolau, in dalliance at Waialua, in visiting historic points of interest, and in completing a journey of something less than one hundred miles.

Starting from Honolulu, the empty carriages were carefully lowered down the steep, ragged and narrow Pali road leading to the valleys below, and the first evening found us at rest by the beautiful shores of Kaneohe. Entering the district of Koolauloa the next day, and approaching the coast over a broad stretch of grassy meadow but slightly above the level of the ocean, our party was suddenly brought to a halt beside a pool of clear water, nearly round, and perhaps a hundred feet in diameter. The surface of the pool was ten or twelve feet below the level of the surrounding plain, and its even banks of solid rock dropped almost perpendicularly into water of unknown depth. The volume of the pool is affected neither by rain nor drought, and the native belief is that it is fed by springs at the bottom, and has a subterranean drainage to the ocean, some two or three miles distant.

This, we learned, was the celebrated pond of Waiapuka, around which so many strange legends have been woven. All of them speak of a cavern somewhere beyond the walls of the pool, and to be reached only by diving into the water and finding the narrow passage leading up into it.

While listening to fragments of the story of Laieikawai and of other legends connected with the mysterious cavern, and seriously doubting the existence of the secret chamber so prominently referred to in the early folk-lore of Oahu, an old native, who had joined the party at Kaneohe, quietly and without a word dismounted, divested himself of his upper garments and plunged into the pool. Swimming to the northern wall, he clung for a moment to a slight projection, and then disappeared. It was suggested for the first time that he was in search of the cavern of Laieikawai, and all eyes were turned toward the point where he was last seen above the water.

Three or four minutes elapsed, and fears for his safety began to be exchanged, when the salutation of "*aloha!*" greeted us from the opposite wall, and the next moment a pair of black eyes were seen glistening through a small opening into the cavern, not before observed, about four feet above the surface of the water.

The swimmer then returned to the pool by the passage through which he had left it, and we were compelled to admit that the cavern of Laieikawai was a reality, however wild and visionary may have been the stories connected with it. Not a single person present, including the governor, had ever before seen the passage to the cavern attempted, and the natives were overjoyed at what they had witnessed.

To the many questions with which he was pressed the old man returned but brief answers on his return, and when importuned to explain the method of his entrance to the cavern, that the secret might not be lost, he pointed significantly to the sea, and declared that there would be found the bodies of those who sought to solve the mystery of the passage and failed.

This rediscovery of the entrance to the cavern of Laieikawai created a renewed interest in the legends associated with it, and thenceforth during our journey many of the old stories were rehearsed. The most interesting related to Laieikawai. It is a recklessly fanciful recital, and gives expression to the extravagant conceits of the early Hawaiian bards. Following is presented a condensation of the legend of Laieikawai, as more elaborately told by Haleole.—EDITOR.

I.

The father of Laieikawai was Kahauokapaka, chief of the two Koolau districts, comprising the entire windward side of the island of Oahu, and her mother's name was Malaekahana. Soon after their marriage he made a vow that if her children should prove to be girls they were to be put to death, at least until a son should be born to them.

In accordance with this savage vow the first four of Malaekahana's children, all being daughters, were slain without mercy. When her time again drew near, by the advice of a priest she sent her husband to the coast to bring her some *ohua palemo*, a small fish of which she was exceedingly fond.

In his absence she was delivered of twin girls, who were named Laieikawai and Laielohelohe. They were surpassingly beautiful children, and, desirous of saving their lives, the mother consigned the first-named to the care of Waka, the child's grandmother, and the other to Kapukaihaoa, a priest of discretion and sanctity.

On the return of the husband he was told that the expected child came into the world without life. He knew that a birth in his house had occurred during his absence, for he had heard two distinct claps of thunder.

Waka took her foster-child to the cavern which opens into the pond of Waiapuka, and which can be entered only by diving. Laielohelohe was taken by her priestly protector to the sacred enclosure of Kukaniloko, on the western side of the island, and there tenderly cared for.

The moment Waka entered the cavern of Waiapuka with Laieikawai a rainbow appeared over the place, and was constantly visible so long as the child remained there. Even when the sun was obscured by clouds the rainbow could be seen.

At length the rainbow was observed by the great prophet Hulumaniani on the distant island of Kauai. For twenty days in succession he saw it, and knew its significance. He secured a canoe and fifteen men from Poloula, the chief of Wailua, provided himself with a black pig, white fowl and red fish for sacrifice, and, when the star Sirius rose, set sail for Oahu.

Reaching that island, he landed at Waianae, and, guided by the rainbow, in due time arrived at the pool of Waiapuka.

Waka had just dived into the cave, and he noticed ripples on the water. During the day Waka started to leave the cavern, but caught a glimpse of the prophet sitting on the bank, and quickly returned, again ruffling the water.

The prophet remained by the pool all night, and in the morning saw a rainbow over Kukaniloko. Traveling in that direction, he ascended Mount Kaala, when he saw the rainbow over the island of Molokai. Finding a canoe bound thither, he took passage and landed at Haleolono, near the western shore.

In a dream Waka had been directed by Kapukaihaoa to remove Laieikawai to some securer place, and had accordingly taken her to Malelewaa, a secluded spot on the north side of Molokai.

Following the rainbow, the prophet arrived in the evening at Waikolu, just below Malelewaa ; but that night Waka was again advised in a dream to remove at once to the island of Hawaii and dwell with her ward at Paliuli. They departed at dawn, and at Keawanui met a man getting his canoe ready to sail to Lanai, and engaged passage ; but before they could embark Laieikawai accidentally removed the veil which Waka compelled her to wear, and the man was amazed at her beauty.

Instead of starting for Lanai, he invited Waka and her ward to remain at his house until he could secure the services of another rower, and then started around the island, proclaiming to every group of people the great beauty of Laieikawai.

A great crowd had assembled at Kalaupapa to witness a boxing-match, and there the man extolled the beauty of the girl in the presence of the head chief and the prophet in search of her. Not doubting that the girl described was the one he was in quest of, the prophet proceeded to Kawela and saw the rainbow over Hawanui. That night he arrived at Kaamola, the land adjoining, and went to rest, for he had journeyed far and was weary.

Meanwhile Waka, again warned in a dream, obtained a canoe and sailed across the channel to Lanai, landing at Maunalei. Three days of fog and rain followed, and on the fourth the prophet saw the rainbow over Maunalei. It did not remain there, however. Ten days later he discerned something peculiar on the high peak of Haleakala, on the island of Maui. He proceeded thither, but found nothing there but fog and rain.

He next journeyed to Kauwiki, a hill near Hana, and there

erected a small *heiau*, or temple, for the worship of his patron deity. After the dedication, seeing nothing on Hawaii, and receiving no inspiration, he remained for some time at Kauwiki.

At length, in the early days of the seventh month of the year, he saw faintly with the rising of the sun a rainbow on the windward side of Hawaii. At sunset on the third day of the next month he entered his *heiau* and prayed fervently, and there appeared before him the wraiths of Waka and Laieikawai. His patron god then informed him that the persons whose shadows he had seen were living in the forest of Puna, in a house thatched with the yellow feathers of the *oo*.

With this information the prophet set sail for Mahukona, on the island of Hawaii. There he prayed in the temple of Pahauna, and was directed to Waipio, where he offered sacrifices in the famous *heiau* of *Paakalana*. He proceeded thence to Kaiwilahilahi, near Laupahoehoe, where he remained for some years, unable to obtain any further information of the persons of whom he was in search.

II.

It was during the sojourn of Hulumaniani, the prophet, at Kaiwilahilahi, that Kauakahialii, king of Kauai, with his queen, Kailikelauokekoa, returned from a wedding tour of the group. A great assemblage of chiefs and commoners had met to welcome them home with music, dancing and other festivities.

In relating his adventures the king referred to a meeting with the mysterious princess of Paliuli, whose beauty, he declared, was something more than human. The meeting occurred at Keaau, in Puna. The *kahu* of the king first met the princess and her companion, and, when requested by him to favor his royal master with a visit, the princess informed him that she might possibly comply with his request the night following. "If I come," she said, "I will give you warning."

"Now, listen and heed," she continued. "If you hear the voice of the *ao* I am not in its notes, and when you hear the caw of the *alala* I am not in its voice. When the notes of the *elepaio* are heard I am getting ready to descend. When you hear the song of the *apapane* I shall have come out of my house. Listen, then, and if you hear the *iiwipolena* singing I am outside of your house. Come forth and meet me."

And so it came to pass. In the *kihi*, or first watch of the evening, resounded the cry of the *ao*, in the second watch the caw of the *alala*, at midnight the chirruping of the *elepaio*, in the *pili* of the morning the song of the *apapane*, and at daybreak the voice of the *iiwipolena*. Then a shadow fell on the door, "and we were enveloped," said the king, "in a thick fog, and when it cleared away the princess was seen in her glorious beauty, borne on the wings of birds." The name of the divine being, he said, was Laieikawai.

Among the chiefs who listened to this story of the king was Aiwohikupua, chief of Wailua, who was of foreign birth. He had made a vow that he would not marry a Hawaiian woman, and, expressing the opinion that the princess described by the king was a daughter of other lands, he resolved to make her his wife.

To this end he sought out the late *kahu* of the king and made him his confidant and chief officer. They talked of little else than Laieikawai. He had a vision of her in a dream, and drank *awa* successively for many days, in the hope of inspiring a repetition of the vision. He chanted a *mele* in praise of the unknown princess, renewed his resolution to possess her, and then prepared to go to Hawaii in search of her.

He fitted out two double canoes, with sixteen rowers and two steersmen, and, when the augurs and soothsayers declared the omens favorable, on the rising of Sirius he set sail for Hawaii. On his way thither he stopped at many places, and at length arrived in the harbor of Haneoo, in the district of Hana, Maui.

A number of surf-riders were amusing themselves on the beach, among them Hinaikamalama, the famous chiefess of Hana. Aiwohikupua was smitten with her charms, and accepted her invitation to join the bathing party in their sports. In turn she became enamored of him, and invited him to visit her house and play *konane*—a game resembling draughts—with her.

When about to begin the game she asked him what he was willing to wager on his success, and he pointed to one of his double canoes. She declined the condition, and proposed, instead, that they should stake their persons. To this he agreed, and, playing, lost the game. To avoid paying the forfeit he declared that he had made a vow to give himself in love to no woman until after he had made the circuit of the island of Hawaii, and admonished her to remain faithful to him while he was absent.

The chief and his party left Haneoo, and the next day arrived at Kauhola, in the district of Kohala, Hawaii, where a boxing-match was in progress. Aiwohikupua was challenged to a contest by Ihuanu, the champion of Kohala. The challenge was accepted, and in the struggle Ihuanu was killed.

They next landed at Paauhau, in Hamakua, to witness another boxing-match. The local champion was Haunaka. He was invited to a contest with Aiwohikupua, but, learning something of the prowess of the chief, he declined the conflict. They then sailed for Laupahoehoe, where the prophet Hulumaniani was still residing.

That evening the prophet was watching the clouds for omens, and discerned in them that a chief's double canoe was approaching, bearing nineteen men. The next morning he saw a mist on the sea, and prepared his black pig, white fowl and bunch of awa. Then followed peals of thunder, and Aiwohikupua's canoes came in sight, with the *puloulou* insignia of a chief ; whereupon the prophet offered sacrifices, and prayed for the chief and himself.

Landing, the chief and prophet embraced, and spent the night together, but Aiwohikupua did not disclose the real object of his voyage. They then sailed for Makahanaloa, from which place could be seen the rainbow over Paliuli. They landed at Keaau, where the people were surf-bathing.

In the evening Aiwohikupua left his men with the canoes, taking with him only his confidant, the *kahu*, carrying a rich feather mantle as a present to the lady of Paliuli. After a long and wearisome journey through the thick jungle they heard the crowing of a cock, and soon after came to a clearing, at the farther end of which was the house of Laieikawai, all covered with the choice yellow feathers of the *oo*

Aiwohikupua was amazed and humiliated. Said he : " I brought my royal feather cloak as a present to her, and behold ! it is not equal to the thatch of her house ! " Then turning to his *kahu*, he said : " I will stay here no longer. Let us return."

In spite of the remonstrances of his companion, Aiwohikupua returned to Keaau without seeing Laieikawai, and sailed at once for Kauai. They did not stop to visit the prophet at Laulapa-hoehoe. When off the coast of Hamakua they saw a woman of extraordinary beauty reclining on a cliff by the shore. She was graceful in every movement, and wore a snow-white mantle.

They landed and made her acquaintance. Her name was Po-liahu, of Mauna Kea. As usual, the chief began to talk to her at once of love. In reply she asked him if he had not sworn by the names of his gods not to marry a woman born on the Ha-waiian group, and whether he had not engaged himself to Hinai-kamalama, of Hana. She informed him that, like himself, she too was of *kupua* descent and possessed supernatural powers. She promised to marry him, however, so soon as he could be released from his oath and would return to claim her. She accompanied them as far as Kohala, where she exchanged mantles with the chief in pledge of their betrothal, and then took her departure.

Crossing the channel to Maui, the chief put into the harbor of Haneoo, but did not land. Hinaikamalama hailed him from the shore, and demanded the fulfilment of his promise; but he be-guiled her by declaring that he had not yet completed the circuit of Hawaii, having sailed only along the windward side of it, and that bad news from home compelled his immediate return to Kauai.

She believed him and was pacified. In the middle of the Oahu channel he enjoined secrecy on his crew, and then hastened to Kauai, fully determined to return to Hawaii and secure an audience with the princess of Paliuli.

Reaching home, he informed his five sisters of what he had seen at Paliuli, and they agreed to accompany him to Hawaii and assist him in his suit with the beautiful Laieikawai.

The next day Aiwohikupua selected a fresh crew of fourteen rowers and two pilots, who, with his sisters and confidential coun-selor, made a party of twenty-three in all, and set sail for Hawaii. They were detained a month at Honuaula, Maui, by stormy weather, but finally reached Kaelehuluhulu, in the district of Kona, Hawaii. Poliahu saw their canoes there, and was disap-pointed when they left for Hilo.

They arrived at Keaau, in Puna, about the middle of the day, and Aiwohikupua made his arrangements and started inland at once with his five sisters and trusted *kahu*. At midnight the party reached Paliuli.

The chief stationed his eldest sister, Maile-haiwale, at the door of Laieikawai. She sent forth the delicate fragrance of the plant of her name, which awoke Laieikawai.

"Waka ! Waka ! " exclaimed the princess.

" Here ! " answered Waka. " What wakes you in the night ? "

" A fragrance, a strange, cool fragrance, which goes to my heart," returned the girl.

" It is not a strange fragrance," said Waka. " It is certainly Maile-haiwale, the sweet-scented sister of Aiwohikupua, who has come to ask you to be his wife."

" Pshaw ! I will not marry him," was the petulant response of Laieikawai.

Aiwohikupua heard her refusal, and was so thoroughly disheartened that he proposed to abandon his sisters and return to Keaau, but his trusty *kahu* intervened and advised another trial. So the next in age, Maile-kaluhea, took a position by the door. Her fragrance was different and more penetrating; but nearly the same exchange of words as before occurred within the house.

The chief again proposed to leave, but the *kahu* insisted on trying the powers of Maile-laulii ; but no better success followed.

" Try again," said the counselor, " and if they all fail I myself will undertake to persuade her."

So Maile-pakaha was sent to the door, but with no better result, and, speaking loudly enough to be heard without, Laieikawai said : " Whoever may come, I will not consent to marry Aiwohikupua."

Hearing this, and regarding any further attempt as useless, Aiwohikupua ordered his sisters to remain behind in the woods as a punishment for their failure, and started on his return to the coast. The youngest sister, whose powers had not been tried, called after him and touched his heart. He offered to take her and leave the rest behind, but she would not consent to abandon her sisters. One of them chanted a *mele* to soften his heart, but he remained obdurate.

He proceeded to the coast, the sisters following as best they could, and when they saw him and his attendants seated in the canoes and ready for departure, Maile-kaluhea chanted a touching *mele ;* but he heeded it not and put out to sea.

The sisters traveled by land and met Aiwohikupua as he was about to go ashore at Punahoa, but he avoided them by again setting sail. They then traveled overland to Honolii, where their brother had stopped for supplies. They watched during the night, and when Aiwohikupua was about to embark in the morning his sisters drew near, and Kahalaomapuana chanted a pathetic song, and with so great effect that her brother invited her into his canoe, placed her on his knee and wept over her.

Ordering his rowers to pull out to sea with his youngest sister, whom he still held in his embrace, she begged him to return for the others, and when he refused she chanted a farewell song, leaped overboard and swam ashore.

The sisters then decided to return to Paliuli, scarcely knowing where else to go on the island of Hawaii, where they were strangers. Arriving there, they found shelter in a clump of *hala* trees near the house of Laieikawai, the doors of which were kept continually closed. Failing to attract the attention of the inmates, the sisters concluded to keep a fire burning at night and to sing by turns—Maile-haiwale the first night, Maile-kaluhea the second, and so on for four nights ; but no notice was taken of them.

On the fifth night it was the turn of the youngest sister to sing. She lighted the fire, made a musical instrument of a *ti* leaf and played upon it. She did this in the evening and morning watches for two nights. Laieikawai had never heard the instrument before, and it delighted her. So she sent her *kahu*, a hunchback, to first spy out the musician, and then bring before her the person who was capable of making such music.

Following the *kahu*, Kahalaomapuana found Laieikawai resting on the wings of birds, with two *iiwipolenas* perched upon her shoulders. She was kindly received, played before her, and told her of her sisters. Touched by the recital, Laieikawai ordered a house to be built for them, and formally adopted them as her companions and guards. They were fed by birds and lived as in an enchanted bower.

On the return to Kauai of Aiwohikupua from his second voyage he had a great feast prepared, and all the guests were made drunk on *awa*. Under the influence of the liquor Aiwohikupua divulged the secret of his mission to Hawaii, and told all about his unsuccessful efforts in seeking to secure an interview with the princess of Paliuli.

Hauailiki, a handsome young chief of Mana, rose to his feet and boasted that he could achieve without difficulty what Aiwo-

hikupua had failed to accomplish ; whereupon the latter offered
to furnish him with a canoe and men to sail it if he would undertake to make good his boast, and each made a wager of his
lands on the result.

Hauailiki set sail for Hawaii the next day, and on his arrival
at Keaau was greatly admired for his manly beauty. The following morning a dense fog enveloped the place, and when it
cleared away he saw seven women sitting by the seaside, one of
whom was Laieikawai.

To attract her attention Hauailiki for four successive days
appeared before her in the surf, performing many difficult feats
of swimming and diving, but she gave him no heed. On the
fifth day he exhibited his skill in surf-swimming, and won applause from all but Laieikawai. He then showed himself as a
surf-swimmer without a board. His skill was then recognized
by Laieikawai, and she beckoned him to approach, and threw
around his neck a *lei lehua*, or garland of *lehua* blossoms. Immediately the fog settled down, and when it cleared Laieikawai
and her party had left for Paliuli.

Hauailiki and his guide determined to follow the party at
once, and, traveling all night, they reached Paliuli in the morning. Approaching the house, they were met by Maile-haiwale,
the first sentinel, who ordered them to retire. But they passed
her by force, as they did the second, third and fourth guards,
until they met Kahalaomapuana near the door of the house, resting on the wings of birds. She ordered them back, threatening
that the birds should pick their bones, and they returned in haste
to Keaau.

Undecided what course to pursue, Hauailiki dreamed of meeting Laieikawai several nights in succession, and at last resolved
to visit Paliuli again and without an attendant. Reaching the
spot, he approached the house by a back path without encountering the sentinels, and found Kahalaomapuana asleep at the
door. He pushed aside the feather curtain, entered the room,
and found Laieikawai asleep, resting on the wings of birds. He
awoke her, and she ordered him away. He pleaded with her
and told her of his dreams, but she insisted upon his departure.
Kahalaomapuana then came to the assistance of her mistress,
and drove the importunate suitor back to Keaau.

Abandoning the undertaking as hopeless, Hauailiki returned

to Kauai.   Arriving at Wailua, he was welcomed by a large
gathering of chiefs, and when he had told his story Aiwohikupua
generously forgave him his wager.

Rejoiced to learn that his sisters had become the attendants
of Laieikawai, Aiwohikupua resolved to revisit Paliuli. He assembled a fleet of twenty double and thirty single canoes, forty
peleleus for his attendants, and a triple canoe for himself and
counselor, and set sail for Hawaii.

Waka knew of the arrival of the fleet at Keaau, and admonished Laieikawai not to visit the coast.   The sisters were put on
guard, and Kahalaomapuana summoned to their defence their
terrible patron god Kihanuilulumoku, a *moo*, or gigantic lizard.

The night following these preparations Aiwohikupua and his
guide made their appearance at Paliuli.   Five *tabu* sticks, covered with white *kapa*, had been set at intervals beyond the
house ; but the invaders disregarded them and pushed on, until
they encountered Maile-haiwale, the first sentinel.   She ordered
them to retire, and sent a bird to summon the rest of her sisters.
The youngest came, borne on the wings of birds, and drove her
brother back, telling him that they were no longer sisters of his.

Aiwohikupua returned to Keaau, resolved to secure by force
what he had been unable to effect by strategy.   He therefore
sent up to Paliuli a detachment of ten warriors, but they were
promptly slain by the lizard god.   After waiting for two days he
sent another detachment of twenty warriors, with a competent
officer, and all of them shared the same fate.   He next sent forty
men, and still other forties, until eight forties in all had perished.

He next despatched his two swift messengers to inquire
about the fate of his warriors.   They met a bird-catcher above
Olaa, who told them of the *moo* and his dreadful work.   Pre-
sently they heard the roaring of the wind and the crash of falling
trees, and the monster appeared in the path before them.   They
reassumed their bird forms, however, and escaped by flying.

Aiwohikupua then summoned Kalahumoku, the man-eating
dog from Kahiki, to kill the *moo* and bring to him Laieikawai ;
and with the dog he sent his two bird messengers, to bring him
early tidings of the result.

As the two monsters met, a column of fog rose and drifted
toward the sea.   This warned Aiwohikupua that the dog had
been defeated.   Late in the day the animal returned, badly

wounded and with ears and tail missing, and the whole party set sail for Kauai.

Arriving home, Aiwohikupua thought of his engagement with the beautiful Poliahu, and began to perform certain expiatory rites to relieve himself of the oath he had taken not to marry a woman of the Hawaiian Islands. He then sent his two bird messengers to Poliahu, to inform her that he was preparing to fulfil his engagement.

By mistake the birds flew to Hana. They inquired for the betrothed of the Kauai chief, and were directed to Hinaikamalama. They informed her that three months were to be spent in preparation, and that in the fourth month, in the night of *kulu*, Aiwohikupua would come to claim his bride. These were the words they had been instructed to speak to Poliahu, but by mistake they were told to another, who joyously replied : " He remembers, then, the game of *konane* which we played together."

On the return of the bird messengers the blunder was discovered, and they were banished from the court. Then the *koae*, or tropic bird, was sent to Poliahu with the same message with which the others had been entrusted.

Aiwohikupua, relieved of his oath, waited until the 24th day of the third month, and then set sail in great state, with forty double and eighty single canoes, and twenty *peleleus*. On the 11th day of the fourth month he arrived at Kawaihae, and despatched the *koae* to inform Poliahu, who named Waiulaula as the place for the marriage.

To give brilliancy to the ceremony Aiwohikupua dressed his petty chiefs, male and female, in feather cloaks, and many of his female attendants in fine mats. He wore the white mantle given to him by Poliahu, and a red feather helmet. His rowers were clad in fine red *kapas*. On the platform of the chief's double canoe was raised an *anu*, covered with yellow cloaks, and above it stood the *tabu puloulou*. Around this canoe were ten others, carrying musicians skilled in playing the *hula* drum and other instruments.

On the day of *kulu* the three great mountains were covered with snow, which was the sign promised by Poliahu. On the arrival of Aiwohikupua and his party at Waiulaula they were met by Poliahu, Lilinoe, Waiau and Kahoupokane, the three latter being mountain goddesses. The men suffered from cold but on being apprised of the fact Poliahu and her friends removed their snow mantles, causing the snow on the mountains to retire to its usual limits.

Aiwohikupua and Poliahu were then made man and wife. Feasting and music followed, and the happy pair returned together to Kauai, making their residence above Honopuwai.

In revenge for their dismissal the banished bird messengers informed Hinaikamalama of the marriage of her betrothed. Angered at his perfidy, she persuaded her parents to make a visit with her to Kauai.

There was a gathering of chiefs at Mana, Kauai, to celebrate the nuptials of Hauailiki and Makaweli. The night was spent in games, dancing and other pastimes. A game of *kilu* was in progress. At midnight Hinaikamalama entered the *kilu* shed and sat down among the circle of players. Observing her, Hauailiki requested the *mea ume* (drawer) to tell Aiwohikupua to stop the *hula kaeke* and take part in the game of *kilu*, in order to enable him to make her his prize. Accordingly, when Hauailiki won at the game, the *mea ume* went around the circle and threw the *maile* wreath over him. The wreath was then removed and placed over the shoulders of Hinaikamalama. She rose to her feet and requested permission to speak. She asked in whose honor the festival was being given, and, on being informed of the occasion, requested Hauailiki to delay the fulfilment of the *ume*, and then proceeded to tell her story of the faithlessness of Aiwohikupua.

The story created a great sensation, and the conduct of Aiwohikupua was universally condemned. Poliahu was enraged and returned to Mauna Kea, and the chief agreed to fulfil his engagement with Hinaikamalama. The night of their marriage Poliahu sent the chill of her snow mantle upon her rival, and she was benumbed with cold. Her teeth chattered, and it was with difficulty that she could be kept from freezing.

A second time, when she and Aiwohikupua came together, an intense chill came over her. She was frightened, and inquired the cause. The chief answered : " The cold is sent by your rival. Betake you at once to a fire, that you may not perish."

The next day at noon they met, as had been previously arranged. Poliahu put on her sun mantle, and a scorching heat almost consumed her rival. Again they met, but were unable to remain together, and Hinaikamalama unceremoniously left Kauai, without even touching noses with Aiwohikupua.

Before she left for Maui, however, a *kilu* game was arranged at Puuapapai, and Hauailiki, still mindful of his success at Mana, endeavored to secure the fruits of his victory. But Hinaikamalama refused to yield, unless the victor would come to Hana in proper state and formally make her his wife.

During the game Poliahu and her companions appeared in glittering robes of snow and chilled the assemblage, and the next morning they returned to Mauna Kea, while Hinaikamalama set sail for Hana.

III.

The king and queen of Kauai both dying a short time after the events just before recorded, they left the sovereignty of the island to their son, Kekalukaluokewa. They also left in his charge a magical bamboo (*ohe*) called Kanikawi, and enjoined upon him a promise to seek out and marry Laieikawai, of whom many reports had reached Kauai.

The new king ordered an immense fleet of canoes for his trip to Hawaii, and sailed in the month of *Mahoemua*, or August. At Makahanaloa he saw the rainbow over Keaau, and sailed thither. Waka foresaw his coming and advised Laieikawai to marry him and become the queen of a whole island.

After waiting four days Laieikawai and her *kahu*, the hunch-back, went down to Keaau, and watched the king and his two favorite companions sporting in the surf. They knew the king by his not carrying his own surf-board when he landed. She returned to Paliuli and informed Waka that she would accept him for a husband.

Waka then arranged that Kekalukaluokewa should go at sunrise the next morning and play in the surf alone ; that a dense fog should settle down, under cover of which Laieikawai would join him in the surf ; that when the fog raised the two would be seen by all riding in together on the same roller, and then they were to touch noses. A fog would again envelop them, and then birds would bear the pair to Paliuli. She was forbidden to speak to any one after leaving the house.

Now, it appears that Halaaniani, a young man of Puna, noted

for his debaucheries, had often seen Laieikawai at Keaau, and ardently longed to possess her. Learning that she was about to marry the king of Kauai, he implored his sister, Malio, to exert her magical powers in his behalf. She consented, and by her direction they both went to sleep, and when they awoke related to each other their dreams. She dreamed that she saw a bird building a nest and leaving it in the possession of another, which was a sure omen in favor of Halaaniani. Malio declared that her magic powers would prevail over those of Waka, and gave her brother minute instructions, which he strictly observed, as will appear.

They went to the beach and saw Kekalukaluokewa swimming alone in the surf. Soon the fog of Waka settled down on the land. A clap of thunder was heard as Laieikawai reached the surf. A second peal resounded, invoked by Malio. The fog lifted, and three persons instead of two were seen in the surf. This was noted with surprise on shore.

When the first roller came the king said, "Let us go ashore," and he rode in on the breaker with Laieikawai, while Halaaniani remained behind. At that moment the king and his companion touched noses. Three times they rode in on the waves, while Halaaniani, as directed by his sister, remained outside among the rollers.

The fourth time Laieikawai asked the king why he desired to repeat the sport so often. "Because," said he, "I am not used to the short surf; I prefer to ride on the long rollers." The fifth was to be the last time for the Kauai king and his promised bride.

As soon as the two started for the shore Halaaniani seized Laieikawai by the feet and held her back, so that the surf-board slipped from her grasp, and Kekalukaluokewa was borne to the shore without her. She complained of the loss of her surf-board, and it was restored to her.

Halaaniani persuaded her to swim farther out to sea with him, telling her not to look back, as he would let her know when they reached *his* surf. After swimming for some time she remonstrated, but he induced her to continue on with him. At last he told her to look back.

"Why," said she, in amazement, "the land is out of sight, and Kumukahi, the sea-god, has come to stir the waves!"

" This is the surf of which I told you," he replied ; " we will wait and go in on the third roller. Do not in any case let go of your surf-board."

Then he prayed to his patron deity, and the breakers began to rise. As the third came thundering on, he exclaimed, " *Pae kaua !* " and, mounting the roller, they started for the shore. Laieikawai was in the overhanging arch of the wave, and, looking up, saw Halaaniani poised with great skill on the crest. At that moment she began to yield to the seductive fascination of Halaaniani.

As they came in, Waka supposed her companion to be Kekalukaluokewa, and she sent down the birds in the fog ; and when it cleared away Laieikawai and Halaaniani were occupants of the feather-house at Paliuli, where their union was consummated.

Waka wondered why her granddaughter did not come to her that night or the next day, as had been promised, and the day following she went to the house to learn if anything serious had happened. Laieikawai and her husband were sleeping soundly. Waka was enraged, for the man was not the one she had selected.

Waking her granddaughter and pointing to the man, she exclaimed, " Who is this ? "

" Kekalukaluokewa," was the answer.

" No," returned Waka ; " this is Halaaniani, the brother of Malio ! "

Angered at the deception, Waka declared that she would deprive Laieikawai of her powers and privileges, and desired never to behold her face again.

Abandoning Laieikawai, Waka resolved to assume the charge of her twin-sister, Laielohelohe, and wed her to the king of Kauai. She had been left, it will be remembered, with the priest of Kukaniloko, on the island of Oahu. To this end Waka had a new house erected, and, borrowing a double canoe from Kekalukaluokewa, sailed at once for Oahu.

Arriving at Kukaniloko, she offered a pig as a propitiation, and explained her errand to Kapukaihaoa, who approved her plans and delivered Laielohelohe into her charge.

After an absence of thirty-three days Waka returned to Keaau with the sister of Laieikawai. At her command the fog gathered, and they were secretly borne by birds to their new

house at Paliuli. Within three days she had a consultation with
Kekalukaluokewa in relation to his marriage with Laielohelohe.
She directed him to build a large *kilu* shed, and there assemble
the people of the district, that the ceremony might be celebrated
with becoming pomp.

Meanwhile, Halaaniani had seen Laielohelohe, and determined
to secure her for himself. With this object he persuaded Laieikawai to go down to Keaau with him for a few days of sea-
bathing, leaving her faithful attendants behind. Arriving there,
he told her that he was about to visit his sister, Malio, and if he
did not return in two days she might consider him dead.

On the twelfth day the five sisters went down to Keaau and
joined their mistress in wailing over her husband, whom she believed to be dead. Soon after they all had dreams of Halaaniani
with another woman, and concluded to cease their mourning and
return to Paliuli.

Halaaniani visited his sister and induced her to assist him in
his designs concerning Laielohelohe. She advised him to watch
her for four days, and report his observations. He did so, and
reported that her chief occupation was stringing *lehua* flowers ;
and he climbed a tree to observe her, while his sister sounded the
pulai, or *ti*-leaf trumpet, five times, and again five times ; but
Laielohelohe did not take the slightest notice of it.

The next morning they went there again, and he climbed a
tree with a mass of *lehua* blossoms, and threw them down before
her, while his sister played the *hano*, a sweet-toned wind instrument. This attracted the attention of Laielohelohe, and, without
seeing the musician, she expressed her thanks.

The morning following they repeated these manœuvres three
times. Then Laielohelohe spoke and said : " If the musician
is a woman, let us touch noses."

With this Malio showed herself, and proposed that she should
touch noses with her brother first. This angered her, and she
ordered both of them to leave.

Malio admitted her failure, but promised to resort to supernatural agencies, and win Laielohelohe for her brother on her
wedding-day, as had been done with Laieikawai.

About this time Waka went down to communicate to Kekalukaluokewa her programme for the marriage ceremonies, fixed for
the day following. He was to order the people and his court to

assemble at the appointed place, and at noon was to retire to his own house. She would then cover the land with a thick mist, and the singing of birds would be heard ; first the quack of the *alae* and the chirruping of *ewaewaiki*, on hearing which he would step without the house. Next he would hear the singing of the *oo*, which would indicate that she was about to send to him Laie-lohelohe. Then would be heard the notes of the *iiwipolena*, and his bride would be near him. Lastly, he would hear the singing of the *ka'huli*, and they would meet apart from the assemblage, when thunder would peal, the earth would quake, and the people would tremble. Then the two would be borne upward by birds, the mist would clear away, and they would be seen resting upon the birds in glory.

Laieikawai and the five sisters were anxious to witness the coming display, of which they had heard, and Kahalaomapuana engaged the *moo* god, Kihanuilulumoku, to convey them thither at the appointed time.

Malio assured her brother again that her power would prevail over the efforts of Waka, and the preliminaries of the ceremony began. At noon Kekalukaluokewa, dressed as became the occasion, entered his house, as had been arranged. He heard the singing of birds, came forth in the fog, and awaited the coming of his bride. A clap of thunder followed, when the fog lifted, and Laielohelohe and Halaaniani were seen rising in the air on the wings of birds. Laieikawai and her attendants witnessed the ascension, sitting on the tongue of the great *moo*.

Believing that he had again lost his bride, Kekalukaluokewa sought Waka, to chide her for the failure. " She is not his yet," said Waka, " for she has obeyed my command not to speak to or touch noses with him " ; and, to reassure the king, she offered to stake her life that all would yet be well.

As they approached the place of assembly Waka again enveloped it in fog, and immediately sent Kekalukaluokewa upward in the air on the wings of birds. When the fog cleared away, Kekalukaluokewa and Laielohelohe were beheld sitting together, upborne by birds, and the multitude shouted, " *Hoao na 'lii ! e !* " (" the chiefs are married ! ")

When Waka heard these acclamations she appeared before the congregation and denounced Laieikawai in the most oppro-brious terms. The latter departed in shame and rage, and was carried by the *moo*, together with the five sisters, to Olaa, where she took up her residence.

Halaaniani's misdemeanors finally brought him into great contempt, and he was despised and condemned by all. The Kauai king returned home with his bride, taking with him Waka. On their way they stopped at Oahu to take on board the priest Kapukaihaoa, who became the prime minister of Kauai.

IV.

The sisters of Aiwohikupua, chagrined at what had befallen their mistress, resolved to send Kahalaomapuana to Kealohilani, in a far-distant land, to bring their brother, Kaonohiokala, to marry Laieikawai, in order that she might triumph over Waka.

Accordingly, she started on her voyage, being carried by the gigantic *moo* god, Kihanuilulumoku. Meantime, Laieikawai and her train made a pleasure trip around Hawaii, first to Kau, then to Kona, and next to Kohala.

Becoming discouraged, the old prophet of Kauai had left Kaiwilahilahi, Hawaii, and started for his native island. Touching at Waimea, he saw the well-known rainbow over Kaiopae, a half-hour's journey north of Kawaihae, and followed it to Moolau, and then to Puakea, in Kohala, where he finally met and conversed with Laieikawai.

He procured a double canoe for the party, and they sailed together to Laie, Oahu, where he learned the history of Laieikawai. That night his guardian deity informed him in a dream that she was the person he had been seeking for so long, and directed him to take the party to Haena, Kauai. In the morning he offered a pig and fowl before her, and obtained her consent for him to become her guardian. They then sailed for Kauai, and settled at Honopuwaiakua.

In one of his subsequent tours the prophet found, on arriving at Wailua, that all the virgin daughters of the petty chiefs and courtiers on Kauai had been collected there, in order that Aiwohikupua might select two new wives to take the places of Poliahu and Hinaikamalama.

The prophet spoke so contemptuously of the girls brought there for inspection, and boasted so loudly of the beauty and graces of his adopted daughter, that a quarrel arose and he was

thrown into prison. He escaped during the night, however, and
it was reported to the chief that he was dead. He had left a
banana trunk wrapped in cloth, and it was offered on the altar
of the *heiau* in the place of his body.

At the moment when the deception was discovered the prophet made his appearance on the platform of a double canoe at
the mouth of the river, with Laieikawai and the five sisters on
board Then Laieikawai stepped upon the platform, surrounded with the insignia of a *tabu* chief, and the winds ceased, the
sea rose, thunders reverberated, lightnings flashed, and the *heiau*
and altar were shaken almost to ruins.

The assembled multitude shouted in admiration of the
beauty of Laieikawai, and Aiwohikupua, after recovering from
the shock of what he had witnessed, sent a herald to demand her
in marriage. But the prophet proudly answered that she was
not for such as he, and would marry no one of lower rank than
the sovereign of an island. They then returned to Honopuwaiakua.

We will now return to Kahalaomapuana, who was sent to a
far-distant land in search of her brother, in the hope of making
him the husband of Laieikawai. For four months the great *moo*
swam with her in his mouth, and they arrived at last at Kealohilani. But the guardian of the place was absent on a visit to the
Moon, and they awaited his return for twenty days.

On his arrival he was greatly alarmed at the sight of the gigantic reptile, lying with his head in the house and his tail in the
sea, and without a word flew to Nuumealani to consult Kaeloikamalama, the powerful *kupua*, who shut the door of the *pea kapu*
of the *Kukulu o Kahiki*, where Kaonohiokala was concealed.

They returned together, the *kupua* armed with a *laau palau* a
hundred paces long with which to slay the *moo*. Just as he was
preparing to strike, the *moo* stirred his tail in the ocean and sent
a tremendous breaker rolling inland, and they both started to
retreat. At that moment the *moo* cast out Kahalaomapuana on
the neck of her uncle, Kaeloikamalama. He asked her who she
was and the object of her visit, which she explained, and also
their relationship. Then both embraced her affectionately, for
they were brothers of her mother.

In furtherance of the purposes of her visit, Kaeloikamalama
took his niece with him on a ten days' journey to the place of

ascent, where he called upon Lanalananuiaimakua to let down the ladder. Before long a sort of spider's web, branching through the air, descended. He then gave his niece full directions, as follows : " Here is your way to ascend until you see a single house standing in the Moon, in the land of Kahakaekaea, where dwells Moanalihaikawaokele, your father, an old man with long hair and bent head. If he is awake do not approach him, lest he see you first, and you die before you have a chance to speak. Wait until he is asleep on his back ; then cautiously approach from the leeward, spring on his breast, grasp him tightly by the beard, and chant the *mele* in which I will instruct you." Instructing her in the *mele*, he continued : " Explain to him the object of your visit, and all will be well." She was about to begin the ascent when he imparted this final information : " In ascending, if fine rain falls and you are chilly, fear not ; it is caused by your father. Climb on, and, should you smell fragrance, know that it is caused by your mother and that you are approaching the end of your journey. If the sunbeams pierce you and the heat beats upon your head, do not fear. Persevere, and you will enter the shelter of the Moon and be safe in Kahakaekaea."

With these instructions she boldly began the ascent. Climbing upward without ceasing, toward evening she encountered fine rain and mist ; early next morning she smelt the fragrance of the shrub *kiele ;* at midday she suffered from the heat of the sun, and in the evening entered the cool shade of the Moon, in the land of Kahakaekaea.

Observing a large house standing alone, she proceeded to the lee side, and waited until the old man fell asleep on his back. She then grasped his beard and chanted the *mele*, as instructed by her uncle. He awoke, but she held him where lay his strength, and his struggles were vain. He asked her who she was, and about her relatives, and her answers were satisfactory. She then let go his beard and he took her on his knee and wailed over her.

He then inquired the object of her visit, and she related the whole story. He informed her that it was not within his power to grant her request, and that she must apply to her mother, who lived with her son, Kaonohiokala, in a sacred, inaccessible place, and only visited Kahakaekaea once every month.

By stratagem she obtained an interview with her mother, Laukieleula, and after great persuasion secured her assistance in advancing the purposes of her visit. The old woman then summoned the bird-god, Haluluikekihiokamalama, to take them up into the *pea kapu* of the *Kukulu o Kahiki*. The bird reached down a wing, upon which they both mounted and were carried to Awakea (noon), the god who opens the gate of the Sun, where dwelt Kaonohiokala (the eye-ball of the sun).

They found the place shut in by thunder-clouds. They called upon Awakea, who rose with intense heat and dispersed the clouds, disclosing to their view the prince asleep in the very centre of the Sun, where the air was white with heat. He awoke. His eyes were like lightning, and his body gleamed like molten lava.

Laukieleula called to him and said : "Your favorite sister is here." He looked up, and then summoned the guardians of the shade to appear and stand before him. This they promptly did, and the heat of the sun was mitigated. His resting-place being thus shaded, he called his sister to him and wailed over her, for they had been separated for a long time. He inquired the object of her visit, and about their sisters, and brother Aiwohikupua, and was interested in all that related to them.

Through the advice of his mother he consented to descend and marry Laieikawai, and the signs of his coming, he explained, would be as follows : First, there would be a heavy rain and high surf before he started. Next, there would be strong wind for ten days, followed by thunder without rain ; then he would be in Kahakaekaea. When it thundered again twice he would be at Nuumealani, and when it thundered thrice he would be in Kealohilani. There he would lay aside his *tabu* supernatural form and assume the human shape as a high chief. After this there would be many portents, such as thunder, lightning, rain, fog, rainbows, high seas and mist on the ocean, and in one month thereafter he would appear on the mountain ridge at dawn. When the sun rose a halo would surround him, and in the evening, when the full moon rose in the night of *Mahealani*, he would appear and marry Laieikawai. After this he would punish the enemies of his sisters and his bride. As a token he gave to his sister for Laieikawai a rainbow-robe.

Kahalaomapuana was a month in returning to Kealohilani,

where she found the *moo* in waiting for her. He swam with her across the great waters to Hawaii, but, not finding their friends at Olaa, he hunted all through the islands, like a dog scenting for his master, until he found them at Honopuwaiakua, Kauai. The whole trip occupied eleven months and fourteen days.

Kahalaomapuana gave her friends a full history of her extraordinary journey, to the dismay of Laieikawai, who was awed at the thought of her intended husband. The prophet, who knew nothing of the mission of the sister until her return, had predicted the coming of Kaonohiokala a month before ; and now he traveled around the island warning the people, and advising Aiwohikupua, in particular, to set up *tabu* flags all around his place and collect his family within the precinct ; but he was repelled with insult. He gave the same advice to Kekalukaluokewa, who obeyed it in spite of the opposition of Waka.

Ten days after the return of Kahalaomapuana the portents began to appear in the order already named, and in due time Kaonohiokala appeared, surrounded by a halo. Shouts of acclamation and homage were heard throughout the island, and Laieikawai put on her rainbow robe.

In the evening, as the full moon rose, the prince descended from the mountain and came within the circle of the prophet, and they all prostrated themselves before him. He spoke graciously to them, and told Laieikawai that he had come to make good the promise made to her through his sister. Then all shouted, "*Amana! ua noa, lele wale aku la !*"

A rainbow appeared, and on it the prince and his bride were suddenly drawn upward to the moon. A few nights after, as the moon was directly overhead, a rainbow was let down like a ladder, on which they descended. Summoning the prophet, the prince directed him to travel around the island and make proclamation for all to assemble at the end of ten days at Pihanakalani. The five sisters, and afterwards the prophet, were taken up to dwell in the coolness of the moon.

One morning the assemblage at Pihanakalani saw the rainbow again let down from the moon, and standing upon it were the prince and his bride, the five sisters and the prophet.

Vengeance was executed upon Waka, who was killed by a thunderbolt, and upon Aiwohikupua, who was reduced to poverty and contempt. Laielohelohe and Kekalukaluokewa were retained in favor under Kahalaomapuana, who was designated as the regent of her brother, and the four other sisters were made the governesses of the rest of the islands of the group.

The affairs of state being thus summarily settled, Kaonohiokala again departed with his bride up the rainbow beyond the clouds, to dwell in the *pea kapu o Kukulu o Kahiki*, above the land called Kahakaekaea.

V.

Kaonohiokala made quarterly visits to his earthly dominions, to see that all went well with their rulers. Laielohelohe had grown more beautiful than her sister, and he became enamored of her.

To promote his designs he made Kahalaomapuana joint regent with Mokukelekahiki in Kealohilani, and appointed Kekalukaluokewa to the regency of the entire group. He then requested the regent to make a tour of the islands, leaving Laielohelohe at Pihanakalani. He next applied to her guardian, Kapukaihaoa, and gained his consent to aid in her seduction.

After Kaonohiokala had made two more trips to earth in furtherance of this intrigue, Laielohelohe resolved to seek her husband, and set sail, accordingly, for the windward islands. She found him at Honokalani, Maui, engaged in an amour with Hinaikamalama, the Hana chiefess who had abandoned Aiwohikupua. After unavailing efforts to reclaim him she returned to Kauai.

Kaonohiokala then renewed his visits, and at last remained a year with the deserted wife. The forsaken Laieikawai appealed to her father-in-law, who directed her to go to the *tabu heiau* when old Laukieleula was asleep, and consult the bowl of knowledge. It was a wooden bowl, covered with wicker-work, the edge of the lid being decorated with feathers, and with carved images of birds standing on the rim. She was to remove the lid, insert her face in the bowl, and call "Laukapalili!" to give her the knowledge she required.

She followed these directions and saw what her husband was doing on earth. His father and mother also looked, and observed for themselves the treachery of their son. Straightway the ladder was let down to the presence of Kaonohiokala. The sky was darkened and filled with uncanny forms, and ghastly voices wailed through the air, " *Ua haule ka lani !* "—" the heaven has fallen ! "

Then the three were seen standing together upon the rainbow ladder, and Moanalihaikawaokele proceeded to pronounce judgment on Kaonohiokala. He was never to return to the upper world, and was doomed to become a *lapu*—a spectre or wandering ghost—and live on butterflies.

Kahalaomapuana took his place in the sun. Laieikawai, at her earnest request, was restored to earth to live with her sister, and the government of the group was entrusted to the prophet.

Laieikawai had her name changed to *Ka wahine o ka liula*—" the lady of the twilight "—under which title she was worshipped by certain families after her death.

LOHIAU, THE LOVER OF A GODDESS.

CHARACTERS.

PELE, the goddess of the volcanoes.

HIIAKA, one of the sisters of Pele.

HOPOE, a friend of Hiiaka.

PAUO-PALAE and
OMEO, } traveling companions of Hiiaka.

LONOIKAONOLII, one of the brothers of Pele.

LOHIAU, a prince of Kauai.

PAOA, a chief of Kauai.

MILU, king of the regions of death.

KANEMILOHAI, a god from Kahiki.

KALAMAINU and
KILEOA, } female demons of Kauai.

OLEPAU, king of Maui.

WAIHIMANO, queen of Maui.

LOHIAU, THE LOVER OF A GODDESS.

THE LEGEND OF HIIAKA, THE IMMORTAL, AND THE PRINCE OF KAUAI.

I.

OF all the legends of the adventures with mortals of Pele, the dreadful goddess of the volcanoes, the most weird and dramatic is the one relating to her love for Lohiau, a prince of the island of Kauai, whose reign was probably contemporaneous with that of Kealiiokaloa, of Hawaii, during the early part of the sixteenth century. The story is not only a characteristic relic of the recklessly imaginative and highly-colored *meles* of the early poets, but an instructive reflex as well of the superstitions controlling the popular mind of the Hawaiian group at that period, when the forests abounded in mischievous gnomes and fairies, when the streams were guarded by nymphs and monsters, and when the very air was peopled with the spirits of the departed. But a thin veil then divided the living from the dead, the natural from the supernatural, and mortals were made the sport of the elements and the playthings of the gods.

As the *mele* relates, Pele and her brothers and sisters, to amuse themselves with a taste of mortal enjoyments, one day emerged from their fiery chambers in the crater of Kilauea, and went down to the coast of Puna to bathe, surf-ride, sport in the sands, and gather edible sea-weed, squid, limpets and other delicacies washed by the waves. They assumed human forms for the occasion, and therefore had human appetites.

While the others were amusing themselves in various ways— eating, laughing and sporting in the waves in the manner of mortals—Pele, in the guise of an old woman, sought repose and sleep in the shade of a *hala* tree. Her favorite sister was Hiiaka, her full name being Hiiaka-ika-pali-opele. She was younger than Pele, and frequently occupied the same grotto with her under the burning lake of Kilauea.

Hiiaka accompanied her sovereign sister to the shade of the *hala* tree, and, sitting devotedly beside her, kept her cool with a *kahili*. Her eyelids growing heavy, Pele instructed Hiiaka to allow her under no circumstances to be disturbed, no matter how long she might sleep, whether for hours or days, and then closed her eyes in slumber.

Scarcely had the ears of the sleeper been closed by the fingers of silence before she heard the sound of a drum—distant, but distinct and regular in its beat, as if to the impulse of music. Before leaving the crater she had heard the same sound, but paid little attention to it. Now, however, when hearing it in her dreams, her curiosity was aroused, and, assuming her spiritual form, she resolved to follow it.

Leaving her slumbering earthly body under the eye and care of her sister, Pele mounted the air and proceeded in the direction whence the sound seemed to come. From place to place she followed it over the island of Hawaii; but it was always before her, and she could not overtake it. At Upolu it came to her from over the sea, and she followed it to the island of Maui. It was still beyond, and she sped to Molokai; still beyond, and she flew to Oahu; still beyond, and she crossed the channel and listened on the shores of Kauai, where it was more distinct than she had heard it before. Now encouraged, she continued the pursuit until she stood upon the mountain peak of Haupu, when she discovered at last that the sound came from the beach at Kaena.

Proceeding thither, and hovering over the place unseen, she observed that the sound she had so long been following was that of a *pahu-hula*, or *hula* drum, beaten by Lohiau, the young and comely prince of Kauai, who was noted not only for the splendor of his *hula* entertainments, participated in by the most beautiful women of the island, but for his personal graces as a dancer and musician. The favorite deity of Lohiau was *Lakakane*, the god of the *hula* and similar sports, who in a spirit of mischief had conveyed the sound of the drum to the ears of Pele.

The beach was thronged with dancers, musicians and spectators, all enjoying themselves under the shade of the *hala* and cocoa trees, with the prince as master of ceremonies and the centre of attraction. Assuming the form of a beautiful woman, Pele suddenly appeared before the festive throng. Attaching to her person every imaginable charm of form and feature, her presence was immediately noted ; and, a way being opened for her to the prince, he received her most graciously and invited her to a seat near him, where she could best witness the entertainment.

Glancing at the beautiful stranger from time to time in the midst of his performances, Lohiau at length became so fascinated that he failed to follow the music, when he yielded the instrument to another and seated himself beside the enchantress. In answer to his inquiry she informed the prince that she was a stranger in Kauai, and had come from the direction of the rising sun. Gazing into her face with a devouring passion, Lohiau smilingly said :

"You are most welcome, but I cannot rejoice that you came."

"And why, since I do not come as your enemy ?" inquired Pele, archly.

"Because, until now," returned the prince, "my thought has been that there were beautiful women in Kauai ; but in looking at yours I find their faces are plain indeed."

"I see you know how to speak flattering words to women," said Pele, casting a languishing look upon the prince.

"Not better than I know how to love them," replied Lohiau, with ardor. "Will you be convinced ?"

"Lohiau is in his own kingdom, and has but to command," answered Pele, with a play of modesty which completed the enthralment of the prince.

Thus Pele became the wife of Lohiau. He knew nothing of her or her family, and cared not to inquire. He saw only that she was beautiful above all women, and for a few days they lived so happily together that life seemed to be a dream to him. And Pele loved the prince scarcely less than he loved her ; but the time had come for her return to Hawaii, and, pledging him to remain true to her, she left him with protestations of affection and the promise of a speedy return, and on the wings of the wind was wafted back to the shores of Puna, where she had left her sister waiting and watching in the shade of the *hala*.

Lohiau was inconsolable. Every day he thought she would be with him the next, until more than a month passed, when he refused food and died of grief at her absence. The strange death of the prince occasioned much comment, for he was naturally strong and without disease. Some said he had been prayed to death by his enemies, and others that he had been poisoned ; but an old *kaula*, who had seen Pele at Kaena and noted her actions, advised against further inquiry concerning the cause of Lohiau's death, offering as a reason the opinion that the strangely beautiful and unknown woman he had taken as a wife was an immortal, who had become attached to her earthly husband and called his spirit to her.

The prince was greatly beloved by his people, and his body, carefully wrapped in many folds of *kapa*, was kept in state for some time in the royal mansion. It was guarded by the high chiefs of the kingdom, and every night funeral hymns were chanted around it, and *meles* recited of the deeds of the dead sovereign and his ancestors. Thus lying in state we will leave the remains of Lohiau, and follow Pele back to Hawaii.

II.

During all the time the spirit of Pele was absent the family kept watch over the body left by her under the *hala* tree, not daring to disturb it, and were overjoyed when it was at last re-animated, for the fires of the crater of Kilauea had nearly died out from neglect. Pele rose to her feet in the form of the old woman she had left asleep under the care of Hiiaka, and, without at the time mentioning her adventures in Kauai or the cause of her protracted slumber, returned with all but one of the family to Kilauea, and with a breath renewed the dying fires of the crater. Hiiaka asked and received the permission of Pele to remain for a few days at the beach with her much-loved friend Hopoe, a young woman of Puna, who had been left an orphan by an irruption from Kilauea, in which both of her parents had perished.

On leaving Kauai it is probable that Pele, notwithstanding her fervent words to the contrary, never expected or particularly desired to see Lohiau again ; but he had so endeared himself to her during their brief union that she did not find it easy to forget him, and, after struggling with the feeling for some time, she resolved to send for him. But to whom should she entrust the important mission ? One after another she applied to her sisters at the crater, but the way was beset with evil spirits, and they refused to go.

In this dilemma Pele sent her favorite brother, Lonoikaonolii, to bring Hiiaka from the beach, well knowing that she would not refuse to undertake the journey, however hazardous. Hiiaka accepted the mission, with the understanding that during her absence her friend Hopoe should be kept under the eye and guardianship of Pele.

Arrangements were made for the immediate departure of Hiiaka. Pele conferred upon her some of her own powers, with an injunction to use them discreetly, and for a companion and servant gave her Pauo-palae, a woman of approved sagacity and prudence.

With a farewell from her relatives and many an admonition from Pele, Hiiaka took her departure for Kauai, accompanied by Pauo-palae. They traveled as mortals, and were therefore subject to the fatigues and perils of humanity. Proceeding through the forests toward the coast of Hilo, they encountered an old woman, who accosted them politely and expressed a desire to follow them. Her name was Omeo, and she was leading a hog to the volcano as a sacrifice to Pele. No objection being made, she hurried to the crater with her offering, and returned and followed Hiiaka and her companion.

Not long after, their journey was impeded by a demon of hideous proportions, who threw himself across their path in a narrow defile and attempted to destroy them. Pele knew their danger, however, and ordered her brothers to protect them with a rain of fire and thunder, which drove the monster to his den in the hills and enabled them to escape.

After a little time they were joined by another woman, whose name was Papau. She desired to accompany them, and proceeded a short distance on the way, when they were confronted by a ferocious-looking man who was either insane or under the influence of evil spirits. He lacked either the power or the disposition to molest the party, however, and they passed on unharmed ; but Papau screamed with fright and hastily returned to her home, where she was turned into a stone as a punishment for her cowardice.

Coming to a small stream crossed by their path, they found the waters dammed by a huge *moo*, or lizard, lying in the bed. He was more than a hundred paces in length, and his eyes were of the size of great calabashes. He glared at the party viciously and opened his mouth as if to devour them ; but Hiiaka tossed into it a stone, which became red-hot when it touched his throat, and, with a roar of pain which made the leaves of the trees tremble, he disappeared down the stream.

After many other adventures with monsters and evil spirits, which Hiiaka was able to control and sometimes punish, the party reached the coast at a place called Honoipo, where they found a number of men and women engaged in the sport of surf-riding. As they were about to start for another trial, in a spirit of mischief Hiiaka turned their surf-boards into stone, and they fled in terror from the beach, fearing that some sea-god was preparing to devour them.

Observing a fisherman drawing in his line, Hiiaka caused to be fastened to the submerged hook a human head. Raising it to the surface, the man stared at it for a moment with horror, then dropped the line and paddled swiftly away, to the great amusement of Hiiaka and her companions.

Embarking in a canoe with two men as assistants, the travelers sailed for the island of Maui, which they reached without delay or accident. Landing at Kaupo, they traveled overland toward Honuaula, near which place, in approaching the palace of the king, whose name was Olepau, and who was lying within at the point of death, Hiiaka observed a human spirit hovering around the outer enclosure. Knowing that it was the half-freed soul or spirit of the *moi*, she seized and tied it up in a corner of her *pau*.

Passing on with the soul of the king in her keeping, she met the queen, Waihimano, and told her that her husband had just died. But the queen denied that Olepau was dead, for she was a worshipper of two powerful lizard divinities, and the gods had assured her that morning that her husband would recover.

Saying no more, Hiiaka and her companions went on their way, and the queen, returning to the palace, found her husband insensible and apparently dead. Trying in vain to restore him, she hastily consulted a *kaula*, telling him what the strange woman had said to her. The seer by the description recognized at once the sister of Pele, who had come to heal the king, but had been deterred in her errand of mercy by the queen's obstinate assurances of his recovery. He therefore advised that she be followed by a messenger with a spotless pig to be placed as an offering in the path before her, when she perchance might return and restore the king to life. But Hiiaka dropped behind her companions and assumed the form of an old woman, and, as the messenger did not recognize her, he returned with the report that the object of his search could not be found.

"Did you meet no one?" inquired the seer.

"No one answering the description," replied the messenger. "I saw only an old woman, so infirm as to be scarcely able to walk."

"Fool!" exclaimed the *kaula*. "That old woman was Hiiaka in disguise. Hasten back to her, if you would save the life of your king!"

The messenger again started in pursuit of Hiiaka, but the pig was obstinate and troublesome, and his progress was slow. Seizing the struggling animal in his arms, the messenger ran until he came within sight of the women, who were again traveling together, when Hiiaka struck the fold of her *pau* against a rock, and that instant the king expired.

Reaching the coast and embarking with a fisherman, Hiiaka and her companions sailed for Oahu. Landing at Makapuu, they journeyed overland to Kou—now Honolulu—and from Haena made sail for Kauai. Arriving at Kaena, Hiiaka saw the spirit hand of Lohiau beckoning to her from the mouth of a cave among the cliffs. Turning to her companions, she said:

"We have failed; the lover of Pele is dead! I see his spirit beckoning from the *pali!* There it is being held and hidden by the lizard-women, Kilioa and Kalamainu."

Instructing her companions to proceed to Puoa, where the body of Lohiau was lying in state, Hiiaka started at once for the *pali*, for the purpose of giving battle to the female demons and rescuing the spirit of the dead prince.

Ascending the cliff and entering the cave, Hiiaka waved her *pau*, and with angry hisses the demons disappeared. Search was made, and the spirit of Lohiau was found at last in a niche in the rocks, where it had been placed by a moonbeam. Taking it tenderly in her hand, she enclosed it in a fold of her *pau*, and in an invisible form floated down with it to Puoa.

Waiting until after nightfall, Hiiaka entered the chamber of death unseen, and restored the spirit to the body of Lohiau. Recovering his life and consciousness, the prince looked around with amazement. The guards were frightened when he raised his head, and would have fled in alarm had they not been prevented by Hiiaka, who at that instant appeared before them in mortal form. Holding up her hand, as if to command obedience, she said :

"Fear nothing, say nothing of this to any one living, and do nothing except as you may be ordered. The prince has returned to life, and may recover if properly cared for. His body is weak and wasted. Let him be secretly and at once removed to the sea-shore. The night is dark, and it may be done without observation."

Not doubting that these instructions were from the gods, the guards obeyed them with so much prudence and alacrity that Lohiau was soon comfortably resting in a hut by the sea-shore, with Hiiaka and her companions ministering to his wants.

The return of the prince to health and strength was rapid, and in a few days he reappeared among his friends, to their amazement and great joy. In answer to their inquiries he informed them that he owed to the gods his restoration to life. This did not entirely satisfy them, but no further explanation was offered.

After celebrating his recovery with feasts and sacrifices to the gods, Lohiau announced to the chiefs of his kingdom that he was about to visit his wife, whose home was on Hawaii, and that he should leave the government of the island in the hands of his friend, the high-chief Paoa, to whom he enjoined the fealty and respect of all during his absence.

In a magnificent double canoe, bearing the royal standard and equipped as became the *kaulua* of an *alii-nui*, Lohiau set sail for Hawaii, accompanied by Hiiaka and her companions, and taking with him his high-priest, chief navigator, and the customary staff of personal attendants.

Touching at Oahu, Hiiaka ascended the Kaala mountains, and saw that her beautiful *lehua* and *hala* groves near the beach of Puna, on the distant island of Hawaii, had been destroyed by a lava flow. Impatient at the long absence of Hiiaka, and jealous as well, Pele had in a fit of rage destroyed the beautiful sea-shore retreats of her faithful sister. She scarcely doubted that Hiiaka had dared to love Lohiau, and in her chambers of fire chafed for her return.

After bewailing her loss Hiiaka rejoined her companions, and Lohiau embarked for Hawaii. Landing at Kohala, the prince ordered his attendants to remain there until his return, and started overland for Kilauea with Hiiaka and her two female companions. Before reaching the volcano Hiiaka learned something of the jealous rage of Pele, and finally saw from a distant eminence her dear friend Hopoe undergoing the cruel tortures of volcanic fire, near the beach of Puna, which ended in her being turned into stone.

Approaching the crater with apprehensions of further displays of Pele's fury, Hiiaka sent Omeo and Pauo-palae in advance to announce to the goddess her return with Lohiau. In her wrath she ordered both of the women to be slain at once, and resolved to treat her lover in the same manner.

Aware of this heartless resolution, and unable to avert the execution of it, on their arrival at the verge of the crater Hiiaka threw her arms around the neck of the prince, whom she had learned to love without wrong to her sister, and, telling him of his impending fate, bade him a tender farewell.

This scene was witnessed by Pele. Enraged beyond measure, she caused a gulf of molten lava to be opened between Hiiaka and the prince, and then ordered the instant destruction of Lohiau by fire.

While the sisters of Pele were ascending the walls of the crater to execute her orders, Lohiau chanted a song to the goddess, avowing his innocence and pleading for mercy ; but her rage was rekindled at the sound of his voice, and she turned a deaf ear to his entreaties.

Approaching Lohiau, and pitying him, the sisters merely touched the palms of his hands, which turned them into lava, and then retired. Observing this, Pele ordered them to return at once, under the penalty of her displeasure, and consume the body of her lover.

Lohiau again appealed to Pele, so piteously that the trees around him wept with grief; but her only answer was an impatient signal to her sisters to resume their work of destruction. In his despair he turned to Hiiaka and implored her intercession, but she answered in agony that she could do nothing.

The sisters returned to Lohiau, and reluctantly touched his feet, which became stone ; then his knees ; then his thighs ; then his breast. By the power conferred upon her by Pele, and of which she had not yet been deprived, Hiiaka rendered the body of the prince insensible to pain, and it was therefore without suffering that he felt his joints hardening into stone under the touch of his sympathizing executioners.

As the remainder of his body was about to be turned into lava, Hiiaka said to the prince :

" Listen !   When you die go to the leeward, and I will find you ! "

The next moment Lohiau was a lifeless pillar of stone.

Observing that the cruel work of her sister had been accomplished, and that all that remained of the shapely form of Lohiau was a black mass of lava, Hiiaka caused the earth to be opened at her feet, and started downward at once for the misty realm of *Milu* to overtake the soul of Lohiau, and, with the consent of the god of death, restore it to its body.

Passing downward through each of the five spheres dividing the surface of the earth from the regions of *Po*, where *Milu* sits in state in the gloomy groves of death, Hiiaka finally stood in the presence of the august sovereign of the world of spirits.

The king of death welcomed her to his dominions, and, in response to her inquiry, informed her that the soul of Lohiau had not yet reached the abode of spirits. Having no desire to return to earth, Hiiaka accepted the invitation of *Milu*, and, watching and waiting for the soul of Lohiau, remained for a time in the land of spirits.

III.

The attendants of Lohiau remained in Kohala until they learned of his fate at the hands of Pele, when they returned to Kauai in the royal *kaulua*, and horrified the friends of the prince by relating to them the story of his death.

Enraged and desperate, Paoa, the faithful and sturdy chief to whom Lohiau had confided the government of his kingdom, started at once for Hawaii with a small party of retainers, determined, even at the sacrifice of his life, to denounce the powers that had slain his royal friend.

Landing on the coast of Puna, he ascended to the crater of Kilauea, and, standing upon the brink of the seething lake of fire, denounced the cruelty of Pele and defied her power. He contemptuously threw to her offerings unfit for sacrifice, and stigmatized all the volcanic deities as evil spirits who had been driven with *Kanaloa* from the presence of *Kane* and the society of the gods.

Paoa expected to be destroyed at once, and recklessly courted and awaited death. The brothers and sisters of Pele, with their several agencies of destruction, were momentarily expecting an order from the goddess to consume the audacious mortal in his tracks. Never before had such words of reproach and defiance been uttered by human tongue, and they could not doubt that swift vengeance would be hurled upon the offender.

But Pele refused to harm the desperate champion of Lohiau, for circumstances had convinced her of the innocence of Hiiaka and the fidelity of the prince. Therefore, instead of punishing the brave Paoa, Pele and her relatives received him with friendship, gently chided him for his words of insult and defiance, and disarmed his anger by forgiving the offence.

Satisfied of the great wrong she had done her faithful sister, and longing for her presence again in the chambers of the crater, Pele restored Pauo-palae and Omeo to life, and, endowing the latter with supernatural powers, sent her down to the regions of the dead to induce Hiiaka to return to earth.

Descending through the opening made by Hiiaka, Omeo was stopped at the intervening spheres, owing to the aspects of mortality which she unconsciously retained, and encountered many difficulties in reaching the kingdom of *Milu*. Arriving there and making known the object of her visit, Omeo was neither assisted nor encouraged in her search for Hiiaka. *Milu* was not anxious to part with his distinguished guest, and attempted to deceive Omeo by intimating that Hiiaka had returned to earth and was then on a visit to some of the relatives of her family in Kahiki.

Omeo was about to return, disappointed, to earth, when she discovered Hiiaka as she was listlessly emerging from a thick grove of trees where she had spent the most of her time since her arrival there in quest of the soul of Lohiau. Their greeting was most friendly, and when Omeo informed her of what had occurred at the volcano since her departure, she consented to leave the land of death and rejoin her relatives at the crater.

The brothers and sisters of Hiiaka were overjoyed at her return, and Pele welcomed her with assurances of restored affec-

tion. Paoa was still there. He was at once recognized by Hiiaka, and the next day she descended from Kilauea and embarked
with him for Kauai in search of the soul of Lohiau.

The canoe of Paoa had scarcely left the shores of Puna before a strange craft swept in from the ocean, and was beached at
the spot from which Hiiaka and her companion had embarked
less than half a day before. It was a huge cowrie shell, dazzling
in the brilliancy of its colors, and capable of indefinite expansion.
Its masts were of ivory, and its sails were mats of the whiteness of
milk. Both seemed to be mere ornaments, however, since the shell
moved quite as swiftly through the water without wind as with it.

The sole occupant of the little vessel was the god *Kanemilohai.* He was a relative of the Pele family, and came from Kahiki on a visit to the volcanic deities of Hawaii. Remaining two
or three days with Pele, and learning all that had happened to
the family since they left Kahiki, the god started for Kauai to
extend a greeting to Hiiaka.

Proceeding in a direct route, when about midway between the
two islands the god caught the soul of Lohiau, which had misun-
derstood the final directions of Hiiaka and was on its way to
Kauai. Not having gone to the land of spirits, it had been
searching everywhere for Hiiaka, and had at last taken flight for
Kauai, when it was intercepted by *Kanemilohai.*

The god returned to the crater with the captured spirit, and,
finding the pillar of stone into which Lohiau had been turned,
restored the prince to life. As he recovered his consciousness
and opened his eyes he recognized Pele standing before him.
Apprehensive of further persecution, he was about to appeal to
her again for mercy when she said, in a tone as tender as that in
which she had first replied to his welcome on the beach at
Kaena :

" Fear me no longer. I have been unjust to you as well as to
Hiiaka. After what I have done I cannot expect your love.
Find Hiiaka and give it to her. She loves you, and knows how
to be kind to a mortal."

Lohiau would have thanked the goddess, but when he looked
again she was gone, and in her place stood *Kanemilohai,* who
told him to take the shell vessel he would find at the beach below, and proceed to Kauai, where he would probably meet Hii·
aka and his friend Paoa.

Lohiau hesitated, for there was something in the appearance of *Kanemilohai* that inspired a feeling of awe.

" Go, and fear nothing," said the god, who knew the thoughts of the prince. " The shell was not made in the sea or by human hands, but it will bear you safely on your journey, no matter how rough the waves or great its burden."

" The coast of Puna is a day's journey in length," said Lohiau. "Where and how will I be able to find the shell?"

" Hasten to the shore at Keauhou," returned the god, " and you will see me there."

Arriving at the beach designated, the prince was surprised to find *Kanemilohai* already there ; but he found something more to excite his wonder when the god took from a crevice in the rocks, where it had been secreted, a shell no larger than the palm of his hand, and passed it to him with the announcement that it was the barge in which he was to sail for Kauai.

Lohiau examined the little toy with something of a feeling of amusement, but more of perplexity, and was about to return it to his strange companion, when the latter instructed him to place the shell in the edge of the waters. The prince obeyed, and instantly found before him the beautiful craft in which the god had made his journey from Kahiki.

The power being conferred upon him by the god to contract or extend the proportions of the shell at his will, Lohiau entered the enchanted vessel of pink and pearl, and, directing its course by simply pointing his finger, was swiftly borne out into the ocean.

Rounding the southern cape of Hawaii, Lohiau thought of proceeding directly to Kauai ; but he pointed too far to the northward, and the next morning sighted Oahu. Passing the headland of Leahi, he turned and entered the harbor of Hou. Landing, he contracted to the dimensions of a limpet, and secreted in a niche in the rocks, his obedient barge, and then proceeded to the village, where, he learned to his great joy, Hiiaka and Paoa were tarrying on a visit. Hou was at that time the scene of great merriment and feasting. It had become the temporary residence of the *alii-nui*, and high-chiefs, *kahunas*, adventurers, and noted surf-riders and *hula* performers had congregated there from all parts of the island.

Ascertaining that an entertainment of great magnificence was to be given that evening by a distinguished chiefess in honor of Hiiaka and her companion, Lohiau resolved to be present. Had he made himself known he would have been entitled to the consideration of the highest—would have been, indeed, the guest of the *alii-nui*, with the right of entrance anywhere ; but fancy prompted him to hide his rank and appear in disguise among the revelers.

Early in the evening the grounds of the chiefess were lighted with hundreds of torches, and under a broad pavilion, festooned and scented with fragrant vines and flowers, the favored guests, enwreathed and crowned with leaf and blossom, partook without stint of such delicacies as the land and sea produced. After the feast, song and music filled the air, and bands of gaily-decked dancers kept step among the flaring torches, while around the doors of the mansion white-bearded bards chanted wild legends of the past and sang the *mele-inoas* of the hostess and her distinguished guests.

In the midst of this inspiring revelry the guests divided into groups as their several tastes suggested. Some strolled out among the dancers, others listened to the stories of the bards, and one party, including Hiiaka, Paoa and the hostess, entered the mansion to engage in the game of *kilu*. It was a pastime of which singing or chanting was a part, and the chiefess was noted for her proficiency in the popular amusement.

Lohiau entered the grounds at the close of the feast, and stood watching the festivities when the party of *kilu* players retired to the mansion. He had turned inward the feathers of his mantle of royal yellow, and, with his long hair falling over his face and shoulders, was readily mistaken for a *kahuna*.

Quite a number of persons thronged around the *kilu* players to witness the game, and Lohiau entered the room without hindrance. Approaching the players, he screened himself behind the *kapas* of two old chiefs who were so intently regarding the performance that they did not observe him.

The game progressed until the *kilu* fell to Hiiaka, and as she threw it she chanted a song of her own composing, in which the name of Lohiau was mentioned with tenderness. The song ceased, and from behind the spectators came the answering voice of the prince. As he sang he brushed back the hair from his handsome face and turned outward the yellow feathers of his mantle. The throng divided, the singer advanced, and before the players stood Lohiau, the prince of Kauai.

He was recognized at once. Hiiaka threw herself into his arms, and the faithful Paoa wept with joy. Informed of the rank of the distinguished visitor, the guests vied with each other in showing him honor, and the festivities were renewed and carried far into the night.

Learning the next day of the presence near his court of the sovereign of Kauai, the *alii-nui* would have entertained him in a manner befitting the high rank of both ; but Lohiau was anxious to return to his people, and set sail for Kauai at once in the shell barge of *Kanemilohai*, expanded to adequate dimensions, taking with him Hiiaka and Paoa.

Although Hiiaka soon after returned to Hawaii and effected a complete reconciliation with her sister, while Lohiau lived she spent much of her time in Kauai. Hopoe was restored to life, and Omeo, or Wahineomeo, was given an immortal form for what she had done, and became thereafter the mediator between the volcanic deities.

KAHAVARI, CHIEF OF PUNA.

CHARACTERS.

PELE, goddess of volcanoes.
KAHAVARI, chief of Puna.
AHUA, companion of Kahavari.
KAPOHO and } children of Kahavari.
KAOHE,

KAHAVARI, CHIEF OF PUNA.

A STORY OF THE VENGEANCE OF THE GODDESS PELE.

BETWEEN Cape Kumakahi, the extreme eastern point of the
island of Hawaii, and the great lava flow of 1840, which
burst forth apparently from a long subterranean channel connecting with the crater of Kilauea, and went down to the sea at
Nanawale over villages and groves of palms, is a small historic district which, notwithstanding the repeated volcanic disturbances
with which it has been convulsed in the past, the chasms with
which it has been rent, and the smoke and ashes that have shut
out the light of the sun and driven its people to the protection of
their temples, still possesses many fertile nooks and natural attractions. Within a few miles of each other, not far inland, are a
number of extinct craters ; but the rains are abundant in Puna,
and spring is eternal, and the vegetation grows rank above hidden patches of lava, and is constantly stretching and deepening
its mantle of green over the vitreous rivers of Kilauea and the
lower and lesser volcanic vents clinging to its base like so many
cauterized ulcers.

The valleys are green in that part of Puna now, and there the
banana and the bread-fruit grow, and the *ohia* and pineapple
scent the air. But so has it not always been, for the mango
ripens over fields of buried lava, and the palms grow tall from the
refilled chasms of dead streams of fire. The depression of Kapoho, now sweet with tropical odors, marks the site of a sunken
mountain, and where to-day sleep the quiet waters of a lake once
boiled a sea of liquid lava, in a basin broader, perhaps, than the
mighty caldron of Kilauea.

We are now about to speak of one of the many irruptions
which at intervals in the past poured their desolating torrents of
fire through the district, alternately loved and hated by Pele, the
dreadful goddess of the volcanoes. In connection with it tradi-

tion has brought down a tale combining elements of simplicity and grandeur strikingly characteristic of the mythological legends of Polynesia—legends equaling the Norse in audacity, but lacking the motive and connecting causes of the Greek. They are simply legendary epics, beginning in caprice and abruptly ending, in many instances, in grandest tumult. They are like chapters torn from a lost volume—patches of disturbed elements and gigantic forms and energies clandestinely cut from a passing panorama and placed in the foreground of strange and inharmonious conditions. They embrace gods reminding us of Thor, monsters more hideous than Polyphemus, demi-gods mighty as the son of Thetis, and kings with strains reaching back to the loins of gods ; but in motive and action they were independent of, and not unfrequently hostile to, each other. No celestial synod shaped their course or moved them to effort, and to no authority higher than their individual wills were they usually responsible. Many of them were created with no reference to the necessity of their being or the maintenance of divine respect or authority, and not a few seem to have been the creations of accident.

As an example the demi-god *Maui* may be mentioned. As told by tradition, his principal abode was Hawaii, although his facilities for visiting the other islands of the group will be considered ample when it is stated that he could step from one to another, even from Oahu to Kauai, a distance of seventy miles. When he bathed—and bathing was one of his greatest delights— his feet trod the deepest basins of the ocean and his hair was moistened with the vapor of the clouds. Neither his creator nor the purpose of his creation is mentioned ; but he was blest with a wife with proportions, it is presumed, somewhat in keeping with his own, and as an evidence of their attachment it is related that at one time he reached up and seized the sun, and held it for some hours motionless in the heavens, to enable his industrious spouse to complete the manufacture of a piece of *kapa* upon which she was engaged.

And *Kana* was another gigantic being of similar proportions. He, too, was partial to Hawaii, and could step from island to island, and frequently stood for his amusement with one foot on Oahu and the other either on Maui or Kauai. Tradition may have confounded these two monsters ; but, as *Kana* was wifeless,

we are constrained to regard them as distinct ; and, being without
the care of a wife, he was enabled to devote his entire attention
to himself and the inhabitants of the islands crawling at his feet.
Hence, when the king of Kahiki, who was the keeper of the sun,
shut its light from the Hawaiians for some trivial offence, *Kana*
waded the ocean to the home of the vindictive monarch, and by
threats compelled him to restore the light to the Hawaiian group.
This done, he waded back and hung his mantle to dry on Mauna
Kea, which was then an active volcano. Another demi-god of the
same name is also referred to in some of the early *meles* of Hawaii. He was the son of Hina, who went with his brother to the
rescue of their mother, who had been during their infancy abducted by the son of the king of Molokai. He was endowed by
his grandmother, a sorceress from one of the southern islands,
with the faculty of so elongating and contracting his person as
to be able to pass through the deepest waters with his head at
all times above the surface.

The shadows of these and other monsters are seen far back
in the past ; but human beings of gigantic proportions, of natural birth and claiming no connection with the gods, are mentioned in Hawaiian folk-lore as having lived as late as the beginning of the sixteenth century. Thus, during the reign of
Umi, king of Hawaii, whose romantic ascent to the throne is the
theme of chant and song, and to whom the past and present dynasties of united Hawaii trace their descent, lived the giant Maukaleoleo. He was one of Umi's warriors, and must have been a
mighty host in himself. His measure in feet is not recorded, but
he stood upon the ground and plucked cocoanuts from the tallest trees, and once, without wetting his loins, strode out into
six fathoms of water and saved the life of his chief. As the traditions relating to Umi are quite elaborate and circumstantial,
the existence of Maukaleoleo cannot well be doubted, however
greatly we may feel disposed to curtail his proportions.

But, in groping among these monsters of the Hawaiian past,
we have been led somewhat from the story of the irruption in
Puna, to which reference has been made. However, as pertinent to it, and to the goddess whose wrath invoked it, it may be
mentioned that many centuries ago a family of gods and goddesses came to Hawaii from Tahiti and took possession of the
volcanic mountains of that island. The family consisted of five

brothers and nine sisters, of which Pele was the principal deity.
The others possessed specific powers and functions, such as controlling the fires, smoke, steam, explosions, etc., of the volcanoes
under their supervision.   Although they frequently dwelt in
other volcanoes, their principal and favorite abode was the crater
of Kilauea.   Almost without exception they were destructive
and merciless.   Temples were erected to Pele in every district
menaced by volcanic disturbance, and offerings of fruits, animals, and sometimes of human beings were laid upon her altars
and thrown into the crater to secure her favor or placate her
wrath.   In the legend of "The Apotheosis of Pele" a more extended reference is made to the goddess and her family.

With this knowledge of the power and disposition of Pele, the
reader will be prepared for the story of the exhibition of her
wrath in Puna, which will now be related nearly in the language
of tradition.   The event occurred during the reign of Kahouka-
pu, who from about 1340 to 1380 was the *alii-nui*, or governing
chief, of Hawaii.   The chief of the district of Puna was Kahavari, a young noble distinguished for his strength, courage and
manly accomplishments.   How he came to be chief or governor
of Puna is not stated.   As his father and sister lived on Oahu, he
was probably a native of that island, and may have been advanced to his position through military service rendered the Hawaiian
king, since it was customary in those days, as it was at later
periods, for young men of martial tastes to seek adventure and
employment at arms with the kings and chiefs of neighboring
islands.

The grass-thatched mansion of the young chief was near Kapoho, where his wife lived with their two children, Paupoulu and
Kaohe; and at Kukii, no great distance away, dwelt his old
mother, then on a visit to her distinguished son.   As his *taro*
lands were large and fertile, and he had fish-ponds on the sea-
shore, he entertained with prodigality, and the people of Puna
thought there was no chief like him in all Hawaii.

It was at the time of the monthly festival of *Lono*.   The day
was beautiful.   The trade-winds were bending the leaves of the
palms and scattering the spray from the breakers chasing each
other over the reef.   A *holua* contest had been announced between the stalwart young chief and his favorite friend and companion, Ahua, and a large concourse of men, women and chil-

dren had assembled at the foot of the hill to witness the exciting pastime. They brought with them drums, *ohes*, *ulilis*, rattling gourds and other musical instruments, and while they awaited the coming of the contestants all frolicked as if they were children —frolicked as was their way before the white man came to tell them they were nearly naked, and that life was too serious a thing to be frittered away in enjoyment. They ate *ohias*, cocoanuts and bananas under the palms, and chewed the pith of sugar-cane. They danced, sang and laughed at the *hula* and other sports of the children, and grew nervous with enthusiasm when their bards chanted the *meles* of by-gone years.

The game of *holua* consists in sliding down a sometimes long but always steep hill on a narrow sledge from six to twelve feet in length, called a *papa*. The light and polished runners, bent upward at the front, are bound quite closely together, with cross-bars for the hands and feet. With a run at the top of the sliding track, slightly smoothed and sometimes strewn with rushes, the rider throws himself face downward on the narrow *papa* and dashes headlong down the hill. As the sledge is not more than six or eight inches in width, with more than as many feet in length, one of the principal difficulties of the descent is in keeping it under the rider ; the other, of course, is in guiding it ; but long practice is required to master the subtleties of either. Kahavari was an adept with the *papa*, and so was Ahua. Rare sport was therefore expected, and the people of the neighborhood assembled almost in a body to witness it.

Finally appearing at the foot of the hill, Kahavari and his companion were heartily cheered by their good-natured auditors. Their *papas* were carried by attendants. The chief smiled upon the assemblage, and as he struck his tall spear into the ground and divested his broad shoulders of the *kihei* covering them, the wagers of fruit and pigs were three to one that he would reach the bottom first, although Ahua was expert with the *papa*, and but a month before had beaten the champion of Kau on his own ground.

Taking their sledges under their arms, the contestants laughingly mounted the hill with firm, strong strides, neither thinking of resting until the top was gained. Stopping for a moment preparatory to the descent, a comely-looking woman stepped out from behind a clump of undergrowth and bowed before them. Little attention was paid to her until she approached still nearer

and boldly challenged Kahavari to contest the *holua* with her instead of Ahua. Exchanging a smile of amusement with his companion, the chief scanned the lithe and shapely figure of the
woman for a moment, and then exclaimed, more in astonishment
than in anger : " What ! with a woman ? "

" And why not with a woman, if she is your superior and you
lack not the courage ? " was the calm rejoinder.

" You are bold, woman," returned the chief, with something
of a frown. " What know you of the *papa ?* "

" Enough to reach the bottom of the hill in front of the chief
of Puna," was the prompt and defiant answer.

" Is it so, indeed ? Then take the *papa* and we will see ! " said
Kahavari, with an angry look which did not seem to disturb the
woman in the least.

At a motion from the chief, Ahua handed his *papa* to the
woman, and the next moment Kahavari, with the strange contestant closely behind him, was dashing down the hill. On, on
they went, around and over rocks, at break-neck speed ; but for
a moment the woman lost her balance, and Kahavari reached the
end of the course a dozen paces in advance.

Music and shouting followed the victory of the chief, and,
scowling upon the exultant multitude, the woman pointed to the
hill, silently challenging the victor to another trial. They mounted the hill without a word, and turned for another start.

" Stop ! " said the woman, while a strange light flashed in her
eyes. " Your *papa* is better than mine. If you would act fairly,
let us now exchange ! "

" Why should I exchange ? " replied the chief, hastily. " You
are neither my wife nor my sister, and I know you not. Come " !
And, presuming the woman was following him, Kahavari made
a spring and dashed down the hill on his *papa.*

With this the woman stamped her foot, and a river of burning
lava burst from the hill and began to pour down into the valley
beneath. Reaching the bottom, Kahavari rose and looked behind him, and to his horror saw a wide and wild torrent of lava
rushing down the hillside toward the spot where he was standing ; and riding on the crest of the foremost wave was the woman—now no longer disguised, but Pele, the dreadful goddess
of Kilauea—with thunder at her feet and lightning playing with
her flaming tresses.

Seizing his spear, Kahavari, accompanied by Ahua, fled for his life to the small eminence of Puukea. He looked behind, and saw the entire assemblage of spectators engulfed in a sea of fire. With terrible rapidity the valleys began to fill, and he knew that his only hope of escape was in reaching the ocean, for it was manifest that Pele was intent upon his destruction. He fled to his house, and, passing it without stopping, said farewell to his mother, wife and children, and to his favorite hog Aloipuaa. Telling them that Pele was in pursuit of him with a river of fire, and to save themselves, if possible, by escaping to the hills, he left them to their fate.

Coming to a chasm, he saw Pele pouring down it to cut off his retreat. He crossed on his spear, pulling his friend over after him. At length, closely pursued, he reached the ocean. His brother, discovering the danger, had just landed from his fishing canoe and gone to look after the safety of his family. Kahavari leaped into the canoe with his companion, and, using his spear for a paddle, was soon beyond the reach of the pursuing lava. Enraged at his escape, Pele ran some distance into the water and hurled after him huge stones, that hissed as they struck the waves, until an east wind sprang up and carried him far out to sea.

He first reached the island of Maui, and thence by the way of Lanai found his way to Oahu, where he remained to the end of his days. All of his relatives in Puna perished, with hundreds of others in the neighborhood of Kapoho. But he never ventured back to Puna, the grave of his hopes and his people, for he believed Pele, the unforgiving, would visit the place with another horror if he did.

Pele had come down from Kilauea in a pleasant mood to witness the *holua* contest; but Kahavari angered her unwittingly, and what followed has just been described.

KAHALAOPUNA, THE PRINCESS OF MANOA.

CHARACTERS.

KAHAUKANI, male, and
KAUAHUAHINE, female, } children of supernatural birth.

KOLOWAHI, guardian of Kahaukani.

POHAKUKALA, guardian of Kauahuahine.

KAHALAOPUNA, daughter of Kahaukani and Kauahuahine.

KAUHI, the betrothed of Kahalaopuna.

KEAWAAWAKIIHELEI and
KUMAUNA, } inferior chiefs.

MAHANA, a young chief.

AKAAKA, father of Kahaukani and Kauahuahine.

KAEA, a sorcerer.

ELEPAIO, a bird-god.

KAHALAOPUNA, THE PRINCESS OF MANOA.

A LEGEND OF THE VALLEY OF RAINBOW

I.

MANOA is the most beautiful of all the little valleys leaping abruptly from the mountains back of Honolulu and cooling the streets and byways of the city with their sweet waters. And it is also the most verdant. Gentle rains fall there more frequently than in the valleys on either side of it, and almost every day in the year it is canopied with rainbows. Sometimes it is called, and not inappropriately, the Valley of Rainbows.

Why is it that Manoa is thus blessed with rains, thus ornamented with rainbows, thus cradled in everlasting green ? Were a reason sought among natural causes, it would doubtless be found in a favoring rent or depression in the summit above the valley, and overlooking the eastern coast of Oahu, where wind and rain are abundant. But tradition furnishes another explanation of the exceptionally kind dealings of the elements with Manoa—not as satisfactory, perhaps, as the one suggested, but very much more poetic.

Far back in the past, as the story relates, the projecting spur of Akaaka, above the head of Manoa Valley, was united in marriage with the neighboring promontory of Nalehuaakaaka. A growth of *lehua* bushes still crowns the spur in perpetual witness of the union. Of this marriage of mountains twin children were born—a boy named Kahaukani, which signified Manoa wind, and a girl called Kauahuahine, which implied Manoa rain. At their birth they were adopted by a chief and chiefess whose names were Kolowahi and Pohakukala. They were brother and sister, and cousins, also, of Akaaka. The brother took charge of the boy, and the sister assumed the custody and care of the girl. Reared apart from each other, and kept in ignorance of their close relationship, through the management of their foster-parents they were brought together at the proper age and married. The fruit of this union was a daughter, who was given the name of Kaha-laopuna, and who became the most beautiful woman of her time. Thus it was that the marriage of the Wind (Kahaukani) and Rain (Kauahuahine) of Manoa brought to the valley as an inheritance the rainbows and showers for which it has since been distinguished.

To continue the story of the ancient bards of Oahu, Kahalaopuna—or Kaha, as the name will hereafter be written—grew to a surpassingly beautiful womanhood. A house was built for her in a grove of sandal-trees at Kahaiamano, where she lived with a few devoted servants. The house was embowered in vines, and two *poloulou*, or *tabu* staves, were kept standing beside the entrance, to indicate that they guarded from intrusion a person of high rank. Her eyes were so bright that their glow penetrated the thatch of her *hale*, and a luminous glimmer played around its openings. When bathing a roseate halo surrounded her, and a similar light is still visible, it is claimed, whenever her spirit revisits Kahaiamano.

In infancy Kaha was betrothed to Kauhi, a young chief of Kailua, whose parents were so sensible of the honor of the proposed union that they always provided her table with *poi* of their own making and choice fish from the ponds of Kawainui. The acceptance of these favors placed her under obligations to the parents of Kauhi and kept her in continual remembrance of her betrothal. Hence she gave no encouragement to the many chiefs of distinction who sought to obtain glimpses of her beauty and annoyed her with proffers of marriage. The chief to whom she was betrothed was, like herself, of something more than human descent, and she felt herself already bound to him by ties too sacred to be broken.

The fame of her beauty spread far and near, and people came from long distances to catch glimpses of her from lands adjoining, as she walked to and from her bathing-pool or strolled in the shelter of the trees surrounding her house. Among those who many times approached her dwelling but failed to see her were Keawaawakiihelei and Kumauna, two inferior chiefs, whose eyes were disfigured by an unnatural distention of the lower lids. In ungenerous revenge, and envious of those who had fared better, they decked themselves with *leis* of flowers, and, repairing to the bathing-place at Waikiki, boasted that the garlands had been placed around their necks by the beautiful Kaha, with whom they affected the greatest intimacy.

Among the bathers at that popular resort was Kauhi. Although the day fixed for his marriage with Kaha was near at hand, he had never seen her—this being one of the conditions of the betrothal. The stories of the two miscreants were repeated until Kauhi at length gave them credence, and in a fit of jealous fury he resolved to kill the beautiful enchantress who had thus trifled with his love.

Leaving Waikiki in the morning, he reached Kahaiamano about midday. Breaking from a pandanus-tree a heavy cone of nuts with a short limb attached, he presented himself at the house of Kaha. She had just awoke from a nap, and was about to proceed to her bathing-pond, when she was startled at observing a stranger at her door. He did not speak, but from frequent descriptions she at length recognized him as Kauhi, and with some embarrassment invited him to enter. Declining, and admitting his identity, he requested her to step without, and she unhesitatingly complied. His first intention was to kill her at once ; but her supreme loveliness and ready obedience unnerved him for the time, and he proposed that she should first bathe and then accompany him in a ramble through the woods.

To this she assented, and while she was absent Kauhi stood by the door, moodily watching the bright light playing above the pond where she was bathing. He was profoundly impressed with her great beauty, and would have given half the years of his life to clasp her in his arms unsullied. The very thought intensified his jealousy ; and when his mind reverted to the disgusting objects upon whom he believed she had bestowed her favors, he resolved to show her no mercy, and impatiently awaited her return.

Finishing her bath and rejoining him at the door, her beauty was so enrapturing that he was afraid to look at her face, lest he might again falter ; it was therefore with his back turned to her that he declined to partake of food before they departed, and motioned her to follow him. His actions were so strange that she said to him, half in alarm :

"Are you, indeed, angered with me ? Have I in any way displeased you ? Speak, that I may know my fault ! "

"Why, foolish girl, what could you have done to displease me?" replied Kauhi, evasively.

"Nothing, I hope," returned Kaha; "yet your look is cold and almost frightens me."

"It is my mood to-day, perhaps," answered Kauhi, increasing his pace to give employment to his thoughts; "you will think better of my looks, no doubt, when we are of longer acquaintance."

They kept on together, he leading and she following, until they reached a large rock in Aihualama, when he turned abruptly, and, seizing the girl by the arm, said:

"You are beautiful—so beautiful that your face almost drives me mad; but you have been false and must die!"

Kaha's first thought was that he was making sport with her; but when she looked up into his face and saw that it was stern and smileless, she replied:

"If you are resolved upon my death, why did you not kill me at home, so that my bones might be buried by my people? If you think me false, tell me with whom, that I may disabuse your mind of the cruel error possessing it."

"Your words are as fair as your face, but neither will deceive me longer!" exclaimed Kauhi; and with a blow on the temple with the cone of *hala* nuts, which he was still carrying, he laid her dead at his feet. Hastily digging a hole beside the rock, he buried the body and started down the valley toward Waikiki.

He had scarcely left before a large owl—a god in that guise, who was related to Kaha and had followed her—unearthed the body, rubbed his head against the bruised temple, and restored the girl to life. Overtaking Kauhi, Kaha sang behind him a lament at his unkindness. Turning in amazement, he observed the owl flying above her head, and recognized the power that had restored her to life.

Again ordering Kaha to follow him, they ascended the ridge dividing the valleys of Manoa and Nuuanu. The way was beset with sharp rocks and tangled undergrowth, and when Kaha reached the summit her tender feet were bleeding and her *pau* was in tatters. Seating herself on a stone to regain her breath, with tears in her eyes she implored Kauhi to tell her whither he was leading her and why he had sought to kill her. His only reply was a blow with the *hala* cone, which again felled her dead to the earth. Burying the body as before he resumed his way toward Waikiki.

Again flying to the rescue of his beautiful and sinless relative, the owl-god scratched away the earth above her and restored her once more to life. Following Kauhi, she again chanted a song of lament behind him, and begged him to be merciful to one who had never wronged him, even in thought. Hearing her voice, he turned, and without answer conducted her across the valley of Nuuanu to the ridge of Waolani, where he killed and buried her as he had done twice before, and the owl-god a third time removed the earth from the body and gave it life.

She again overtook her merciless companion, and again pleaded for life and forgiveness for her unknown fault. Instead of softening his heart, the words of Kaha enraged him, and he resolved not to be thwarted in his determination to take her life. Leading her to the head of Kalihi valley, where she was for the fourth time killed, buried and resurrected as before, he next conducted her across plains and steep ravines to Pohakea, on the Ewa slope of the Kaala mountains. He hoped the owl-god would not follow them so far, but, looking around, he discovered him among the branches of an *ohia* tree not far distant.

As Kaha was worn down with fatigue, it required but a slight blow to kill her the fifth time, and when it was dealt to the unresisting girl her body was buried under the roots of a large *koa* tree, and there left by Kauhi, satisfied that it could not be reached by the owl-god. Repairing to the spot after the departure of Kauhi, the owl put himself to the task of scratching the earth from the body ; but his claws became entangled with the roots, which had been left to embarrass his labors, and, after toiling for some time and making little or no progress, he abandoned the undertaking as hopeless, and, reluctantly left the unfortunate girl to her fate, following Kauhi to Waikiki.

But there had been another witness to these many deaths and restorations of Kaha. It was a little green bird that had flitted along unobserved either by Kaha or her companion, and had followed them from Kahaiamano, flying from tree to tree and making no noise. Noting with regret that the owl-god had abandoned the body of Kaha, the little bird, which was a cousin to the girl and a supernatural being, flew with haste to the

parents of Kaha, and informed them of all that had happened to
their daughter.

The girl had been missed, but as some of her servants had
recognized Kauhi, and had seen her leave the house with him,
her absence occasioned no uneasiness ; and when the little green
bird, whose name was Elepaio, recounted to the parents the story
of Kaha's great suffering and many deaths, they found it difficult to believe that Kauhi could have been guilty of such fiend-
ish cruelty to the radiant being who was about to become his
wife. They were convinced of Elepaio's sincerity, however, and
with great grief prepared to visit the spot and remove the remains of Kaha for more fitting interment.

Meantime the spirit of the murdered girl discovered itself to
Mahana, a young chief of good address, who was returning from
a visit to Waianae. Directed by the apparition, he proceeded to
the *koa* tree, and, removing the earth and roots, discovered the
body of Kaha. He recognized the face at once, notwithstanding
the blood and earth stains disfiguring its faultless regularity.
He had seen and become enraptured with its beauty at Kahaiamano, and on one occasion, which lived in his memory like a
beautiful dream, he had been emboldened by his love to approach sufficiently near to exchange modest words and glances
with it.

Gently removing the body from the shallow pit in which it
had been buried, Mahana found to his great joy that it was still
warm. Wrapping it in his *kihei*, or shoulder scarf, and covering
it with *maile* ferns and ginger, he tenderly bore it in his arms to
his home at Kamoiliili. As he walked he chanted his love and
scarcely felt his burden. Reaching home, he laid the body upon
a *kapa-moe*, and earnestly implored his elder brother to restore it
to life, he being a *kahuna* and having skill in such matters.

Examining the body and finding that he could do nothing
unaided, the brother called upon their two spirit-sisters for assistance, and through their instrumentality the soul of Kaha was
once more restored to its beautiful tenement. But it was some
time before she fully recovered from the effects of her cruel
treatment—some time, in fact, before she was able to walk without support. In her convalescence Mahana was her considerate
and constant companion, and found no greater pleasure than in
providing her with the delicacies to which she had been accus-

tomed. She was greatly benefited by the waters of the under-
ground cave of Mauoki, to which she was frequently and secretly taken, and under the watchful care of Mahana she was at
length restored to health.

II.

With her recovery, in the home of her new friends at Kamoiliili, Kaha was introduced to a life that was new to her; but it
was by no means an unpleasant change from the restraints of
her listless and more sumptuous past behind the protecting
shadows of her *puloulous*, where she was jealously watched, and
where rank closed her doors to congenial companionship. She
repaired to an unfrequented beach, and, unobserved, played with
the shifting sands and sang to the waves, and at night went with
Mahana to the reef with torch and spear in search of fish and
squid.

Knowing that her restoration to life could not be long kept
from her relatives, Mahana told her that his love for her was
great, and asked her to become his wife.

" I shall never love any one better than Mahana," replied
Kaha; " but from infancy I have been betrothed to Kauhi; my
parents, the Wind and Rain of Manoa, have promised that I shall
be his wife, and while he lives I can be the wife of no other."

The argument that Kauhi had forfeited all right to her by
his cruelties failed to shake her resolution, and the brother of
Mahana advised him to in some manner compass the death of
Kauhi. To this end they apprised the parents of Kaha of her
restoration to life, and conspired with them to keep secret the
information for a time. This they were the more disposed to do
because of their uncertainty concerning what Kauhi might again
attempt should he find the girl alive.

In pursuance of the plan adopted, Mahana learned from
Kaha all the songs she had chanted to mollify the wrath of
Kauhi while she was following him through the mountains, and
then sought the *kilu* houses of the king and chiefs in the hope of
encountering his rival. It was not long before they met, under
just such circumstances as Mahana desired. He discovered
Kauhi engaged with others in the game of *kilu*, and joined the
party as a player. The *kilu* passed from the hand of Kauhi to

Mahana, who, on receiving it, began to chant the first of Kaha's songs.

Surprised and embarrassed, Kauhi, in violation of the rules of the game, stopped the player to inquire where he had learned the words of the song he was singing. The answer was that he had learned them from Kaha, the noted beauty of Manoa, who was a friend of his sister, and was then visiting them at their home. Knowing that she had been deserted by the owl-god, and feeling assured that Kaha was no longer living, Kauhi denounced as a falsehood the explanation of the player. Bitter words followed, and but for the interference of friends there would have been bloodshed.

They met the next day at the *kilu* house, and in the evening following, when similar scenes occurred between Mahana and his rival, Kauhi became so enraged at length that he admitted that he had killed the beautiful Kaha of Manoa, and declared the Kaha of Mahana to be an impostor, who had heard of the death of the real Kaha and audaciously assumed her name and rank. He then challenged Mahana to produce the woman claiming to be Kaha, agreeing to forfeit his life should she prove in flesh and blood to be the one whom he knew to be dead, and subjecting Mahana to a like penalty in the event of the claimant proving to be other than the person he represented her to be.

It had been the purpose of Mahana to provoke his rival to a combat with weapons, but the challenge of Kauhi presented itself as a more satisfactory means of accomplishing the object of his aim, and he promptly accepted it ; and, that both might be more firmly bound to its conditions, they were repeated and formally ratified in the presence of the king and principal chiefs of the district.

The day fixed for the strange trial arrived. It was to be in the presence of the king and a number of distinguished chiefs, and Akaaka, the grandfather of Kaha, had been selected as one of the judges. *Imus* had been erected near the sea-shore by the respective friends of the contestants, in which to roast alive the vanquished chief, and dry wood for the heating was piled beside them.

Fearing that the spirit of the murdered girl might be able to assume a living appearance, and thus impose upon the judges,

Kauhi had consulted the priests and sorcerers of his family, and was advised by Kaea to have the large and tender leaves of the ape plant spread upon the ground where Kaha and her attendants before the tribunal were to be seated. "When she enters," said the *kaula*, "watch her closely. If she is of flesh her weight will rend the leaves; if she is merely a spirit the leaves where she walks and sits will not be torn."

On her way to Waikiki, the place designated for the trial, Kaha was accompanied by her parents, friends and servants, and also by the two spirit-sisters of Mahana, who had assumed human forms in order to be better able to advise and assist her, if occasion required. They informed her of Kaea's proposed test with ape leaves, and advised her to quietly tear and rend them as far as possible for some distance around her, in order that the spirit-friends beside her, who would be unable to do as much for themselves, might thereby escape detection. If discovered, they would be exposed to the risk of being killed by the *poe-poi-uhane*, or spirit-catchers.

Arriving at Waikiki, Kaha and her companions repaired to the large enclosure in which the trial was to take place. The king, chiefs, judges and advisers of Kauhi were already there, and thousands of spectators were assembled in the grounds adjoining. The ape leaves had been spread, by the consent of the king, as advised by Kaea, and Kaha entered with her friends and advanced to the place reserved for them. Not far from her stood Kauhi. As he bent forward in anxiety and looked into her star-like eyes, with a sinking heart he saw that their reproachful gleam was human, and knew that he had lost the wager of his life.

Observing her instructions, Kaha took pains to quietly rend and rumple the ape leaves under and around her. So far as she was concerned, the test was satisfactory. The evidence of the leaves torn by her feet could not be questioned. Kaea was therefore compelled to admit that Kaha was a being of flesh and bone; but in his disappointment he declared that he saw and felt the presence of spirits in some manner connected with her, and would detect and punish them.

Irritated at the malice of the *kaula*, Akaaka advised him to look for the faces of the spirits in an open calabash of water. Eagerly grasping at the suggestion, Kaea ordered a vessel of clear water to be brought in, and incautiously bent his eyes over it. He saw only the reflection of his own face. Akaaka also caught a glimpse of it, and, knowing it to be the spirit of the seer, he seized and crushed it between his palms, and Kaea fell dead to the earth beside the calabash into which he had been peering.

Akaaka then turned and embraced Kaha, acknowledging that she was his granddaughter, and that her purity and obedience rendered her worthy of the love of the bold upland of Akaaka, and of her parents, the Wind and Rain of Manoa.

The curiosity of the king was aroused, and he demanded an explanation of the strange proceedings he had just witnessed. Kaha told her simple story, and Kauhi, on being interrogated, could deny no part of it. As an excuse for his barbarous conduct, however, he repeated, and attributed his jealous rage to, the boastful assertions of Kumauna and Keawaawakiihelei. The slanderers were sent for at once, and, on being confronted by Kaha, admitted that they had never seen her before, and that they had boasted of their intimacy with her to make others envious of their good fortune.

"Well," replied the king, after listening to the confessions of the miscreants, "as your efforts in exciting the envy of others have brought terrible suffering to an innocent girl, I now promise you something of which no one, I think, will envy you. You will be baked alive with Kauhi! If you have friends among the gods, pray to them that the *imus* may be hot and your sufferings short !"

The *imus* were ordered to be heated at once, and Kauhi and the two calumniators were thrown into them alive and roasted. The first went to his death bravely, chanting a song of defiance as he proceeded to the place of execution, but the others vainly struggled and sought to escape. The retainers of Kauhi were so disgusted with his cruelty to Kaha that they transferred their allegiance to her, and the lands and fishing rights that had been his were given to Mahana at once.

"And how do you intend to reward the young chief who hazarded his life for you?" inquired the king, pleasantly addressing Kaha as he rose to depart.

"With my own, O king!" replied the girl, advancing to Mahana and laying her head upon his breast.

"So shall it be, indeed," returned the king. "I have said it, and you are now the wife of Mahana."

In his gratitude the happy young chief threw himself at the feet of the king and said :

"I am your slave, great king ! Demand of me some great service or sacrifice, that you may know that I am grateful ! "

"Even as you desire," returned the king, "I will put you to a task that will tax to the utmost your patience."

"I listen, O king ! " said Mahana, resolutely.

"The sacrifice I ask," resumed the king, with a merry twinkle in his eye, " is that for full three days from this time you embrace not your bride."

"A sacrifice, indeed ! " exclaimed Mahana, catching the kindly humor of the request, and slyly glancing at the downcast face of Kaha. "It is—"

"Too great, I see, for one whose beard is not yet fully grown," interrupted the king. "Well, I withdraw the request. The girl is yours ; take her with you without conditions ! "

Here the story of the trials of Kaha should end ; but it does not. Some time during the night following the death of Kauhi a tidal wave, sent by a powerful shark-god, swept over and destroyed the *imus* in which the condemned men had been roasted, and their bones were carried into the sea. Through the power of their family gods Kumauna and Keawaawakiihelei were transformed into two peaks in the mountains back of Manoa Valley while Kauhi, who was distantly related to the shark-god, was turned into a shark.

For two years Kaha and her husband lived happily together, surrounded by many friends and enjoying every comfort. Her grandfather, Akaaka, visited her frequently, and, knowing of Kauhi's transformation and vindictive disposition, admonished her to avoid the sea. For two years she heeded the warning ; but one day, when her husband was absent and her mother was asleep, she ventured with one of her women to the beach to witness the sports of the bathers and surf-riders. As no harm came to the swimmers, and the water was inviting, she finally borrowed a surf-board, and, throwing herself joyfully into the waves, was carried beyond the reef.

This was the opportunity for which Kauhi had long waited. Seizing Kaha, and biting her body in twain, he swam around with the head and shoulders exposed above the water, that the bathers might note his triumph. The spirit of Kaha at once returned to the sleeping mother and informed her of what had befallen her daughter. Waking and missing Kaha, the mother gave the alarm, and with others immediately proceeded to the beach. The bathers, who had fled from the water on witnessing the fate of Kaha, confirmed the words of the spirit, and canoes were launched in pursuit of the shark, still exhibiting his bloody trophy beyond the reef.

Swimming with the body of Kaha just far enough below the surface to be visible to the occupants of the canoes, the monster was followed to Waianae, where in shallow waters he was seen, with other sharks, to completely devour the remains. This rendered her restoration to life impossible, and the pursuing party returned sadly to Waikiki.

With the final death of Kaha her parents relinquished their human lives and retired to Manoa Valley. The father is known as Manoa Wind, and his visible form is a small grove of *hau* trees below Kahaiamano. The mother is recognized as Manoa Rain, and is often met with in the vicinity of the former home of her beloved and beautiful daughter.

The grandparents of Kaha also abandoned their human forms, Akaaka resuming his personation of the mountain spur bearing his name, and his august companion nestling upon his brow in the shape of a thicket of *lehua* bushes. And there, among the clouds, they still look down upon Kahaiamano and the fair valley of Manoa, and smile at the rains of Kauahuahine, which day by day renew their beauty, and keep green with ferns and sweet with flowers the earthly home of Kahalaopuna.

Appendix.

APPENDIX.

HAWAIIAN LEGENDS: GLOSSARY.

EXPLANATORY NOTE.

THE Hawaiian alphabet proper contains but twelve letters, five vowels and seven consonants, namely : A, E, I, O, U, H, K, L, M, N, P, W. To these are sometimes added R, T and B. No appreciable distinction, however, is observed between the sounds of R and L, T and K, and B and P.

The almost invariable sound of A is as pronounced in *father*; of E as in th*ey*; of I as in mar*i*ne; of O as in m*o*le; of U as in m*u*te. The only general deviation is in giving the vowels long and short sounds. W takes the sound of V in most cases.

Every word and every syllable of the language ends in a vowel, and no two consonants occur without a vowel sound between them.

The accent of nine-tenths of the words in the language is on the penultimate.

The indefinite article is *he;* the definite article *ka* or *ke;* the plural takes the prefix of *na.*

The "O" beginning the metrical lines of chants and *meles* is not always employed as an interjection. It is used chiefly as a prefix to personal nouns and pronouns in the nominative case.

A.

Aa, the root of any vegetation.
Ae, the affirmative; yes.
Ao, light.
Aakoko, a vein or artery.
Auwina la, afternoon.
Akane, an intimate friend.
Aole, the negative; no.
Ai, food of any kind.
Auhau, any tax due to a chief.
Au, a current; the gale.
Auwae, the chin.
Aumoe, midnight.
Aouli, the sky.
Aumakua, the spirit of a deceased ancestor.
Ailo, chiefs permitted to eat with the king.
Ahiahi, evening.
Aha-alii, chiefs of accepted and irrevocable rank.
Aha, a sacred *tabu* prayer, during which any noise was death.

Ahi, fire.
Ahinahina, the color of gray.
Aka, a shadow.
Akua, a spirit or god.
Akepaa, the liver.
Akemama, the lungs.
Aku, a mythical bird, sacred to the high priesthood.
Ala, a path, road or way.
Ala-nui, a great path.
Alaula, the red path ; the dawn.
Aho; a breath.
Aha-ula, a feather cape worn by chiefs.
Alae, a sacred bird.
Alii-koa, a military leader ; a general.
Aloha, love; love to you; a greeting or salutation.
Alii, a chief.
Alii-nui, a great or principal chief.
Alii-niaupio, Alii-pio, Alii-naha, Alii-wohi and *Lo-alii,* different grades of chiefs.

Anu, a receptacle in the inner temple from which issued the oracles.

Anaana, the process of praying another to death.

Anuenue, a rainbow.

Ana, a cave or cavern.

Apapani, a little song-bird.

Awa, a plant ; an intoxicating drink made of *awa;* a harbor.

Awakea, noon.

E.

Ea, breath ; air; a fish *tabu* to women.

Eleele, black, or dark blue.

Eha, pain.

I.

Ia, general name for fish.

Ie, a vine for decorating idols.

Iu, a sacred or tabued place.

Ihe, a javelin used in war.

Io, the human flesh.

Ihimanu, a fish *tabu* to women.

Ihu, the nose.

Iku-nuu, of the royal strain.

Iku-pau, of the priestly or sacred strain.

Ili, the smallest division of land ; the bark ; the skin.

Imu, an oven for cooking.

Ilio, a dog ; a stingy person.

Imu-loa, an oven for baking men.

Ipu, a calabash ; a vessel ; a container.

Iliahi, sandal-wood.

Iwi, a small bird with yellow feathers ; the bone.

O.

O, a fork, or pointed implement used in eating.

Oo, a bird with yellow feathers, used in making royal mantles.

Oa, the rafters of a house.

Oi-e, a name for the godhead.

Oala, a club thrown in battle.

Ohia, a native apple-tree ; the fruit of the *ohia*.

Ohia-apane, a species of *ohia* wood used in making idols.

Oho, hair.

Ohu, fog.

Oho-kui, a bushy wig sometimes worn in battle.

Ola, life.

Omaomao, green.

One, sand.

Onionio, striped.

Olai, an earthquake.

Onini, a surf-board.

Omo, a narrow stone adze.

Oma, a space between two armies where sacrifices were made ; the prime minister, or first officer under the king.

Opelu, a fish sacred to the priesthood.

Opu, the stomach.

Owili, a surf-board made of *wiliwili* wood.

U.

Ua, a sea-bird ; rain.

Uau, a large marine bird.

Uala, a potato.

Uila, lightning.

Uha, the thigh.

Uhi, a yam.

Ulu, the bread-fruit.

Ukeke, an ancient pulsatile musical instrument.

Ulili, a bamboo flute.

Uliuia, a beer made of cane-juice or the *ti* root.

Ulu-maika, a game of rolling round stone disks.

Ulaula, red ; the sacred color.

Uliuli, blue.

Ulunu, a pillow or head-rest.

Unauna, a *tabu* mark.

Unihipili, the spirit of a deceased person.

Umiumi, the beard or whiskers.

H.

Hanai, a foster-child.

Haiao, a day sacrifice.

Haole, a foreigner.

Hanuhanu, an ancient pastime.

Hala, the pandanus-tree.

Hakaolelo, a chief's spy ; informer ; reporter of events.

Haa, a singing dance.

Haipo, a night sacrifice.

Haku, a lord ; a master.

Hakoko, wrestling, with a variety of holds.

Hailima, the elbow.

Hanauna, a relative.

Hale, a house or dwelling.

Hale-alii, the house of the chief ; the royal mansion.

Hale-lole, a tent or cloth house.
Hale-koa, a fort or house of war.
Hale-lua, a grave or sepulchre.
Haili, a ghost ; a name for a temple.
Hawane, the cocoa palm.
Hau, a lascivious dance, or *hula*.
Hekili, thunder.
Heenalu, surf-riding.
Heihei, foot-racing ; a large drum.
Heie, the servant of a seer who reported his prophecies.
Heiau, a temple or place of worship.
Hikiee-moe, the stand for a bed.
Hia, fire made by friction.
Hika-po-loa, a name for the godhead.
Hiua, a game played on a board with four squares.
Hiiaka, a general name for volcanic deities.
Hikini, sunrise ; the east.
Hili, a dye, made of barks, for coloring *kapa*.
Hoa, a companion.
Hoalii, a companion of the chief.
Hoku, a star.
Hoku-paa, the north star.
Hoku-hele, a planet or " wandering star."
Hoku-lele, a meteor.
Hoku-welowelo, a comet.
Honua, the earth.
Holua, the pastime of sliding down precipitous hills on sledges.
Hoao, the ancient marriage contract among the chiefs.
Hoalauna, a friendly companion.
Hoe, a paddle.
Hoeuli, a rudder or steering-oar.
Hoewaa, an oarsman.
Hooilo, the rainy season.
Hookama, an adopted child.
Hokio, a musical instrument.
Honu, a turtle.
Hookupu, gifts to chiefs by their subjects.
Hoopalau, a single combat in battle.
Hua, an egg.
Hue, a water-calabash or container.
Hula, a dance, of which there were many varieties.
Hulu, a feather.
Hulumanu, aids of a chief or king wearing plumes.

K.

Kaai, a girdle put around the loins of a god by a chief.

Kao, the star Antares.
Kaunoa, a pointed, poisonous shell, making a dangerous wound.
Kapu, or *Tabu*, a command, or interdict, of which there were several kinds ; a prerogative pertaining to chiefs, priests and temples.
Kane, a husband ; the name of one of the godhead.
Kauwa, a servant.
Kai, the sea.
Kaa-i, the neck.
Kanaka, a man ; a male.
Kanaka-wale, a private citizen.
Kanaka-maoli, an actual slave.
Kaikamahine, a girl or daughter.
Kaiki-kane, a male child.
Kaikunane, a brother.
Kaikuahine, a sister.
Kaliko, spotted.
Kaioloa, the ceremony of putting a *maro* on a god by the women of a chief.
Kaumaha, a sacrifice to the gods.
Kaumihau, a *tabu* by the high-priest, when a hog was baked, and men were temporarily separated from their wives.
Kakuai, an offering to the gods at daily meals, generally of bananas.
Kahoaka, the spirit of a living person, claimed to be visible to certain classes of priests.
Kamakini, a *tabu* worship for the chief alone.
Kaula, a prophet.
Kaula-wahine, a prophetess.
Kao, a tradition ; a dart or javelin.
Kaua, war ; a battle ; an army marching to battle.
Kaualau, a plantain.
Kakaka, a bow for shooting arrows, not used in war.
Kaukaualii, inferior chiefs with titled fathers and untitled mothers.
Kanikau, a funeral dirge ; a mournful song.
Kapa, a native cloth.
Kalo, or *Taro*, a bulbous root from which *poi* is made.
Kahili, a standard of feathers; an emblem of high rank.
Kani, music.
Kahuna, a priest, doctor or sorcerer.
Kahu, a nurse or guardian of a child.
Kahu-alii, chiefs of the lesser nobility acting as personal attendants to the king.

Kapua, a wizard.
Kaike, a large sacrificial drum.
Kamaa, sandals.
Kapuna, a grandparent.
Kapuna-kah·ko, ancestors.
Kau, the dry season.
Keiki, a child.
Keena, a room or apartment.
Keokeo, white.
Kekuielua, a war implement.
Kino, the body.
Kilo, a prophet.
Kihi, the native sweet potato.
Kilu, an indoor game of amusement.
Kihei, a cloth worn over the shoulders.
Konane, a game resembling draughts.
Koa, coral; a species of wood; a warrior.
Koilipi, an axe for cutting stone.
Ko, sugar-cane.
Koelo, a garden of a chief, cultivated by his people.
Koheoheo, a poisonous mixture producing speedy death.
Koipohaku, a stone axe.
Koloa, a duck.
Kona, a south wind; the south side of an island.
Koolau, a windward district or division.
Kua, the back of a person.
Kuli, the knee.
Kuekue, the heel.
Kumu, a fish *tabu* to women.
Kuoha, a prayer to incite sexual love in another.
Kupua, a sorcerer.
Kuai, a war implement.
Kuleana, a small landed possession within the boundaries of an estate belonging to another.
Kupee, a string of shells; a bracelet; an ornament.
Kuahive, high lands.
Kumu, a teacher.
Kuahana, a war messenger despatched when a general call to arms was made.
Kukui, a light; a torch made from the nuts of the *kukui* tree.

L.

Laau, a tree; wood.
Lau, a leaf.
Lala, a limb.
Lae, the forehead.

La, the sun.
Lani, the heavens.
Laau-palau, a knife used in husbandry, sometimes in war.
Lanahu, coals.
Lanai, a veranda, or house with open sides.
Lehelehe, the lips.
Lenalena, yellow, the royal color.
Lei, a wreath of flowers or feathers.
Lepa, a flag or ensign.
Lehua, an aromatic shrub.
Liliha, the fat of hogs.
Loko, a lake or pond.
Lima, the hand.
Lou, a hook; a fish-hook.
Loulu, a cocoanut.
Luawai, a well.
Luakina, the house of sacrifice in a temple.
Luau, a feast.
Lua, an ancient practice of killing by breaking bones.
Luna, an overseer.
Lunapai, a war messenger of a king or chief.

M.

Maa, a sling for throwing stones.
Mahu, steam.
Maiuu, the finger-nails.
Mahioli, a feather helmet worn by chiefs.
Maili, a fragrant and greatly esteemed plant.
Mauka, toward the hills or mountains.
Malama, a month; a purveyor in traveling.
Mapuna, a spring.
Maka, the eye.
Manamana-lima, a finger.
Manamana-wawae, a toe.
Manu, general name for birds.
Makuakane, a father or uncle.
Makuahine, a mother or aunt.
Mahini, the moon.
Mahini-hou, the new moon.
Mahini-peopeo, the full moon.
Makani, the wind.
Makani-ino, a storm.
Makalii, the beginning of the Hawaiian new year.
Maliu, a deified deceased chief.
Maia, a general name for plantains and bananas, *tabu* to women.
Malaolao, evening twilight.

Mano, the shark; every species was *tabu* to women.

Makaainani, the common people.

Maro, a cloth worn around the loins of males.

Mamo, a bird; a royal feather mantle; descendants.

Manele, a palanquin for chiefs, with four bearers.

Mahele, circumcision.

Mahana, chiefs near the throne.

Mele, an historical chant or song.

Mele-inoa, a personal chant or song.

Moa, a fowl.

Moo, a lizard.

Maikai, toward the sea.

Mooolelo, a narrative of past events.

Mookaao, an historical legend.

Moko, boxing.

Moko-moko, a boxer.

Momi, a pearl.

Moae, the trade winds.

Moi, a king, or principal chief.

Mu, the person who procured men for sacrifice.

Muliwai, a stream, or river.

Mumuku, a violent gust of wind.

N.

Naua, a pedigree.

Nene, a goose.

Niu, the cocoanut tree and fruit.

Ninalo, the fruit of the *hala* tree.

Noho, a seat.

P.

Pa, a dish or platter; a fence or wall.

Pau, a short skirt worn by women; completed, finished.

Pahale, a lawn or other enclosure.

Pahu, a general name for a drum.

Papa, a board; a sledge used in the pastime of *holua.*

Papalina, the cheek.

Paliuli, paradise.

Pahi, general term for a knife or cutting instrument.

Pakiko, an ancient war implement.

Palala, any tax paid to a chief.

Panalaau, a distant possession of lands.

Papataina, a table of any kind.

Pahoa, a dagger, generally of wood.

Palaoa, a carved ivory talisman worn around the neck by chiefs.

Pali, a precipice.

Paiai, pounded *taro* for making *poi.*

Pahoehoe, lava.

Pawa, a garden; a small cultivated field.

Pea, an elevated cross before a *heiau,* signifying sacred.

Peleleu, a large double war canoe.

Pepeiao, the ear.

Pipi, an oyster; clam; shell-fish.

Poi, the paste of *taro.*

Po'i, a cover or lid.

Poo, the head.

Poohiwi, the shoulder.

Poni, purple.

Pokahu, a stone.

Pouli ka la, an eclipse.

Po, night; darkness; the realms of death; chaos.

Pola, a raised platform over double canoes.

Pololu, a long war spear.

Pua, a flower.

Puka, a door.

Puuwai, the heart.

Puaa, a hog.

Puaa-keiki, a pig.

Puahiohio, a whirlwind.

Puhenehene, an indoor pastime.

Punipeki, a child's game.

Pueo, an owl.

Puana, a leader in *meles;* a starter of words.

Pukaua, an officer in the army; a captain; a champion.

Pule, a prayer.

Pulelelua, a butterfly.

Punahele, a friend or companion.

Puloulou, a *tabu* staff, crowned with balls of *kapa.*

Puuku, inferior chiefs, personal attendants of the king.

W.

Waa, a general name for canoe.

Wai, a general name for water.

Waiali, the platform from which chiefs addressed the people.

Wahine, a woman; females generally.

Wahi-moe, a bed.

Wahie, wood for burning.

Wanaao, the dawn.

Wawae, a leg or foot.

Waipuilani, a waterspout.

Wauti, the inner bark of a tree from which cloth is made.

Wahine-hoao, the real wife.

Wili, lightning.

Wiliwili, a light wood from which surf-boards were made.

CARDINAL NUMBERS.

One, *Akahi.*
Two, *Alua.*
Three, *Akolu.*
Four, *Aha.*
Five, *Alima.*
Six, *Aono.*
Seven, *Ahiku.*
Eight, *Awalu.*
Nine, *Aiwa.*
Ten, *Umi.*
Eleven, *Umikumamakahi.*
Twelve, *Umikumamalua.*
Thirteen, *Umikumamakolu.*
Fourteen, *Umikumamaha.*
Fifteen, *Umikumamalima.*
Sixteen, *Umikumamaono.*
Seventeen, *Umikumamahiku.*
Eighteen, *Umikumamawalu.*
Nineteen, *Umikumamaiwa.*
Twenty, *Iwakalua.*
Twenty-one, *Iwakaluakumamakahi.*
Twenty-two, *Iwakaluakumamalua.*
Twenty-three, *Iwakaluakumamakolo.*
Twenty-four, *Iwakaluakumamaha.*
Twenty-five, *Iwakaluakumamalima.*
Twenty-six, *Iwakaluakumamaono.*
Twenty-seven, *Awakaluakumamahiku.*
Twenty-eight, *Awakaluakumamawalu.*
Twenty-nine, *Awakaluakumamaiwa.*
Thirty, *Kanakolu.*
Forty, *Kanaha.*
Fifty, *Kanalima.*
Sixty, *Kanaono.*
Seventy, *Kanahiku.*
Eighty, *Kanawalu.*
Ninety, *Kanaiwa.*
One hundred, *Hookahi haneri* (modern).
One thousand, *Hookahi tausani* (modern).

NAMES OF THE MONTHS.

January, *Makalii.*
February, *Kaelo.*
March, *Kaulua.*
April, *Nana.*
May, *Welo.*
June, *Ikiiki.*
July, *Kaaona.*
August, *Hinaieleele.*
September, *Hilinehu.*
October, *Hilinama.*
November, *Ikuwa.*
December, *Welehu.*

NAMES OF THE DAYS OF THE MONTH.

1st, *Hilo.*
2d, *Hoaka.*
3d, *Kukahi.*
4th, *Kulua.*
5th, *Kukolo.*
6th, *Kupau.*
7th, *Olekukahi.*
8th, *Olekulua.*
9th, *Olekukolu.*
10th, *Olekupau.*
11th, *Huna.*
12th, *Mohalu.*
13th, *Hua.*
14th, *Akua.*
15th, *Hoku.*
16th, *Mahealani.*
17th, *Kulu.*
18th, *Laaukukahi.*
19th, *Laaukulua.*
20th, *Laaupau.*
21st, *Olekukahi.*
22d, *Olekulua.*
23d, *Olepau.*
24th, *Kaloakukahi.*
25th, *Kaloakulua.*
26th, *Kaloapau.*
27th, *Kane.*
28th, *Lono.*
29th, *Mauli.*
30th, *Muku.*

Other TUT BOOKS available: